THE ORIGENIST
CONTROVERSY

To some readers—students of early Christian history—the themes of *The Origenist Controversy* will seem an archaic throwback to those of the second and third centuries: then, defending the resurrection body and free will and debating the "unforgivable sin" engaged the intellectual energies of Christians. To other readers, my rendition of the controversy's issues will carry contemporary resonance: the status of representation; the ways in which the body is inscribed with cultural value; the constitution of the "self"; how praxis both creates and challenges theory. Both sets of readers read well.

Around the turn of the fifth century, Christian theologians and churchmen contested each other's orthodoxy (and good repute) by hurling charges of "Origenism" at their opponents. Although the alleged deficiencies of Origen's theology—centering on the Trinity, creation, and eschatology—served as the base for the dispute, the controversy was marked both by contemporary Origenist speculation (derived most notably from Evagrius Ponticus) and by the religious contests of the later fourth century. Shaped by the Trinitarian and ascetic debates, and in turn leaving its impact on the clash between Pelagians and Augustine, the Origenist controversy of the 390s and first years of the fifth century thus stands at the juncture of several theological contestations. It also threads its way amidst Christian campaigns against pagan "idolatry" and Manichean and astrological determinism as well as networks of alliance and enmity.

Those who approach the Origenist controversy from the perspective of late antiquity will find that its issues hark back to the pre-Nicene era. Then, pastors reassured their congregations that although pagan persecutors might kill the body, they could not destroy it; "orthodox" polemicists denounced the Gnostics' depreciation of materiality and reputed "determinism" (i.e., the Gnostic election theology); churchmen pondered whether denial of the faith—or murder, or adultery—might put a Christian beyond the pale of the redeemed community. In part, the archaic tone of the controversy stems from the location of its central emblem, Origen, as a third-century theologian, not a fifth-century bishop. Yet Origen's centrality does not entirely explain why the issues of early third-century Christianity returned in new form to capture the theological imagination of late fourth- and early fifth-century writers.

The fourth century, immersed in debates pertaining to the doctrine of God—the subordination or nonsubordination of the Son to the Father, the divinity or creaturehood of the Holy Spirit—had bypassed several pressing concerns of earlier Christianity in its single-minded quest for Trinitarian definition. These concerns, abeyant while Nicene and anti-Nicene forces raged, emerged in new dress in the 380s and beyond. Of these, theodicy in particular—the reconciling of God's justice, power, and goodness with the evils and inequities of life—returned to haunt the Origenist debate. Moreover, readers familiar with early Christian history will here recognize the recurrence of questions concerning the worth of the material world, human freedom in relation to divine benevolence, sin and forgiveness.

Other readers will perceive the themes of this book as strikingly modern. An early stage of the controversy among the monks in Egypt concerned what we today would call the status of representation. In its ancient guise, this debate centered on the validity and usefulness of the image. Influenced by Origenist speculation, the monks asked whether God could be "imaged" in humans (as Genesis 1:26 suggested) or in other ways. Were images of *any* sort conducive to spiritual progress, or was the Christian's goal a kind of "mental iconoclasm"? Yet if the mind is conceived as a picture-making machine, how could worship and contemplation proceed *without* representation? That this debate was set in the historical framework of the demolition of pagan "idolatry" in Egypt is not, I think, accidental.

Likewise, those readers interested in the cultural coding of the body will find much to ponder in the ways that social and moral hierarchy left its mark on late ancient Christians' understanding of the body. As advocates of the "social construction" of the body, Origenists explored the extent of the body's transformability both here and in the hereafter, an exploration that linked ascetic practice with theories of the afterlife. More radically, Origen's view of the body's constant flux suggested that there *is* no such thing as "the body": physiology itself conspires to support the claims of social constructionists. Yet if, as Origenists believed, the origin and final destiny of the rational creature was bodiless, in what does the truth of the "self" lie?

Last, this study asks how theory (theology) and praxis (liturgical and ascetic practice) intersected to reinforce or challenge one another. How, for example, did the Church's practice of the Eucharist or prayer techniques relate to its doctrine of divine incorporeality? How did aspects of baptism, such as the exorcism and exsufflation of infants, buttress arguments concerning sin and salvation? And if the developing practice of penance suggested to Christians of late antiquity that *all* sins were forgivable, was the devil a candidate for salvation? Although these questions are rooted in ancient theological debates, their themes, in broader perspective, strike a modern chord.

Students of early Christianity will nonetheless note that the issues that resurfaced in the Origenist controversy were transmuted by changed religious and cultural needs. Thus, for example, although Valentinians and other Gnostics posed a minimal threat to Christians in late fourth-century Italy, Palestine, and North Africa, the "determinism" of which they had been accused was reborn in Manicheanism and in late antiquity's flirtation with astrological speculation. Likewise, the "fleshly" interpretation of the resurrection that some second-century Christians deemed essential for the refutation of Gnosticism now came under question: was it necessary to confess the resurrection of all the hairs of one's head, or of one's genital organs, in order to be counted as a Christian? Would an affirmation of the "spiritual body" (I Corinthians 15:44) suffice? Last, the arguments relating to God's incorporeality that characterized the Trinitarian controversy resonated in the Origenist debates over "Anthropomorphism" and "the image of God."

The central religious controversy of the later fourth century that marked the Origenist debate as forever different from second-century inquiry, however, concerned asceticism. The ascetic disputes of the 380s and 390s, for Western Christianity centering on Jerome, have never been considered "high theology" and hence have not been accorded the status of the Trinitarian controversy by most scholars of the patristic era. Although this inattention can be explained in several ways—for example, by the centrality of the "history of ideas" in theology or the lack of interest exhibited by Protestant scholars in the "Catholic" topic of asceticism—it has contributed, I think, to a misconstrual of Christianity in the later fourth and early fifth centuries.

The most important effect of the ascetic controversies was to concentrate Christian attention again on "the body": its discipline, its transformability, its usefulness as a tool for spiritual improvement. Proponents of asceticism claimed that a different body could make a different "self"; their opponents rejoined that asceticism promoted an elitism discordant with the confession that we are "all one in Christ Jesus" (Galatians 3:28). The major participants in the Origenist controversy were themselves ascetics: Epiphanius of Salamis, Theophilus of Alexandria, John of Jerusalem, Jerome, Rufinus, and their women companions—not to speak of Origen himself. Yet they differed sharply in their assessments of asceticism's implications for Christian teaching on marriage, reproduction, creation, and eschatology.

In the late fourth century, debates over asceticism coincided with a heightened critique of Origen's theology. Did not Origen's theory of the "fall" of rational creatures imply that embodied existence and reproduction are a defect? If the best we can claim for our present bodies is that they provide a means for our discipline and improvement, why *should* they be preserved into eternity when our perfection will be complete? Ought Origen's egalitarianism (all rational creatures were created in and shall return to a condition of equal blessedness) bow to Jerome's theory of a hierarchy of merit based on ascetic renunciation? Points of the ascetic debate thus found support or challenge in the newly centered attention on Origen's theology.

Moreover, just as the Origenist controversy refocused theological issues of earlier Christianity, so it contributed to the Pelagian debate in the decade after its own official demise in the West. When Origen's theory of the origin and fall of creatures was rejected by Western ecclesiastical authorities at the turn of the fifth century, the central question that had stimulated his theology (how to square the justice, goodness, and power of God with the miseries and inequalities of the present life) remained open. It is my contention that the debate between Pelagians and Augustine over original sin can profitably be reread as one resolution to the Origenist controversy in the West: Augustine's theory of original sin becomes the functional equivalent of Origen's notion of the precosmic sin and "fall" of the rational creatures. In my reconstruction, the dispute between Pelagians and Augustinians is thus a latter-day episode in the Origenist controversy . . . or, conversely, Origenism stands as the prehistory of the Pelagian debate.

Yet a nagging question remains: was the debate really over Origen? In some ways, the answer is no: "Origen" served as a code word for various theological concerns problematic to Christians at the turn of the fifth century.

As will be readily evident to readers of this book, each participant in the controversy had a somewhat different view of what the dispute was "about." I was indeed tempted to title the book *Origenisms* in order to convey that there is neither a stable personal identity that can be definitively labeled Origen nor a uniform set of doctrines that can be called Origenism, as is made manifest in the pages that follow. Perhaps more than any other early Christian "heresy," Origenism prompts post-structuralist reflection. Moreover, many arguments between pro- and anti-Origenist forces centered not on theology at all, but on personal alliances, hatreds, and jealousies that were carried on across three continents. Indeed, when I began my research on the Origenist controversy in 1985, before I had encountered Evagrius Ponticus, I imagined that I might explain the contro-

versy with little reference to theological "ideas" of any sort. But my introduction to Evagrius's *Kephalaia gnostica* in its unexpurgated form
challenged my early, purely social understanding of the Origenist dispute.
By situating Evagrius as a central force in the Western (i.e., Latin-speaking) Origenist debate, I signal my chastened reconsideration of the importance of both theology and an ascetic spirituality for the controversy.

This aspect of my project has, I think, produced some surprising results.
For one, I am now convinced that despite Jerome's enthusiasm for Egyptian asceticism and his translation of four lengthy denunciations of Origenism by Theophilus of Alexandria, he knew nothing of Evagrian theology
circa 400: he completely missed Theophilus's veiled references to Evagrius,
though to be sure, Theophilus did not lend him much assistance. Only in
the midst of the Pelagian controversy—414 and later—did an enraged Jerome at last perceive the centrality of Evagrius for the Origenist debates in
which he had so heatedly participated. Despite the propensity of previous
scholars to focus the Origenist controversy on the conflict between Jerome
and Rufinus of Aquileia, the former seems less aware of the contemporary
contested issues that we might have expected.

It is not to Jerome but to Rufinus that we turn to note the influence of
Origenism on Western theology. Here, Gabriel Bunge's commentary on
the Syriac version of Evagrius's letters has been of prime importance for
my study. The Evagrian connection with Rufinus and Melania that
emerges from these investigations does much to illumine the relationship
between Eastern and Western (i.e., Greek and Latin) Origenism. Through
networks of friendship and correspondence as well as his own study and
translation of Origen's writings, Rufinus was positioned to serve as conduit for Origenist theology and spirituality to a Latin-speaking audience.

As my research proceeded, Rufinus became still more important for my
argument. Attempting to situate the controversy historically, I was led to
ponder whether the ancient participants in the debate themselves were able
to read Origen's theology in historical perspective. Of the controversy's
main participants, it was only Rufinus, I concluded, who did so. Only Rufinus understood the religious issue confronting Origen that had prompted
the writing of *On First Principles*: the need to construct a polemic against
Gnostic and astrological determinism that would "save" human free will
and God's justice.[1] To be sure, Rufinus had a vested interest in reading *On
First Principles* positively, for his translation of the work into Latin had left
him vulnerable to charges of Origenist heresy. Jerome, in contrast, could

---

[1] Marguerite Harl, "La Préexistence des
âmes dans l'oeuvre d'Origène": "The problematic of the *Peri Archōn* is that of the inequality of conditions: Origen must respond
to the Gnostic doctrine of a determinism of
'natures,' fixed in different and unequal conditions" (241). As Harl clearly sees, Origen's
positing of the preexistence of souls is his
way of explaining that God is not responsible for evil (252).

see the dispute only through the lens of his own day: for him, the ascetic program to uphold hierarchy among Christians both here and in the hereafter was all-determining. In his zeal to proclaim his own orthodoxy, Jerome forgot (conveniently?) the pressing theological and philosophical questions that had prompted Origen to write *On First Principles*, questions that had by no means vanished in the century and a half since Origen's death.

Thus it was in Rufinus's interest to opt for a "minimalist" definition of Christian orthodoxy. Over and again, he claimed that if the doctrines defined up to his time by the Church—the Creator God, the Incarnation, the Trinity—were faithfully confessed, there was freedom to discuss points that had not been so defined, such as the origin of the soul and the fate of the devil. Jerome, in contrast, embraced a more rigid notion of doctrinal definition, claiming that there is only one acceptable position on the soul's origin (creationism) and one orthodox view of the resurrection body (that we receive back for eternity our very hair, bones, and genital organs). Whereas Jerome had earlier espoused a kind of exegetical freedom that encouraged the reader to select his or her preferred interpretation, in the midst of the Origenist controversy with his own correctness under suspicion, he urged a far less generous view of orthodoxy's requirements than did Rufinus.

Situating the Origenist controversy historically has brought to the fore a number of its important features that have sometimes been backgrounded. It was, for example, a controversy in which many notable women participated: Paula, Marcella, Melania the Elder, Melania the Younger, Olympias, and others. As patrons of Jerome, Rufinus, and John Chrysostom, they provided the material base that enabled their "clients" to write numerous treatises and letters that furnish much of our evidence. Although we only occasionally catch glimpses of them as participants in the debate itself, their centrality should not be underestimated simply because *their* letters were not preserved nor many of their conversations recorded.

A second historical dimension of the Origenist controversy I have highlighted is the role that pagan-Christian conflict played in it. Thus the disputes over "Anthropomorphism" and "images" in Egypt are set in the framework of the Christian attack on pagan "idolatry" in the 390s, most notably represented in the destruction of the Serapeum. As my colleague Annabel Wharton reminds me, we have here a dispute over power, over who controls the production of the image. Although churchmen were concerned to eradicate pagan devotion to "images," they were divided among themselves as to the usefulness of the image for Christian worship and contemplation.

Moreover, the prominence of pagan astrological speculation even in the later fourth century emerges as an important theme. Not only was the desire to refute astrological (and other forms of) determinism central to Origen's own theology: it was the expressed (and usually forgotten) reason for Rufinus's translation of *On First Principles*—the work best suited, he claimed, to refute the ravings of the *mathematici*. Nor was Augustine's youthful fascination with astrology entirely abandoned in his later career: he imported classic antiastrological arguments to his discussion of original sin—to construct a new "determinism," complained his Pelagian opponents.

Last, in exploring the social networks involved in the controversy, I have attempted to detail the alliances and enmities that provided much of the controversy's heat. Rivalries between bishops such as Theophilus of Alexandria and John Chrysostom of Constantinople, and over issues of ecclesiastical jurisdiction, such as whether Epiphanius had inappropriately ordained Jerome's brother within the ecclesiastical territory controlled by John of Jerusalem, added rancor to the debate. Indeed, in the case of Theophilus, one could easily argue that his campaign against Origenism merely provided a foil for his political machinations: having tamed the desert monks to his own purposes and having helped to engineer the downfall of John Chrysostom from the bishopric of Constantinople, he resumed the study of Origen he had enjoyed before the controversy's outbreak. The fragments of Theophilus's writings recovered in the last decades strengthen the thesis that he (unlike Jerome) knew the Evagrian form of Origenism. Fragments of his letters indicating that his agents circulated among the desert monks to ferret out "suspicious" points of theology lend weight to the claims of fifth-century church historians that Theophilus played the major role in hounding Origenists out of Egypt. That he was not entirely successful is suggested by the discovery of Origenist speculation among monks in fifth-century Egypt, combated by Shenute.

In investigating the charges and countercharges concerning Origenism, I have proceeded in chronological order through the writings of Epiphanius, Theophilus, Jerome, and Rufinus. Although this approach may strike the reader as less than exciting, it has enabled me to track shifts in argumentation influenced by contemporary debates. Thus I have highlighted how by the mid-390s, Epiphanius's attack on Origen had moved from the Trinitarian issues of the 370s to one centered on the body and reproduction, and how, in a brief four-year span, Theophilus refocused his entire argument on the latter issue. As for Jerome, a chronological tour through his writings reveals both how belatedly (only in 398 or thereafter) he recognized that he must defend *himself* against charges of Origenism, and how lightly he dismissed (until pressed by Rufinus) the Origenist concern with

God's justice. Likewise, a chronological survey of Rufinus's treatises and translations discloses the consistency of his theological opinions before, during, and after the controversy: the points he defended appear as considered theological judgments, however unpopular they may have been with his opponents.

Thus I have situated the Origenist controversy amid debates between pagans and Christians, "Anthropomorphites" and spiritualists, champions and opponents of asceticism. I have examined how the activities of aristocratic ascetic women affected its course, and how the West's rejection of Origenism marked the debate between Pelagians and Augustine. Throughout I have foregrounded figures such as Evagrius Ponticus and Theophilus of Alexandria, who have received little attention in the English-speaking world.

My approach, as even the inattentive reader will soon note, is admittedly partisan. Although I have brought all the relevant documents of which I am aware to bear upon my interpretation of events, I have been concerned throughout to give a sympathetic reading to the Origenist side of the debate. Evagrius Ponticus, Rufinus, and the Pelagians are thus the "heroes" of my account—not Epiphanius, Jerome, and Augustine. Mine is not the approach of most theology textbooks. It is, rather, an attempt to raise up for consideration a defeated theology that for a few years stirred the Christian world to new intellectual creativity.

Elite Networks and Heresy
Accusations: Towards a
Social Description of the
Origenist Controversy

Ont night in A.D. 397, the Roman nobleman Macarius had a dream. Macarius, who had been attempting (without apparent success) to compose a refutation of astrological determinism through an appeal to God's benevolence, saw a ship approaching across distant seas that would, God promised, solve his difficulties with the *mathematici*. Macarius later realized that his dream had portended Rufinus of Aquileia's arrival from Palestine and translation, at his request, of Origen's *On First Principles*.[1] Jerome, Rufinus's chief antagonist in the Origenist controversy, took a different and dimmer view: the trireme carrying that vast treasure of Egyptian and Eastern teaching[2] might better have sunk en route, for although it had come to Rome to "solve the puzzle of the *mathematici*," it had in fact "unloosed the faith of Christians."[3]

As is well known, Origen's *Peri Archōn* entertained a variety of theories that fourth-century Christians found reprehensible. Jerome catalogues them as follows: that within the Godhead, the Son was subordinated to the Father and the Holy Spirit to both;[4] that rational creatures fell from a

---

[1] Rufinus, *Apologia contra Hieronymum*, I, 11 (*CCL* 20, 44–45). Macarius is identified as a Roman by Jerome, in *Apologia contra Rufinum* III, 32 (*CCL* 79, 102), and as a noble (*vir nobilis*) in III, 24 (*CCL* 79, 96). (Book III of Jerome's *Contra Rufinum* is identified as *Epistula adversus Rufinum* in the *CCL* edition; Jerome's and Rufinus's defenses against each other will hereafter be cited simply as *Apologia*.) Is Macarius to be identified with a man of the same name who is described by Palladius as an "ex-vicar" (*Historia Lausiaca* 62 [Butler ed., 2: 157])?

For a detailed study of the controversy's chronology, see Karl Holl, "Die Zeitfolge der ersten origenistischen Streits." Holl dates Rufinus's departure from Palestine for the West to early 396, and his translations of *On First Principles* to late spring and summer of 398 (317, 322, 324).

[2] Jerome, *Apologia* III, 29 (*CCL* 79, 101).
[3] Jerome, *Apologia* III, 32 (*CCL* 79, 102).
[4] Jerome, *Ep.* 124, 2; 13 (*CSEL* 56, 97–98, 115–116); *Contra Ioannem Hierosolymitanum* 7 (*PL* 23, 376).

heavenly, incorporeal preexistence to acquire bodies, identified with the "coats of skins" of Genesis 3:21;[5] that the devil could resume his angelic status and be saved;[6] that demons could be transformed into humans, and *vice versa*;[7] that since bodily substance was destined to pass away, there would be no physical resurrection;[8] that a succession of worlds may have already existed and may exist in the future;[9] that hellfire is not external to us, but the pangs of guilty conscience;[10] that Christ may come again to suffer for the demons;[11] and that allegorical exegesis is preferable to literal for those of advanced spirituality.[12] These theories and others—most notably, an approach to the material body that implied a denigration of reproduction[13]—constituted the main grounds for the attack on Origenism by Jerome, Epiphanius, and Theophilus, as is detailed in Chapter Three.

When charged with Origenism Rufinus's first response was to affirm Nicene doctrine,[14] which Jerome scathingly rejected as a totally irrelevant affirmation.[15] Rufinus next confessed his belief in a bodily resurrection.[16] He refused to pronounce on the origin of souls, however, asserting (correctly) that since the Church had not declared any one opinion as orthodox to the exclusion of others, Christians were entitled to continue debate.[17] As a further defense, Rufinus claimed that dubious theological motifs in Origen's books had been inserted there by heretics and did not reflect Origen's considered opinion.[18] Moreover, he charged, Jerome himself had earlier en-

---

[5] Jerome, *Ep.* 124, 3; 9 (*CSEL* 56, 98–99, 108–109); *Contra Ioannem* 7 (*PL* 23, 376).

[6] Jerome, *Ep.* 124, 3 (*CSEL* 56, 98); *Contra Ioannem* 7 (*PL* 23, 376).

[7] Jerome, *Ep.* 124, 3; 10 (*CSEL* 56, 99, 111–112).

[8] Jerome, *Ep.* 124, 4; 5; 9; 10 (*CSEL* 56, 99–100, 101–102, 109–110, 111–112).

[9] Jerome, *Ep.* 124, 5; 9 (*CSEL* 56, 101–103, 107–108).

[10] Jerome, *Ep.* 124, 7 (*CSEL* 56, 104–105).

[11] Jerome, *Ep.* 124, 12 (*CSEL* 56, 114–115).

[12] Jerome, *Contra Ioannem* 7 (*PL* 23, 376).

[13] See the criticisms made by Epiphanius, Theophilus, and Jerome, detailed in Chap. 3.

[14] Rufinus, *Apologia ad Anastasium* 2 (*CCL* 20, 25); *Apologia* I, 4 (*CCL* 20, 39). The same charge is raised against John of Jerusalem by Jerome in *Contra Ioannem* 8 (*PL* 23, 377).

[15] Jerome, *Apologia* II, 4 (*CCL* 79, 36): Rufinus may cite his faith in the Trinity all he likes, but the issue is Origen, not Arius. Al-

though Rufinus had changed what Origen had written on the Trinity to make it more orthodox, this was hardly the only part that needed "emendation" (Jerome, *Apologia* I, 6 [*CCL* 79, 6]).

[16] Albeit a spiritual and incorporeal body, following I Corinthians 15:35–54: Rufinus, *Prologus in Apologeticum Pamphili Martyris pro Origene* (*CCL* 20, 234); *Apologia ad Anastasium* 3; 4 (*CCL* 20, 26); *Apologia* I, 4–9 (*CCL* 20, 39–43). Rufinus holds Jerome guilty of dispensing with the resurrection body in his *Commentary on Ephesians: Apologia* I, 24–25; 41 (*CCL* 20, 58–60, 75–77).

[17] Rufinus, *Apologia ad Anastasium* 6 (*CCL* 20, 27). Jerome tried to make it sound as if the Church had ruled in favor of creationism: *Contra Ioannem* 22 (*PL* 23, 389); *Apologia* III, 28; 30 (*CCL* 79, 99–100, 101–102). Jerome is more cautious after the heat of the controversy died; see *Ep.* 126, 1 (*CSEL* 56, 143), dated to A.D. 412.

[18] Rufinus, *De adulteratione librorum Origenis* 1–2, 6–9, 14–16 (*CCL* 20, 7–8, 10–14, 16–17); *De principiis, praefatio,* 3 (*CCL* 20, 246); *Apologia ad Anastasium* 7 (*CCL*

gaged in extensive translation of and commentary upon Origen's works.[19] Had not Jerome deceived his readers, who expected on the basis of his extravagant encomia to encounter Origen in the heavenly halls after they died?[20]

Most important, Rufinus—unlike Jerome—vigorously affirmed that the motivation undergirding Origen's enterprise should be lauded: he had wished to uphold both God's justice and benevolence, and human free will, against the determinism of Gnostics and astrologers. Under attack, Rufinus maintained that *any* theology worth credence must protect these teachings of the Christian tradition at all costs.[21] Thus for Rufinus, the scheme of *On First Principles* was as relevant to Macarius's dilemma in 397 as it had been in Origen's milieu.

A thumbnail sketch of the conflict between Jerome and Rufinus—as traditionally conceived—might go as follows:[22] the first round of dispute occurred in the mid-390s in Palestine, when Epiphanius of Salamis charged John of Jerusalem with Origenism, and Rufinus aligned himself with John. John appealed to Theophilus of Alexandria—not yet an opponent of Origenism—who sent an emissary, Isidore, to assess the situation; but Isidore's partisan support of John served only to arouse Jerome's ire when he heard of it.[23] Jerome, rallying to Epiphanius's side, translated his admonitory letter to John for a private readership, but (according to Jerome) Rufinus's allies bribed someone for a copy and misused it to promote controversy.[24] Jerome then began composing a fiercely anti-Origenist tract against John, but abandoned it when he and Rufinus patched up their relationship just before Rufinus's departure for the West in 397.[25] When

---

20, 27–28); *Apologia* I, 12 (*CCL* 20, 45). Rufinus testifies that he sometimes supplanted these interpolated views with orthodox ones that Origen expressed elsewhere.

[19] Rufinus, *De principiis, praefatio*, 1–2 (*CCL* 20, 245–246); *Apologia* I, 24–25; 28; 36; 39; 41–43; II, 16–21, 23–25, 49–50 (*CCL* 20, 58–59, 62–63, 70, 73–74, 75–79, 95–98, 99–102, 121–122). Jerome tries to reduce the extent of his association with Origen. Although he admits he has translated "many tomes," he insists he was interested in the Biblical commentary, not the dogma: *Apologia* I, 22; 24 (*CCL* 79, 21–22, 24). In *Apologia* II, 16 (*CCL* 79, 50), he says he possesses all (*omnia*) of Origen's works and has read a great many of them. Jerome speaks of his work on Origen in *Epp.* 33, 4–5 (*CSEL* 54, 255–259); 43, 1–2 (*CSEL* 54, 318); 61, 1–2 (*CSEL* 54, 575–578); 82, 7 (*CSEL* 55, 113–114); 84, 2–3; 7; 8; 11 (*CSEL* 55,

121–125, 128–131, 133–134); 85, 3 (*CSEL* 55, 136–137); 124 (*CSEL* 56, 96–117); 130, 16 (*CSEL* 56, 196–197), and in many of his Biblical commentaries.

[20] Rufinus, *Apologia* I, 22; 25 (*CCL* 20, 56–57, 58–60).

[21] See Chap. 4.

[22] For an overview of the controversy, see Brochet, *Saint Jérôme et ses ennemis* pt. 2; Maurice Villain, "Rufin d'Aquilée—La querelle autour d'Origène," 5–37, 165–195; Francis X. Murphy, *Rufinus of Aquileia (345–411)*, 59–157; or J.N.D. Kelly, *Jerome: His Life, Writings, and Controversies*, chaps. 18, 20–22.

[23] Jerome, *Contra Ioannem* 4; 37–39 (*PL* 23, 374–375, 406–409); *Ep.* 82, 9 (*CSEL* 55, 116).

[24] Jerome, *Ep.* 57, 2–4 (*CSEL* 54, 504–508).

[25] Jerome's *Contra Ioannem* breaks off un-

Rufinus arrived in Italy, Macarius prevailed upon him to translate Origen's *On First Principles* into Latin, as described above. An uproar resulted among Jerome's Roman friends, who sent Jerome a copy of the translation and requested that he act.[26] Now under attack, Rufinus defended his theological orthodoxy in a statement to Pope Anastasius and in a treatise, the *Apology against Jerome*. Before Jerome had the text of Rufinus's *Apology* in hand, he wrote two books against Rufinus on the basis of reports reaching Palestine; a third book followed after Jerome had obtained a complete copy of Rufinus's work. Only through the intervention of other parties and the passage of time did the controversy abate.

Rufinus continued to translate Origen's writings until the time of his death in about 410. Jerome, who could not relinquish a grudge, continued to slander Rufinus, dubbing him with nicknames such as "Grunnius Corocotta Porcellius" ("Porky the Grunter").[27] Only belatedly, more than a decade after the controversy's height, did Jerome realize that Evagrius Ponticus's theology had been central to its outbreak and that some important issues of the Origenist dispute were resurfacing in the then-developing debate between Pelagian and Catholic Christians.[28] These two recognitions, essential for a wider understanding of the Origenist controversy, claims our attention in Chapters Two and Five. Yet theological issues were not all that was at stake.

Students of early Christianity can readily guess that other, nontheological issues lay only slightly beneath the surface of the controversy. Not surprisingly, only portions of Jerome's and Rufinus's diatribes on these subjects actually concern Origen. We hear much, for example, about a struggle over ecclesiastical jurisdiction: had bishop Epiphanius of Salamis overstepped his rights when he ordained Jerome's brother Paulinianus in Palestine, allegedly within the episcopal jurisdiction of John of Jerusalem?[29] A second disputed question was who had authored the famous *Apology* for Origen—the blessed martyr Pamphilus (as Rufinus claimed) or the wretched Arian historian, Eusebius of Caesarea (a view Jerome found attractive).[30]

---

finished. Jerome says that he and Rufinus joined hands in peace at the Church of the Resurrection (*Apologia* III, 33 [*CCL*, 79, 103]).

[26] Pammachius and Oceanus, *Ep. ad Hieronymum* (= Jerome, *Ep.* 83) (*CSEL* 55, 119–120).

[27] Jerome, *Comm. in Esaiam*, praefatio (*CCL* 73A, 465). Jerome refers to Rufinus as "Grunnius" also in *Ep.* 125, 18 (*CSEL* 56, 137) and in *In Hieremiam Prophetam*, prologus 4 (*CCL* 74, 2).

[28] Jerome, *Dialogus adversus Pelagianos*, prologus 1 (*PL* 23, 518); *Ep.* 133, 3 (*CSEL* 56, 244–246).

[29] Epiphanius, *Ep. ad Iohannem Episcopum* (= Jerome, *Ep.* 51) 1–2 (*CSEL* 54, 396–399): Epiphanius claims that Paulinianus was not ordained in a place within John's jurisdiction. Also, see Jerome, *Contra Ioannem* 10; 40; 41 (*PL* 23, 379, 410–411); *Ep.* 82, 4; 8 (*CSEL* 55, 111, 114–115).

[30] Rufinus, *Prologus in Apologeticum Pamphili Martyris pro Origene* (*CCL* 20, 233); Jerome, *Ep.* 84, 11 (*CSEL* 55, 133–134); *Apologia* I, 8–11; 13; II, 15; 23; III, 12 (*CCL* 79, 7–11, 12, 48–49, 59–60, 83–85).

A third point concerned correct principles of translation. Jerome and Rufinus each thought his own style of translation to be correct, if not always literal, and each wished to impugn the translating abilities of the other.[31] Jerome faulted Rufinus for altering the *Peri Archōn* in the direction of orthodoxy[32] and ridiculed the clumsy yet pretentious style of his opponent.[33] Rufinus countered that Jerome, in his earlier translations of Origen's works, had sometimes proceeded in less than literal fashion.[34] More nastily, he insinuated that Jerome's study of Hebrew and subsequent translation of the Hebrew Scriptures into Latin was a covert condemnation of the Septuagint, an attempt to sneak "Jewish" views into the purity of Christian teaching.[35] Fourth, Rufinus assumed the role of Tertullian *redivivus* and challenged Jerome's constant citation of secular literature, contending that Cicero, Virgil, and Horace had nothing to do with Christian truth.[36] Jerome's snide rejoinder was to claim that Rufinus's writings made obvious that *he* had never studied literature at all:[37] Origen's souls falling from the heavens to be clothed with bodies on earth were less knocked about, said Jerome, than the souls Rufinus described, struck on all sides by his barbaric phrases.[38]

Last, the quarrel over asceticism resurfaced. Rufinus pounced upon the "Manichean" tone of Jerome's *Epistle* 22 to the virgin Eustochium and his *Against Jovinian*,[39] delighting to remind his readers that Jerome had been so transported by ascetic enthusiasm that he had blasphemously called his friend Paula, the mother of the letter's recipient, "the mother-in-law of God."[40] Jerome's response was to question Rufinus's ascetic rigor, comparing his wealth to that of Croesus and Sardanapalus,[41] and hinting that the soft life prevailed in Rufinus's and Melania the Elder's Jerusalem monas-

---

[31] Jerome, *Apologia* I, 19; II, 18 (*CCL* 79, 19, 52–54); *Ep.* 57, 5–6; 12 (*CSEL* 54, 508–512, 524–526); Rufinus, *Apologia* II, 31 (*CCL* 20, 106–107); *De principiis* I, *praefatio*, 1 (*CCL* 20, 245). Recall how ardently Jerome desired a Ciceronian style: *Ep.* 22, 30 (*CSEL* 54, 189–191). For a detailed examination of Rufinus's and Jerome's translating styles, see Gustave Bardy, *Recherches sur l'histoire du texte*, Book II; also Friedhelm Winkelmann, "Einige Bemerkungen zu den Aussagen des Rufinus von Aquileia," II, 532–547.

[32] Jerome, *Apologia* I, 6; II, 11 (2); III, 14 (*CCL* 79, 5–6, 45–46, 86–87). In his preface to *De principiis* I, 2, Rufinus says that Jerome emended Origen's language in translating so that nothing would be at variance with the faith (*CCL* 20, 245–246).

[33] Jerome, *Apologia* I, 17; III, 6 (*CCL* 79, 16, 78–80).

[34] Rufinus, *Apologia* II, 8; 31 (*CCL* 20,

89, 106–107).

[35] Rufinus, *Apologia* II, 36–41 (*CCL* 20, 111–116). Jerome defended himself long before the controversy (in 388) in his preface to *Hebraicae quaestiones* (*CCL* 72, 2) as well as later, during the controversy, *Apologia* II, 24–33 (*CCL* 79, 60–70).

[36] Rufinus, *Apologia* II, 6; 7; 9; 11 (*CCL* 20, 87–89, 90–91, 91–92); cf. Tertullian, *De praescriptione haereticorum* 7, 9 (*CCL* 1, 193): "Quid ergo Athenis et Hierosolymis? quid academiae et ecclesiae?"

[37] Jerome, *Apologia* I, 30 (*CCL* 79, 30–31); *Ep.* 70 (*CSEL* 54, 700–708).

[38] Jerome, *Apologia* II, 10 (*CCL* 79, 41).

[39] Rufinus, *Apologia* II, 5; 42–43 (*CCL* 20, 86–87, 116–117).

[40] Rufinus, *Apologia* II, 13 (*CCL* 20, 93).

[41] Jerome, *Ep.* 57, 4; 12 (*CSEL* 54, 507, 526); *Apologia* I, 17; III, 4 (*CCL* 79, 16, 76); *In Naum* III (vv. 8–12) (*CCL* 76A, 564).

teries.[42] That Jerome later came to a different insight on Origenism's ascetic stringency is revealed in his attack on Evagrius Ponticus's advocacy of *apatheia*, the attainment of an equanimity undisturbed by the passions.[43] As we shall see, Jerome's critique of Origenism was strongly influenced by his claim that superlative merit accrued to ascetic renunciation, both here and in the hereafter: hierarchy had to be preserved at all costs.[44]

Yet beneath the theological and extratheological issues mentioned above lies another consideration that would be considered decisive by many social scientists: the principals in the controversy, who had known each other for many years, had their coteries of supporters well in line before the controversy ever erupted. If there is anything surprising about the way the conflict developed, it is the degree to which the factions lined up precisely on the basis of old friendship and association. Only a few "switch" characters can be noted in the entire complex drama, Theophilus of Alexandria being the most important. In fact, some might argue that the multifaceted relations to be examined—kinship, marriage, hospitality proffered and received, religious mentorship, gift-giving, and literary and financial patronage—illumine the developing antagonisms with less recourse to theological debate than students of Christian history would have imagined.

Two points need emphasis before we unravel the social webs undergirding the controversy. First, although contemporary social scientists assume that network description proceeds through direct observation, interviews, and questionnaires, the literature from the Origenist controversy is so abundant that a scholar working fifteen centuries later need not despair at ferreting out the relationships through which the controversy evolved. Although some pieces of evidence have been lost and other points remain obscure in the extant materials, more documents pertinent to social analysis remain for the Origenist debate than for any other early Christian controversy.

In part, the abundance of our material stems from the letter-writing proclivities of the disputants: here, Jerome's letters (and his translation of some of Epiphanius's and Theophilus of Alexandria's) comprise an invaluable source for the reconstruction of the networks. Unfortunately, neither the letters written by women to Jerome nor those composed by Rufinus are extant. Moreover, letters often went astray: the Origenist controversy constitutes an exemplary case of a dispute fueled by letters that never reached their destination. It must also be admitted that ecclesiastical "men

---

[42] Jerome, *Epp.* 57, 12 (*CSEL* 54, 526); 125, 18 (*CSEL* 56, 138). Is the distinction to be correlated with a possible difference of *Rules* used in the monasteries? Recall that Jerome translated the *Rule of Pachomius* for Eustochium to use with her nuns (*S. Pachomii Regula, praefatio* 1 [Boon ed., 3–5]),

while Rufinus translated the milder *Rule of St. Basil*. See Murphy, *Rufinus*, 61–62.

[43] Jerome, *Dialogus adversus Pelagianos, prologus*, 1 (*PL* 23, 517–519); *Ep.* 133, 3 (*CSEL* 56, 244, 246).

[44] See discussion below, pp. 128–132.

of letters," like their secular counterparts, sometimes wrote to people whom they knew little, if at all. Such letters cannot always be taken as evidence of close relationships, but perhaps are better understood as a manifestation of ancient patronage systems in a new Christian environment.

Throughout the Origenist controversy, the giving and receiving of favors was sustained among a highly "internationalized" Christian elite by means of exchanging letters. From the remains of such correspondence, we learn how wealthy men and women provided funds for the building of churches and monasteries, commissioned (usually by "requesting") works of Christian literature, and lent social prestige to the activities of theologians who were low on cash but high on learned reflection. Despite the problems that separate the analysis of ancient networks from that of modern ones, the abundant literary remains from the Origenist controversy provide sufficient material to inspire at least limited confidence in the reconstruction of the social networks involved.

Second, the amenability of the Origenist controversy to exploration through a network analysis most associated with the social sciences in no way dampens its high drama: the relationships revealed are replete with friendships gone awry, jealousy, betrayal, larceny, bribery, vanity, and sheer pigheadedness. Above the prejudice and calumny soars Origen's admittedly heterodox genius, a genius that produced the first coherent piece of speculative theology in the Christian tradition.

The considerations that sparked the development of social network theory make it a particularly productive approach to the types of relationships involved in the Origenist controversy. Abandoning structuralist/functionalist analysis as inadequate for examining relations *within* groups[45] and faulting its assumption of a static social model,[46] social scientists sought an approach that better lent itself to the consideration of societies and relationships characterized by hierarchy, asymmetry, and inequality, without reverting to an individualistic, psychological analysis. The examination of networks was the result of this quest, and sociologists agree that the method has proven especially fruitful in the study of friendships, disputes, and patronage[47]—precisely the topics relevant to an examination of the Origenist controversy.

---

[45] E.g., J. Clyde Mitchell, "The Concept and Use of Social Networks," 1; J. Clyde Mitchell, "Networks, Norms and Institutions," 9, 15; Boissevain, *Friends of Friends*, 4–7; Noble, "Social Network" 4; Eisenstadt and Roniger, "Patron-Client Relations as a Model of Structuring Social Exchange," 47.

[46] Mitchell, "Concept and Use," 9; Noble, "Social Network," 4; Boissevain, *Friends of*

Friends, 4–19; Eisenstadt and Roniger, "Patron-Client Relations," 47; Mitchell, "Social Networks," 281. Boissevain accuses the structuralist/functionalist approach of serving conservative ends, of supporting a colonialist mentality: *Friends of Friends*, 13, 19.

[47] E.g., Eisenstadt and Roniger, "Patron-Client Relations," 48–51, 56, 72–73; Boissevain, *Friends of Friends*, chaps. 3, 6, 7;

Network Theory

The determining concept of network theory is, as J. Clyde Mitchell explains, that "the variations in behaviour of people in any one role relationship may be traced to the effects of the behaviour of other people, to whom they are linked in one, two or more steps, in some other quite different relationship."[48] Structures of relationships—who is linked to whom and how, and which persons are linked to each other through third parties—are held to be more decisive than issues of motivation or belief in explaining behavior. Thus researchers such as Rodney Stark have argued, with good evidence, that in some contemporary religious groups, interpersonal ties are far more effective than ideology both in recruitment to the group and in maintenance of commitment.[49]

Network analysts, measuring the density of a network (i.e., "the number of links that actually exist expressed as a proportion of the maximum number of links that could possibly exist"),[50] claim that dense networks, in which many persons are connected with each other, make probable that an individual's actions are as strongly conditioned by relationships with others in the network as by the ideas that constitute the alleged matter at hand—in the case of the Origenist controversy, by points of theology. Asking whether individuals in a network are linked with each other in one role or in many,[51] network analysts argue that the greater the multiplexity of ties, the stronger the likelihood that a person's action in any particular situation is conditioned by his or her links with others in the network. Thus in the Origenist controversy, the sheer multiplicity of ties existing among network members—ties of kinship, friendship, hospitality given and received, literary and financial patronage, religious mentorship, traveling companionship—helps to predispose the theological positions they will adopt.

Network researchers also speak of the "brokers" and "gatekeepers" who provide access between the more and the less powerful persons in a network.[52] In the case of the Origenist controversy, the liaison persons did

---

Thoden van Velzen, "Coalition and Network Analysis," 219–250; Wolf, "Kinship, Friendship, and Patron–Client Relations in Complex Societies," 1–22; Wellman, "Network Analysis: Some Basic Principles," 157, 172; Weingood, "Patronage and Power," 41–51; and other essays in this book. For the application of these issues to cases in contemporary religious life, see especially Boissevain, "When the Saints Go Marching Out," 81–96; and Stark and Bainbridge, "Networks of Faith," 1376–1395. For a helpful analysis of ancient material by a classicist familiar with network theory, see Saller, *Personal Patronage under the Early Empire.*

[48] Mitchell, "Concept and Use," 46.
[49] Stark and Bainbridge, "Networks," 1376–1391.
[50] Mitchell, "Concept and Use," 35.
[51] Barnes, *Social Networks*, 13; Mitchell, "Concept and Use," 17–18, 24–25, 35; Boissevain, *Friends of Friends*, 30–39; Mitchell, "Social Networks," 288–289; Niemeijer, "Some Applications of the Notion of Density to Network Analysis," 46–49.
[52] E.g., Barnes, *Social Networks*, 10; Mitchell, "Concept and Use," 38; Boissevain, *Friends of Friends*, chap. 6; Adrian C. Mayer, "The Significance of Quasi-Groups in the Study of Complex Societies," 114.

not always mediate between those of unequal status, but often operated on a "horizontal" plane between persons of roughly equal power who, because of geographic separation, were dependent on intermediaries to carry messages, literature, and information for them. Many developments of the Origenist controversy rested on the success or failure (mostly failure) with which these "go-betweens" performed their tasks. In many cases, the go-betweens provide, in Mark Granovetter's phrase, the "weak ties" (the relations between acquaintances, as contrasted with those of friends) essential to relations *between* groups,[53] serving as the bridges that connect clusters of friends.[54] Granovetter's theory of "the strength of weak ties" does not seem applicable to the Origenist controversy at first glance, both because the "Gesellschaft" type of relations it was designed to explain[55] is foreign to the material under investigation, and, more importantly, because Jerome's and Rufinus's networks are composed chiefly of "strong-tied relations," where the principle of "transitivity" holds: the friends of friends tend to be one's own friends as well.[56] Yet if ties are seen from the viewpoint of the larger social structure, not from that of individual relationships, they appear as the links, the form of "brokerage," that join the parts of a social system. Thus in the Origenist controversy, mere acquaintances sometimes serve as the "bridges" or "brokers" between groups of friends—or enemies. Such concepts help to illuminate the historical material pertaining to the Origenist controversy without, I think, dismissing the fact that theological affirmation played a far more central role in the lives of these ancient Christian disputants than it does in those of contemporary social scientists. Rather, the themes emphasized by network analysts serve to enrich our historical understanding by calling attention to relationships that might otherwise be insufficiently noticed.

The sheer density of the relationships constituting the two major networks involved in the Origenist controversy is striking: the network analysts' stress on the importance of density of ties within and among networks is here strongly borne out. For a world in which written communication and travel were far slower and more complex than our own, the participants remained surprisingly connected. In part, these connections testify to the still-important roles that wealthy laypeople—such as Jerome's friend Pammachius, or Macarius, who implored Rufinus to translate *On First Principles*—enjoyed in late fourth-century Christian society. Bishops such as John of Jerusalem and Theophilus of Alexandria moved

---

[53] Mark S. Granovetter, "The Strength of Weak Ties," 1360, 1376; Mark S. Granovetter, "The Strength of Weak Ties: A Network Theory Revisited," 201.

[54] Granovetter, "Strength," 1364–1365, 1367–1368, 1378; Granovetter, "Strength Revisited," 202, 219.

[55] Granovetter, "Strength Revisited," 203–204, 209: Granovetter discusses such issues as the passage of information about jobs and the mobilization of citizens for or against urban renewal.

[56] Granovetter, "Strength Revisited," 218.

with ease in circles of monks and pious laypeople as well as of their fellow clerics. Heiresses such as Paula, Fabiola, and the two Melanias, who lavished their fortunes on Christian causes, proved welcome companions to ascetic males struggling to found monasteries and to bishops seeking funds for the Church's extensive charity work. Male and female speakers of Greek and of Latin joined in a truly international society, traveling between Italy, North Africa, Egypt, Palestine, and Asia Minor. To unpack the social connections—connections that provided the material foundation for the dispute of ideas—among this sophisticated group is the task at hand.

As young adults, Rufinus and Jerome had been best of friends, perhaps fellow students in Rome. Jerome then departed for Gaul, but did not forget Rufinus: at Rufinus's request, he had two treatises of Hilary copied out for him.[57] After Jerome's return to Italy, the two probably mingled in the religious community at Aquileia, which included the priest Chromatius.[58] Here Rufinus was baptized by Chromatius.[59] In 371 or 372, their paths again diverged. Jerome went to Antioch, Rufinus to Egypt.[60] One of Jerome's first extant letters is addressed to Rufinus in Egypt: he yearns to kiss Rufinus, who "so often in the past joined me in error or in wisdom."[61] Ironically, in light of later events, Jerome closes with the sentiment, "the friendship which can come to an end has never been genuine."[62] In this letter, Jerome reports that among the people with him in Syria was Hylas, "the servant of the holy Melanium."[63] This notice establishes that Jerome had at least secondhand knowledge of Melania the Elder from the early 370s. Later, he describes her as a second Thecla.[64] Likewise, in his *Chronicle* for 377, Jerome calls Rufinus a model monk.[65]

Soon after his departure from Aquileia, Rufinus met Melania, either in Rome or in Egypt.[66] Visiting Nitria, they encountered some of the "Tall Brothers," four monks and priests associated with Evagrius Ponticus, who later would suffer for their allegedly Origenist views.[67] According to the

[57] Jerome reports this detail later in *Ep.* 5, 2 (*CSEL* 54, 21–22).

[58] So inferred from Jerome's early correspondence; see Kelly, *Jerome*, 30–33; Murphy, *Rufinus*, 19–27.

[59] Rufinus, *Apologia* I, 4 (*CCL* 20, 39).

[60] The circumstances of Jerome's departure are obscure and hint at unpleasant developments of an unknown sort: see Kelly, *Jerome*, 33–35; F. Cavallera, *Saint Jérôme. Sa vie et son oeuvre*, C, vol. 2: 75–77.

[61] Jerome, *Ep.* 3, 1 (*CSEL* 54, 13).

[62] Jerome, *Ep.* 3, 6 (*CSEL* 54, 18).

[63] Jerome, *Ep.* 3, 3 (*CSEL* 54, 18). This instance of a masculine ending appended to her name may relate to the issue of whether she was the recipient of Evagrius Ponticus's

so-called *Letter to Melania*: see below, pp. 191–192.

[64] Rufinus, *Apologia* II, 29 (*CCL* 20, 105); Jerome, *Chronicon* for 374 (*GCS* 24, 247). Jerome also had praised Melania in *Epp.* 39, 5 and 45, 4–5 (*CSEL* 54, 305, 325–327).

[65] Jerome, *Chronicon* for 377 (*GCS* 24, 248).

[66] Francis X. Murphy, "Melania the Elder: A Biographical Note," 67, opts for Alexandria.

[67] Palladius, *Historia Lausiaca* 46 (Butler ed., vol. 2: 134); for Melania's relation with Pambo, teacher of the Tall Brothers, see 10 (Butler ed., vol. 2: 29–31); on Ammonius, see 11 (Butler ed., vol. 2: 32–34). Rufinus is at Nitria in Jerome, *Ep.* 3, 2 (*CSEL* 54, 14).

Coptic version of the *Lausiac History*, Melania also went to Scete, where she built a church for the priest Isidore.[68] During Melania and Rufinus's Egyptian sojourn, the Arian-sympathizing emperor Valens ordered a persecution of Nicene Christians in Egypt. Melania fled to Diocaesarea in Palestine with a group of the Nitrian monks—including Evagrius's friend, Ammonius "the Earless," and Isidore of Alexandria—all of whom she supported.[69] Rufinus reports that he was jailed during the Arian outburst,[70] but whether he spent six years in Egypt (as he later claimed) is uncertain.[71] Jerome's assumption that Rufinus was already in Palestine by 374 (he writes asking to have a commentary copied)[72] may have been mistaken.

By the late 370s, Rufinus had joined Melania in Palestine, where they built monasteries for men and women on the Mount of Olives. In the years following, they entertained a steady stream of visitors at their monastic establishment.[73] Melania's extraordinary generosity was well noted by Palladius: he writes that from her own fortune, she made donations to churches, monasteries, and private individuals,[74] and that upon her death, she endowed her monastery.[75] Rufinus's wealth, to which Jerome often alludes,[76] can thus be better assigned to Melania. An heiress of the *gens Antonia*[77] who had married into the *gens Valeria*,[78] she was enormously wealthy. We do not know, however, how many of the mansions and estates owned by her granddaughter Melania the Younger in Rome and its suburbs, Campania, Sicily, Spain, Africa, Mauretania, Britain, Numidia, Aquitania, and Gaul[79] were inherited through Melania the Elder's side of the family.

There can be no doubt that Melania the Elder and Rufinus were a very well-connected monastic pair. They were on the best of terms with John of Jerusalem,[80] bishop of the city since 386, whose rebuff to and mockery of Epiphanius enraged Jerome.[81] They were linked to Constantinople so-

---

[68] *Historia Lausiaca* (Coptic) 2 (Pamo) (Amélineau ed., 96).

[69] Palladius, *Historia Lausiaca* 46 (Butler ed., vol. 2: 134–135); Paulinus of Nola, *Ep.* 29, 11 (*CSEL* 29, 257–258). For the adventures of Isidore, later to be hated by Theophilus of Alexandria, see Chap. 2.

[70] Rufinus, *Apologia ad Anastasium* 2 (*CCL* 20, 25).

[71] Rufinus, *Apologia* II, 15 (*CCL* 20, 94).

[72] Jerome, *Ep.* 5, 2 (*CSEL* 54, 21–22).

[73] Palladius, *Historia Lausiaca* 46 (Butler ed., vol. 2: 135–136). Exactly when Rufinus arrived in Palestine is a matter of speculation; see Murphy, *Rufinus*, 44.

[74] Palladius, *Historia Lausiaca* 54 (Butler ed., vol. 2: 146).

[75] Palladius, *Historia Lausiaca* 54 (Butler ed., vol. 2: 148).

[76] E.g., Jerome, *Epp.* 57, 4; 12 (*CSEL* 54, 507, 526); 125, 18 (*CSEL* 56, 137–138); *Apologia* III, 4 (*CCL* 79, 76), among other references.

[77] *PLRE* I, 592.

[78] *PLRE* I, 592.

[79] *Vita Melaniae Junioris* 7; 11; 14; 19 (*SC* 90, 140, 146, 154, 166, 168); Palladius, *Historia Lausiaca* 61 (Butler ed., vol. 2: 156).

[80] Jerome charged that John associated daily with "Romans" (*Ep.* 82, 7 [*CSEL* 55, 113–114]); Epiphanius linked John and Rufinus through their mutual esteem for Origen (*Ep. ad Iohannem Episcopum* [= Jerome, *Ep.* 51] 6 [*CSEL* 54, 406–407]).

[81] Jerome, *Contra Ioannem* 11 (*PL* 23, 380): Jerome was an eyewitness to John's mockery of Epiphanius.

ciety in several ways. Melania served as religious mentor to the wealthy heiress Olympias of Constantinople,[82] who renounced "the world" around A.D. 390 and gave her fortune to the church;[83] according to her *Vita*, she virtually supported the operations of the Church of Constantinople under John Chrysostom's bishopric.[84] Chrysostom was brought back into the circuit of Origenism when the Tall Brothers and their supporters, after Theophilus's rout of Origenists from the Egyptian desert, fled to Constantinople; his tolerance of their presence in the city gave Theophilus the opportunity to raise charges against Chrysostom that ultimately led to his downfall.[85]

Evagrius Ponticus, now recognized as the prime theoretician of late fourth-century Origenism, provided connection between the Olivet monasteries and Constantinople. Evagrius fled a threatening love affair in the Eastern capital and journeyed to Melania and Rufinus's monastery, where Melania converted him to the ascetic life.[86] In all likelihood, Evagrius's *Rule for Nuns* was written for Melania's use;[87] whether his important treatise called *The Letter to Melania* was really composed for her has been debated.[88] After a stay on the Mount of Olives, Evagrius went to live among the monks of Egypt[89] and was instrumental in imbuing them with Origenist sentiments.[90] His extraordinary contributions to later Origenism are detailed in Chapter Two, and the means by which his writings reached monastic communities in Palestine, in Chapter Four.

Another sojourner at the Jerusalem monastery who subsequently traveled to Egypt was Palladius,[91] who lavished praise on Melania in his *Lau-*

---

[82] Palladius, *Historia Lausiaca* 56 (Butler ed., vol. 2: 149–150).

[83] See the *Vita Olympiadis* 5–7 (*SC* 13 bis, 416–420).

[84] *Vita Olympiadis* 7; 8; 14 (*SC* 13 bis, 420, 422, 436).

[85] Socrates, *HE* VI, 7; 9; 15; 17 (*PG* 67, 684–688, 692–693, 708–712); Sozomen, *HE* VIII, 13; 14; 17 (*PG* 67, 1549, 1552–1553, 1557–1560), and see below, pp. 45–46, 50. An intriguing topic that could bear further research is the link of Chrysostom to Evagrius Ponticus through Heraclides: according to Sozomen (*HE* VIII, 6 [*PG* 67, 1529]), Heraclides was a disciple of Evagrius; Chrysostom ordained him as bishop of Ephesus in 401, which event served as one of the charges against Chrysostom at the Synod of the Oak (see Photius, *Bibliotheca*, codex 59 [*PG* 103, 105, 109]).

[86] Palladius, *Historia Lausiaca* 38 (Butler ed., vol. 2: 117, 118–120).

[87] Joseph Muyldermans, ed., tr., *Evagriana Syriaca. Textes inédits du British Mu-*

seum et de la Vaticane, 30. Rufinus may have translated the work into Latin; see the hints in Jerome, *Ep.* 133, 3 (*CSEL* 56, 246–247); Gennadius, *De scriptoribus ecclesiasticis* 17 (*PG* 58, 1070); D. A. Wilmart, "Les Versions latines des Sentences d'Evagre pour les vierges," 143–144, 148–151. See now Susanna Elm, "Evagrius Ponticus' *Sententiae ad Virginem*," 283.

[88] See discussions below, pp. 191–192.

[89] Palladius, *Historia Lausiaca* 38; 11 (Butler ed., vol. 2: 120, 34).

[90] Including John Cassian, who emerges later in the Origenist controversy as a partisan of John Chrysostom. For Evagrius and the Nitrian monks, see Antoine Guillaumont, *Les "Kephalaia Gnostica" d'Evagre le Pontique et l'histoire de l'Origénisme chez les Grecs et chez les Syriens*, 57ff., 77ff. Guillaumont argues (81–123) that Jerome's complaints against John of Jerusalem's views concern Evagrian theology.

[91] Palladius, *Historia Lausiaca* 55 (Butler ed., vol. 2: 148–149), with Melania and Sil-

siac History.[92] Ephiphanius warns against Palladius in the conclusion of his letter to John of Jerusalem,[93] an indication that the latter was accused of Origenist sympathies early in the controversy. Palladius's *Dialogus de vita S. Ioannis Chrysostomi*[94] reveals the decisive link that he provided between the alleged Origenists and John Chrysostom. The *Dialogus* also shows him in contact with "Westerners" such as John Cassian (now known to be sympathetic to Evagrian Origenism),[95] and Aemelius of Beneventum, the father-in-law of the Pelagian theologian Julian of Eclanum.[96] In his *Lausiac History*, Palladius reports that during his trip to Rome to plead on behalf of Chrysostom, he was given hospitality by Melania the Younger and her husband Pinianus.[97]

Highly placed visitors came as well to the Mount of Olives monasteries. Silvia, sister-in-law of the praetorian prefect of the East, Flavius Rufinus, arrived around 394. In Melania's monastery she met Palladius, with whom she traveled to Egypt.[98] Perhaps Silvia influenced the decree that in late 394 ordered banishment for Jerome's monks in Bethlehem;[99] nothing came of the decree, however, perhaps because Count Rufinus was assassi-

---

via on their way out of Jerusalem; 7 (Butler ed., vol. 2: 24–25). In Egypt, Palladius met Evagrius Ponticus and the Tall Brothers (Palladius, *Historia Lausiaca* 11; 23; 35 [Butler ed., vol. 2: 34, 75, 101]). For an important study of Palladius's chronology and activities, see Eduard Schwartz, "Palladiana," 161–204.

[92] Palladius, *Historia Lausiaca* 46; 54; part of 55 is also now judged to be about Melania (Butler ed., vol. 2: 134–136, 146–148, 148–149). That she, along with other Origenists, receives less attention in the B and G manuscripts of the *Lausiac History* (on which Butler largely based his critical edition of the text) than in the Coptic version has now been demonstrated by Gabriel Bunge, "Palladiana I: Introduction aux fragments coptes de l'Histoire Lausiaque," 79–129; cf. Adalbert de Vogüé, "Palladiana II: La Version copte de l'Histoire Lausiaque," esp. 334–336.

[93] Epiphanius, *Ep. ad Iohannem Episcopum* (= Jerome, *Ep.* 51) 9 (*CSEL* 54, 411–412). That Palladius's Origenist ties are brought out more clearly in the Coptic version of the *Lausiac History* is shown by Bunge, "Palladiana I," 82.

[94] Palladius details Chrysostom's reception of and dealings with the exiled Origenist monks in *Dialogus* VII, 24 (Coleman-Norton ed., 39–40). Three interesting studies of Chrysostom in relationship to the Origenist

controversy are Jean-Marie Leroux, "Jean Chrysostome et la querelle origéniste," 335–341; Charles Pietri, "Esquisse de conclusion: l'aristocratie chrétienne entre Jean de Constantinople et Augustin d'Hippone," 283–305; Matthieu-Georges de Durand, "Evagre le Pontique et le 'Dialogue sur la vie de saint Jean Chrysostome'," 191–206.

[95] Palladius, *Dialogus* III, 13 (Coleman-Norton ed., 17–18); Cassian was part of a delegation from the Constantinople clergy to Innocent of Rome, pleading on Chrysostom's behalf. For Cassian's link to Evagrius, see especially D. Salvatore Marsili, *Giovanni Cassiano ed Evagrio Pontico*, and Hans-Oskar Weber, *Die Stellung des Johannes Cassianus zur Ausserpachomianischen Mönchstradition*.

[96] Palladius, *Dialogus* IV, 15 (Coleman-Norton ed., 22); cf. Paulinus of Nola's *Carmen* 25, on the occasion of Julian's wedding.

[97] Palladius, *Historia Lausiaca* 61 (Butler ed., vol. 2: 157).

[98] Palladius, *Historia Lausiaca* 55 (Butler ed., vol. 2: 148–149); see E. D. Hunt, "St. Silvia of Aquitaine: The Role of a Theodosian Pilgrim in the Society of East and West," 353–354, 357.

[99] Jerome, *Contra Ioannem* 43 (*PL* 23, 411); *Ep.* 82, 10 (*CSEL* 55, 116–117); see Hunt, "Silvia," 358. Jerome blames the decree on John of Jerusalem in *Ep.* 82, 10 (*CSEL* 55, 116–117).

nated shortly thereafter.[100] Rufinus of Aquileia promised to translate the Pseudo-Clementine *Recognitions* for Silvia, but she died before he accomplished his task.[101] Another highly placed friend of Rufinus and Melania, who may have influenced the Constantinople regime against Jerome, was Bacurius, *dux Palestinae* from 378–394; a former king of the Iberians, he fought against Eugenius at the battle of the Frigidus.[102] Finally, according to the historian Gennadius, Rufinus also corresponded with the women of what was arguably the wealthiest family of the Western Empire, the Anicii.[103] The family received other eager addresses from Jerome (who did not know the family),[104] from Augustine (who killed a blossoming relationship with the Anician women through his hostility to Pelagian views),[105] and from Pelagius himself (who seems on good terms with the family).[106]

Melania and Rufinus journeyed westward at the end of the fourth century and reestablished contacts with family and friends there. Melania's arrival in Italy dates to A.D. 399–400,[107] two years after Rufinus's.[108] According to Palladius, her return was motivated in part by her desire to rescue her granddaughter, Melania the Younger, from falling prey to "heresy."[109] Given the predilections of both the author and the subjects of the account, this can mean only one thing: Melania the Elder wished to prevent her granddaughter from falling into the hands of Jerome's anti-Origenist faction in Rome. Upon her disembarkment, Melania the Elder was greeted and entertained by Paulinus of Nola, with whom her entire family enjoyed a close relationship.[110] To Paulinus, Melania brought a coveted

---

[100] Zosimus, *Historia nova* V, 7, 5–6 (Mendelssohn ed., 225).

[101] Rufinus, *Prologus in Clementis Recognitiones* (CCL 20, 281).

[102] Rufinus, *HE* X, 11; XI, 33 (*GCS* 9², 976, 1038–1039; Socrates, *HE* I, 20 (*PG* 67, 133); Zosimus, IV, 57, 3 (Mendelssohn ed., 213); *PLRE* I, 144.

[103] So Gennadius, *De scriptoribus ecclesiasticis* 17 (*PL* 58, 1070).

[104] Jerome, *Ep.* 130, 2 (*CSEL* 56, 176).

[105] Augustine, *Epp.* 130; 131; 150; 188; *De bono viduitatis*. See also Elizabeth A. Clark, "Theory and Practice in Late Ancient Asceticism: Jerome, Chrysostom, and Augustine," esp. 41–44.

[106] Pelagius, *Ad Demetriadem* (*PL* 30, 15–45). For Pelagius and the Anicii, see Georges de Plinval, *Pélage, ses écrits, sa vie et sa réforme* 214–215; Peter Brown connects the Pelagian treatise, *De malis doctoribus* XXIV, 3 (Caspari ed., 112) with the Anician family in "Pelagius and His Supporters: Aims and Environment," 93–114, reprinted in *Religion and Society in the Age of Saint Augustine*, ci-

tation at 192. Since Jerome reports that he knew Pelagius in Rome (i.e., pre-385), Pelagius would have had ample time in the city to know at least some leaders of the Christian aristocracy (see Jerome, *In Hieremiam* IV, 1, 6 [*CCL* 74, 175] and Yves-Marie Duval, "Pélage est-il le censeur inconnu de l'Adversus Iovinianum à Rome en 393? ou: du 'Portrait-Robot' de l'hérétique chez S. Jérôme," 538).

[107] The highly complex dating of Melania's history rests ultimately on that of correspondence between Paulinus and others. See Nicole Moine, "Melaniana," esp. 25–27; and Elizabeth A. Clark, *The Life of Melania the Younger: Introduction, Translation, Commentary*, 195n.9, 196n.18.

[108] Moine, "Melaniana," 25–45; cf. Jerome, *Apologia* II, 24.

[109] Palladius, *Historia Lausiaca* 54 (Butler ed., vol. 2: 146).

[110] Paulinus of Nola, *Epp.* 29, 6; 12–13 (*CSEL* 29, 251–252, 258–261); 45, 2–3 (*CSEL* 29, 380–381); *Carmen* 21, 60–83, 210–325 (*CSEL* 30, 160–161, 165–168).

present, a piece of the True Cross that John of Jerusalem had given her.[111]

Melania the Elder also met in the West several new family members, including her cousin's husband, Turcius Apronianus, whom we are told she converted.[112] Apronianus was to play an important role as "go-between" for Rufinus. It was from Apronianus that Rufinus received a copy of Jerome's letter to Pammachius and Oceanus attacking Rufinus's views;[113] Apronianus was the rare owner of a corrected copy of Rufinus's translation of the *Peri Archōn*;[114] to Apronianus, Rufinus dedicated his *Apology against Jerome*;[115] and it was Apronianus whom Rufinus beseeched to intercede with Jerome through Pammachius that the controversy be laid to rest.[116] Later, Rufinus dedicated to Apronianus his translation of nine sermons by Gregory Nazianzen[117] and of Origen's *Explanatio super Psalmos XXXVI–XXXVIII*.[118]

In Italy, Melania the Elder also met her granddaughter's wealthy and aristocratic husband Pinianus for the first time.[119] Rufinus became enamored of the young man, calling him "*amantissimus filius noster*,"[120] and planned to dedicate to him a translation of Origen's *Homilies on Deuteronomy*,[121] a project he contrived while on Melania's estates in Sicily shortly before his death.[122] The younger generation also learned to revere the friends of the elder: when Palladius fled to Rome in 404–405 to plead on behalf of the exiled John Chrysostom, he was given hospitality by the younger Melania and Pinianus.[123]

This brief description of Rufinus's circle suggests how tightly the group was linked by kinship, marriage, patronage, religious mentorship, ascetic devotion, gift-giving, and hospitality. Jerome's circle, although not com-

---

[111] Paulinus of Nola, *Ep.* 31, 1 (*CSEL* 29, 267–268).

[112] Palladius, *Historia Lausiaca* 54 (Butler ed., vol. 2: 146–147).

[113] Rufinus, *Apologia* I, 1 (*CCL* 20, 37).

[114] Rufinus, *Apologia* I, 19 (*CCL* 20, 54).

[115] Rufinus, *Apologia* I, 1 (*CCL* 20, 37). Caroline Hammond (Bammel) refers to Apronianus as Rufinus's "literary agent" in Rome during Rufinus's stay in Aquileia: "A Product of a Fifth-Century Scriptorium Preserving Conventions Used by Rufinus of Aquileia," 371.

[116] Rufinus, *Apologia* II, 48 (*CCL* 20, 120).

[117] Rufinus, *Praefatio in Gregorii Nazianzeni orationes* (*CCL* 20, 255); also a translation of Basil's *Homilies* (*Praefatio in omelias Sancti Basilii* [*CCL* 20, 237]).

[118] Rufinus, *Prologus in explanationem Origeniis super Psalmos XXVI–XXVIII* (*CCL* 20, 251).

[119] See *PLRE* I, 702.

[120] Rufinus, *Prologus in omelias Origenis super Numeros* (*CCL* 20, 285).

[121] Rufinus, *Prologus in omelias Origenis super Numeros* (*CCL* 20, 285).

[122] Rufinus, *Prologus in omelias Origenis super Numeros* (*CCL* 20, 285): This was the next project Rufinus planned to undertake. The date of 410 is fixed by the reference to the barbarians' burning of Rhegium across the strait from Sicily.

[123] Palladius, *Historia Lausiaca* 61 (Butler ed., vol. 2: 157). Melania the Younger retained contact with Palladius's mentor Lausus, to whom the *Lausiac History* is dedicated: he sent funds for the construction of a bath in her Jerusalem monastery and entertained her when she visited Constantinople in 436 (*Vita Melaniae Junioris*) (Latin 41 [Rampolla ed., 24], Greek 53 [*SC* 90, 230]; cf. Latin 53 [Rampolla ed., 30]).

manding the favor of as many highly placed individuals,[124] similarly consisted of persons with long-standing, multifaceted relationships with each other. The density and complexity of ties within the two networks goes far to explain the ardor with which their members argued over Origenist ideas.

Paula played the role in Jerome's circle that Melania the Elder did in Rufinus's. There can be no doubt that Paula was the soul mate of Jerome's life:[125] he dedicated many of his commentaries and translations to her,[126] and confessed his inability to estimate the number of letters he sent her, since he wrote daily.[127] When Jerome first met Paula in Rome in 382, she was an aristocratic widow with five children.[128] Although of senatorial rank, she may not have been as wealthy as Melania the Elder;[129] nonetheless, she probably provided much of the money for the Bethlehem monasteries. In Palestine, Paula and Jerome searched three years for funding to erect their establishments,[130] but even then, Jerome was later forced to sell some family property to help with costs.[131]

The year 382 saw another important arrival in Rome: Epiphanius attended a bishops' council in Rome that year and stayed at Paula's mansion for the duration.[132] Her hospitality was reciprocated when, in 385, she and Jerome stopped to see him on their way East. On Cyprus, Paula visited "all" the monasteries and left funds for them, such as she could afford.[133] Paula and Jerome stayed in touch with Epiphanius after they reached Palestine. Once when Paula was ill, Jerome secretly appealed to Epiphanius, asking him to convince her to take some wine. According to Jerome, Paula

---

[124] Jerome's only entrée to the Constantinople aristocracy and court had been Nebridius (briefly the husband of Olympias); in *Ep.* 79 he writes to Salvina, the elder Nebridius's daughter-in-law. Nebridius was long dead when the Origenist controversy flared, and Olympias, by virtue of her relationship with John Chrysostom, would in any case have been on the opposite side of the controversy from Jerome.

[125] See Jerome's revealing comments in *Ep.* 45, 3 (*CSEL* 54, 325): Paula was the only woman who had the power to "subdue" him, yet with this one woman to whom he was so attracted, he never even ate dinner.

[126] To Paula are dedicated Jerome's translations of Job (*PL* 29, 63); Psalms (*PL* 29, 122); the books of Solomon (*PL* 29, 426); Samuel and Kings (*PL* 28, 604); Esther (*PL* 28, 1504); Isaiah (*PL* 28, 828); Jeremiah (*PL* 28, 904); Daniel (*PL* 28, 1360); the twelve Minor Prophets (*PL* 28, 1072); of Origen's *Commentary on Luke* (*PL* 26, 229); and Jerome's *Commentaries* on Ephesians

(*PL* 26, 4667); Philemon (*PL* 26, 639); Titus (*PL* 26, 590); Galatians (*PL* 26, 331); Micah (*CCL* 76, 473); Nahum (*CCL* 76A, 526); Zephaniah (*CCL* 76A, 655); and Haggai (*CCL* 76A, 713).

[127] Jerome, *De viris illustribus* 135 (*PL* 23, 759).

[128] Jerome, *Ep.* 108, 4; 5 (*CSEL* 55, 309–310).

[129] Jerome's attempt to link Paula's family with the Scipios, Gracchi, and Agamemnon (*Ep.* 108, 3 [*CSEL* 55, 308]), probably a bogus genealogy, may indicate Paula's family was *nouveau riche*. See Anne Ewing Hickey, *Women of the Roman Aristocracy as Christian Monastics*, 21–24.

[130] Jerome, *Ep.* 108, 14 (*CSEL* 55, 325).

[131] Jerome, *Ep.* 66, 14 (*CSEL* 54, 665).

[132] Jerome, *Ep.* 108, 6 (*CSEL* 55, 310–311); for Jerome's arrival along with Epiphanius, see Jerome, *Ep.* 127, 7 (*CSEL* 56, 150).

[133] Jerome, *Ep.* 108, 7 (*CSEL* 55, 312).

saw through the ruse and almost (but not quite) persuaded Epiphanius never to take a drop again.[134] From the beginnings of the controversy in Palestine, Epiphanius aligned Jerome with his side[135] and Jerome defended Epiphanius's views.[136]

Although Paula did not star in the Origenist controversy in Palestine to the degree Marcella did in Rome, she nonetheless had her bouts with Origenists. When an unnamed man tried to trick her with questions about the bodily resurrection, the status of infants' souls before birth, and other disputed topics, Paula turned the matter over to Jerome, who by his own account speedily bested the opposition. But Jerome reveals that Paula "publicly" proclaimed the man and his supporters to be enemies of God.[137]

Paula had another strong relationship in Jerome's circle: the Roman senator Pammachius married her second daughter, Paulina.[138] When Paulina died in 395, Pammachius adopted an ascetic life while still performing his senatorial duties.[139] Perhaps a schoolmate of Jerome,[140] Pammachius was by all accounts a friend of long standing.[141] Jerome reports that Pammachius had served as a proconsul[142] and was a member of the *gens Furia*, thus a distant relative of Paula.[143] He was also a cousin of Marcella,[144] the principal Hieronymian actress in the Origenist drama. Pammachius may not have been of the highest rank in the senatorial aristocracy;[145] nonetheless, he used his abundant income for such charitable projects as a *xenodochium* at Portus[146] and church buildings in Rome.[147] It is not clear whether it was at Pammachius's *xenodochium*, or at his house in Rome, that Pelagius's supporter Caelestius heard Rufinus the Syrian deny the transmission of sin, a view that Caelestius found compatible.[148]

Pammachius served as Jerome's key advocate in the controversy. He informed Jerome in Bethlehem of the disturbances that had erupted in the Western capital as a result of Rufinus's translation of the *Peri Archōn* and requested a literal rendition of the work from Jerome.[149] To Pammachius

---

[134] Jerome, *Ep.* 108, 21 (*CSEL* 55, 337).

[135] Epiphanius, *Ep. ad Iohannem Episcopum* (= Jerome, *Ep.* 51) 1 (*CSEL* 54, 396).

[136] Jerome, *Contra Ioannem* 11 (*PL* 23, 380–381).

[137] Jerome, *Ep.* 108, 23; 25 (*CSEL* 55, 339–341, 344).

[138] Jerome, *Ep.* 108, 4 (*CSEL* 55, 309–310); *Ep.* 66 on the occasion of Paulina's death.

[139] Jerome, *Ep.* 66, 6 (*CSEL* 54, 654).

[140] Jerome calls Pammachius his "former fellow-learner" in *Ep.* 49 (48 Vall.), 1 (*CSEL* 54, 351).

[141] Jerome, *Ep.* 49 (48 Vall.), 1 (*CSEL* 54, 351).

[142] Jerome, *Ep.* 66, 7 (*CSEL* 54, 655).

[143] Jerome, *Ep.* 66, 6 (*CSEL* 54, 654); Paula was related to Furia, according to Jerome in *Ep.* 54, 2 (*CSEL* 54, 467).

[144] Jerome, *Ep.* 48 (49 Vall.), 4 (*CSEL* 54, 349): "*consobrina tua.*"

[145] Jerome says that some senators ranked above him: *Ep.* 66, 7 (*CSEL* 54, 655).

[146] Jerome, *Epp.* 66, 11 (*CSEL* 54, 661); 77, 10 (*CSEL* 55, 47).

[147] See *PLRE* I, 663.

[148] See the testimony in Augustine, *De gratia Christi et de peccato originali* II, 3, 3 (*CSEL* 42, 168). See below, p. 202.

[149] Pammachius and Oceanus, *Ep. ad Hieronymum* (= Jerome, *Ep.* 83) (*CSEL* 55, 119–120).

(and Marcella), Jerome sent his *Apology against Rufinus*[150] and his translation of Theophilus of Alexandria's Paschal Letter of 402 condemning Origenism.[151] Most important, Pammachius was responsible for suppressing the friendly letter of reconciliation that Jerome wrote to Rufinus in mid-controversy and for circulating instead the hostile one that Jerome had intended only for the eyes of his intimate supporters.[152] Thus Rufinus did not know until much later that Jerome was, in 399, ready for reconciliation. Here it is helpful to recall that Pammachius had earlier suppressed material from Jerome with which he disagreed: shocked by Jerome's *Against Jovinian*, he had hastened about Rome in 394 to remove all the copies from circulation.[153] To Pammachius, Jerome addressed his tirade *Against John of Jerusalem*[154] and dedicated many of his commentaries on the minor prophets.[155]

Three other Roman friends of Jerome played significant roles in the controversy: Oceanus, Fabiola, and Marcella. Fabiola, perhaps Oceanus's housemate, had been visiting Jerome in Bethlehem when the first phase of the controversy erupted in Palestine.[156] We are told that she enriched many monasteries through her generosity;[157] no doubt the Bethlehem foundations stood high on her gift list. Fabiola shared with Pammachius the expense of building the aforementioned *xenodochium* at Portus.[158] Jerome reports that an important document in the Origenist controversy mysteriously appeared in her and Oceanus's dwelling, but does not identify it.[159]

Of Oceanus's involvement in the controversy we know more. Jerome was informed by another correspondent how ardently Oceanus was battling Origenism in Rome.[160] Along with Pammachius, he wrote to Jerome in Bethlehem asking for a literal translation of the *Peri Archōn*, his request

---

[150] Jerome, *Apologia* (CCL 79, 1).

[151] Jerome, *Ep.* 97 (CSEL 55, 182–184).

[152] Jerome, *Ep.* 81 to Rufinus (CSEL 55, 106–107); Pammachius circulated *Ep.* 84 (CSEL 55, 121–134), which criticized Origen and Rufinus.

[153] Jerome, *Ep.* 48 (49 Vall.), 2 (CSEL 54, 347).

[154] Jerome, *Contra Ioannem* 1 (PL 23, 371).

[155] Jerome's dedications to Pammachius: the *Commentaries* on Hosea (CCL 76, 1), Joel (CCL 76, 159), Amos (CCL 76, 256), Obadiah (CCL 76, 350), Jonah (CCL 76, 300), and Daniel (CCL 75A, 772).

[156] Jerome, *Ep.* 77, 8 (CSEL 55, 46). In *Apologia* III, 4 (CCL 79, 76), Jerome speaks of how a document mysteriously appeared in the "chambers of Fabiola and Oceanus," and in *Ep.* 77, 8 (CSEL 55, 46), he writes that when Fabiola returned to her native land

from Palestine, she "lodged in another's house." Conceivably, she lived in the hospice she and Pammachius had built at Portus (Jerome, *Ep.* 77, 10 [CSEL 55, 47]); also see *Ep.* 66, 11 (CSEL 54, 661). For Fabiola, Jerome wrote on the garments of the high priest (*Ep.* 64) and on the forty-two stopping places on the Exodus (*Ep.* 79).

[157] Jerome, *Ep.* 77, 6 (CSEL 55, 44): there was not a monastery not sustained by her riches. Fabiola was of the Fabian family: *Ep.* 77, 2 (CSEL 55, 38).

[158] Jerome, *Ep.* 77, 10 (CSEL 55, 47).

[159] Jerome, *Apologia* III, 4 (CCL 79, 76).

[160] Tranquillinus has so informed Jerome: Jerome, *Ep.* 62, 2 (CSEL 54, 583). Earlier, Jerome had counseled Oceanus against taking too harsh a line against remarriage (*Ep.* 69)—an interesting document to find in the dossier, given Fabiola's checkered marital history (*Ep.* 77, 3 [CSEL 55, 39–40]).

prompted by Rufinus's removal or correction of the offending passages in his translation.[161] Jerome replied, attempting to dissociate himself from Origen as much as possible[162]—but he presumably sent Pammachius and Oceanus his own more literal translation.[163] Assuming that this is the same Oceanus whom Jerome later commends to Count Marcellinus and his wife Anapsychia in North Africa—an Oceanus who owns a copy of the *Apologia Adversus Rufinum*—we see him brought into the controversy over the origin of the soul that fueled the Pelagian dispute.[164] Oceanus wrote to Augustine three times about the issue of the soul's origin, and finally received Augustine's *Epistle* 180 in response.[165] Here we see an intriguing link between the networks involved in the Origenist controversy and those of the Pelagian debate.

Another important Roman partisan of Jerome was Marcella, whom he had first met on his arrival in the capital in 382.[166] A wealthy widow with a palace on the Aventine,[167] Marcella was a cousin of Pammachius;[168] Jerome credits her with being the religious mentor of Paula's daughter Eustochium.[169] Probably the most scholarly of Jerome's women friends, Marcella plied him with questions about Scripture both before and after his departure from Rome.[170] Never successful in luring Marcella to Palestine,[171] Jerome nonetheless composed Biblical commentaries for her.[172]

Most important for our purposes, Jerome attributes to Marcella the initiating of the condemnation of Origenists at Rome. Although she had at first been reluctant to assume a public role, her indignation grew at the number of innocents (including Pope Siricius) who had been duped by Origenist "heretics." She moved to public action: she found witnesses who had been led astray by Origenism, especially by Rufinus's "emended" translation of the *Peri Archōn*, and wrote "countless" letters asking the Origenists to defend themselves publicly—but, according to Jerome, they never would.[173] To Marcella as well as Pammachius,[174] Jerome sent his translation of Theophilus's Easter Letter of 402, a tirade against Origenism.[175]

Rufinus's assessment of Marcella's activity is understandably different.

[161] Pammachius and Oceanus, *Ep. ad Hieronymum* (= Jerome, *Ep.* 83 [*CSEL* 55, 119–120]).

[162] Jerome, *Ep.* 84 (*CSEL* 55, 121–134).

[163] Jerome, *Ep.* 84, 12 (*CSEL* 55, 134).

[164] Jerome, *Ep.* 126, 1 (*CSEL* 56, 143).

[165] Augustine, *Ep.* 180, 1 (*CSEL* 44, 697–698).

[166] Jerome, *Ep.* 127, 7 (*CSEL* 56, 150–151).

[167] Jerome, *Ep.* 47, 3 (*CSEL* 54, 346).

[168] Jerome, *Ep.* 48 (49 Vall.), 4 (*CSEL* 54, 349): Marcella is *consobrina tua*.

[169] Jerome, *Ep.* 127, 5 (*CSEL* 56, 149).

[170] Jerome, *Ep.* 127, 7 (*CSEL* 56, 151); see also Jerome's prefaces to his *Commentar-ies* on Galatians and to Books 2 and 3 of Ephesians (*PL* 26, 331, 507, 546–547), for praise of Marcella. Jerome's letters to Marcella on Scriptural questions she had raised are numbered 32, 34, 59 (and letters 37, 38, 40–44, on other topics).

[171] Despite the invitation from Jerome, Paula, and Eustochium in *Ep.* 46.

[172] In addition to the mini-commentaries found in his exegetical letters, Jerome also dedicated the *Commentary on Daniel* to Marcella and Pammachius (*CCL* 75A, 772).

[173] Jerome, *Ep.* 127, 9–10 (*CSEL* 56, 152–153).

[174] Jerome, *Ep.* 97.

[175] In Jerome, *Ep.* 98.

He writes that "that woman Jezebel" exceeded even Eusebius of Cremona in wickedness: it was she who supplied the allegedly falsified copy of the *Peri Archōn* to Eusebius, which he then broadcast throughout Italy to Rufinus's dismay. In his account, Rufinus reveals that he did not know Marcella personally: after he mentions her, he adds, "whoever she may be."[176] Rufinus and Marcella thus constitute two of the few unconnected partisans in the controversy.

Two bishops of Rome were also involved in the controversy: Siricius, who approved Rufinus's statement of faith and gave him a letter of commendation,[177] and Anastasius, his successor in 399, of the opposite persuasion. Although Anastasius claimed (astonishingly enough) that he did not know who Origen was nor did he wish to know,[178] he apparently rejected Rufinus's appeal.[179] He condemned Origen's writings and furnished Eusebius of Cremona with a letter of the church at Milan so testifying.[180] He also corresponded with others involved in the controversy: Jerome, Theophilus of Alexandria,[181] and John of Jerusalem.[182]

Other partisans of Jerome included his monastic companions, four of whom served as Jerome's emissaries to Italy in the years just before and during the eruption of the Origenist controversy in Rome: Paulinianus, Vincentius, Eusebius, and another Rufinus.[183] Through them, Jerome doubtless wished to strengthen his influence on Western Christians. His brother Paulinianus accompanied Jerome out of Rome in August 385[184] and reemerged in the Bethlehem monastery. In Palestine, Paulinianus was ordained by Epiphanius,[185] an ordination that may have given rise to the

---

[176] Rufinus, *Apologia* I, 19 (CCL 20, 54): "*de qua ego, quaecumque illa est, nihil dico*"— a puzzling admission, since Marcella was one of the first women ascetics in Rome. Even if Jerome overestimates the years of her ascetic devotion (from the 340s: *Ep.* 127, 5–6 [*CSEL* 56, 149–150]), the 360s probably are not too early. See Georg Grützmacher, *Hieronymus: Eine biographische Studie zur alten Kirchengeschichte*, vol. 1: 227n. 3. On the link between Eusebius of Cremona and Marcella on the falsification of the *Peri Archōn*, see Yves-Marie Duval, "Le 'Liber Hieronymi ad Gaudentium': Rufin d'Aquilée, Gaudence de Brescia et Eusèbe de Crémone," 168–171. Duval argues that the "book" to Gaudentius was in fact written by Rufinus, and close to the time that Gaudentius journeyed to Constantinople to support the case of John Chrysostom (185). Here we have yet another link between Rufinus and the circle of John Chrysostom.
[177] Jerome, *Apologia* III, 21; 24 (CCL 79, 92, 96); derived from a lost letter of Rufinus to Jerome.

[178] Anastasius, *Ep. ad Ioannem Episcopum* 3 (*PL* 20, 69–70). His disclaimer is especially surprising since Jerome in the 380s reports that Origenism had been condemned at Rome (*Ep.* 33, 5 [*CSEL* 54, 259]). I disagree with Basil Studer's claim that Origen's theology was well known in the West before the outbreak of the controversy ("Zur Frage des westlichen Origenismus," pt. 3, 270–287).
[179] That the appeal was rejected is gathered from the fact that Anastasius condemned Origen's writings; see n. 180. Rufinus appealed to Anastasius in A.D. 400 (*Apologia ad Anastasium*).
[180] Anastasius, *Ep. ad Simplicianum* (= Jerome, *Ep.* 95) 2–3 (*CSEL* 55, 158).
[181] Seen in Jerome, *Ep.* 88 (*CSEL* 55, 141).
[182] Anastasius, *Ep. ad Ioannem Episcopum* (*PL* 20, 68–73); referred to in Jerome, *Apologia* III, 21 (CCL 79, 92–93).
[183] Jerome, *Apologia* III, 24 (CCL 79, 96).
[184] Jerome, *Apologia* III, 22 (CCL 79, 93).
[185] Jerome, *Ep.* 82, 4; 8 (*CSEL* 55, 111, 114–115).

original hostilities between Epiphanius and John of Jerusalem.[186] Later we find Paulinianus living in Cyprus, presumably near Epiphanius, but frequently visiting Jerome in Bethlehem.[187] Jerome sent him as his emissary to Italy in 397 or 398;[188] while in Rome, he memorized parts of Rufinus's *Apology against Jerome*, which he recited to his brother upon his return to Bethlehem.[189] Jerome also honored Paulinianus with his translation of Didymus the Blind's treatise on the Holy Spirit.[190]

Another long-standing friend and monastic companion of Jerome who played an important role in the controversy was the presbyter Vincentius. Apparently at the Council of Constantinople with Jerome in 381–382,[191] Vincentius journeyed to Rome with Jerome and left with him (and thus with Paulinianus) in 385. Traveling to Cyprus with them, he enjoyed Epiphanius's hospitality.[192] In 394, while at Jerome's monastery,[193] Vincentius served as a significant intermediary: letters from Isidore, a pro-Origenist emissary from the Alexandrian church to John of Jerusalem, were misdelivered to Vincentius, who showed them to Jerome. Although Isidore (whose activities are further detailed in Chapter Two) had supposedly been sent to Palestine as a peacemaker, his letters were decidedly partisan: they encouraged John of Jerusalem not to fear Jerome's "dirges" and promised that he, Isidore, would come to Jerusalem and crush John's adversaries.[194] Needless to say, the letters discouraged friendly relations between the Bethlehem and the Jerusalem religious establishments. A few years later, probably in 396 or 397, Jerome sent Vincentius to Rome on a mission.[195] Thus he was in the Western capital when the controversy erupted and reported to Jerome upon his return to Palestine.[196] Jerome dedicated his translations of Eusebius of Caesarea's *Chronicle*[197] and of Origen's *Homily on Ezekiel*[198] to Vincentius.

A third monastic friend and advocate of Jerome was Eusebius of Cremona. Eusebius first surfaces in Jerome's monastery in 394, where he ex-

[186] Jerome, *Contra Ioannem* 10; 40 (*PL* 23, 379, 410).

[187] Jerome, *Contra Ioannem* 41 (*PL* 23, 410).

[188] Jerome, *Apologia* III, 24 (*CCL* 79, 96); perhaps this was the journey to sell family property mentioned in *Ep.* 66, 14 (*CSEL* 54, 665).

[189] Jerome, *Apologia* I, 21; 23; 28 (*CCL* 79, 20, 22–23, 27). In *Ep.* 66, 14 (*CSEL* 54, 665), Paulinianus has already gone, in 397; although in *Apologia* III, 24 (*CCL* 79, 96) Jerome claims that he didn't send Paulinianus until a year after Rufinus left Palestine. Paulinianus had not yet returned in 399, the date of Jerome's friendly (and suppressed) letter to Rufinus: he thinks Rufinus will see Paulinianus at Chromatius's house in Aqui-

leia (*Ep.* 81, 2 [*CSEL* 55, 107]).

[190] Rufinus, *Apologia* II, 26–27 (*CCL* 20, 102); Jerome, *Translatio libri Didymi de Spiritu Sancto, praefatio* (*PL* 23, 107).

[191] Jerome, *Contra Ioannem* 41 (*PL* 23, 410).

[192] Jerome, *Apologia* III, 22 (*CCL* 79, 93).

[193] Revealed by Epiphanius in his letter to John of Jerusalem (= Jerome, *Ep.* 51) 1 (*CSEL* 54, 396).

[194] Jerome, *Contra Ioannem* 37 (*PL* 23, 407).

[195] Jerome, *Apologia* II, 24 (*CCL* 79, 96).

[196] Jerome, *Ep.* 88 (*CSEL* 55, 142).

[197] Jerome, *Chronicon* (*GCS* 24, 1).

[198] Jerome, *Translatio homiliarum Origenis in Jeremiam et Ezechielem, prologus* (*PL* 25, 583).

tolled the high character and ascetic devotion of Paulinus of Nola to Jerome.[199] At Eusebius's behest, Jerome translated into Latin Epiphanius's
letter criticizing John of Jerusalem. The letter was supposed to remain private, but a "pretended monk" either bribed or stole the letter from Eusebius and gave it to John,[200] thus exacerbating the friction between the
Bethlehem and the Jerusalem monasteries. Jerome did not hesitate to claim
that Rufinus stood behind the theft of the document.[201]

Eusebius of Cremona also starred in the Roman act of the controversy.
Although Jerome later claimed that he had sent Eusebius to Rome a year
after Rufinus's arrival and on a mission unrelated to Origenism,[202] yet, according to Rufinus, it was Eusebius who changed his translation of the
Peri Archōn and circulated the faulty copy.[203] We also know that Eusebius
journeyed to Milan and in Rufinus's presence read out the allegedly falsified copy, which he claimed he had received from Marcella;[204] Rufinus
hotly contended that the version from which Eusebius read was not the
version *he* had produced.[205] And Eusebius took more to Milan with him
than the *Peri Archōn*: he carried to bishop Simplicianus of Milan the letter
from Anastasius of Rome condemning the works of Origen, in which Anastasius divulges that it was Eusebius who pointed out to him the "blasphemous" passages in the *Peri Archōn*.[206] Jerome dedicated his *Commentary
on Matthew* to Eusebius and gave him an extra copy for Marcella's monastic
housemate in Rome, Principia.[207] In addition, Jerome dedicated his *Commentary on Hebrew Questions* to Eusebius.[208]

A fourth emissary of Jerome, a priest named Rufinus,[209] does not
emerge in the writings of Jerome or Rufinus of Aquileia as a participant in
the Origenist debate. Yet the possible identification of this Rufinus with
the "Rufinus the Syrian" mentioned by Macarius Mercator and the assignment of the *Liber de fide* to "Rufinus the Syrian"—scholarly attributions
detailed in Chapter Five—afford us a glimpse of the strongly anti-Origenist cast of Rufinus the Syrian's theology. And given this Rufinus's influence
on the Pelagian Caelestius's denial of the transmission of an original sin,[210]

---

[199] Jerome, *Ep.* 53, 11 (*CSEL* 54, 464).

[200] Jerome, *Ep.* 57, 2 (*CSEL* 54, 504–
505); *Apologia* III, 4 (*CCL* 79, 76).

[201] Jerome, *Ep.* 57, 3; 4 (*CSEL* 54, 506–
508).

[202] Jerome, *Apologia* III, 24 (*CCL* 79, 96).

[203] Rufinus, *Apologia* I, 19; 21 (*CCL* 20,
53–54, 55).

[204] Rufinus, *Apologia* I, 19 (*CCL* 20, 54).
See Duval, "Le 'Liber Hieronymi,'" 168–
169.

[205] Rufinus, *Apologia* I, 19–20 (*CCL* 20,
54–55).

[206] Anastasius, *Ep. ad Simplicianum* (= Jerome, *Ep.* 95) 2–3 (*CSEL* 55, 158). See Du-

val, "Le 'Liber Hieronymi,'" 170. Only a
few years earlier, Simplicianus was the recipient of Augustine's first major attempt to
work out a theory of original sin: see below,
p. 230.

[207] Jerome, *Comm. in Matheum* (*CCL* 77,
4, 6); for Principia's relationship with Marcella, see Jerome, *Ep.* 127, 1; 8; 13 (*CSEL*
56, 145, 151, 155).

[208] Jerome, *In Hieremiam, prologus* 1 (*CCL*
74, 1).

[209] Jerome, *Apologia* III, 24 (*CCL* 79, 96);
cf. *Ep.* 81, 2 (*CSEL* 55, 107).

[210] See below, p. 202.

we have a link from Jerome's circle to "pre-Pelagianism," a link that no doubt would have later irritated Jerome, had he thought to comment on it.[211] Since Augustine reports that, on Caelestius's own testimony, the discussion with Rufinus the Syrian took place in Pammachius's house,[212] the association of Rufinus the Syrian with Jerome's circle in Rome is sure. Although the identification of Rufinus the Syrian with Jerome's emissary named Rufinus cannot be proved, it remains a plausible hypothesis that is further explored in Chapter Five.

Two members primarily associated with Rufinus of Aquileia's circle also retained cordial relations with Jerome. One was bishop Chromatius of Aquileia, who baptized Rufinus[213] and presumably knew Jerome at Aquileia during the same period.[214] When Rufinus returned to the West in 397, he spent some years in Aquileia and vicinity.[215] Chromatius had the distinction of serving as literary patron to both Rufinus and Jerome. He asked Rufinus to translate Eusebius of Caesarea's *Church History* into Latin,[216] perhaps assuming that this massive project would remove Rufinus from controversy for a few years.[217] Yet Chromatius also commissioned Jerome to write commentaries on Chronicles, Jonah,[218] and Habakkuk, and to translate Proverbs, Ecclesiastes, Song of Songs, Tobit, and Judith.[219] In the preface to his translations of the first three books, Jerome reveals that Chromatius (and Heliodorus) had sent him the necessary supplies for the task and had supported his secretaries and copyists:[220] here we have documentation of genuine literary patronage. During the heat of the Origenist controversy, however, Chromatius wrote to Jerome, begging him to lay aside his enmity and make peace with Rufinus.[221]

A second friend of Rufinus who at least briefly enjoyed cordial relations with Jerome was Paulinus of Nola. A latecomer to Italy, Paulinus had apparently received a cool reception from Pope Siricius when he journeyed

---

[211] It is of interest that Jerome never mentions Rufinus the Syrian's *Libellus fide* in his anti-Pelagian polemic. Although this point could be used to argue that Jerome's emissary Rufinus was a different "Rufinus" from the one mentioned by Marius Mercator, the case could also be made that Jerome either remained ignorant of Rufinus's book or (conveniently) chose to overlook it in his construction of an anti-Pelagian polemic from 414 on.

[212] Augustine, *De gratia Christi* II, 3, 3 (*CSEL* 42, 168).

[213] Rufinus, *Apologia* I, 4 (*CCL* 20, 39).

[214] Inferred from Jerome's letters of the period; see above, p. 20.

[215] For a careful study of Rufinus's activities after his return to the West, see C. P. Hammond, "The Last Ten Years of Rufinus'

Life and the Date of his Move South from Aquileia," 372–427.

[216] Rufinus, *In libros historiarum Eusebii, prologus* (*CCL* 20, 267).

[217] Suggested by Hammond, "The Last Ten Years," 392.

[218] In the Preface to Book III of his *Commentary* on Amos, however, Jerome states that the Jonah *Commentary* was written at the request of Pammachius (*CCL* 76, 300).

[219] Jerome dedicated to Chromatius translations of Proverbs, Ecclesiastes, and Song of Songs (*PL* 28, 1305), Tobit (*PL* 29, 23), Judith (*PL* 29, 42); and *Commentaries* on Jonah (*CCL* 76, 379) and Habakkuk (*CCL* 76A, 579).

[220] Jerome, *In libros Salomonis, praefatio* (*PL* 28, 1307).

[221] Jerome, *Apologia* III, 2 (*CCL* 79, 75).

from Spain to take up residence at Nola.[222] Paulinus deeply admired Melania the Elder (possibly his relative),[223] whom he entertained upon her return from Palestine and commemorated in *Epistle* 29.[224] Melania in turn brought Paulinus a sliver of the True Cross that John of Jerusalem had given her; Paulinus generously shared his bit with his friend Sulpicius Severus, whose establishment at Primuliacum was awaiting Silvia's promised gift of relics.[225] Melania's entire family, especially her granddaughter's husband Pinianus, receive lavish commendation in Paulinus's *Carmen* 21.[226] Through his relationship with Melania, Paulinus also became close friends with Rufinus.[227] A great admirer of Rufinus's translating talent, he asked him to translate the Pseudo-Clementines (which Rufinus still had not done, despite Silvia's earlier request); Paulinus himself had attempted the task, but found his skills inadequate.[228] He also requested that Rufinus write a commentary on the blessings of the patriarchs in Genesis, a request Rufinus was pleased to honor.[229] He may also have been a correspondent of the Macarius for whom Rufinus of Aquileia translated *On First Principles*.[230]

Despite these strong links with Rufinus's circle, Paulinus was also an acquaintance of Jerome's Roman friend Pammachius. He composed a moving letter of condolence to Pammachius upon the death of his wife Paulina,[231] thus beating Jerome by a year in expressing his sympathy.[232] Moreover, Paulinus had corresponded with Jerome during 394–395, using Vigilantius as carrier,[233] and had sent Jerome gifts, for which Jerome thanked him in *Epistles* 53 and 85.[234]

---

[222] Paulinus of Nola, *Ep.* 5, 14 (*CSEL 29*, 33); see Pierre Fabre, *Saint Paulin de Nole et l'amitié chrétienne*, 37.

[223] Paulinus of Nola, *Ep.* 29, 5 (*CSEL 29*, 251).

[224] Paulinus of Nola, *Ep.* 29, 6; 8–14 (*CSEL 29*, 251–252, 253–262).

[225] Paulinus of Nola, *Epp.* 31, 1; 32, 11 (*CSEL 29*, 268, 287).

[226] Paulinus of Nola, *Carmen* 21, esp. lines 60–83, 210–325 (*CSEL 30*, 160–161, 165–168).

[227] Paulinus of Nola, *Ep.* 28, 5; *Epp.* 46 and 47 are addressed to Rufinus (*CSEL 29*, 245–246, 387–389).

[228] Paulinus of Nola, *Ep.* 46, 2 (*CSEL 29*, 387–388).

[229] Paulinus of Nola, *Ep.* 47, 2 (*CSEL 29*, 389); Rufinus, *De benedictionibus patriarchum* I, *praefatio*; II, *praefatio* (*CCL* 20, 189, 203).

[230] See Paulinus of Nola, *Ep.* 49 to Macarius (*CSEL 29*, 390–404); cf. Palladius, *Historia Lausiaca* 62 (Butler ed., vol. 2: 157), where Macarius is described as an *ex-vicarius*;

Pierre Fabre, *Essai sur la chronologie de l'oeuvre de Saint Paulin de Nole*, 86–87; Bardy, *Recherches*, 91.

[231] Paulinus of Nola, *Ep.* 13 (*CSEL 29*, 84–107).

[232] Paulinus's epistle is dated early 396, while Jerome let two years pass before he wrote to Pammachius (*Ep.* 66, 1 [*CSEL 54*, 648]): probably Jerome thus *meant* his letter as a literary tribute. It is interesting to note Paulinus's extended discussions on how souls don't survive without bodies and on the real flesh of Jesus. Although Paulinus makes out that he is describing positions of the philosophical schools, surely there is resonance of the Origenist debate, given the choice of topics (*Ep.* 13, 25–26 [*CSEL 29*, 105–106]).

[233] Jerome, *Ep.* 61, 3 (*CSEL 54*, 580). On Paulinus's relationship with Jerome, see Pierre Courcelle, "Paulin de Nole et Saint Jérôme," 250–280. On Vigilantius as an emissary, see Fabre, *Essai*, 22.

[234] Jerome, *Epp.* 53, 1 (*CSEL 54*, 442); 85, 6 (*CSEL 55*, 138).

In *Epistle* 85, Jerome responds to Paulinus's query about "the hardening of Pharaoh's heart"—that is, to a question about free will in relation to God's predetermination, based on the classic Biblical text. Surprisingly enough, Jerome here, in the very midst of the Origenist controversy (A.D. 400), advises Paulinus that his question is answered in Origen's *Peri Archōn*; Paulinus can borrow a copy of the work from Pammachius, if he wishes to read a Latin translation, although Jerome is sure that Paulinus can manage the Greek original.[235] Jerome's nonchalance in suggesting that Paulinus read the *Peri Archōn* at the very moment when tempers were aflame and friendships breached raises an unsettling doubt about the centrality of theology in Jerome's attack on Origenism.

In addition to providing a link between Rufinus's network and Jerome's, Paulinus of Nola was also an important link between Pelagius and Augustine, as is detailed in Chapter Five. He was in friendly correspondence with Augustine before the outbreak of the Origenist controversy,[236] and was an admirer of Augustine's anti-Manichean writings.[237] Whether the break in their correspondence—from early 397 to 408—was a deliberate rupture of friendship or is simply to be explained by the loss of their respective letters, is not clear.[238]

Yet Paulinus was also tightly connected with Julian of Eclanum and his family; for Julian's wedding, probably before 404, Paulinus wrote an *epithalamium*.[239] It is tempting to posit that it was from Paulinus of Nola's library that Julian first got access to Augustine's anti-Manichean writings.[240] Moreover, Augustine himself testifies to the warm friendship that had existed between Pelagius and Paulinus of Nola—a friendship that Augustine, writing in 417, hopes is no longer flourishing.[241] That Paulinus and Pelagius had been in touch from about 405 is revealed by Augustine in *De gratia Christi*.[242] Paulinus thus emerges as a figure whose interests and relationships inform both the Origenist and the Pelagian debates, and the links between the two.

Last, two people who played "turncoat" roles in the controversy must

---

[235] Jerome, *Ep.* 85, 2–3 (*CSEL* 54, 136–137).

[236] See Paulinus of Nola, *Epp.* 4; 6; Augustine, *Epp.* 27; 31; 42.

[237] Paulinus of Nola, *Epp.* 3, 2; 4, 2 (*CSEL* 29, 14–15, 20).

[238] See Fabre, *Saint Paulin*, 239–240. The last evidence of their correspondence dates to 417 (Augustine, *Ep.* 186), but in 421, Augustine addressed his treatise *De cura pro mortuis gerenda* to Paulinus, in which he refers to a letter he had received from him (1, 1 [*PL* 40, 591–592]); see Fabre, *Essai*, 74.

[239] Paulinus of Nola, *Carmen* 25 (*CSEL* 30, 238–245); on the dating (that revolves around Julian's father-in-law's trip to Con-

stantinople), see Fabre, *Essai*, 122–123.

[240] See Albert Bruckner, *Julian von Eclanum. Sein Leben und seine Lehre. Ein Beitrag zur Geschichte des Pelagianismus*, 85, on Julian's knowledge of these writings; and Otto Wermelinger, *Rom und Pelagius. Die theologische Position der Römischen Bishöfe im Pelagianischen Streit in den Jahren 411–432*, 227.

[241] Augustine, *Ep.* 186, 1, 1 (*CSEL* 57, 45). Augustine testifies that Pelagius was a correspondent of Paulinus.

[242] Augustine, *De gratia Christi* I, 35, 38 (*CSEL* 42, 154): Augustine cites Pelagius's report that the letter was "some three hundred lines" long.

be briefly considered: Theophilus of Alexandria and Vigilantius. Vigilantius first comes to our attention as a letter carrier between Paulinus of Nola and Sulpicius Severus, and between Paulinus and Jerome.[243] In *circa* 395, Jerome calls his messenger Vigilantius a "reverend presbyter."[244] About a year later, Jerome changed his mind: Vigilantius had returned West and spread the report that Jerome held Origenist views, and had indicted Oceanus, Vincentius, Paulinianus, and Eusebius of Cremona as well.[245] Jerome lashed out bitterly against this "Judas."[246] He is puzzled how Paulinus of Nola's judgment could have been so mistaken. Jerome had assumed that since Vigilantius was Paulinus's "little client" (*clientulus*), he was trustworthy; Jerome should have trusted his own first impressions instead.[247] Jerome concludes his letter with an apt curse on Vigilantius: may he receive pardon when the devil obtains it[248]—which to anti-Origenists meant "never."

Most importantly, Jerome drops a revealing comment about Vigilantius in his *Apology against Rufinus*: it was Rufinus, he claims, who stirred up Vigilantius against Jerome.[249] The reference may pertain only to the Origenist controversy—or it may not. Here recall that Rufinus had taken pains to remind Jerome that his ascetic views were considered "Manichean,"[250] and that within a few years, Vigilantius's critique of Jerome's asceticism[251] would lead Jerome to assert that Jovinian had been reborn in Vigilantius.[252] It is not unlikely that Vigilantius's retreat from Jerome on the Origenist issue may have been coupled with his growing discomfort about Jerome's fanatic asceticism. Rufinus, despite his own monastic vocation, disagreed with Jerome on both issues as well. Thus Vigilantius, at first consideration an unimportant character in the controversy, may have been more central to it than has heretofore been imagined.

[243] Paulinus of Nola, *Ep.* 5, 11 (*CSEL* 29, 32); Jerome, *Ep.* 61, 3 (*CSEL* 54, 580). On Vigilantius, see Claire Stancliffe, *St. Martin and His Hagiographer: History and Miracle in Sulpicius Severus*, 274, 297–306.

[244] Jerome, *Ep.* 58, 11 (*CSEL* 54, 541): "*sanctum presbyterum.*"

[245] Jerome, *Ep.* 61, 3 (*CSEL* 54, 579).

[246] Jerome, *Ep.* 61, 1 (*CSEL* 54, 575–576).

[247] Jerome, *Ep.* 61, 3 (*CSEL* 54, 580). Saller (*Personal Patronage*, 9) offers the interesting observation that the term "clients" was usually reserved for the "humble members of the lower classes." Since the term implied "social inferiority and degradation," a writer like Pliny would never use it to refer to his protégés. Jerome not only uses the term of Vigilantius, but puts it in the diminutive, thus doubling the insult.

[248] Jerome, *Ep.* 61, 4 (*CSEL* 54, 582).

[249] Jerome, *Apologia* III, 19 (*CCL* 79, 91).

[250] Rufinus, *Apologia* II, 43 (*CCL* 20, 117). Rufinus criticizes Jerome's ascetic views also in *Apologia* II, 5; 42; 48 (*CCL* 20, 86–87, 116–117, 120–121).

[251] Jerome, *Contra Vigilantium* 2; 17 (*PL* 23, 355–356, 368).

[252] Jerome, *Contra Vigilantium* 1 (*PL* 23, 355). Jerome's evident delight in repeating the story (designed to humiliate Vigilantius) of Vigilantius's terrified prayer in the nude during an earthquake in Palestine suggests that Jerome was enraged at his opponent: *Contra Vigilantium* 11 (*PL* 23, 364). We learn from Jerome's report of Rufinus's nonextant letter that Jerome had apparently claimed Vigilantius was defiled by his communion with "heretics" (no doubt Origenists) at Alexandria: Jerome, *Apologia* III, 19 (*CCL* 79, 91).

Last we come to Theophilus of Alexandria, to whom extensive attention is given in Chapters Two and Three. In the first phase of the Origenist controversy in Palestine, Theophilus had shown decidedly Origenist tendencies, expressing his contempt for the narrow theological viewpoints Epiphanius had championed in a letter to Pope Siricius.[253] At the outbreak of hostilities in Palestine, Theophilus sent an emissary, Isidore, to calm the dispute, but Isidore's neutrality was rightly called into question when letters Isidore had written to John of Jerusalem counseling resistance to Jerome fell into the hands of Jerome's friend Vincentius.[254] Moreover, Isidore refused to deliver letters Theophilus had written to Jerome, and did so allegedly at John of Jerusalem's request.[255] Although Theophilus's immediate response to Jerome after these events was cool, Jerome nonetheless kept up a decidedly one-sided correspondence.[256] In a letter dating probably from 397, Jerome told Theophilus that "many people" considered his stand on Egyptian Origenism too lax, and urged him to greater activity.[257] A year or two later, Theophilus wrote to Jerome, adopting a peacemaker's role.[258] Jerome responded that he also desired peace, but only if it were based on genuine agreement.[259] In passing, Jerome mentions the loving concord that prevailed between Theophilus and the monks of the Egyptian desert.[260] Indeed, Theophilus had so admired the Tall Brothers that he had coerced them into ecclesiastical service.[261]

As is further detailed in Chapter Two, Jerome did not have to wait long for Theophilus to change his mind. In his Easter letter of 399, Theophilus had discussed God's incorporeality, a point that angered the simple monks given to Anthropomorphism. They flocked to Alexandria and riots erupted; Theophilus was in serious danger for both his post and his life. He thus made a *volte-face*: he agreed with the monks that God had ears, eyes, and other parts (after all, Scripture said so), and blamed his former friends the Tall Brothers and other Origenists for their disagreement. A time of persecution followed. The Tall Brothers and about eighty other monks fled to Palestine and then to Constantinople, where their cause became tied to that of John Chrysostom.[262]

---

[253] Palladius, *Dialogus* 16 (Coleman-Norton ed., 99); Socrates, *HE* VI, 10 (*PG* 67, 693–696); Sozomen, *HE* VIII, 14 (*PG* 67, 1552).

[254] Jerome, *Contra Ioannem* 37 (*PL* 23, 407).

[255] Jerome, *Contra Ioannem* 39 (*PL* 23, 408–409).

[256] Jerome, *Ep.* 63, 1 (*CSEL* 54, 585).

[257] Jerome, *Ep.* 63, 3 (*CSEL* 54, 586).

[258] Jerome, *Ep.* 82, 1 (*CSEL* 55, 107–108).

[259] Jerome, *Ep.* 82, 2 (*CSEL* 55, 108–109).

[260] Jerome, *Ep.* 82, 3 (*CSEL* 55, 109–110).

[261] Socrates, *HE* VI, 7 (*PG* 67, 684–685); Sozomen, *HE* VIII, 12 (*PG* 67, 1545).

[262] Socrates, *HE* VI, 7 (*PG* 67, 684–685, 688); Sozomen, *HE* VIII, 11–13 (*PG* 67, 1544–1549); Theophilus to Epiphanius (= Jerome, *Ep.* 90). Ammonius and Dioscorus, two of the Tall Brothers, died at Constantinople and were buried in the Church at Chalcedon called "Rufinianae," that is, the church dedicated by Flavius Rufinus, Silvia's brother-in-law (Palladius, *Historia Lausiaca* 11 [Butler ed., vol. 2: 34]; Socrates, *HE* VI,

Meanwhile, Theophilus aligned himself with the anti-Origenists, even enlisting Epiphanius, whose views he had earlier censured.[263] He wrote to Jerome, reporting his rout of the Nitrian monks;[264] he wrote a synodical letter to bishops in Palestine and Cyprus;[265] he wrote to Anastasius of Rome.[266] In the next years, Jerome translated Theophilus's Paschal letters, heavy with criticism of Origenism.[267] There is, however, very little evidence that Theophilus's anti-Origenism had much basis in anything but political expediency. As soon as he had regained his power at home and abroad had engineered the opposition that would lead to Chrysostom's downfall, he quickly reconciled himself to the Origenist monks he had hounded out of Egypt[268]—and resumed his study of Origen's writings. When asked why he now read the books he had so recently condemned, Theophilus allegedly replied that Origen's works could be compared to a meadow: one could pluck the beautiful flowers and step over the thorny ones,[269] a view identical with that held by both Jerome[270] and Rufinus[271] in their more rational moments.

This last point again brings home the extent to which the antagonists agreed in their approach to Origen: to use what was edifying and discard what was not. So once more we ask, why did the controversy develop as it did? Here the network concepts of density, multiplexity, brokerage, and "the strength of weak ties" illumine the historical data. Using the formula

---

17 [*PG* 67, 716], and Sozomen, *HE* VIII, 17 [*PG* 67, 1560]. For an overview of Theophilus's role in these events, see J.H.W.G. Liebeschuetz, *Barbarians and Bishops: Army, Church, and State in the Age of Arcadius and Chrysostom*, chap. 19. Chrysostom's consecration of Heraclides, a pupil of Evagius Ponticus, as bishop of Ephesus provides another link to Origenist circles: see Liebeschuetz's discussion of the incident (214–215) and n. 85 above.

[263] Theophilus, *Ep. ad Epiphanium* (= Jerome, *Ep.* 90 [*CSEL* 55, 143–145]); also see Socrates, *HE* VI, 10; 12 (*PG* 67, 693, 696, 700–701); Sozomen, *HE* VIII, 14 (*PG* 67, 1552–1553); Palladius, *Dialogus* 16 (Coleman-Norton ed., 99).

[264] Theophilus, *Ep. ad Hieronymum* (= Jerome, *Ep.* 87 [*CSEL* 55, 140]). According to Theophilus in a letter to Jerome (= Jerome, *Ep.* 89 [*CSEL* 55, 143]), the Nitrian monks were subdued.

[265] Theophilus, *Synodica epistula ad Palaestinos et ad Cyprios episcopos* (= Jerome, *Ep.* 92 [*CSEL* 55, 147–155]).

[266] Mentioned in Jerome, *Ep.* 88 to Theophilus (*CSEL* 55, 141): Jerome's information was relayed by Vincentius, returning from Rome to Bethlehem. See also Anastasius's letter to Simplicianus of Milan (= Jerome, *Ep.* 95) 2 (*CSEL* 55, 158).

[267] Theophilus's Paschal Letters are translated in Jerome as *Epp.* 96, 98, and 100 (*CSEL* 55, 159–181, 185–211, 213–232).

[268] Sozomen, *HE* VIII, 17 (*PG* 67, 1560); Socrates, *HE* VI, 16 (*PG* 67, 712).

[269] Socrates, *HE* VI, 17 (*PG* 67, 715).

[270] Jerome, *Ep.* 61, 1 (*CSEL* 54, 576): Jerome reads many authors, including Origen, and culls their flowers, holding fast to what is good in them. *Ep.* 61, 2 (*CSEL* 54, 577): we should accept what is good in Origen's writings and cut away what is evil; cf. *Apologia* II, 23; III, 9; 27 (*CCL* 79, 59–60, 82, 98); *Epp.* 62, 2 (*CSEL* 54, 583–584); 84, 2 (*CSEL* 55, 121–122).

[271] Rufinus's attitude toward Origen is shown in *De adulteratione* (*CCL* 20, 7–17); *De principiis* II, *praefatio* (*CCL* 20, 245–246); *Apologia ad Anastasium* 7 (*CCL* 20, 27–28).

employed by network analysts to calculate the density of a network,[272] and counting only those relationships that are documentable from the sources, I conclude that both Jerome and Rufinus were operating within very thick networks: around 83 percent density in Jerome's case, and about 78 percent in Rufinus's.[273] These figures would be considered strong indicators even by present-day investigators whose subjects are available for interviews; the density becomes remarkable for subjects who have been dead close to fifteen hundred years and who are known only from incompletely preserved literary sources.[274] Moreover, if all the probable but nondocumentable relationships were charted, the figures would be higher, and if second-order relationships were calculated (A and C's indirect relationship through their individual associations with B), the density would be higher still, approximating 100 percent. Network analysts would claim that the sheer density of these clusters largely explains the complexity and the heat of the controversy: almost everybody knew everybody else directly or through a third party.

The multiplexity of ties in the network is a second factor to note. When I charted seven possible ties (marriage/kinship; religious mentorship; hospitality; traveling companionship; financial patronage, money, and gifts; literature written to, for, or against members of the network; and carriers of literature and information), the strong connections *within* clusters became immediately obvious.[275] To take three examples: Paulinianus is linked to Jerome by six of the seven categories: as kin, religious advisee, recipient of hospitality, traveling companion, receiver of literature, and carrier of information. As for Epiphanius of Salamis, he was host to Paula, Paulinianus, Vincentius, and Jerome, and was himself hosted by Paula in Rome and by Jerome in Bethlehem; he served as a religious mentor to Paulinianus and Paula; his writings were read and used by Jerome and Theophilus of Alexandria in the construction of their own anti-Origenist polemic; his monastery was patronized by Paula; and he emerges in Constantinople as a companion of Theophilus. His associations and theological influence are detailed in Chapters Two and Three.

Likewise, turning to Rufinus's cluster, we can see that Melania the Elder is linked to Apronianus by kinship and by religious mentorship; insofar as she undoubtedly stayed with family members when she returned to Rome

---

[272] The density calculation formula is: (200 × actual number of links) ÷ (number in cluster × number in cluster − 1).

[273] Density calculation for Jerome's cluster: (200 × 55) ÷ (12 × 11) = 11,000 ÷ 132 = 83.3% density. Density calculation for Rufinus's cluster is: (200 × 71) ÷ (14 × 13) = 14,200 ÷ 182 = 78.0% density. Charts detailing the known relationships

among the controversy's participants can be found in my article "Elite Networks and Heresy Accusations."

[274] The fact that Rufinus's correspondence has not been preserved probably accounts for the slightly lower density calculation.

[275] The charts documenting these ties are printed in Clark, "Elite Networks."

in A.D. 400, we are probably safe in adding the link of hospitality. To Paulinus of Nola, Melania was perhaps related by kinship. She received his hospitality, was the subject of his laudations, and gave him gifts. To Evagrius Ponticus, she served as religious mentor, providing both hospitality and financial support; he in turn directed letters and treatises to her from Egypt. She was also in the 380s instructed by the Tall Brothers, with some of whom she fled Egypt for Palestine, and for whom she there provided material resources and political protection. These intercrossings illustrate the multiplex relations that obtained among these late-antique friends and disputants, who were often separated from each other by considerable distances. Although Rufinus's cluster appears to contain fewer multiplex relations than Jerome's, the difference can probably be accounted for by the relative lack of epistolary evidence for Rufinus's circle and the abundance of it for Jerome's.

The role of "brokers" was also of decisive importance in the early stages of the Origenist controversy. Separated at first by small distances (Jerusalem and Bethlehem) and then by more extensive ones (Italy and Palestine), Rufinus and Jerome were in need of speedy and faithful emissaries. Both the development and the rancor of the controversy were influenced by the questionable behavior of their intermediaries. The deliberate nature of the liaisons' misguided actions undoubtedly resulted from the passionate loyalty they gave their respective patrons, and hence their patrons' opinions: as Rodney Stark observed in his studies, religious commitments tend to follow the lines of personal loyalties to friends and relatives. That seemingly unimportant persons, unknown to the pages of theology textbooks, so strongly influenced the controversy's development is a fact that network analysis has brought to light—a fact obscured by concentration on the theological dimensions of the debate alone. The following examples illustrate the point.

First, the controversy might not have smoldered on in Palestine had Isidore of Alexandria served as peacemaker, the role in which he had been sent by bishop Theophilus. By allowing his own pro-Origenist letter opposing Jerome to fall (accidentally?) into the hands of Jerome's friend Vincentius, Isidore is at least partially responsible for the deteriorating relations of the Jerusalem and Bethlehem factions. His failure to play his "liaison" role is further indicated by his refusal to deliver letters from Theophilus to Jerome, as he had been directed.

A second case concerns Pammachius, Jerome's supporter in Rome. Instead of delivering Jerome's letter attempting reconciliation with Rufinus, as he had been instructed to do by his mentor, he suppressed it and circulated in its place Jerome's hot letter against Rufinus, meant only for the eyes of Pammachius and a few of Jerome's Roman intimates. Thus Rufinus composed his *Apology against Jerome*, Jerome responded with his rancorous *Apology against Rufinus*, and the controversy escalated.

As a third example, Jerome was poorly served by the actions of his emissary Eusebius of Cremona, whom he had sent on an allegedly private mission to Rome. According to Rufinus, Eusebius while in Rome pirated an uncorrected copy of Rufinus's translation of the *Peri Archōn*, "emended" it to accentuate its theological unorthodoxy, and trumpeted citations from this falsified version before bishops and aristocrats in Italy. With intermediaries behaving so irresponsibly, it is understandable how difficult it was for Jerome and Rufinus to resolve their feud. The infrastructure of the network depended upon the smooth functioning of these "weak-tied" associations, and when the ties unraveled, the controversy was prolonged and intensified.

A fourth example illustrates how the sheer fact of a person's place in the network's structure, quite aside from his or her relative importance in the larger history, may have influenced the course of events in important ways: "brokers" need not be—and in the case of the Origenist controversy, usually were not—the prime theological disputants. Take the case of Sylvia, a virtual nonentity except for her kinship with Count Rufinus, praetorian prefect of the East and briefly the central Eastern wielder of power during Theodosius's Western trip in 394. The few pieces we know of Sylvia's story (her journey from Constantinople to Jerusalem, her meeting of Palladius and subsequent travel with him to Egypt, and her role as intended recipient of Rufinus of Aquileia's translation of the Pseudo-Clementine *Recognitions*) suggest that she may have been a (indeed, *the*) missing link in a seemingly mysterious affair: the issuing of an edict of banishment against Jerome. Her "structural" position as intermediary between the Jerusalem religious establishment and the Eastern court may provide a key to an otherwise puzzling aspect of the controversy.[276]

The prime person in the Origenist controversy who exemplifies the importance of "weak-tied relationships" is perhaps Paulinus of Nola. Paulinus was linked by many ties with partisans of both Jerome's and Rufinus's circles—and with circles of both Pelagians and Augustinians in the debate that later ensued. During the Origenist controversy, Paulinus was doubtless most connected with Rufinus's group: as a relative of Melania the Elder who lauded her ascetic virtues for posterity, Paulinus reached out to her whole circle of relatives and companions (Rufinus, Melania the Younger and Pinianus, Apronianus and Avita). So likewise was he linked both personally and through letters with major disputants on the Pelagian

---

[276] The other possible link of the Jerusalem group to the Eastern court is through their friend Bacurius, *dux Palestinae*. Quite possibly, the Jerusalem group mobilized both of these allies against Jerome.

side of the controversy (Pelagius himself, Julian of Eclanum, and the latter's family) as well as with the anti-Pelagians Augustine, Alypius, and Jerome. Yet throughout the Origenist dispute, Paulinus managed to maintain relations with Jerome's circle as well as Rufinus's. He and Jerome corresponded,[277] and he was close enough to the senator Pammachius, Jerome's friend and Paula's son-in-law, to compose for him a moving memorial upon the death of Pammachius's wife Paulina.[278] Likewise, he was connected with Jerome's monastic circle in Bethlehem through Vigilantus, who after serving as a letter carrier between Paulinus and Jerome, took up residence at the Bethlehem monastery—only to desert to Rufinus's camp. Although Paulinus of Nola cannot be considered a significant theologian in the controversy, as Chapter Five indicates, as a correspondent and friend of many he nonetheless served as a link between the warring camps.

The advantages of tracing the social networks involved in the Origenist controversy have, I hope, become obvious. They show how previous loyalties—and enmities—could influence the theological positions adopted by participants in the controversy. Furthermore, they bring to light the allegedly minor characters in the dispute, including many women, whose roles emerge as more central to the debate's development than we ever could have imagined from presentations in theology textbooks. I would not, however, follow those network analysts who claim that the ideas argued about in any dispute are inconsequential factors, as the chapters to follow demonstrate. Living in a world more deeply committed to religious faith than is our own, at least some of the disputants did care passionately about the theological points involved, or, more correctly, about their own interpretations of theological points. Yet their eager desire for orthodoxy, as defined at the turn to the fifth century, was always tempered by their respect for Origen's monumental stature as an exegete and a thinker. The chapters that follow detail the theological issues of the controversy and note how they passed through and by means of the networks outlined above: the networks, in other words, furnish the historical and material contextualization for contested ideas. Let us begin not with Jerusalem, Bethlehem, Cyprus, or Alexandria—the conventional sites usually mentioned first in introductions to the Origenist controversy—but with the Egyptian desert.

---

[277] Jerome, *Epp.* 53; 58; 85; Paulinus's letters to Jerome have not been preserved.

[278] Paulinus of Nola, *Ep.* 13.

Image and Images:
Evagrius Ponticus and the
Anthropomorphite
Controversy

The desert father Sopatros, upon being asked for a commandment, offered the following: "Do not let a woman come into your cell and do not read apocryphal literature. Do not speculate about the image. Although this is not heresy, there is too much ignorance and love of dispute on both sides. It is impossible for any creature to understand this matter."[1] That Sopatros's advice went unheeded is all too clear from the many accounts pertaining to the desert monks' discussions of "the image of God." Moreover, Sopatros incorrectly assured his petitioner that the topic held no possibilities for heresy accusations: the debate over the "image of God" served as one focus for Theophilus of Alexandria's charge of Origenism against some of the monks[2] and his rout of the Nitrian community. An investigation of the distinctive form assumed by the Origenist controversy in Egypt, the subject of this chapter, reveals that to concentrate merely on the structure of Origenist and anti-Origenist networks without exploring the ideas circulating through them obscures the complexity of the dispute. The contested ideas did not, however, float free, as theology textbooks sometimes seem to presume: the intensity of the clash is explained not only by the personal associations of its contestants (as network analysts would argue), but also by the tight link

[1] *Apophthegmata patrum* (Alphabetical), Sopatros (*PG* 65, 413).
[2] The long-lasting effect of Theophilus's action is mixed. That by the end of the sixth century, Evagrius Ponticus was remembered at Cellia as a heretic is revealed by John Moschus, *Pratum spirituale* 177. On the other hand, Evagrius's books were still being requested for reading in the seventh or eighth century; see W. E. Crum, *Coptic Ostraca from the Collections of the Egypt Exploration Fund, the Cairo Museum and Others*, #252 (46 Coptic; 63 English).

between theological speculation and religious praxis manifested in this branch of the Origenist debate.

Although the church historians of the period systematically downplay the theological issues involved by blaming the controversy entirely on Theophilus of Alexandria's dubious behavior, I contend that deeper theological issues attend the dispute than they lead us to expect—issues that stemmed from religious controversies of the later fourth century, whose repercussions extended to ritual, anthropology, and ascetic praxis. I also argue that the theology of Evagrius Ponticus is central to the controversy[3]—although its centrality could not have been inferred from the church historians' narrations of Theophilus's dealings with the Egyptian monks in 399, from which Evagrius is conspicuously absent.[4] They were, however, correct in noting the short life of Theophilus's anti-Origenist campaign, a brevity that lends support to their allegation that his attack on Origenism was not entirely sincere or theologically motivated. Had ecclesiastical politics not intervened, Theophilus might well have remained closely aligned with the alleged Origenists.

Three Christian commentators of the fifth century describe the events of 399: Socrates, Sozomen, and Palladius. Although their accounts differ somewhat in the details they offer to explain Theophilus's behavior, all three lead their readers to assume that theology was not central to the debate, and the little of it that appears was served up by the bishop of Alexandria as a guise to further his ecclesiastical politics. All three are noticeably hostile to Theophilus, who, through their assessments, comes down in the annals of church history as a thoroughly unscrupulous character. Most important, all three side with the theological opinions espoused by the suspect Origenists. Thus much, but not all, of our evidence is furnished by writers who wished to present the campaign against Origenism in the least favorable light. For example, they consistently interpret the debate over the "image of God" in such a way as to suggest that their opponents believed that God possessed bodily parts. Whether their opponents, dubbed "Anthropomorphites" by the Origenist-oriented historians, would necessarily have so construed their own position remains debatable.[5]

---

[3] Among the few scholars pressing this point are Antoine and Claire Guillaumont, "Le Texte véritable des 'Gnostica' d'Evagre le Pontique," 203; see also François Refoulé, "Evagre fut-il origéniste?" 398–399. The definitive statement of this argument is pronounced by Antoine Guillaumont in Les "Kephalaia Gnostica," 120–123.

[4] The absence of reference to Evagrius in the controversy is noted by J. G. (Gabriel) Bunge, "Origenismus—Gnostizismus: Zum geistesgeschichtlichen Standort des Evagrios Pontikos," 25–26, but Bunge uses the ab-

sence of explicit mention as a support for Evagrius's basic orthodoxy, rather than as a stimulus for inquiry about other possible interpretations of this silence. Two monographs on Theophilus of Alexandria never mention the name of Evagrius Ponticus: Giuseppe Lazzati, Teofilo d'Alessandria, and Agostino Favale, Teofilo d'Alessandria (345c.–412): Scritti, Vita e Dottrina.

[5] A point highlighted by Graham Gould in his paper, "Doctrines of the Image: Origenism and the Monks." Nonetheless, it is important to note that Theophilus and Je-

Socrates reports that the question of whether God had a human shape or was in any way corporeal had been debated in the Egyptian desert for some time. When Theophilus expounded the view that God was incorporeal (presumably in his festal letter of 399, no longer extant), rioting broke out among those desert monks who believed that God had a body. Leaving their monastic retreats, they flocked to Alexandria where they raised a tumult and even threatened to kill Theophilus. The bishop unhesitatingly changed his stance (God indeed had a body), and pacified the angry monks by telling them, "In seeing you, I behold the face of God." Since the notion of God's incorporeality had been bolstered by appeals to Origen's theology, the monks allegedly asked Theophilus to anathematize Origen's books (presumably including *On First Principles*), a request to which the bishop readily agreed. Theophilus then sent letters to the monastic communities of the desert, informing their inhabitants that since Scripture portrays God as having bodily parts, they should accept its authoritative testimony as binding. Socrates concludes his account by reporting that Theophilus went with a "multitude" to Nitria and armed the Anthropomorphite monks against those of the opposite persuasion, who fled.[6] The Nitrian community was thus supposedly purged of Origen's supporters.

According to Socrates, Theophilus's action was entirely motivated by church politics, not by theology. Indeed, in Socrates' judgment, Theophilus had not really changed his mind at all, but had disingenuously espoused Anthropomorphite opinions to win the support of bishop Epiphanius of Salamis, whom he believed ascribed to this position—even though Theophilus had earlier scorned Epiphanius's "lowly" understanding of God.[7]

The occasion that had prompted Theophilus's *volte-face* and appeal for Epiphanius's support, Socrates states, concerned the famous "Tall Brothers."[8] Honored for their erudition as well as their sanctity, they had been

---

rome—self-proclaimed opponents of Origenism—both testify that there were monks called "Anthropomorphites." See below, pp. 120, 149.

[6] Socrates, *HE* VI, 7 (*PG* 67, 684–688). For a summary of events as described by Socrates and other contemporary historians see Hugh G. Evelyn-White, *The Monasteries of the Wâdi 'N Natrûn. Part II: The History of the Monasteries of Nitria and of Scetis*, chap. 8. For an overview of Socrates and Sozomen, and their Origenist proclivities, see Glenn F. Chesnut, *The First Church Histories. Eusebius, Socrates, Sozomen, Theodoret and Evagrius*, chaps. 7 and 8. On the histories of the monasteries at Nitria and Cellia, see (in addition to Evelyn-White) Antoine Guillaumont, "Histoire des moines aux Kellia," 187–203.

[7] Socrates, *HE* VI, 10 (*PG* 67, 693). According to Palladius, Theophilus in the 380s had charged Epiphanius with heresy (*Dialogus* 16 [56] [Coleman-Norton ed., 99]). Whether or not Epiphanius was truly an "Anthropomorphite," we have evidence that he performed the iconoclastic action of tearing down a church curtain that had an image of a man on it (Epiphanius, *Ep. ad Ioannem Episcopum* (= Jerome, *Ep.* 51) 9 (*CSEL* 54, 411). That John of Jerusalem attempted to pin a charge of "Anthropomorphism" on Epiphanius is stated by Jerome in *Contra Ioannem* 11 (*PL* 23, 380); apparently Rufinus shared this view (Jerome, *Apologia*, III, 23 [*PL* 23, 495–496]).

[8] On the Tall Brothers, see Lazzati, *Teofilo*, chaps. 4 and 6, and Favale, *Teofilo*, 96–103, 115–120, 133–135.

solicited by Theophilus for ecclesiastical service. One of the four, Diosco-rus, had been "forced" into the bishopric of Hermopolis, and two others were pressed to help manage the affairs of the Alexandrian church.[9] We learn from the *Lausiac History* as well as from Socrates that the fourth brother, Ammonius, escaped ordination by cutting off his ear,[10] thus ren-dering himself unfit for ecclesiastical service by the church's interpretation of Levitical regulations governing priestly "wholeness."[11] When the two brothers with Theophilus (presumably Eusebius and Euthymius)[12] wit-nessed the corruption of financial and other affairs in the Alexandrian church—Theophilus is said to have been concerned only with the amassing of wealth—they tried to return to the purer air of the desert. Theophilus, however, ascertained their true motivation for wishing to depart and began to menace them. According to Socrates, he charged them with "anti-An-thropomorphism" and instructed the desert monks to "pay no heed" to their opinions concerning God's incorporeality. In Socrates' account, the more educated of the monks resolutely affirmed the opinions of Dioscorus and Origen, but the majority of the "simple" monks, whom he calls illit-erate, were aroused to riot against them.[13] The Tall Brothers fled the per-secution of their attackers, ultimately landing in Constantinople, where their fates became entwined with that of John Chrysostom.[14]

There were, however, still further complexities to the plot. According to Socrates, Theophilus had earlier campaigned for his own presbyter, Isi-dore, to be chosen bishop of Constantinople when that seat became vacant upon the death of Nectarius in September 397.[15] The imperial chamber-lain, Eutropius, who favored the candidacy of John Chrysostom over that of Isidore, allegedly threatened that he would reveal unsavory details of Theophilus's behavior, and stood ready with formal accusations, if The-ophilus did not agree to Chrysostom's appointment.[16]

---

[9] Socrates, *HE* VI, 7 (*PG* 67, 684–685).

[10] Socrates, *HE* IV, 23 (*PG* 67, 521); *His-toria Lausiaca* 11, 1 (Butler ed., vol. 2: 33); *Historia monachorum* 20, 14 (Festugière ed., 122–123: three of the brothers are here said to have cut off their ears).

[11] Leviticus 21:16–24.

[12] Palladius, *Dialogus* 7 (23) (Coleman-Norton ed., 38, 12 [app.]); Socrates, *HE* VI, 7 (*PG* 67, 684); Sozomen, *HE* VIII, 12 (*PG* 67, 1545).

[13] Socrates, *HE* VI, 7 (*PG* 67, 685, 688). If the monks were truly of the low educa-tional level that Socrates states, the relative lack of treatises and other documents ema-nating from "anti-Origenists" is more easily explained.

[14] That Origenism did not disappear from the Egyptian desert with their departure is revealed in fragments of two letters by The-ophilus, preserved in Justinian's *Liber adver-sus Origenem* (*PG* 86, 967), one dated from the summer of 400 and the second, from late 400 or early 401, on the issue of Origenist monks still present. See also Shenute's *Con-tra Origenistas*, discussed below, pp. 151–156.

[15] Socrates, *HE* VI, 2; 5 (*PG* 67, 661, 663, 673, 676); Sozomen elaborates the story in *HE* VIII, 2; 12 (*PG* 67, 1517, 1520, 1545). Isidore is described as guest master of the church of Alexandria by Palladius, *Historia Lausiaca* 1, 1 (Butler ed., vol. 2: 15). On Is-idore, see Lazzati, *Teofilo*, 27–30, 35, 43–44; Favale, *Teofilo*, 96–102.

[16] Socrates, *HE* VI, 2 (*PG* 67, 664).

In the meantime, however, Theophilus had turned against Isidore. Socrates reports that Theophilus expelled Isidore from the Alexandrian church for not supporting Theophilus's version of a story regarding the admission of a convert from Manicheanism to "the sacred mysteries."[17] Sozomen, whose account generally follows that of Socrates,[18] adds two other stories to explain Theophilus's renunciation of his former trusted associate. Isidore, we learn, refused to attest the existence of a legacy in which Theophilus's sister was the named beneficiary. Moreover, Sozomen adds, when Isidore refused Theophilus's request to hand over money that had been given to the Alexandrian see for poor relief to enhance Theophilus's church-building program, Theophilus excommunicated him in a fury.[19] (Theophilus's "lithomania" is also noted by Palladius[20] and by Isidore of Pelusium.)[21] According to Sozomen, Isidore then returned to the desert and joined the circle of the Tall Brothers, who interceded on Isidore's behalf. When Theophilus imprisoned one of the monks, the others voluntarily joined him, thus forcing an apology from a highly annoyed Theophilus. These incidents, writes Sozomen, were the prime motivating factors for Theophilus's attacks on the Origenism of the anti-Anthropomorphite faction.[22] Upon Theophilus's rout of the Nitrian monks in 399, Isidore fled along with the Tall Brothers, first to Palestine and then to Constantinople.[23]

Both Socrates and Sozomen suggest that in this affair, church politics, not theology, was at stake. In Socrates' view, the accusation of Origenism was simply Theophilus's device to deflect accusations about his violence that were rumored to be circulating in the Eastern capital.[24] Theophilus's more immediate motivation, he alleges, was the wish to discredit the Tall Brothers;[25] thus his and Epiphanius's engineering of the Tall Brothers' excommunication in a synod held at the Church of the Apostles in Constantinople was the logical outcome of his campaign against them.[26] For Socrates, Theophilus's duplicity was confirmed by his genial rescinding of this degree of excommunication after he had orchestrated the downfall of John Chrysostom.[27] The Alexandrian bishop then returned to his study of Ori-

---

[17] Socrates, *HE* VI, 9 (*PG* 67, 692).

[18] Sozomen, *HE* VIII, 11–15 (*PG* 67, 1544–1556).

[19] Sozomen, *HE* VIII, 12 (*PG* 67, 1545, 1547).

[20] Palladius, *Dialogus* 6 (22) (Coleman-Norton ed., 35).

[21] Isidore of Pelusium, *Ep.* I, 1, 151 (*PG* 78, 285).

[22] Sozomen, *HE* VIII, 12 (*PG* 67, 1548–1549). Evelyn-White (*Monasteries* II: 135–137) agrees that Theophilus's personal animosity toward Isidore and the Tall Brothers,

who came to Isidore's defense, was the motivating factor prompting Theophilus's attack upon the Origenist monks.

[23] Sozomen, *HE* VIII, 13 (*PG* 67, 1549); cf. Socrates, *HE* VI, 9 (*PG* 67, 693). For a discussion of the subsequent fortunes of the Tall Brothers, see Evelyn-White, *Monasteries* II: 142–144.

[24] Socrates, *HE* VI, 9 (*PG* 67, 692–693).

[25] Socrates, *HE* VI, 10 (*PG* 67, 696).

[26] Socrates, *HE* VI, 14 (*PG* 67, 705): Epiphanius was in charge of the proceedings.

[27] Socrates, *HE* VI, 16 (*PG* 67, 712).

gen, claiming that he could pick the beautiful flowers from the "meadow" of Origen's writings but step over the thorns.[28] In sum, Socrates is thoroughly convinced that theology was a mere cover for Theophilus's devious ecclesiastical politics, and to this charge Sozomen adds the motivating factor of Theophilus's greed.[29]

The third and earliest source, also hostile to Theophilus, is Palladius, who was an eyewitness to some of the events described above. Palladius adds one further intriguing accusation to those supplied by Socrates and Sozomen: in his attempt to ruin Isidore, Theophilus accused him of having committed sodomy with a youth eighteen years earlier. Theophilus bribed a young man with fifteen pieces of gold—delivered by Theophilus's sister—to support the trumped-up tale, but the alleged victim's pious mother revealed the plot to Isidore, and the young man, instead of testifying against him, fled to the church for sanctuary. Theophilus then excommunicated Isidore without a hearing, since evidence had vanished with the revelation of the plot, and Isidore returned to the desert, where he had lived before his time of service in the Alexandrian church.[30] Theophilus next wrote to neighboring bishops urging the expulsion from the desert monasteries of some leading ascetics; when a delegation journeyed to Alexandria to inquire the reasons for this request, Theophilus refused to discuss the issue but bloodied the nose of Ammonius, one of the Tall Brothers, shouting at him, "Anathematize Origen, you heretic!"[31] From Palladius's account we would infer that the "true" reasons for the dispute were nonreligious but that the wicked bishop of Alexandria cloaked his immoral behavior with theological sanctity by levelling a charge against Origenists. Here, as so often in church history, accusations of heresy are linked to those of sexual deviation.

In Palladius's version, it was these events that prompted Theophilus's attack upon the monastic community at Nitria, an attack that led to the forcible expulsion of Dioscorus from his see, the burning of the monastic cells, along with the books they contained, and the flight of more than three hundred monks from the monastery.[32] (That the books pertained to

---

[28] Socrates, *HE* VI, 17 (*PG* 67, 716). As Evelyn-White phrased it, Theophilus had probably taken a liberal view of Origen "until he saw fit to trim his sails to catch another breeze" (*Monasteries* II: 128). For an overview of Theophilus's theology, see Favale, *Teofilo*, 179–210.

[29] See Sozomen's addition of two stories to Socrates' account in *HE* VIII, 12 (*PG* 67, 1545, 1547).

[30] Palladius, *Dialogus* 6 (22–23) (Coleman-Norton ed., 35–37). Palladius's special interest in Isidore may well stem from the

fact that, according to Palladius, Isidore initiated him to the monastic life in Egypt: *Historia Lausiaca* 1, 1; 1, 5; 2, 1 (Butler ed., vol. 2: 15, 16). For a discussion of the debate over the identification of Isidore, see Favale, *Teofilo*, 96–97.

[31] Palladius, *Dialogus* 6 (23) (Coleman-Norton ed., 37–38).

[32] Palladius, *Dialogus* 7 (24) (Coleman-Norton ed., 39). According to Evelyn-White (*Monasteries* II: 140), the anti-Origenists obtained a decree from Arcadius and Honorius that prohibited "servants of God" from

Origenist theology is suggested by Sulpicius Severus.)[33] Some of the expelled monks ended up in Constantinople, where they made known that they were prepared to file formal charges against Theophilus.[34] Thus Palladius, like Socrates and Sozomen, ascribes to Theophilus a purely political motivation, although his version centers entirely on vindicating his friend John Chrysostom through his report of Theophilus's machinations.

As might be expected, Theophilus's own summary of events is quite different: theology—or more precisely, heresy—is at the center of his account. Theophilus claims that he was rightfully alarmed at some of Origen's teachings. When he condemned his writings, the advocates of Origenist theology rioted in anger. As for the role of Isidore, Theophilus alleges that the Origenists were creating a *cause célèbre* over a man who, in Theophilus's recounting, "for various reasons had been cut off by many bishops from the communion of the saints."[35] The story Palladius tells of Theophilus's raising a false sodomy charge against Isidore is here desexualized: the boy and his mother, in his version, tried to arouse pagans against Theophilus for his role in "the destruction of the Serapeum and other idols."[36] When the woman pressed a charge of an unspecified nature against Isidore, clerical friends attempted to secure her silence by allowing her to be enrolled in the rank of the widows, that is, to receive financial support from the church. Moreover, Theophilus states, Isidore used his great wealth to furnish provisions for the fleeing Nitrian monks. Theophilus concludes his recitation with a sarcastic jibe: "Where rage and slaughter are necessary, they don't need anyone's help; where money and various expenses are involved, nothing is handier than to have a treasury!"[37] As is clear, Theophilus has turned the allegations of false charges and greed away from himself and onto others. In this and other letters[38] he paints himself as a staunch defender of orthodoxy in the face of rioting and heretical Origenist monks. And by noting his own role in the campaign against Egyptian "idolatry," Theophilus hints at the alignment of iconoclasm with anti-Origenism—an alignment that will be severely challenged by his Origenist

---

reading the works of Origen (see Anastasius, *Ep.* 1, 5 [*PL* 20, 72]; cf. Jerome, *Apologia* I, 12 [*PL* 23, 425]), and probably appealed to this decree to obtain the assistance of the secular authorities stationed in Egypt for the attack on the Nitrian monks.

[33] Sulpicius Severus, *Dialogus* I, 6–7 (*PL* 20, 187–188).

[34] Palladius, *Dialogus* 7 (24; 26) (Coleman-Norton ed., 40, 42).

[35] Theophilus, esp. *Synodica epistula* (= Jerome, *Ep.* 92) 1; 3 (*CSEL* 55, 147–148, 150).

[36] Theophilus, *Synodica epistula* (= Jerome, *Ep.* 92) 3 (*CSEL* 55, 150).

[37] Theophilus, *Synodica epistula* (= Jerome, *Ep.* 92) 3 (*CSEL* 55, 151).

[38] Of the complete letters for which we have full translations, see Theophilus, *Ep. ad Hieronymum* (= Jerome, *Ep.* 89 [*CSEL* 55, 142–143]); *Ep. ad Epiphanium* (= Jerome, *Ep.* 90 [*CSEL* 55, 143–145]); *Ep. paschalis* (16) (= Jerome, *Ep.* 96 [*CSEL* 55, 159–181]); *Ep. paschalis* (17) (= Jerome, *Ep.* 98, 8–22 [*CSEL* 55, 192–208]); *Ep. paschalis* (21) (= Jerome *Ep.* 100, 11–13 [*CSEL* 55, 224–227]).

opponents.[39] Each network, in effect, attempted to represent itself as the supremely iconoclastic party.

That theological controversy, but not a controversy centering on Origen's writings pure and simple, played a more significant role than is suggested by the accounts of the church historians seems clear, for the dispute over the imaging of God had widespread ramifications that extended to the realms of worship and ascetic praxis, as well as of anthropology and theology *per se*. It was a dispute with a past,[40] a past located *historically* in the conversion of native Egyptians from paganism ("idolatry") to Christianity, and *theologically* in the later Arian controversy, especially with the refinement of language about God that attended the debates between Arians and the Cappadocian Fathers. Nonetheless, I shall argue that the controversy is focused not only on these events of the recent past or on the theology of Origen as we know it from his writings, but also on the Origenist views under discussion in the Egyptian desert at the turn of the fifth century—and this is the theology of Evagrius Ponticus, whose name figures not once in the historians' reports of the events of 399, although all three elsewhere reveal that they knew either Evagrius himself[41] or his writings.[42] Through networks of Origenists and anti-Origenists, the ideas of this speculative theologian and ascetic practitioner—himself nearly unacknowledged in the debate—began to circulate throughout the Mediterranean world.

Two other sources lead us deeper into the theological issues involved. The first is provided by John Cassian, who claims to have been present when Theophilus's festal letter of 399 arrived at Scete.[43] According to Cassian, Theophilus's letter was directed against the Anthropomorphites. Many of the monks, he reports, became agitated at hearing Theophilus refer to God's incorporeality, since "in their simplicity" they believed that God had human form: if humans were created in "God's image," did not God have human shape and characteristics? Cassian adds the revealing detail that three of the four priests of the churches at Scete opposed The-

---

[39] For an important linking of the iconoclastic impulse in early Christianity to the influence of Origen, see George Florovsky, "Origen, Eusebius, and the Iconoclastic Controversy," 77–96. Theophilus's insinuation appears as an illogical and polemical attempt to link his "antipagan" and "antiheretical" concerns.

[40] That it also was a controversy with a future is shown by Cyril of Alexandria's attention to the issue in his treatise, *Against the Anthropomorphites* (PG 76, 1065–1132); and Agatonicus, "On Anthropomorphism," 217–218.

[41] Palladius reveals his personal relationship to Evagrius in *Historia Lausiaca* 12, 1–2; 23, 1; 24, 2; 35, 3; 38, 3; 47, 3 (Butler ed., vol. 2: 35, 75, 78, 101, 117, 137).

[42] For Socrates' knowledge of Evagrius's writings, see *HE* IV, 23 (PG 67, 516–521); III, 7 (PG 67, 396) (Socrates quotes from several of Evagrius's writings); Sozomen mentions some details of Evagrius's life in *HE* VI, 30 (PG 67, 1584–1588).

[43] John Cassian reports that the letters arrived at Epiphany, to announce the dates for Lent and Easter: *Conlationes* X, 2 (SC 54, 75).

ophilus's anti-Anthropomorphite teaching; only the priest of the congregation to which Cassian was attached, Paphnutius, affirmed the incorporeality of God.[44] Some of the monks, says Cassian, were shocked at the "novelty" of Theophilus's opinion.[45]

A second source providing clues about the theological dimensions of the debate is a Coptic document first published in 1883 and republished, with a French translation, by Etienne Drioton in 1915–1917.[46] The text concerns the life of Aphou, an Egyptian monk from Oxyrhynchus (Pemdjé) in Upper Egypt, who three years after the event described was reputedly raised to the episcopal throne by Theophilus.[47] The text reports the reception given Theophilus's anti-Anthropomorphite festal letter of 399 at Pemdjé.

We are told that it was Aphou's custom to journey from his monastic retreat to the town of Pemdjé once a year to hear the paschal letter from the bishop of Alexandria read aloud to the congregation.[48] When Theophilus's letter of 399 was read out, Aphou was so shaken that he heeded an angel's summons to undertake the trip to Alexandria to correct the bishop. For three days, Aphou stood at Theophilus's door before he gained an audience.[49] Upon being admitted, Aphou told Theophilus his reasons for disagreement (to be examined below) and speedily convinced him of his error in imagining that humans had lost God's "image."[50] The repentant Theophilus wrote to "every region" to repudiate his earlier opinion. Aphou graciously refrained from blaming Theophilus directly: it was rather the devil's ploy to let the bishop scandalize the faithful so that they would give no heed to the rest of his "holy teaching." By Theophilus's retraction, the devil was foiled and a praiseworthy example of episcopal humility was provided by Theophilus's admission of error.[51]

In Drioton's view, the triumph of what he understands as Anthropomorphitism in this account is to be read as a vindication of the views of the Audian monks who lived at Pemdjé in the later fourth century.[52] He be-

---

[44] John Cassian, *Conlationes* X, 2 (*SC* 54, 76). Paphnutius is identified as the disciple of Macarius the Great in *Apophthegmata Patrum*, Macarius the Great 37 (*PG* 65, 277); and in the Coptic document, "The Virtues of St. Macarius," Am. 178, 9, translated in *Les Sentences des Pères du désert. Troisième recueil et tables*, ed. Lucien Regnault, 180.

[45] John Cassian, *Conlationes* X, 3 (*SC* 54, 76). Specific points of Cassian's account will be discussed below, pp. 52, 58–59, 66.

[46] Etienne Drioton, "La Discussion d'un moine anthropomorphite Audien avec le patriarche Théophile d'Alexandrie en l'année 399," 92–100, 113–128.

[47] Drioton, "La Discussion," 94.

[48] Drioton, "La Discussion," 94.

[49] Drioton, "La Discussion," 95–96.

[50] Drioton, "La Discussion," 96–100.

[51] Drioton, "La Discussion," 114–115.

[52] Drioton, "La Discussion," 116–117. According to Drioton, the Audians differed on two points with the Catholics: on calculating the date for Easter, and on their view of God's corporeality, a view they justified by an appeal to Genesis 1:26 and 9:6. Antoine Guillaumont, however, has cautioned against attaching the Anthropomorphite faction in Egypt to the Audians, originally from Mesopotamia: see *Les "Kephalaia Gnostica,"* 61n. 62. It is in any case questionable whether we should necessarily label those

lieves that the story recounts an actual event, but argues that Theophilus must have been mentally converted to the Anthropomorphite cause even before hearing Aphou's arguments.[53] Although Drioton's assessment of the account seems historically naive,[54] this document, when coupled with Cassian's report, alerts us to the presence of more complex religious issues underlying the possible events of 399, issues not evident from the accounts of Socrates, Sozomen, and Palladius.

Cassian offers a clue that helps to situate the incidents described by the church historians in the wider religious context of late fourth-century Egypt. He hints that the Anthropomorphite position was not a Christian one at all, nor a new illusion prompted by demons, but a remnant of older "heathenism" formerly practiced by these simple Egyptians, who upon conversion to an ascetic variety of Christianity had taken up monastic retreat in the desert. These new converts had been accustomed to thinking of a god as something that could be grasped and held onto, who could furnish them with an image to which they could address their devotions.[55] The background of Egyptian paganism indeed seems a significant factor to be reckoned with when we consider Theophilus's antipagan activities earlier in the 390s.

Several sources report Theophilus's zealous campaign to eradicate pagan idolatry.[56] They differ in the pagan commentators' dismay at Theophilus's activities,[57] in sharp contrast with the Christian writers' jubilation. More-

---

who believed that humans retained the "image of God" as "Anthropomorphites," even though the sources sympathetic to Origenism tend to name them thus.

[53] Drioton, "La Discussion," 121–122.

[54] Drioton's reading of this point, which lacks any other confirmation, appears historically naive. The document seems designed rather to serve to elevate the role of the bishop of Pemdjé vis-à-vis the archbishop of Alexandria. Missing from the story regarding Aphou are all the references by Socrates, Sozomen, and Palladius to Isidore and the Tall Brothers. Nonetheless, the document about Aphou and Theophilus shows the *kinds* of Scriptural and theological justifications that could be given for the Anthropomorphite position (these will be considered below, pp. 59–60). Drioton, doubtless writing before 1915, seems completely unaware of the role Evagrius's theology played in the controversy. See also Guillaumont's doubt about associating Anthropomorphites and Audians, n.52 above. In Tito Orlandi's opinion, the *Dialogue* is "plainly a monastic creation" ("Theophilus of Alexandria in Coptic

Literature," pt. 2, 101).

[55] John Cassian, *Conlationes* X, 5 (*SC* 54, 78–79). Annabel Wharton has suggested that the controversy could be construed as occurring not so much between pagan "materialists" and Christian "spiritualists," as between pagans and Christians fighting over *whose* image should be revered. Her suggestion seems apt on the level of popular culture; Christian theological writers, however, were all on the "antimaterial" side of the debate.

[56] For summaries, see Lazzati, *Teofilo*, 14–18; Favale, *Teofilo*, 61–68: H. G. Opitz, "Theophilos von Alexandrien," col. 2151; Johannes Geffcken, *The Last Days of Greco-Roman Paganism*, 170–174.

[57] Most notably Eunapius, *Vitae philosophorum et sophistorum* 471–473; Theophilus is compared to Eurymedon, king of the "overweening Giants" in *Odyssey* VII, 59. For Zosimus (IV, 37–38; 59), Theodosius's attempt to eradicate the ancestral religion led to the decay and degeneration of the Empire. Writing probably in 390, before the destruction of the Serapeum, Libanius in the *Pro*

over, the Christian sources themselves vary regarding details and the chronology of events.[58] In Rufinus of Aquileia's continuation of Eusebius's *Church History*, we have an extensive account of Theophilus's assault against paganism, most notably expressed in the destruction of the Serapeum in Alexandria.[59] According to Rufinus, Theophilus's antipagan moves began when Christians uncovered a Mithraeum while they were clearing ground, under Theophilus's direction, to build a new church. According to Rufinus, pagans rioted upon this perceived desecration of a holy site, attacking the Christians; when the Christians (whom Rufinus says were in the majority) appeared to prevail, the pagan attackers took refuge in the Serapeum. Rufinus reports that the emperor Theodosius next decreed that the pagans should be released if they surrendered, but that pagan idols should be destroyed.[60] Rufinus notes the actual destruction of the Serapeum very briefly,[61] but takes the occasion to describe at some length the immoral practices and outright crimes that occurred in connection

---

Templis exonerates Theodosius and blames the monks ("these men clad in black, who eat more than elephants" [8]) for the shutting of the temples: see René Van Loy, "Le 'Pro Templis' de Libanius," 7–39, 388–404, esp. 11–19 for the dating of Libanius's treatise and of the attack on the Serapeum.

[58] Socrates appears to have been furnished with some different details by Helladius and Ammonius, pagans who defended the Serapeum and later moved to Constantinople where they became Socrates' teachers: *HE* V, 16 (*PG* 67, 605). The status of an imperial decree is also unclear: *Codex Theodosianus* XVI, 10, 11, to which commentators usually appeal for a legal authorization for temple demolition, mentions only the suppression of pagan worship, not the destruction of temples. Yet another point on which the sources vary is in whether only the statue of Serapis was torn down, or the entire Serapeum. The most satisfying explanation of various divergences has now been given by Tito Orlandi, who utilizes Coptic sources and traditions in addition to the Greek and Latin ones used by other commentators. Our extant sources, he concludes, are based on at least two separate accounts (one of which, now not extant in Greek, stems from Theophilus himself); the confusion in Rufinus's long recitation (*HE* II, 22–30) is thus partially accounted for by his use of separate and diverging sources ("Uno scritto di Teofilo di Alessandria sulla distruzione del Serapeum?"

295–304). See Orlandi's "Un frammento copto Teofilo di Alessandria," 23–26, for more on the story of Athanasius's wanting to build a martyrion. Other helpful reconstructions of events include Jacques Schwartz, "La Fin du Serapeum d'Alexandrie," 98–111; Françoise Thelamon, *Païens et Chrétiens au IV⁰ siècle: L'apport de l' 'Histoire ecclésiastique' de Rufin d'Aquilée*, 157–279; and Antonio Baldini, "Problemi della tradizione sulla 'distruzione' del Serapeo di Alessandria," 97–152. Our earliest reference to the destruction of the Serapeum comes from Jerome: writing in 392 or 393, he mentions that a volume had been composed "On the Overthrow of Serapis" (*De viris inlustribus* 134).

[59] Rufinus, *HE* XI, 22–30 (*GCS* 9², 1025–1036); for a summary discussion, see Evelyn-White, *Monasteries* II: 89–90, and references in n.58. Garth Fowden notes that Theophilus was deprived of taking further "initiative of his own once the secular authorities had things in hand." His prompting of the crisis, Fowden suggests, illustrates "why bishops were not entrusted with direct authority over the pagan cults" ("Bishops and Temples in the Eastern Roman Empire A.D. 320–435," 78).

[60] Rufinus, *HE* XI, 22 (*GCS* 9², 1025–1026); according to Rufinus, other temples were destroyed at the same time (XI, 25–26, 28 [*GCS* 9², 1031–1033, 1034]).

[61] Rufinus, *HE* XI, 27 (*GCS* 9², 1033).

with pagan worship in Alexandria.[62] The origins of Serapis worship he explains on euhemerist grounds: a dead man was divinized.[63] Given the date at which Rufinus composed his supplement to Eusebius's *Church History*—A.D. 402–403[64]—his treatment of Theophilus is surprisingly favorable. Did Rufinus, then residing at Aquileia, not register the fierceness of Theophilus's attack upon his friends, the Nitrian monks, in 399–400? Did perhaps his own anti-idolatry fervor still, a decade after the destruction of the Serapeum, outweigh his probably negative assessment of Theophilus's anti-Origenist stance?[65] Or, by 402–403, did Rufinus seek to protect himself from charges of heresy by aligning himself with the self-proclaimed opponents of Origenism?

Socrates' report of the event[66] depicts Theophilus securing an imperial edict for the destruction of pagan temples as a first step; then, after demolishing the Mithraeum, he displayed the "tokens of its bloody mysteries" to the public.[67] Next he destroyed the Serapeum and put its cult objects on public view, ordering that the phalli of Priapus be carried through the forum. The pagans most enraged by these activities, according to Socrates, were professors of philosophy—indeed, Socrates' source appears to be the grammar teachers of his youth at Constantinople. When the immediate riot quieted down, the governor of Alexandria and the military commander of Egypt helped Theophilus to destroy the remaining pagan temples, which were razed to the ground. The images of the gods were melted down to make ritual vessels for the use of the Alexandrian church rather than for the relief of the poor, as Theodosius had suggested. Theophilus saved one statue from destruction, however, to be displayed publicly in perpetuity so that pagans could not later claim that they had never engaged in idol worship.[68]

Theodoret's account supplements Socrates' with the note that Theophilus startled the crowd by commanding the enormous statue of Serapis to be struck with an axe; most of the chopped-up parts were burned, but the head was carried through the city to mock the worship of Serapis' devo-

---

[62] Rufinus, *HE* XI, 24–25 (*GCS* 9², 1030–1032): both infanticide and the priest of Saturn's seduction of matrons are mentioned. Paganism is thus aligned with sexual irregularity.

[63] Rufinus, *HE* XI, 23 (*GCS* 9², 1030).

[64] Thelamon, *Païens*, 31n. 3; Schwartz, "La Fin," 98.

[65] It is notable, in any case, that Rufinus ends his *Church History* with the death of Theodosius I (395), and does not narrate the alarming events of 399 and thereafter.

[66] Socrates, *HE* V, 16–17 (*PG* 67, 604–

609).

[67] Socrates' report here raises questions, since it is now believed that the *taurobolium* was *not* practiced by Mithraists, as is commonly imagined. For the modern discussion, see Robert Duthoy, *The Taurobolium. Its Evolution and Terminology*, esp. 63–66.

[68] Socrates, *HE* V, 16 (*PG* 67, 605). The motivation for saving one statue suggests that by Socrates' era, pagans of a more "philosophical" bent were more of a problem for Christian intellectuals than the idol worshipers here depicted.

tees.[69] And Sozomen, for his part, appears to have sources unknown to Socrates: he reports the names of the military commander of Egypt (Romanus) and of the prefect of Alexandria (Evagrius),[70] names he perhaps derived from *Codex Theodosianus* XVI, 10, 11. He also includes a few further details regarding the pagan resistance.[71] Whatever variations in details the historians supply, they nonetheless agree that Theophilus was the instigator and perpetrator of a Christian campaign to eradicate Egyptian paganism in the 390s. The destruction of pagan images, we shall see, was undertaken in the very years during which monks in Egypt debated whether human beings had retained "the image of God" after the first sin and whether mental images deterred us from true worship: the 390s could well have been designated "the decade of the image."

Theophilus's overthrow of the statue of Serapis is also commemorated in legend and folklore. In a saying ascribed to Epiphanius the "idol" is said to have been smashed at the very moment that a charioteer in Alexandria whose mother was named Mary triumphed over his opponents; the crowd cheered the victor with their cry, "The son of Mary has fallen; he rose up again and is the victor!"[72]—words appropriate, in Christian imagination, to Christ's "victory" through his agent Theophilus over Serapis worship. Moreover, so zealous was Theophilus's anti-pagan campaign that a later legend recounting episodes of his childhood portrays pagan statues crashing to the ground merely at the pious boy's presence[73]—a story no doubt intended to foreshadow the statue-bashing activities of Theophilus the bishop. There is, in addition, a homily traditionally (whether or not correctly) ascribed to Theophilus whose major theme is Christianity's triumph over idolatry, both the idolatry of the Israelites, who worshipped the golden calf (Exodus 32) and that of the Egyptians, whose country was the first to be freed from idols at the coming of Christ.[74] Thus in legend as in history, Theophilus is represented as a major combatant of "idolatry."

The legal history of these events remains less clear than the historian

---

[69] Theodoret, *HE* V, 22 (*PG* 82, 1248).

[70] Sozomen, *HE* VII, 15 (*PG* 67, 1453).

[71] Sozomen, *HE* VII, 15 (*PG* 67, 1453–1457); see also Baldini, "Problemi," 114–119.

[72] *Apophthegmata patrum* (Alphabetical), Epiphanius 2 (*PG* 65, 164).

[73] John of Nikiu, *Chronicon* 79 (Zotenberg ed., 316; Charles tr., 75). If John of Nikiu's report that Theophilus was born and raised in Memphis (Zotenberg ed., 315; Charles tr., 75) is correct, we should also recall that Memphis was still renowned for its paganism in the later fourth century: see Jerome, *In Hiezechielem* IX, 30 (*CCL* 75, 421);

RE 15, 1, col. 666–667; discussion in Favale, *Theophilo*, 43–44.

[74] See *Hom. in Petrum et Paulum* (*CPG* II, 2630), edited and translated from an Arabic manuscript by H. Fleisch, "Une Homélie de Théophile d'Alexandrie sur l'honneur de St. Pierre et de St. Paul," 371–419, esp. 380–382. Its authenticity is questioned by R. Delobel and M. Richard, "Théophile d'Alexandrie," col. 526. The reference to Jesus' rooting out idolatry first in Egypt derives from the infancy tales circulating among Coptic Christians that depict statues and temples crashing at the mere presence of the infant Jesus in Egypt.

would like: Theodosius's decree of 391, as we know it, orders the suppression of pagan worship, but not the destruction of temples.[75] Perhaps an edict expressly ordering the destruction of temples was given, but it is not included in the *Codex Theodosianus*, despite the assurances of the church historians cited above who speak of such an edict. In fact, we have from 399 a decree expressly forbidding the destruction of temples that were public monuments,[76] although the wording could be taken to mean that temples which were *not* public monuments stood liable to destruction. Whatever the historical reality, the urge to provide Christian legend with a legal foundation was so great that Theodosius was represented as giving to Theophilus "the keys of the temples of the idols of all Egypt from Alexandria to Assuan, in order that he might take the wealth contained in them and spend it in erecting buildings for the Church of our Lord Jesus Christ."[77] And Theophilus himself affirms that "the cross is that which closes the temples of idols and opens the churches."[78]

The literature pertaining to the desert fathers makes two allusions to the monks' involvement with the destruction of the Serapeum and other temples. From the sayings of Bessarion, we learn that while Bessarion was on a visit to John of Lycopolis, John reported that it had been revealed to him that the temples would be overthrown, and so it was accomplished.[79] Moreover, the "anonymous" version of the *Apophthegmata patrum* states that Theophilus summoned some of the monks to Alexandria "so that he might make a prayer and take down the temple."[80] Monks are thus aligned in the *Apophthegmata* with Theophilus's iconoclastic campaign—a suggestive hint that the authors of this source might dispute the allegations of Cassian and the church historians cited above that many desert monks had retained some vestiges of Egyptian paganism now expressed in the debate over the "image of God."

That the desert fathers were well aware of Egyptian paganism, including its theriomorphic forms—indeed, those from country backgrounds could scarcely *not* be[81]—is evident in several stories. One of the most revealing

---

[75] *Codex Theodosianus* XVI, 10, 11. For a discussion of the somewhat confused evidence, see Evelyn-White, *Monasteries* II: 89–90; Favale, *Teofilo*, 62–65, and the references in n. 58 above. Otto Seeck believed that the 391 law here cited was the legal basis for the destruction of the Serapeum: *Geschichte des Untergangs der antiken Welt* V: 233–234.

[76] *Codex Theodosianus* XVI, 10, 15.

[77] "The Vision of Theophilus," III: Syriac 44; English 8. Also see Franz Joseph Dölger, "Drei Theta als Schatzsicherung u. ihre Deutung durch den Bischof Theophil von Alexandrien," 189–191.

[78] Theophilus, *Hom. de crucifixione et in*

bonum latronem, 244–250, at 249.

[79] *Apophthegmata patrum* (Alphabetical), Bessarion 4 (*PG* 65, 140).

[80] *Apophthegmata patrum* (Alphabetical), Theophilus 3 (*PG* 65, 200). An interesting feature of the story is the implicit condemnation of Theophilus for serving the monks meat; in their simplicity, they did not even know what they were eating.

[81] That some of the desert fathers came from families that had engaged in practices of "idol worship" is revealed in the *Apophthegmata patrum* (rec. Pelagius) (= *Verba seniorum* 5, 39 [*PL* 70, 885]).

accounts is assigned to abba Apollo in the *Historia monachorum*. In this story, Apollo, depicted as converting natives from idol worship, explains why the Egyptians fell into idolatrous practices in the first place. He offers a rationalizing account: the ox was deified because the animal was necessary to produce the Egyptian food supply; the dogs, apes, and other animal forms the Egyptians worship were revered because preoccupation with the images of the beasts had earlier prevented the Egyptians from following Pharaoh to the Red Sea at the time of the Israelites' Exodus, and thus saved them from destruction.[82] Leaving aside the improbability of Apollo's explanation, the connection between "mental preoccupation" and idolatry is nonetheless notable, and doubly so when we consider the pro-Origenist bias of the author of the *Historia monachorum*:[83] these themes will be explored below.

Just as Theophilus's early idol-destroying activities appear to be all-of-a-piece with his original anti-Anthropomorphism, so the furor expressed by Egyptian pagans at the destruction of their temples, statues, and other cult objects forms a significant historical background for the Anthropomorphite view that God can be "imaged." It can be no accident that pro-Origenist authors link mental illusions and "evil thoughts" to idolatry: we set up for ourselves an "image of God" in our minds.[84] Moreover, it is also no accident that our major sources for the controversy, composed by educated "foreign" writers who largely sided with the Origenists, depict the proponents of Anthropomorphism as simple native Egyptian monks,[85] that is, those who came from areas and backgrounds where pagan practices flourished. Further, the sources more representative of the indigenous Egyptian tradition, reveal the distrust felt by the native Egyptian clientele of Origen's views:[86] for the so-called Anthropomorphites, the argument that hu-

---

[82] *Historia monachorum* VIII, 21–29 (Festugière ed., 54–58).

[83] Hammond, "The Last Ten Years," 395, 397; see also Jerome, *Ep.* 133, 3 (*CSEL* 56, 246).

[84] Evagrius Ponticus, Coptic fragment translated and discussed in Hans-Martin Schenke, "Ein Koptischer Evagrius," 219–221.

[85] John Cassian, *Conlationes* X, 2; 5 (*SC* 54, 75–76, 78); Socrates, *HE* VI, 7 (*PG* 67, 684); Sozomen, *HE* VIII, 11; 12 (*PG* 67, 1544, 1548–1549); on the "foreign" element of Nitria, see Evelyn-White, *Monasteries* II: 84.

[86] E.g., *Apophthegmata patrum* (Alphabetical), Lot l (*PG* 65, 253, 256); Ammon, *The Letter of Ammon*. The first Greek *Vita* of Pachomius (chap. 31) claims him as a hater of Origen, a detail absent from the Coptic *Lives: Sancti Pachomii Vitae Graecae*, 20. Jon

F. Dechow has argued that an anti-Origenist Pachomius cannot be traced before about 377, the date of Epiphanius's *Panarion* 64: *Dogma and Mysticism in Early Christianity: Epiphanius of Cyprus and the Legacy of Origen*, 222, cf. 100–102; for the argument that Origen was acceptable in Egypt until the end of the fourth century, see also 170, 181, 187–190, 221–222, 240, 301, 327–329. The authenticity of a letter claiming to be from Theophilus to Horsiesius, head of the Pachomian monasteries in the 380s, has been questioned (W. Hengstenberg, "Pachomiana mit einem Anhang über die Liturgie von Alexandrien," 238–252). Nonetheless, even if the letter *cannot* be ascribed to Theophilus, it reveals a desire to link Theophilus with the Pachomian communities. Also see Guillaumont, *Les "Kephalaia Gnostica,"* 54–56; Evelyn-White, *Monasteries* II: 127.

mans retain the "image of God" may have been in part motivated by a desire to appropriate for our species alone what the pagans assigned to images made by human hands.[87] The themes of iconoclastic rhetoric noted by W.J.T. Mitchell are all present in the episodes and stories here recounted: exclusion, domination, caricature, accusations of obscenity.[88] Yet a far more rigorous approach to iconoclasm awaits us in the writings of Evagrius Ponticus, albeit one less politically driven than Theophilus's assault on Egyptian "idolatry."

A second religious issue—this time, an intra-Christian one—that forms the background of the Anthropomorphite controversy concerns the battle over the doctrine of God that raged throughout most of the fourth century. Although that debate had been ostensibly settled by the Council of Constantinople in 381 with its Trinitarian formula of "one essence, three persons" and by the ratification of this definition by imperial decree,[89] the Cappadocian triumph over Homoiousian, Homoian, and Anomoian positions had its reflex in the Anthropomorphite dispute.

Discussion of Trinitarian theology in the course of the fourth century had sensitized Christian theologians to the use of God-language. They tended to repudiate all analogies drawn from the created order in ways unfamiliar to Christians of an earlier era. This heightened sensitivity expressed itself in various ways in the Anthropomorphite controversy. Most important, the anti-Anthropomorphites pressed the point that to imagine God as possessing human characteristics would be to introduce defects into our notion of the deity. As Socrates explained, the Origenists held to a strict view of God's incorporeality, because to do otherwise would be to ascribe human passions to God.[90] Or as Cassian put it, describing God in human terms would entail affirming that God not only has the bodily parts that enable him to sleep, stand, and sit—but also the mental structures that might allow him to become angry, to forget, to be ignorant. Cassian instructs Christians how to interpret Scriptural language that seemingly accords physical members to God: since Scripture accommodates itself to human understanding, God's "limbs" should be read as his "operations." Nor should the "anger" ascribed to God be taken anthropophatically, for otherwise we would be imputing unworthy human passions to the divine. Yet according to Cassian, there is a moral benefit for Christians in Scrip-

---

[87] The debate can thus be construed as one over who has the "true" image: see n. 55 above. Note this theme also in a seventh-century iconoclastic debate in Armenia: see Paul G. Alexander, "An Ascetic Sect of Iconoclasts in Seventh Century Armenia," 157–160, and S. der Nersessian, "Image Worship in Armenia and Its Opponents," 69–70, and "Une Apologie des images du septième siè-

cle," 58–87.

[88] W.J.T. Mitchell, *Iconology: Image, Text, Ideology*, 113.

[89] Summary of Tome of Council of Constantinople (381) in Theodoret, *HE* V, 9 (*PG* 82, 1212–1218); *Codex Theodosianus* XVI, 1, 2; 1, 3.

[90] Socrates, *HE* VI, 7 (*PG* 67, 685).

ture's use of such expressions: we are prompted to good behavior by hearing of God's "wrath," although, strictly speaking, such language is not appropriate to the Godhead.[91] If Christians since the 380s had been warned
not to misuse the language of "essence" and "persons" in regard to the
Godhead, by how much more they should erase vulgar anthropomor-
phisms from their speech.

The so-called Anthropomorphites, for their part, felt obliged to explain
their way around the charge that they were attributing unworthy characteristics to God. A fascinating defense of the Anthropomorphite position
is given in the account of Aphou's alleged conversion of Theophilus. According to the narrative, Theophilus originally argued against Aphou that
humans at present could not be said to possess the "image of God," for
such an ascription would accord unworthiness to the divine. "How," Theophilus is depicted as asking, "could an Ethiopian [i.e., a black man] be in
the 'image of God,' or a leper, a cripple, or a blind man?" The fact that
humans are subject to sickness and to fatigue raised the question of how
one could posit that ill and weary people were in the "image of God" without ascribing these defects to God. Theophilus is here assigned the position held by the pro-Origenist commentators on the controversy: positing
that humans at present, with all their physical deficiencies, retain the "image of God" implies a theology tainted by Anthropomorphism.

Aphou answers with an analogy that the anonymous author of the text
perhaps adapted from an earlier writer:[92] just as the picture of a king will
be deficient (e.g., the nose will not be in correct relief), yet we not only call
it his "image," we *ought* to say that it is his image, for the king has com-
manded us to do so. Likewise, said Aphou, we must affirm that humans
exist "in God's image," despite the evident dissimilarities. Human deficiencies should not be understood as detracting from the glory of God.[93] The
model, Aphou assures Theophilus, does not contain the defects of human
nature: our defects are present as something "extra" (*epithesis*), beyond
what is in the archetype.[94] Thus for Aphou, God remains without imper-
fection, yet we defective humans can still be said to possess his "image":
difference has not imperilled the basic similarity. Equally important,

[91] John Cassian, *De institutis coenobiorum* VIII, 2–4 (*SC* 109, 338–344).

[92] In describing the unity of the Father and the Son within the Godhead, Athanasius—if he is the author of *Contra Arianos* III—uses the analogy of the emperor and his image. But for the earlier author (unlike Aphou), the image is so exact (*aparallaktos*) that it might even say, "I and the Emperor are one" (*Contra Arianos* III, 5). For the argument that *Contra Arianos* III was not written by Athanasius, but is Apollinarian, see Charles

Kannengiesser, *Athanase d'Alexandrie, évêque et écrivain: une lecture des traités contre les ariens*, 310–368, 405–416. See also Basil, *Hom.* 24, 4.

[93] Drioton, "La Discussion," 97–100, 113. Theophilus's phrase, "This weakness is not the image of God," is perhaps a recollection of Theophilus's 14th Paschal Letter of 399: see Marcel Richard, "Les Ecrits de Théophile d'Alexandrie," 36.

[94] Drioton, "La Discussion," 127.

Aphou's argument hints at the literalist interpretation of Scripture and the notion of Scriptural authority as the final court of appeal that some, perhaps most, of the alleged Anthropomorphites espoused.

Such positions were unacceptable to anti-Anthropomorphites like Evagrius Ponticus: for them, it was preferable to admit that God could in no way be comprehended by the human mind than to introduce the possibility of "failure" into our notion of God. As Evagrius expressed this view, a defective concept cannot convey to humans the perfection of God.[95] And, as might be expected, he and other Origenists practiced an allegorical interpretation that "spiritualized" and dehistoricized not only grossly anthropomorphic Biblical expressions, but Scripture as a whole. Although both sides in the debate appealed to the Bible, their hermeneutical principles differed as much as their views on whether humans retained characteristics sufficiently similar to God to make meaningful use of the phrase, "the image of God."[96]

For sophisticated theologians, however, the discussion of language about God was carried on at a deeper level than the simple affirmation that God should not be envisioned as possessing bodily parts and human passions. Theologians involved in fourth-century Trinitarian discussions, especially the Cappadocian Fathers, had already posited that no image drawn from the human realm could describe God: there was nothing in the realm of created nature, whether nonhuman or human, that could capture that which exists as "one essence, three persons."[97] For the Cappadocians and their successors, orthodoxy entailed not just the refusal to depict God as a human; it also insisted that no analogy could correctly convey an impression of the Godhead. This aspect of the Trinitarian discussion made a dramatic impact on the theology of Evagrius Ponticus.

There are, in addition, historical links that connect the monastic supporters of the Nicene/Cappadocian position in Egypt with the later Origenist cause: some of the Origenist-aligned monks—including Isidore,

---

[95] Evagrius Ponticus, *De octo vitiosis cogitationibus* (PG 40, 1275). Whether this work can be ascribed to Evagrius has been questioned; Nilus may or may not be its author. See J. Muyldermans, *A travers la tradition manuscrite d'Evagre le Pontique. Essai sur les manuscrits grecs conservés à la Bibliothèque Nationale de Paris*, 13, 42.

[96] In the controversy of the eighth and ninth centuries over images, the iconoclastic party sometimes took the line that for an image to be "true," it must be "identical in essence with that which it portrays" (hence no images can convey the divine), while the supporters of icons argued that "difference" between the prototype and the image was al-

lowable. See the discussion and references in Jaroslav Pelikan, *The Christian Tradition: A History of the Development of Doctrine*, Vol. 2: *The Spirit of Eastern Christendom (600–1700)* 109, 119, 130; Gerhart B. Ladner, "The Concept of the Image in the Greek Fathers and the Byzantine Iconoclastic Controversy," 8; and Norman H. Baynes, "Idolatry and the Early Church," 134–135.

[97] Representative statements by the Cappadocian Fathers on this point include, e.g., Gregory of Nyssa, *Ad Ablabium*; Gregory of Nazianzen, *Orationes theologicae* II (= XXVIII), 7–13; V (= XXXI), 11–22, 31–32; Basil of Caesarea, *Ep.* 38.

Paphnutius, Pambo, and Ammonius—had been persecuted by the Arian emperor Valens in the 370s and had fled to the solicitous care of Melania the Elder in Diocaesarea.[98] Rufinus—the friend of Evagrius, Palladius, the Tall Brothers, and other defenders of Origen—reports that he himself spent several years of that decade imprisoned in Egypt for his defence of Trinitarian orthodoxy against the Arianism pressed by the emperor.[99] Moreover, the historical and theological links between the Cappadocian Fathers and Evagrius Ponticus are well known: Evagrius as a young man had Gregory Nazianzen and Basil as his mentors. In fact, the views expressed in an early letter of Evagrius were so akin to Basil's teaching on the Godhead that it was ascribed to Basil and passed into the tradition under his name.

From (probably) Gregory Nazianzen, Evagrius's early sponsor in Constantinople,[100] we have a letter addressed to a "monk Evagrius" replying to questions that he had asked about the nature of the Trinity. If the letter was intended for Evagrius Ponticus—and this hypothesis cannot be proved—we have an indication of Evagrius's early interest in the question of the attribution of names and number to God. The author of the letter had been asked, Is the Trinity simple or compounded? If the nature of the Godhead is simple, how can it admit the number "three," for the simple is something uniform that cannot be numbered? What can be numbered is subject to division, and division is a "passion." Indeed, if the Godhead is simple, how can there even be names for God? Conversely, if names for God are "true," do not the uniformity and simplicity of the Godhead vanish?[101]

---

[98] Palladius, *Historia Lausiaca* 46, 3 (Butler ed., vol. 2: 135); cf. Rufinus, *HE* II, 2–4 (*PL* 21, 509–513); Socrates, *HE* IV, 24 (*PG* 67, 521–525: Rufinus and the two Macarii are named, and Socrates claims Rufinus as one of his sources); Sozomen, *HE* VI, 20 (*PG* 67, 1340–1344: the two Macarii, Pambo, and Heracleides are named); John Cassian, *Conlationes* XVIII, 7 (*SC* 64, 21). The location of Pambo's deathbed is thrown into question by these notices, for *Historia Lausiaca* 10, 5 (Butler ed., vol. 2: 30–31) implies that he died in Egypt, not Palestine. See Guillaumont, *Les "Kephalaia Gnostica,"* 57, on the persecution, and Evelyn-White, *Monasteries* II: 77–83.

[99] Rufinus, *Apologia ad Anastasium* 2 (*CCL* 20, 25); Socrates, *HE* IV, 24 (*PG* 67, 524). That "Origenist" monks suffered on behalf of Nicene orthodoxy at the hands of Arians provides an interesting counterpart to Epiphanius's accusation that followers of Origen are Arians: *Panarion* 64, 2 (*GCS* 31², 410); see also Dechow, *Dogma*, 95–96, 99, and chap. 10; and Guillaumont, *Les "Kephalaia Gnostica,"* 85. That one aim of Basil's and Gregory Nazianzen's compilation of the *Philocalia* (selections from Origen) was to rescue Origen from Arian interpretation is stressed by Guillamont, *Les "Kephalaia Gnostica,"* 49.

[100] On Evagrius's relation to Gregory Nazianzen, see Palladius, *Historia Lausiaca* 38, 2 (Butler ed., vol. 2: 117); Socrates, *HE* IV, 23 (*PG* 67, 516: Evagrius cites a saying of Gregory at 520); Sozomen, *HE* VI, 30 (*PG* 67, 1584). For Evagrius's citing of Gregory's teaching on the four virtues, see *Gnosticus* 44 (*SC* 356, 172, 174) and *Practicus* 89 (*SC* 171, 680–689, with notes). See discussion in Gabriel Bunge, ed. and tr., *Evagrios Pontikos, Briefe aus der Wüste*, 24–28; Michael W. O'Laughlin, *Origenism in the Desert: Anthropology and Integration in Evagrius Ponticus*, 10–14, 20–28.

[101] See the discussion in Irénée Hausherr,

Soon thereafter, Evagrius composed his own answer to these very questions: a letter of his that for centuries was ascribed to Basil ("Basil," *Epistle 8*, now called Evagrius's *Epistula fidei*)[102] examines these same issues. According to this early work of Evagrius,[103] number must be excluded from the Godhead, since everything relating to quantity is linked to bodily nature.[104] Homoian and Anomoian attempts to claim that the Son is either "like" or "unlike" the Father also fail, because these terms are predicated of quality, and the divine is as free from quality as it is from quantity.[105] According to *Epistle 8*, the original Godhead was "naked" (*gymnos*): it received "clothing" only with the Incarnation (Matthew 25:36 is adduced in support).[106] For humans, too, all number will be lost when we join the final Unity.[107]

These views are in accord with those Evagrius expresses elsewhere, in various genres of his work. Thus in *Kephalaia gnostica* VI, 10–13, all number is ruled out in the discussion of the divine;[108] even saying "one" is to utter a number that might imply a corporeal nature.[109] In his epistles as well, Evagrius rejects color and extension as applicable to the Godhead;[110]

"Le Traité de l'oraison d'Evagre le Pontique (Pseudo-Nil)," 117; Hausherr accepts the probable assignment of authorship to Gregory Nazianzen, despite the *Patrologia Graeca*'s assignment of it to Gregory of Nyssa (see *PG* 37, 385–386 and *PG* 46, 1101–1108). After studying the text of this letter, Frederick Norris reports that neither its style nor its content rules out its composition by Gregory Nazianzen.

[102] In the early 1920s, Robert Melcher argued from manuscript, internal, and external evidence that the letter did not belong to Basil's corpus and should rather be assigned to Evagrius: see Melcher's *Der 8. Brief des hl. Basilius, ein Werk des Evagrius Pontikus*. His view now seems to be accepted by all scholars of Evagrius; see Bunge, *Evagrios Pontikos, Briefe*, 169–170. Wilhelm Bousset's hypothesis that Evagrius was a monk in Basil's monastic community appears to go beyond the evidence: *Apophthegmata: Text Überlieferung und Charakter der Apophthegmata Patrum. Zur Überlieferung der Vita Pachomii. Euagrios-Studien*, 336.

[103] The letter most easily fits into the period of Evagrius's life in Constantinople, when he was most centrally concerned with the struggle against Arianism; see Bunge, "Origenismus-Gnostizismus," 26. Would, however, Evagrius be addressed as a "monk"

in the letter mentioned above, before 383?

[104] Evagrius Ponticus, *Ep. fidei* 2 (*PG* 32, 248–249).

[105] Evagrius Ponticus, *Ep. fidei* 3 (*PG* 32, 249), cf. *Kephalaia gnostica supplementum* 19 (Frankenberg ed., 438–439): "difference" can pertain only to things with bodies; *Kephalaia gnostica* I, 2; V, 62 (*PO* 28, 17, 203): "opposition" comes from qualities, and these pertain to the body and to creatures.

[106] Evagrius Ponticus, *Ep. fidei* 8 (*PG* 32, 261).

[107] Evagrius Ponticus, *Ep. fidei* 7 (*PG* 32, 260), citing John 17:21–22; cf. *Kephalaia gnostica* IV, 19 (*PO* 28, 143).

[108] Evagrius Ponticus, *Kephalaia gnostica* VI, 10–13 (*PO* 28, 221); see discussion in Hausherr, "Le Traité de l'oraison," 117; Nicholas Gendle, "Cappadocian Elements in the Mystical Theology of Evagrius Ponticus," pt. 2, 373–375.

[109] Evagrius Ponticus, *Kephalaia gnostica* IV, 19 (*PO* 28, 143).

[110] Evagrius Ponticus, *Ep.* 39, 2 (Frankenberg ed., 592–593; Bunge tr., 252); cf. Evagrius Ponticus, *Ep. ad Melaniam* 5 (Frankenburg ed., 616–617; Parmentier tr., 12): all plurality of names, even those of the Trinity, will be ruled out when God is "all in all" (I Corinthians 15:28).

in Biblical commentaries, number is excluded;[111] and in the gnomic works, all attempts to define God are ruled out, since definition belongs only to bodily things.[112] A formal expression of this view is found in Evagrius's *Gnosticus*, in a passage cited by Socrates, arguing that definition belongs only to things that are compounded:[113] "Every proposition has either a *genus*, which is predicated, or a *species*, or a *differentia*, or a *proprium*, or an *accidens* or that which is compounded of these: but none of these can be the case in regard to the Holy Trinity. Let what is inexplicable be worshipped in silence." There will come a time, according to Evagrius, when even the Scriptural names assigned to God (e.g., Judge, Vindicator) will be removed.[114]

The anti-Arian tenor of Evagrius's teaching is also revealed in an anecdote reported by Palladius in the *Lausiac History*, most fully in its Coptic version.[115] This longer recension recounts the story of Evagrius's nocturnal encounter with three demons (dressed as clerics!) who expound the heresies of Arianism, Eunomianism, and Apollinarianism. To the Eunomian's question of whether the Father is *agennētos* or *gennētos*, Evagrius replies that the question is wrongly conceived, since such terms do not apply to God[116]—the exact answer that he gives in the *Epistula fidei* ("Basil," *Ep.* 8). Thus the Trinitarian discussions that formed the background to Evagrius's anti-Anthropomorphite position resonate clearly: if quantity, quality, extension, definition, and names are ruled out in language about God, most assuredly so are ears and eyes, hands and feet, anger and ignorance.

That this radically anti-imagistic confession of God had consequences for worship, especially for an understanding of the Eucharist and prayer, is suggested by several sources. These areas of Christian practice had become

[111] Evagrius Ponticus, *Scholia in Ecclesiasten* 1:15 (Catena Barberiniana) (Antonio Labate, "L'Esegesi di Evagrio al libro dell' Ecclesiaste," 487: Evagrius comments on the verse, "what is lacking cannot be numbered").

[112] Evagrius Ponticus, *Gnosticus* 27 (SC 356, 132), cited in Socrates, HE III, 7 (PG 67, 396).

[113] Evagrius Ponticus, *Gnosticus* 41 (SC 356, 166), cited in Socrates, HE III, 7 (PG 67, 396); cf. *Kephalaia gnostica* V, 62 (PO 28, 203).

[114] Evagrius Ponticus, *Ep. ad Melaniam* 5 (Frankenberg ed., 617; Parmentier tr., 12).

[115] Palladius, *Historia Lausiaca* 38, 11 (Butler ed., vol. 2: 121–122); Coptic text in *Historia Lausiaca*, Amélineau ed., 121–124; English translation in Butler ed., vol. 1: 132–135, discussion 135–137.

[116] Palladius, *Historia Lausiaca* 33 (Amélineau ed., 122; English translation in Butler ed., 1: 132). Evagrius also speaks against thinking of the *Logos* and the Holy Spirit as creatures, and against the Apollinarian denial of a human *nous* to Christ (Amélineau ed., 123–124). See the discussion in Bunge, "Origenismus-Gnostizismus," 26–28; and Otto Zöckler, *Evagrius Pontikus, Seine Stellung in der altchristlichen Literatur- und Dogmengeschichte*, 75, esp. n.106. Some passages in the *Kephalaia gnostica*, however, imply a subordination within the Trinity. e.g., VI, 4, in which the Father is held to be "considered before the Son, inasmuch as he is Father, and before the Holy Spirit, inasmuch as he is the origin of the Spirit" (PO 28, 219). The S_1 version tones down the obviously "dangerous" direction of this saying (PO 28, 218).

foci of dispute among the monks of the Egyptian desert in ways that relate to the debate over the corporeality or incorporeality of God, and to whether or not humans remained in the "image of God."

The alleged Anthropomorphites, for their part, appealed to the notion of Christ's "real presence" in the Eucharist to argue that God must have, in some sense, a human form. The dialogue between Theophilus and Aphou clearly suggests this position. According to Aphou, anyone who rejects the notion that humans truly image God must also deny the reality of Christ's presence in the Eucharist. Only a Jew would be so misguided as to say of the Eucharist that "it is mere bread that the ground has produced and human labor embellished," thus mocking the belief that it could be the body of the Lord. Aphou's implication is sly: does Theophilus want to be aligned with the Jews?

Theophilus, for his part, implies that Aphou has a deficient understanding of the Eucharistic transformation and repeats the orthodox line that the bread before consecration *is* mere bread; it becomes the body of Christ, and the chalice his blood, only when God is invoked. If Christ said to the disciples, "Take, eat, this is my body and my blood," then we must believe the words simply because Christ said them. Aphou's retort to Theophilus is pointed: if we believe literally what Christ said in the case of the Eucharist, then we must also take literally God's words that even after the sin in Eden, man was made "in his image" (Genesis 9:16).[117] The force of a literal interpretation of Scripture—so literal that Genesis 1:28 and 9:16 are taken to be authoritative propositions requiring our acceptance—is evident in Aphou's discussion. By such arguments, the story reports, Theophilus was converted to the so-called Anthropomorphite cause.

A second tale that links the question of the "image of God" to the Eucharist is found in the *Apophthegmata patrum*, in which abba Daniel repeats a story he had heard from his master, Arsenius. When an old monk from Scete denied Christ's "real presence" in the Eucharist, he was roundly rebuked by the elders who insisted that he affirm Christ to be truly in the bread and the wine. They argued by means of an appeal to the story of creation: just as in the beginning, God formed man from the dust of the earth to be "in his image," even though it doesn't *seem* as if man could be God's image, so likewise the bread "really" is the body of Christ, even if it doesn't appear to be. Their argument was confirmed by a dramatic occurrence: when on the next Sunday the priest began to celebrate the Eucharist,

---

[117] Drioton, "La Discussion," 98–99 (text) and discussion 126. The debate over images in relation to the Eucharist was repeated in the iconoclastic controversy of the eighth and ninth centuries. Although both sides affirmed the presence of Christ in the Eucharist, the supporters of icons claimed that the iconoclasts took an inconsistent position in upholding the "real presence" in the Eucharist but refusing to affirm that other images could bear the divine: see the discussion in Pelikan, *The Christian Tradition* 2: 93–94, 109–110, 125.

the bread appeared to the doubting monk as a child. When the priest broke the bread, an angel descended with a sword and real blood poured into the chalice; when the priest cut the bread, the child was cut; and when the old monk received the elements, he (and he alone) was offered a morsel of bloody flesh. The monk's conversion instantly accomplished, the flesh was changed back into bread, and the brothers returned to their cells rejoicing.[118] Personal experience thus sealed not only the teaching of the "real presence" in the Eucharist, but the reality of human existence "in the image of God." This story, unlike that reported in the dialogue of Aphou and Theophilus, supports the "reality" of Christ in the Eucharist and of God's image in humans *against* the visual evidence that might suggest otherwise. Was the story constructed, one wonders, to confirm the truth of these points over against those who argued the opposite, namely, *for* a purely symbolic interpretation of the Eucharist and *against* the view that humans at present retain the "image"?

As might be expected, the teaching about the Eucharist among the anti-Anthropomorphite monks tends to be spiritualized and allegorized. Thus we learn from Evagrius's *Sentences for Monks* that the "body of Christ" consists of the "active virtues," lending *apatheia* to him who "eats" them; and that the "blood of Christ" consists in the *theōria* of beings, which gives wisdom to those who "drink" them.[119] This same spiritualized interpretation appears also in his *Commentary on Ecclesiastes*[120] and in the *Epistula fidei*.[121] Nowhere does Evagrius treat the Eucharist in the manner suggested by the two stories recounted above.

Another Evagrian passage suggests why the physical ceremony of the Eucharist is defective: it is linked with the formation of images in the mind. When the words about breaking the bread are repeated, Evagrius writes, a form and figure come into the mind, of bread and its fraction. Such an image, however, is contrary to the teaching of John 1:1 ("In the beginning was the Word and the Word was with God and the Word was God . . ."), in which nothing is said about a form or a figure; rather, an (imageless)

---

[118] *Apophthegmata patrum* (Alphabetical), Daniel 7 (PG 65, 156–157, 160). Here it is interesting to recall that the *Apophthegmata* downplay material about Evagrius and the "Origenists," in contrast to the writings of the Greek-educated church historians. A longer variant of the story appears in the Anonymous collection, now published in translation by Regnault in *Les Sentences, Troisième recueil*, 1761B (from Vatican gr. 1599 f° 301 Anast. 52), 55–57.

[119] Evagrius Ponticus, *Sententiae ad monachos* 118–119 (Gressmann ed., 163). Also note Evagrius's spiritualized interpretation of baptism: the baptism propitiatory for the

soul is the remembrance of the future life (*De perfectione* 1 [J. Muyldermans ed., tr., "Evagre le Pontique: *Capita Cognoscitiva* dans les versions syriaque et arménienne," Syriac, 99; French, 103]).

[120] Evagrius Ponticus, *Scholia in Ecclesiasten*, Sch. 13 (Eccles. 2:25), in Paul Géhin, "Un Nouvel Inédit d'Evagre le Pontique: son Commentaire de l'Ecclésiaste," 197.

[121] Evagrius Ponticus, *Ep. fidei* 4 (PG 32, 253); cf. Melcher, *Der 8. Brief*, 61–65. For other references to Evagrius's spiritualized interpretation of "bread," see Gabriel Bunge, *Das Geistgebet. Studien zum Traktat "De Oratione" des Evagrios Pontikos*, 40.

thought is set in the heart.[122] Although there is no extended discussion of the Eucharist in Evagrius's extant works, these passages hint that his spiritualized interpretation of the Eucharist was in part motivated by his call for an "imageless" Christianity. For Evagrius, even imaging the breaking of bread leads the mind away from the God who should be worshipped "in spirit and truth" (John 4:24), that is, without images of any sort.

As has been compellingly argued by others, Evagrius's concern for "imageless" worship was especially manifested in his instructions on prayer that enjoin the devotee to banish from his mind any semblance of an "image." Evagrian scholar Antoine Guillaumont has even suggested that Evagrius's teaching on "pure prayer" was responsible for touching off the Anthropomorphite controversy of the late 390s; he points to specific sections of Evagrius's treatise *On Prayer* as stimuli to the dispute.[123]

Guillaumont illustrates his claim with an anecdote provided by Cassian: Serapion, an old monk, had disagreed with Theophilus's original affirmation of God's incorporeality, calling it a "novelty." When a visiting deacon from Cappadocia, Photinus, declared that the churches of the East interpreted Genesis 1:26 "spiritually" (i.e., that God's nature was simple, incorporeal, uncomposed, and incapable of being seen), Serapion reluctantly accepted this testimony as intellectually correct. Yet when the time of prayer arrived, Serapion's distress was revealed: he burst into sobs, crying out, "They have taken away my God from me, and now I don't have anything to lay hold of; I don't know whom to worship, whom to call upon." Cassian, who found this story disturbing, asked his instructor, abba Isaac, for an explanation. Isaac thus summarized for Cassian the theory of "pure prayer" in which no figure, memory, appearance, or outline is present to the mind.[124] Isaac also offered practical help to the monk troubled by "images of vain figures" coming to his mind at the time of prayer: if he repeat over and again, "O God, make speed to save me; O Lord, make haste to help me," he will be aided in his prayer.[125] In Guillaumont's view, the anecdote reveals both the dissatisfaction felt by some Anthropomorphite monks at Evagrius's "pure prayer" teaching, and the early development of prayer formulas aimed to rid the devotee's mind of images.[126]

For Evagrius, "pure prayer," which in essence he identifies with contem-

---

[122] Evagrius Ponticus, *De diversis malignis cogitationibus* 24 (*PG* 79, 1228). It is of interest that to Evagrius, "bread and wine" do not immediately call to mind the Eucharist, but Christ's role as creator in multiplying the loaves (Matt. 14:15–21; 15:32–38 and parallels) and in producing wine at the wedding in Cana (John 2:1–10): *Kephalaia gnostica* IV, 57 (*PO* 28, 161).

[123] Guillaumont, *Les "Kephalaia Gnostica,"* 61.

[124] John Cassian, *Conlationes* X, 3; 5–6 (*SC* 54, 76–80). Bunge posits that the teaching on "glowing prayer" ascribed to abba Isaac in *Conlationes* X actually comes from Evagrius (Gabriel Bunge, *Akēdia: Die geistliche Lehre des Evagrios Pontikos von Überdruss*, 87).

[125] John Cassian, *Conlationes* X, 10 (*SC* 54, 85–90).

[126] Guillaumont, *Les "Kephalaia Gnostica,"* 59–61.

plation,[127] requires that worshipers rid themselves of both emotions and images from the sense world. Prayer demands a kind of "purgation" that entails a moral, spiritual, and (we would say) psychological discipline. The time of prayer serves as a kind of "mirror" through which we can judge the condition of our own souls:[128] it is, he posits, a "state" (*katastasis*).[129]

Purging the mind of emotions at the time of prayer involves for Evagrius the battle against the "evil thoughts" (*logismoi*). Although numerous types of "evil thoughts" impede prayer (e.g., vainglory,[130] sexual fantasies[131]), he considers anger the chief impediment.[132] Anger, he writes, puts us far away from the realm of "pure prayer";[133] the prayer of an angry man is like frankincense that has no fragrance.[134] He calls anger a "Judas," a betrayer, who hands over the mind to the power of demons.[135] Blurring our spiritual vision,[136] it renders us incapable of seeing spiritual things.[137] This and other emotions must be rooted out in order for a person to pray well: a state of *apatheia* must be cultivated.[138]

Evagrius offers practical as well as theoretical advice on how to achieve this emotionless state. Tears, for example, are recommended.[139] He also suggests a simple test for the monk to judge the seriousness of his distracted state of mind: if "evil thoughts" disturb him for longer than the time he requires to finish saying his Psalms, then he must increase his efforts at mental purgation.[140] To achieve *apatheia*, the monk must free his

---

[127] See discussion in Antoine and Claire Guillaumont, "Contemplation," col. 1784. According to Evagrius, prayer is the activity most worthy of the intellect (*nous*): *De Oratione* 84 (*PG* 79, 1185). Also see John E. Bamberger, "Introduction to *Chapters on Prayer*" (Evagrius Ponticus, *The Praktikos. Chapters on Prayer*, xcii, 45); and Gabriel Bunge, *Geistgebet*, 40, 82, and *passim* for discussions of Evagrius on prayer.

[128] Evagrius Ponticus, *Ep.* 25, 6 (Frankenberg ed., 582–583; Bunge, tr., 237).

[129] See Irénée Hausherr, *Noms du Christ et voies d'oraison*, 138–139, for a discussion of prayer as a *katastasis*, and references. Hausherr claims that Cassian adopts this teaching from Evagrius.

[130] Evagrius Ponticus, *De oratione* 73; 116 (*PG* 79, 1184, 1193).

[131] Evagrius Ponticus, *Antirrheticus* II, 57 (Frankenberg ed., 492–493), and the entire book, in general.

[132] Evagrius Ponticus, *Practicus* 38 (*SC* 171, 586).

[133] Evagrius Ponticus, *De diversis malignis cogitationibus* 16 (*PG* 79, 1217, 1220); cf. 5 (*PG* 79, 1205).

[134] Evagrius Ponticus, *De octo vitiosis cogitationibus* 5 (Ethiopian version) (in Otto

Spies, "Die Äthiopische Überlieferung des Abhandlung des Evagrius, 'Peri tōn oktō logismōn,'" 223). Muyldermans argues that the Ethiopian version was dependent upon a second version of the treatise; the Armenian version, he thinks, is closer to the original: "Une Nouvelle Recension du *De Octo Spiritibus Malitiae* de S. Nil," 263–264.

[135] Evagrius Ponticus, *Ep.* 6,4 (Frankenberg ed., 570–571; Bunge tr., 219). For the special association of the demons with anger, see Antoine and Claire Guillaumont, "Démon," col. 197.

[136] Evagrius Ponticus, *Kephalaia gnostica* VI, 63 (*PO* 28, 243, 245); on the blinding power of *thumos*, also see *Kephalaia gnostica* V, 27 (*PO* 28, 187).

[137] Evagrius Ponticus, *Ep.* 58,3 (Frankenberg ed., 606–607; Bunge tr., 277); cf. *Kephalaia gnostica* V, 39 (*PO* 28, 193).

[138] Evagrius Ponticus, *De diversis malignis cogitationibus* 24 (*PG* 79, 1228); *De oratione* 71 (*PG* 79, 1181).

[139] Evagrius Ponticus, "Letter of Advice" (157ab, 157ba) (Frankenberg ed., 560–561).

[140] Evagrius Ponticus, "Letter of Advice" (157ba) (Frankenberg ed., 560–561).

mind of images, which tend to arouse emotions.[141] The mind should become so "imageless"[142] that it does not entertain even concepts.[143]

The motive for stripping the mind of images and concepts stems directly from Evagrius's anti-Anthropomorphic, iconoclastic theology: since God is an incorporeal being, no shapes drawn from matter can appropriately represent him.[144] Imaging God suggests that he is situated in a place, a suggestion Evagrius labels a delusion.[145] In addition, the *multiplicity* of images from the corporeal world can in no way be consonant with the simplicity of God.[146] According to Evagrius, images of God arise in our minds not only because we are involved with material concerns,[147] but also because the demons stimulate precise sites in the brain to produce the forms that we misidentify with God.[148] How the evil demon of vainglory rejoices if he can make us swell with pride at the thought that we are capturing God in "form and figure"![149] Thus both sense experience and demonic temptation conspire to render our minds unfit for "pure prayer."

Evagrius did not claim originality for his view on "pure prayer." Indeed, we know that John of Lycopolis, whom we encountered earlier predicting the overthrow of pagan "idols," taught that all forms must be removed from the mind at the time of prayer, all recollections of "indecent images" removed.[150] We also know that Macarius the Great, a major influence on Evagrius,[151] was esteemed as an expert on prayer,[152] and that he provided

[141] Evagrius Ponticus, *Kephalaia gnostica supplementum* 6 (Frankenberg ed., 428–429).

[142] Evagrius Ponticus, *Kephalaia gnostica supplementum* 21 (Frankenberg ed., 440–441: probably *aneideos* stands behind the Syriac translation); cf. 23 (Frankenberg ed., 442–443).

[143] Evagrius Ponticus, *Kephalaia gnostica supplementum* 29 (Frankenberg ed., 452–453); *De oratione* 70 (PG 79, 1181). The "unstamped" quality of mind at the time of prayer is also detailed in Evagrius's *Commentary on Psalms*: *In Ps.* 140:2 (P2 [1–2]) (cited by Bunge, from Rondeau's unpublished work, in *Akēdia*, 34). Evagrius's view that even concepts are somehow imagistic suggests later debates on theories of perception. See, e.g., Mitchell, *Iconology*, esp. chap. 1.

[144] Evagrius Ponticus, *De oratione* 66 (PG 79, 1181).

[145] Evagrius Ponticus, *De oratione* 67 (PG 79, 1181).

[146] Evagrius Ponticus, *De oratione* 57 (PG 79, 1180).

[147] Evagrius Ponticus, *De oratione* 70 (PG 79, 1181).

[148] Evagrius Ponticus, *De oratione* 72–73

(PG 79, 1181, 1184). Hausherr suggests John of Lycopolis as a source for this "physiological" exposition ("Le Traité de l'oraison," 121–122).

[149] Evagrius Ponticus, *De oratione* 116 (PG 79, 1193).

[150] *Historia monachorum* I, 23; 62 (Festugière ed., 17, 33–34).

[151] See esp. Gabriel Bunge, "Evagre le Pontique et les deux Macaire," 215–227, 323–360. In the Coptic document, "The Virtues of St. Macarius," Evagrius is represented as asking Macarius for advice on how to allay his "tormented thoughts and bodily passions": Am. 160, 10, in *Les Sentences, Troisième recueil*, Regnault ed., 170–171. See also the discussion between Macarius and Evagrius on forgiveness: Am. 200, 5, in *Les Sentences, Troisième recueil*, Regnault ed., 190–191.

[152] E.g., *Apophthegmata patrum* (Alphabetical), Macarius the Great 19 (PG 65, 269); the "Virtues of St. Macarius" adds other (authentic?) points: see the sayings Am. 160, 1 and 160, 10, translated in *Les Sentences, Troisième recueil*, Regnault ed., 170–171.

short formulas to help the worshiper come near to God by dispelling the distracting demons.[153] That Evagrius adopted some of these techniques from his teachers seems likely. Thus Evagrius writes, "Join to every breath a sober invocation of the name of Jesus," as one of the practices that will greatly profit the soul.[154] Another phrase he recommends for repetition are the words of Psalm 23:4, "I shall fear no evil, for Thou art with me."[155] For Evagrius, uttering the name of Jesus or a short cry for God's help seem not to function so much as prayers of content,[156] but rather as techniques to *rid* the mind of content, of images. Certainly Evagrius does not intend that a cry to God should summon up a mental image of the divine.

Nor did Evagrius claim that he himself had achieved this ideal purity of mind at the time of prayer: he confessed that he "carried around images of the world with him" which impeded his progress in reaching God, since at the time of prayer he "spoke with" the images.[157] Nonetheless, the "stripped" quality of the mind at the time of prayer[158] that he held as an ideal was the closest earthly counterpart to the "naked" state of the mind at the original creation of the rational beings—the state to which we shall eventually return.[159]

Our knowledge of this prayer technique has been enriched by the work of Antoine Guillaumont[160] and Irénée Hausherr,[161] especially by Guillaumont's report on the archeological campaign undertaken at "the Cells" in 1965 that uncovered a long inscription relating to the "Jesus prayer."[162] The Coptic inscription written on a wall of a monastic cell, accompanied by a picture of Jesus,[163] is set in the context of the demons' attack upon the monk while he says the "Jesus prayer." They insinuate, "If you constantly cry out 'Lord Jesus,' you do not pray to the Father or the Holy Spirit"[164]— that is, the demons charge that the monk's prayer undermines the doctrine

---

[153] *Apophthegmata patrum* (Alphabetical), Macarius the Great 19 (*PG* 65, 269); Coptic sayings Am. 160, 1 and 160, 10, given in translation in *Les Sentences, Troisième recueil*, Regnault ed., 170, 171. See discussion in Bunge, "Evagre le Pontique," 345–346.

[154] Evagrius Ponticus, *De octo vitiosis cogitationibus* (*PG* 40, 1275); Guillaumont, however, contests that this saying can be attributed to Evagrius; see Antoine Guillaumont, "The Jesus Prayer among the Monks of Egypt," 66, esp. n. 5: Guillaumont assigns it to Hesychius of Sinai.

[155] Evagrius Ponticus, *De oratione* 97 (*PG* 79, 1189).

[156] Evagrius posits that we do not have to make a request in a prayer or to set forth what seems good to us; God already knows how he will act, always in accord with his providence: *De oratione* 31–32 (*PG* 79,

1173). Also see Bunge, *Geistgebet*, 53.

[157] Evagrius Ponticus, *Ep.* 7,1 (Frankenberg ed., 570–573; Bunge tr., 220).

[158] Evagrius Ponticus, *De oratione* 119 (*PG* 79, 1193): *aktēmōn*.

[159] Evagrius Ponticus, *Kephalaia gnostica* VI, 20; 85; I, 58; II, 77; III, 66; 68; VI, 58; 81 (*PO* 28, 225, 253, 45, 91, 125, 241, 251).

[160] Guillaumont, "The Jesus Prayer," 66–71.

[161] Hausherr, *Noms du Christ*, 123–297.

[162] Antoine Guillaumont, "Une Inscription copte sur la 'Prière de Jésus'," 310–311.

[163] We can be sure that Evagrius would not have approved of the picture as an aid to prayer.

[164] Guillaumont, "Une inscription," Coptic, 316; French, 317.

of the Trinity. The author of the inscription provides an answer to console the troubled monk, namely, that the demons do not know of what they speak: if the monk calls on Jesus, he also is praying to the Father and the Spirit. When we say "Christ Jesus," we refer to Jesus as part of the Trinity, as the Son of the Father.[165] Other inscriptions in the room, as reported by Guillaumont, give similar short prayer formulas: "Jesus Christ, name of the Savior" and "My Lord Christ Jesus, help us!"[166] Although the main inscription Guillaumont examined dates to two or three centuries after the time of Evagrius,[167] he thinks that there can be posited an earlier development of this prayer technique.[168] Thus the practice that Evagrius recommended in his writings for ridding the mind of distracting or evil thoughts at the time of prayer receives archeological support.

The goal of prayer for Evagrius is an experience characterized as one of "light" that has no form—although he sometimes suggests that we "see" the color of sapphires or of the heavens.[169] The question raised in the Evagrian literature is, from whence does the light come? Is it from our own minds? Is it from God? So pressing was the question to Evagrius that he and Ammonius (one of the Tall Brothers) journeyed to ask John of Lycopolis, whose reputation as a "seer" made him a source of wisdom. John's reply to the question was that no human could answer it: what we *do* know, however, is that without God's grace, no mind will be illuminated at the time of prayer.[170]

It appears that Evagrius himself never satisfactorily answered the question of the source of the "light" experienced during pure prayer. Although he writes that the *nous* will become "like light" when it is stripped of the

---

[165] Guillaumont, "Une inscription," Coptic, 316; French, 317.

[166] Guillaumont, "Une inscription," 321.

[167] Guillaumont, "Une inscription," 320: Guillaumont posits that the inscription dates to between the mid-seventh and the mid-eighth centuries.

[168] Guillaumont, "Une inscription," 323–325. Hausherr warned not to posit too early a development of the "Jesus Prayer": even Diadochus of Photica (ca. A.D. 400–486) remains problematic as a witness (*Noms du Christ*, 202–210). Yet see the prayer given by Shenute and translated below, p. 154: does this prayer not qualify as a "Jesus prayer"?

[169] Evagrius Ponticus, *De diversis malignis cogitationibus* 18 (*PG* 79, 1221); *Ep.* 39, 5 (Frankenberg ed., 592–593). It is of interest that Theophilus before his alleged "conversion" to Anthropomorphism said that he

experienced God as "light" (Drioton, "La Discussion," 98). For a discussion of Evagrius's teaching on "light," see Hans-Veit Beyer, "Die Lichtlehre der Mönche des vierzehnten und des vierten Jahrhunderts, erörtert am Beispiel des Gregorios Sinaïtes, des Euagrios Pontikos und des Ps.-Makarios/Symeon," esp. 475–491.

[170] Evagrius Ponticus, *Antirrheticus* VI (Accēdia), 16 (Frankenberg ed., 524–525). It is of interest that in Rufinus's additions to the Greek version of the *Historia monachorum*, John of Lycopolis warns his listeners against shaping for themselves "some kind of appearance or image" in their hearts, a "corporeal likeness." Such imaging is inappropriate because God has no form and no limitations (*PL* 21, 397). This teaching appears to be a logical result of John's teaching on the experience of God as formless light.

passions,[171] will "shine like a star,"[172] or will "glow like a sapphire,"[173] Evagrius does not directly state that the light is from God. The ambiguity is well-expressed in *Gnostikos* 45: building on a teaching of Basil about types of human knowledge, Evagrius explicates the knowledge that comes from God's grace, which at the time of prayer we see as a light shining from the *nous*.[174] Probably Evagrius means that the light of God shines on the *nous* so that it, too, glows: this we gather from his analogy of the *nous* as a lamp that was created to absorb the holy Light (i.e., God).[175]

Whatever the precise resolution of this question concerning the "light" of God in relation to that of the mind, it is clear that God's "light" has no form or shape, occupies no space, and is completely immaterial. This teaching thus serves as yet another indication of Evagrius's insistence on the total "imagelessness" of the mind at the time of contemplative prayer. Any image we have in our minds exists "as a god"[176]—and hence is basically idolatrous.

If God can in no way be "imaged," what can we say about the anthropological referent of the phrase "image of God" used in Genesis 1:26? How is it said that humans were created "in the image of God"? The "image" cannot be our corporeal natures, Evagrius affirms[177]—bodies being, in any case, a secondary addition to the pure *noes* of the original creation.[178] Nor is even "incorporeality" the distinctive quality of the "image," according to Evagrius.[179]

In his technical writings, especially the *Kephalaia gnostica*, Evagrius lays down a theory of creation that provides the foundation for his view of the "image of God" in humans and the loss of that image.[180] At the creation, there was no bodily existence: the "naked *nous*" was all,[181] and it alone was

---

[171] Evagrius Ponticus, *Kephalaia gnostica* V, 15 (*PO* 28, 183).

[172] Evagrius Ponticus, *De diversis malignis cogitationibus* 24 (*PG* 79, 1228).

[173] Evagrius Ponticus, *De diversis malignis cogitationibus* 18 (*PG* 79, 1221).

[174] Evagrius Ponticus, *Gnosticus* 45 (*SC* 356, 178); the saying of Evagrius is cited in Socrates, *HE* IV, 23 (*PG* 67, 520).

[175] Evagrius Ponticus, *Ep.* 28, 1 (Frankenberg ed., 584–585; Bunge tr., 241). Cf. *Kephalaia gnostica* III, 52 (*PO* 28, 119); *Kephalaia gnostica supplementum* 4; 30 (Frankenberg ed., 426–427, 454–455); *De diversis malignis cogitationibus*, recensio longior, 42 (Muyldermans ed., *A travers*, 55). See Bunge, *Akēdia*, 65–66, 96–97.

[176] When we image even the face of an enemy at the time of prayer, we make him "as a

god," for what the mind looks at constantly during prayer should rightly be called its god: *De diversis malignis cogitationibus* 27 (*PG* 79, 1232).

[177] Evagrius Ponticus, *Kephalaia gnostica* III, 32 (*PO* 28, 111).

[178] Evagrius Ponticus, *Kephalaia gnostica* VI, 20; 85 (*PO* 28, 225, 253); also see Guillaumont, *Les "Kephalaia Gnostica,"* 109, n. 131.

[179] Evagrius Ponticus, *Kephalaia gnostica* VI, 73 (*PO* 28, 247).

[180] It should be noted that in his less technical writings, Evagrius occasionally implies that humans still retain the "image," for example, *Ep.* 28, 3; 48 (Frankenberg ed., 584–585; 596–597; Bunge tr., 242, 261).

[181] Evagrius Ponticus, *Kephalaia gnostica* III, 6; 8 (*PO* 28, 101).

in "the image and likeness of God."[182] Since we lacked bodies, we also lacked *thumos* and *epithumia*; all three of these were created only after the rational minds descended into "movement"[183] (Evagrius's word for the precosmic "fall")[184] and hence acquired "fatness."[185] Thus God should not be described as a creator of bodies until after the "movement."[186] Although Evagrius holds that it is blasphemy to speak badly of the body,[187] he also believes that bodies must be discarded again before the *nous* can see the "incorporeals."[188] Although he speaks of a "resurrection body," this bodily change is for him only the first of two transformations.[189] To gain once more "the image of the Son" ("essential knowledge"),[190] we must at the end cast off bodies entirely: bodies will ultimately be destroyed, not just transformed.[191] The haste with which this aspect of Evagrius's theology was modified and "softened" within the Syriac tradition[192] and abandoned totally in the Greek and Latin-speaking worlds makes clear that it was too radical for many Christians.[193]

Perhaps Evagrius's fullest explication of the "image of God" is given in his *Letter to Melania*.[194] Here Evagrius argues that the "image" of Genesis

---

[182] Evagrius Ponticus, "On the Faith of Mar Evagrius," Muyldermans ed., tr., *Evagriana Syriaca*, 168); *De seraphim* (J. Muyldermans ed., tr., "*Sur les Séraphins et sur les chérubins* d'Evagre le Pontique dans les versions syriaque et arménienne," Syriac, 371; French, 374).

[183] Evagrius Ponticus, *Kephalaia gnostica* VI, 85 (*PO* 28, 253).

[184] On the "movement," see Guillaumont, *Les "Kephalaia Gnostica,"* 244; and for a summary of the pre-cosmic world according to Evagrius, Antoine and Claire Guillaumont, "Evagre le Pontique," col. 1739; and Bamberger, "Introduction," lxxv–lxxvii. See Evagrius Ponticus, *Kephalaia gnostica* I, 49; 51 (*PO* 28, 41).

[185] Evagrius Ponticus, *Kephalaia gnostica* IV, 36 (*PO* 28, 151); cf. ("Origen"), *Selecta in Psalmos* 16: 9, 10 (*PG* 12, 1220).

[186] Evagrius Ponticus, *Kephalaia gnostica* VI, 20 (*PO* 28, 225). Also see O'Laughlin, *Evagrius*, 73, 125–126, on the two creations.

[187] Evagrius Ponticus, *Kephalaia gnostica* IV, 60; 62 (*PO* 28, 163).

[188] Evagrius Ponticus, *Kephalaia gnostica* IV, 86 (*PO* 28, 173).

[189] Evagrius Ponticus, *Kephalaia gnostica* VI, 34 (*PO* 28, 231).

[190] Evagrius Ponticus, *Kephalaia gnostica* VI, 34 (*PO* 28, 231).

[191] Evagrius Ponticus, *Kephalaia gnostica* II, 77; III, 66 (*PO* 28, 91, 125).

[192] For an analysis of the two Syriac versions, see Antoine and Claire Guillaumont, "Le Texte véritable," 156–205; A. Guillaumont, *Les "Kephalaia Gnostica,"* esp. 24–30. As a reading of the two versions of the text of the *Kephalaia gnostica* makes clear, the S_1 version "doctors up" Evagrius to make him more orthodox. In the case of the saying just reported (*Kephalaia gnostica* III, 66), S_1 changes the sentence to read that the "last trumpet shall be the renovator of bodies"—not "the destroyer," as in S_2 (*PO* 28, 124–125).

[193] For the later fate of Evagrian texts in various linguistic communities, see Guillaumont, *Les "Kephalaia Gnostica,"* 23–32, 166–170, 333–335. For the Greek world, some of Evagrius's treatises were preserved under the name of Nilus of Ancyra (e.g., *De oratione*; *De malignis cogitationibus*; see *PG* 79).

[194] The *Letter to Melania* was preserved in two parts. Only the first part was known to Frankenberg and published by him (612–619). The second part of the *Letter* was published (Syriac text, French translation) by Gösta Vitestam, "Seconde Partie du traité, qui passe sous le nom de 'Le Grand Lettre d'Evagre le Pontique a Mélanie l'Ancienne,'" 3–29. The entire letter in English translation, with commentary, was published by Martin Parmentier, "Evagrius of Pontus' 'Letter to Melania,'" 2–38. Vitestam (4–5, esp. n.4) thinks that the letter was not really

1:26 refers to the rational beings as "signs" of the Son and the Holy Spirit:[195] the human mind is of the same nature as the divine mind, and thus has the capability to understand "everything."[196] Eventually, body and soul will no longer exist as such, because they will have been raised to the level of *nous*, thus fulfilling the words of John 17:22, "Let them be one in us, as you and I are one." When the plurality and "names" that have come upon the *nous* as the result of the "movement" have been eliminated, so also will the names of God (e.g., Judge, Vindicator, Healer).[197] The minds will flow back to God, as rivers to the sea, becoming completely one with his own nature.[198]

According to Evagrius's *Letter to Melania*, when the soul (technically, the mind) fell, it ceased to be in "the image of God" and voluntarily acquired for itself "the image of the animals." Evagrius cites Romans 1:23, a passage that again links his discussion of the "image" to idolatry. Now the soul shares with the animals the movements of the body; in fact, it makes the "animal" body even worse than it would otherwise be, by introducing it to pride, vainglory, and avarice.[199] Only one creature has preserved God's true "image," capable of knowing the Father, and this is the incarnate Son,[200] whose divine nature remains one of "naked *nous*."[201] *After* "all the worlds"—but not before then—God will make us fit "the resemblance of the image of his Son" (Romans 8:29).[202]

Thus, to sum up Evagrius's teaching on the human possession of the "image of God," we had the "image" only when we existed as unembodied

---

addressed to Melania but to a man; Bunge agrees (*Evagrios Briefe*, 193–195, 199), reassigning it to Rufinus as the addressee. Their argument rests on the fact that in one manuscript, the pronouns referring to the addressee are masculine.

[195] Evagrius Ponticus, *Ep. ad Melaniam* 3; 4 (Frankenberg ed., 614–617; Parmentier tr., 9–11).

[196] Evagrius Ponticus, *Ep. ad Melaniam* 4 (Frankenberg ed., 616–617; Parmentier tr., 11).

[197] Evagrius Ponticus, *Ep. ad Melaniam* 5 (Frankenberg ed., 616–617; Parmentier tr., 11–12); cf. "The Faith of Mar Evagrius" (Muyldermans ed., tr., *Evagriana Syriaca*, 169), citing Psalm 16:5, "You will give me back my heritage" (Septuagint reading).

[198] Evagrius Ponticus, *Ep. ad Melaniam* 6 (Frankenberg ed., 618–619; Parmentier, tr., 12–13); cf. these ideas to those in *Kephalaia gnostica* II, 17, a sentence that Guillaumont thinks forms the basis for Anathema 14 of the Fifth Ecumenical Council at Constantinople (*PO* 28, 67).

[199] Evagrius Ponticus, *Ep. ad Melaniam* 9 (Parmentier tr., 16–17, based on British Museum Ms. Add. 17192).

[200] Evagrius Ponticus, *Ep. ad Melaniam* 4 (Frankenberg ed., 614–615; Parmentier tr., 11).

[201] Evagrius Ponticus, *Ep. ad Melaniam* 6 (Frankenberg ed., 618–619; Parmentier tr., 12).

[202] Evagrius Ponticus, *Kephalaia gnostica* VI, 34 (*PO* 28, 231); cf. VI, 89: in the next world Christ will be "first born with many brothers" (Colossians 1:18; Romans 8:29)—meaning that we will be "brothers" with him. Note that Evagrius distinguishes the Son from Christ or Jesus: Christ is not the Word, but has the Word in him; Christ is not "essential knowledge," but has it in him: *Kephalaia gnostica* IV, 80; V, 46; VI, 14 (*PO* 28, 171, 197, 223). For a full discussion of Evagrius's Christology, see François Refoulé, "La Christologie d'Evagre et l'origénisme," 221–266; also see Paul Géhin, "Introduction," *Evagre le Pontique, Scholies aux Proverbes* (*SC* 340, 48–53).

minds: with the precosmic fall, we lost it. The regaining of the "image" will occur not when we receive a transformed body in the "first resurrection," but only when we cast off bodies totally, when again we exist as "naked minds," unencumbered by bodies that cloud the vision of God, the vision without image.

That anti-Anthropomorphite circles shared Evagrius's view of the loss of the "image of God" seems clear from a number of sources. The pseudo-Macarian *Homilies*[203] often refer to the loss of the "image," comparing it to the lost coin of Luke 15:8–10.[204] In the "image" lay our heavenly inheritance—all now gone with the image's loss.[205] The result of its obliteration, according to the author, was that men worshiped devils,[206] probably pagan idols. That Christ will strip the "powers and the principalities" (Colossians 2:15) is interpreted to mean that he will "strip" our souls, originally created in God's image,[207] and reclothe them with it,[208] thus granting them a status that the author of the *Homilies* understands not just as a recovery of Adam's original condition, but as a conferring of deification.[209]

John Cassian—that unacknowledged Evagrian sympathizer[210]—presents a slightly blurred rendition of the same theme. Although Cassian writes that Adam lost the "glory" that he had received as the Creator's gift,[211] he tends to soften the teaching so that there is not a complete loss but only a "marring" of the "image of God," which like a damaged statue, needs repair.[212]

Especially interesting on this point is the testimony offered by the dialogue between Aphou and Theophilus. We learn from it that before Theophilus "converted" to the Anthropomorphite position, he had taught that although Adam had been granted the "image of God" at creation, humans after him lost it through sin. He notes the various frailties of post-Edenic life that made him hesitate to affirm that humans now share any character-

---

[203] It is now questioned whether the *Homilies* come from Macarius the Great himself or from Messalian circles of the later fourth century: see L. Villecourt, "La Date et l'origine des 'Homélies Spirituelles' attribuées à Macaire," 250–258. Villecourt's thesis was modified by A. J. Mason, in *Fifty Spiritual Homilies of St. Macarius the Egyptian*, who accepted as certain only that Macarius's *Homilies* formed the basis for a book used by Messalians whose propositions were condemned by the council of Ephesus in 431 (xliii). Jon Dechow, in contrast, argues that the similarity of the teaching of the Macarian *Homilies* on the loss of God's image to the Origenist position attacked by Epiphanius "supports their traditional ascription to Macarius of Scete, regardless of their subsequent influ-

ence in Messalian circles": see Dechow, *Dogma*, 308.

[204] Macarius, *Hom.* 11, 4 (*PG* 34, 548); cf. 1, 7 (*PG* 34, 457).

[205] Macarius, *Hom.* 12, 1 (*PG* 34, 557).

[206] Macarius, *Hom.* 11, 5 (*PG* 34, 548).

[207] Macarius, *Hom.* 1, 7 (*PG* 34, 457).

[208] Macarius, *Hom.* 11, 6 (*PG* 34, 548).

[209] Macarius, *Hom.* 26, 2 (*PG* 34, 676).

[210] For the seminal argument establishing the link, see Marsili, *Giovanni Cassiano ed Evagrio Pontico*.

[211] John Cassian, *Institutiones cenobiorum* XII, 5 (*SC* 109, 456).

[212] John Cassian, *Conlationes* V, 6 (*SC* 42, 193); *De incarnatione* VII, 6 (*PL* 50, 213–214).

istics with God.[213] That this in fact *was* Theophilus's early position is attested by Gennadius, who wrote that Theophilus contrasted the incorporeality of God with the corporeality and corruptibility of bodily human life, affirming that there is nothing in the creatures that bears a "*simile per substantiam*" with God.[214]

Aphou's retort to Theophilus is brief and Biblical: we know that humans retain the "image of God" even after Adam's sin because Genesis 9:6 says so:[215] "Whosoever sheds the blood of a man, the same shall be done to him, for man was created in the image of God." These examples suggest that there was a direct correlation between the Anthropomorphite and anti-Anthropomorphite positions regarding the imaging of God, on the one hand, and the debate over whether humans had retained or lost the "image of God" with sin, on the other. For the Anthropomorphites, humans retain the "image of God" despite sin, and they likewise can form an "image" of God in their minds; for anti-Anthropomorphites, neither claim holds. That humans' loss of God's image was believed to be a central tenet of Origenist theology is clear from Epiphanius's attention to the point in *Panarion* 64 (ca. A.D. 376) and in his letter to John of Jerusalem, dated to 394,[216] to be examined in the next chapter.

If, according to Evagrius and his Origenist colleagues, the "image of God" is something no longer available to us in our sinful bodily state, what unfortunately *are* available to us, and in superabundance, are "images" that arise through visual impressions, memory, dreams, fantasies, and demonic inspiration. It is through an investigation of Evagrius's theory of how images affect the human mind that we come, at last, to the ascetic root of Evagrius's anti-iconic theology: his approach to the Eucharist and prayer, to the doctrine of God and anthropology, all revolve around the quest to purge the human mind of "thoughts." The mind itself—construed as an entity receptive to images—provides the final battleground on which the war against "images" is waged. That this internalized form of iconoclasm was fueled as much by ascetic concerns as by theological considerations *per se* will become evident in the discussion to follow.

The fullest statement of Evagrius's "epistemology" (if we may call it that) is found in chapter 24 of the long recension of *De diversis malignis cogitationibus*.[217] According to the theory there presented, sensible things impress themselves upon the human mind as thoughts; the mind then

[213] Drioton, "La Discussion," 97–98.

[214] Gennadius, *De scriptoribus ecclesiasticis* 33 (*PL* 58, 1077–1078).

[215] Drioton, "La Discussion," 98.

[216] See Epiphanius, *Panarion* 64, 4, 9 (*PG* 17, 1059–1063); *Ep. ad Iohannem Episcopum* (= Jerome, *Ep.* 51) 6–7 (*CSEL* 54, 405–410). In the latter, Epiphanius charges Rufinus specifically with holding to the "error" of Adam's loss of the image. For a detailed discussion, see Dechow, *Dogma*, 80, 302–315.

[217] The problem of the two recensions of the treatise is complex; see Muyldermans, *A travers*, 39–41, 42–45.

grasps and judges the thoughts so presented. Since the mind is itself an incorporeal entity, it would not engage in such a "motion" if forms were not presented to it. These forms, however, tend to lead the mind to sin; without them, the incorporeal mind would not think of (for example) committing adultery in the heart (Matthew 5:28).[218]

A second version of the theory is found in chapter 4 of the same treatise. Our "ruling principle" (*hēgemonikon*) is imprinted by what we see or hear, or by memory. The soul introduces the images, whether they come from an external source, memory, demons, or dreams.[219] In yet another discussion, Evagrius posits that the passions, which are "contrary to nature,"[220] when aroused call forth thoughts of corporeal objects that impress themselves upon the mind. For the process to be halted, the passions must be stopped.[221] The wise man, who has extirpated the passions, thus can break the link that produces evil dreams.[222] The pure person, according to Evagrius, has no fantasies such as these.[223]

François Refoulé has argued that Evagrius's epistemological theory depends heavily on a Stoic understanding of the mind's operations: that when the senses or memory imprint the object on the "ruling principle," an image results.[224] Thinking thus proceeds from pictorial representation.[225] His argument seems substantiated by Evagrius's own words. Somewhat less clear than the Stoic influence, however, is the question of whether the "thoughts" excite the passions, or the passions excite the "thoughts." In some passages, Evagrius states that the aroused passions call forth mental images,[226] while in other places, he teaches that memory, the senses, or demons set in motion the passions.[227]

[218] Evagrius Ponticus, *De diversis malignis cogitationibus* 24, long. rec. (Muyldermans ed., *A travers*, 49–50).

[219] Evagrius Ponticus, *De diversis malignis cogitationibus* 4 (PG 79, 1204–1205); Evagrius Ponticus, *Kephalaia gnostica supplementum* 18 (Frankenberg ed., 434–435) (= Muyldermans, Cod. Barberini graecus 515, #9, in "Evagriana" [1931] 52). On the confused relation of the *Kephalaia gnostica supplementum* to other works of Evagrius, see also Muyldermans, "Evagre le Pontique: Les Capita Cognoscitiva" 73–83, 94. Also see the discussion in François Refoulé, "Rêves et vie spirituelle d'après Evagre le Pontique," 502–503.

[220] Evagrius Ponticus, *De diversis malignis cogitationibus* 2 (PG 79, 1201): demonic thoughts that produce *thumos* or *epithumia* are *para physin*; cf. *Skēmmata* 56 (J. Muyldermans ed., "Evagriana: Note Additionelle A," 56).

[221] Cf. Evagrius Ponticus, *Epp.* 6, 4; 39, 3

(Frankenberg ed., 570–571, 592–593; Bunge tr., 219, 253). See discussion in Refoulé, "Rêves," 501.

[222] Evagrius Ponticus, *De diversis malignis cogitationibus* 4 (PG 79, 1204); see Refoulé, "Rêves," 511.

[223] Evagrius Ponticus, *De diversis malignis cogitationibus* 4 (PG 79, 1204).

[224] See Refoulé, "Rêves," 503. Cf. Aristotle, *De anima* III, 7 (431a): "the soul never thinks without a mental image." Clement of Alexandria seems to disagree: *Stromateis* V, 5; *Protrepticus* 4.

[225] For some modern discussions of the pictorial or nonpictorial nature of mental processes, see, for example, *Imagery*, ed. Ned Block; W.J.T. Mitchell, "Spatial Form in Literature: Toward a General Theory," 296; and Mitchell, *Iconology*, 14–19, 42–43.

[226] Evagrius Ponticus, *Epp.* 6, 4; 39, 3 (Frankenberg ed., 570–571, 592–593; Bunge tr., 219, 253).

[227] Evagrius Ponticus, in Cod. Barberini

However the mental mechanism worked, Evagrius wished to avoid the implication that *all* memories, "thoughts," and dreams are evil: there can be good *logismoi*.[228] Angelic as well as demonic powers can stimulate the memory, so that in our minds "we may meet with saints and delight in their company."[229] Moreover, even thoughts of corporeal entities that often serve as temptations to us—for example, thoughts of gold—need not in themselves be demonic. Angels can dispassionately examine gold to discover its nature, and exemplary humans can sometimes picture it without arousing their passions.[230] As Evagrius puts it in his *Commentary on Psalms* (imbedded in Origen's *Selecta in Psalmos*), it is the passion attached to such thoughts that makes them evil; since God made both gold and women,[231] they cannot be evil in themselves. Thus we should consider demonic only those memories, images, and dreams that stir the passionate element.[232] The monk must learn how to differentiate the more "neutral" memories from the ones inspired by demons: one test is that demons excite us or prompt desires that are "contrary to nature"[233]—that is, sinful.

These qualifications duly noted, the fact remains that the evaluation of "thoughts" by Evagrius remains overwhelmingly negative. It is, quite simply, "thoughts" that separate us from God.[234] Evagrius's teaching on the "thoughts" is grounded in a specific anthropology that he shared with other intellectuals of his age. As humans, we are endowed with *nous, thumos,* and *epithumia,* all of which can be excited by demons:[235] Evagrius holds that *thumos* is most characteristic of the devil, *nous* of the angels, and *epithumia* of humans.[236] With the animals, we share the passions stemming from *thumos* and *epithumia,*[237] characteristics we received after—and only

---

graecus 515, #47 (Muyldermans ed., "Evagriana" [1931], 56; Latin translation of the same saying in Cod. Barberini latina 3024, #56, 64). The first part of the work represented by these manuscripts is sometimes referred to as the *Capita cognoscitiva.* See also Muyldermans, "Evagre le Pontique: Les *Capita Cognoscitiva,*" 73–106, and his "Evagriana: Le Vatic. Barb. Graecus 515," 191–226, for a discussion of the relation of this text to the *Kephalaia gnostica supplementum.*

[228] Evagrius Ponticus, in Cod. Barberini graecus 515, #34 (Muyldermans ed., "Evagriana" [1931], 55 = Cod. Barberini latina 3024, #43, 63). The "good *logismoi*" are said to come from three sources: from nature, from a correct *prohairesis,* or from an angel. See Bunge, *Akēdia,* 33.

[229] Evagrius Ponticus, *De diversis malignis cogitationibus* 4 (*PG* 79, 1204).

[230] Evagrius Ponticus, *De diversis malignis cogitationibus* 7 (*PG* 79, 1208–1209).

[231] Evagrius Ponticus, *In Psalmos* 145, 8 (Rondeau 8 + P8), cited in Bunge, *Evagrios Briefe,* 122; cf. *De diversis malignis cogitationibus* 19 (*PG* 79, 1221). On the forthcoming Psalms Commentary, see Marie-Josèphe Rondeau, *Les Commentaires patristiques du Psautier. Vol. I: Les Travaux des pères grecs et latins sur le Psautier. Recherches et bilan,* esp. 121–126, 270–271; and her earlier article, "Le Commentaire sur les Psaumes d'Evagre le Pontique," 307–348.

[232] Evagrius Ponticus, *De diversis malignis cogitationibus* 2 (*PG* 79, 1201).

[233] Evagrius Ponticus, *De diversis malignis cogitationibus* 2 (*PG* 79, 1201): *para physin.*

[234] Evagrius Ponticus, *Scholia in Ecclesiasten* 1:11 (Sch. 3) (Géhin ed., 197).

[235] Evagrius Ponticus, *Kephalaia gnostica* I, 53 (*PO* 28, 43).

[236] Evagrius Ponticus, *Kephalaia gnostica* I, 68; cf. III, 34 (*PO* 28, 49, 111).

[237] Evagrius Ponticus, in Cod. Barberini

after—the fall of the *nous*.[238] (The bestial nature of the various passions, in any case, is often detailed by Evagrius.)[239] The specifically human *logismoi* are stimulated by grief, vainglory, and pride.[240] Special dangers attend the monk, however, for not only does he share in the *logismoi* that affect *all* humans: he is prone to some that afflict monks in particular.[241] For example, anchorites may be especially prone to fantasies of political and ecclesiastical power.[242] According to Evagrius, "thoughts" are a particular problem for ascetics: whereas people in "the world" are tempted mostly by deeds, the monk receives demonic temptation especially in the form of "thoughts."[243]

Evagrius, more than any of his Christian predecessors, is responsible for producing an internalized and mental understanding of sin. Indeed, the medieval notion of the "seven deadly sins" is derived, through Cassian,[244] from Evagrius's teaching on the "eight evil thoughts." Although Irénée Hausherr has argued that Evagrius did not invent either the number (eight) or the concept of the sins (both of these, he posits, were largely derived from Origen),[245] Evagrius does give a rationale for the ordering of the "thoughts" that shows their interconnection.[246] From the first three "thoughts" (gluttony, lust, and avarice) stem all the others. Since gluttony leads to lust, the monastic regime counsels the limitation of food and drink in an effort to curb sexual desire.[247] From avarice (the desire for things), stems anger (presumably we are piqued when we don't possess things and others do), or pride (when we *do* possess them).[248]

Important for our purposes is Evagrius's teaching that sin lies not so much in acts committed, but in the monk's thinking of the acts, of not immediately rooting out "thoughts" from his mind if and when they arise.

graecus 913, #40 (Muyldermans ed., "Evagriana: Note Additionelle A," 378).

[238] Evagrius Ponticus, *Kephalaia gnostica* VI, 85 (*PO* 28, 253); cf. Codex Paris. Graeca 913, #40 (Muyldermans ed., "Evagriana: Note Additionelle A," 378).

[239] For other associations of the passions with "animals," see, e.g., *De diversis malignis cogitationibus* 17; 21 (*PG* 79, 1220, 1224); *Kephalaia gnostica* V, 27 (*PO* 28, 187); *De octo spiritibus malitiae* 10 (*PG* 79, 1156).

[240] Evagrius Ponticus, in Codex Paris. Graeca 913, #40 (Muyldermans ed., "Evagriana: Note Additionelle A," 378).

[241] Evagrius Ponticus, *Skēmmata* 50 (Muyldermans ed., "Evagriana: Note Additionelle A," 379).

[242] Evagrius Ponticus, *De diversis malignis cogitationibus* 22 (*PG* 79, 1224–1225).

[243] Evagrius Ponticus, *Practicus* 48 (*SC*

171, 608).

[244] John Cassian, *Conlationes* V (*SC* 42, 188–217); see also Irénée Hausherr, "L'Origine de la théorie orientale des huit péchés capitaux," 165–166.

[245] Hausherr, "L'Origine," 167–171.

[246] Hausherr, "L'Origine," 171. Cf. Evagrius Ponticus, *Skēmmata* 41–43 (Muyldermans ed., "Evagriana: Note Additionelle A," 378). Also see Bunge, *Akēdia*, 35, and Antoine and Claire Guillaumont, "Introduction," *Évagre le Pontique. Traité Pratique ou Le Moine* (*SC* 170, 90–93).

[247] Evagrius Ponticus, *De diversis malignis cogitationibus* 1 (*PG* 79, 1200); *Antirrheticus* II, 48; 49 (Frankenberg ed., 490–491); *Practicus* 15 (*SC* 171, 536); *De octo spiritibus malitiae* 4 (*PG* 79, 1148).

[248] Evagrius Ponticus, *De diversis malignis cogitationibus* 1 (*PG* 79, 1201).

To be sure, the monk must take care also not to engage in *actual* sinful deeds: feast days may tempt him to overeat in fact, not just in fantasy,[249] just as he might be sexually tempted by a flesh-and-blood woman,[250] not only by a demonic illusion. Nonetheless, the great majority of temptations that come to monks exist within the realm of thought. Thus the monk imagines how pleasant it would be to have tasty tidbits, his familiar beaker of wine, as he did in times past when he frequented taverns.[251] Moreover, the demons, as well as the memories and dreams, introduce images of sex to his mind which he must immediately resist.[252] The demon of anger can summon up for him images of his family and friends being unjustly insulted in order to arouse his passions.[253] The demon of *accēdia* fires in him the desire to live elsewhere, to be again with his family and to enjoy his former way of life.[254]

Even more disturbing, the demons are able to present "thoughts" as if they were something good and beautiful.[255] Thus the demon of avarice leads the monk to believe that he should accumulate goods for the sake of assisting the poor, strangers, and prisoners,[256] that he should obtain more bread in case visitors arrive who need to be shown hospitality.[257] The demon of gluttony makes him think that he should eat in order to preserve his health;[258] the demon of vainglory leads him to imagine how blessed it would be to heal the sick (and thus receive the adulation of crowds).[259] The demon of *porneia* tempts the monk to think that marriage and children are "goods" that he might innocently undertake.[260] The demon of vainglory urges him to lead a crowd of brothers and sisters to the monastic life.[261] And worst of all is the demon of pride, who stimulates him to believe that he is the cause of any good he may do:[262] even helping others can thus become a danger to the monk's salvation.[263]

---

[249] Evagrius Ponticus, *Antirrheticus* I, 3; 25; 29; 40 (Frankenberg ed., 474–475, 476–479, 480–481).

[250] Evagrius Ponticus, *Rerum monachalium rationes* 2 (PG 40, 1253); *De octo spiritibus malitiae* (PG 79, 1148–1149).

[251] Evagrius Ponticus, *Antirrheticus* I, 30; 36 (Frankenberg ed., 478–479).

[252] Evagrius Ponticus, *De diversis malignis cogitationibus* 16 (PG 79, 1217); *Practicus* 75 (SC 171, 662).

[253] Evagrius Ponticus, *De diversis malignis cogitationis* 16 (PG 79, 1220).

[254] Evagrius Ponticus, *Practicus* 12 (SC 171, 520–526).

[255] Evagrius Ponticus, *De perfectione* 16 (Muyldermans ed., tr., "Evagre le Pontique, Les *Capita Cognoscitiva*" [1934] Syriac, 102; French, 106).

[256] Evagrius Ponticus, *De diversis malignis*

cogitationibus 22 (PG 79, 1225); *Rerum monachalium rationes* 4 (PG 40, 1256).

[257] Evagrius Ponticus, *Rerum monachalium rationes* 3 (PG 40, 1253); *Antirrheticus* I, 12 (Frankenberg ed., 476–477).

[258] Evagrius Ponticus, *Practicus* 7 (SC 171, 508–510); *Antirrheticus* I, 19; 33; 44; 56; 59 (Frankenberg ed., 476–477, 478–479, 480–481, 482–483).

[259] Evagrius Ponticus, *Practicus* 13 (SC 171, 528).

[260] Evagrius Ponticus, *Antirrheticus* II, 49 (Frankenberg ed., 490–491).

[261] Evagrius Ponticus, *Antirrheticus* VII, 1 (Frankenberg ed., 530–531).

[262] Evagrius Ponticus, *Practicus* 14 (SC 171, 532).

[263] Evagrius Ponticus, *De octo vitiosis cogitationibus* (PG 40, 1275).

The quality of *vision* associated with these experiences is notable:[264] the mind is plagued by its constitutive receptivity to representation. The *logismoi* are said to "paint on our minds" the images by which the demons hope to lure the monk. Images of our future bodily debilitation are meant to lead the monk away from fasting;[265] the demon of *porneia* brings to the monk's mind the image of a married woman,[266] or the picture of a man and woman engaged in sexual relations.[267] The demon of vainglory depicts its "vile images" within his mind so as to activate his desire and his anger.[268] The demon of avarice "spins a web of fantasy" before his eyes, to make the monk imagine the endless treasures that could be his: significantly, Evagrius compares this demon to an "idol-maker."[269] The very fact that the mind thinks pictorially prompts its downfall: for Evagrius idolatry was not extirpated by Theophilus's antipagan campaign.

In addition to painting these pictures of future or imaginary situations, the demons can stimulate the memory to call up images from our own past experience, such as of the days when we enjoyed food and drink,[270] feasting in the company of beloved relatives.[271] Memory is especially dangerous at the time of prayer,[272] for in it are stored those experiences we had while under the influence of the passions, which live on—as *eidōla*—to deter us from the quest for purity.[273] Thus all situations that fill the monk's mind with images, such as going to the city, should be avoided, for these pictures will surely continue to haunt him.[274]

So many are the ways that the demons attack: they give the monk sexual visions in his dreams at night;[275] they appear to him transformed into beautiful women;[276] they even borrow pretexts from Scripture to lure him to engage in sexual activity[277]—citing (presumably) those passages that affirm the goodness of marriage and childbearing, and that caution against

[264] Especially notable is the link of vision to *porneia*: Evagrius Ponticus, *De octo spiritibus malitiae* 4–6 (*PG* 79, 1148–1152); *Antirrheticus* II, 1; 15; 19; 32; 36; 37; 52; 54; 60 (Frankenberg ed., 484–485, 486–487, 488–489, 490–491, 492–493).

[265] Evagrius Ponticus, *Antirrheticus* I, 56; 59 (Frankenberg ed., 482–483).

[266] Evagrius Ponticus, *Antirrheticus* II, 1 (Frankenberg ed., 484–485).

[267] Evagrius Ponticus, *Antirrheticus* II, 56 (Frankenberg ed., 492–493).

[268] Evagrius Ponticus, *Antirrheticus* VII, 33 (Frankenberg ed., 534–535).

[269] Evagrius Ponticus, *Peri tōn oktō logismōn* (Ethiopian version) 2 (Spies tr., 220–221); cf. *De octo spiritibus malitiae* 8 (*PG* 79, 1153) (comparison of the avaricious man with the "idolmaker").

[270] Evagrius Ponticus, *Antirrheticus* I, 30;

36 (Frankenberg ed., 478–479).

[271] Evagrius Ponticus, *Antirrheticus* I, 39 (Frankenberg ed., 478–479).

[272] Evagrius Ponticus, *De oratione* 44–46 (*PG* 79, 1176).

[273] Evagrius Ponticus, *Practicus* 34 (*SC* 171, 578); *Sententiae ad virginem* 6 (Gressman ed., 146).

[274] Evagrius Ponticus, *Ep.* 41, 2 (Frankenberg ed., 594–595).

[275] Evagrius Ponticus, *Antirrheticus* II, 15; 19; 34; 53; 60 (Frankenberg ed., 486–487, 488–489, 492–493).

[276] Evagrius Ponticus, *Antirrheticus* II, 32 (Frankenberg ed., 488–489); *De diversis malignis cogitationibus* 26 long. rec. (Muyldermans ed., *A travers*, 51).

[277] Evagrius Ponticus, *Antirrheticus*, II, 50 (Frankenberg ed., 490–493).

excessive abstinence.[278] Speech here cooperates with pictorial representation to lure the monk to sin.[279]

Against such demonic wiles, the monk must arm himself. This he can do in several ways. For one, he should mount a verbal attack, equipping himself with Scriptural verses to hurl at the demons when they assault him, after the fashion of Jesus's response to the Tempter.[280] Some of the Scriptural verses Evagrius recommends seem obviously applicable: "But I say to you that every one who looks at a woman lustfully has already committed adultery with her in his heart" (Matthew 5:28),[281] or "Let the dead bury their dead" (Matthew 8:22), used as a warning against the temptation to see one's relatives.[282] Other Scriptural verses that Evagrius offers as apotropaic devices against the demons, however, make sense only when stripped of the historical context that first occasioned them, for example, David's words in II Samuel 3:35, "So do God to me and more also if I eat bread and drink water until the sun goes down."[283] Still other verses acquire a more strongly ascetic connotation than they originally carried by being put in conjunction with other ascetically oriented verses—for example, the command to Jeremiah not to take a wife (Jeremiah 16:1–4) acquires a more universal significance by being joined with Paul's injunction to celibacy in I Corinthians 7:32–34.[284] No interpretation is too forced for Evagrius: even verses that originally carried an antiascetic message can be wrenched free from context to serve the purposes of desert asceticism. Thus I Timothy 5:23, on drinking "a little wine for your stomach's sake and for your frequent ailments"—originally an antiascetic injunction— now is suggested as an appropriate verse with which to rebuff the demon of gluttony, who tempts us to drink wine even when we have no pain in our stomachs.[285]

Evagrius's campaign against the demons, however, is more than verbal. In addition to providing Scriptural quotations that will mar the artistry of the demons' illusions, Evagrius advises a strict regime of ascetic discipline to help the monk resist their temptations. Fasting and the limitation of water is essential,[286] and this to the very end of life.[287] (Evagrius reports

[handwritten margin note: Ascet.]

---

[278] E.g., Genesis 1:28; I Timothy 4:1–5. In *Kephalaia gnostica* VI, 37 (*PO* 28, 233), Evagrius complains that the demons recite words of the fear of God when they don't comprehend it; they are compared to cranes who fly in the formation of letters even though they don't know letters.

[279] Although Evagrius does not, of course, present his views in the discourse of modern philosophy, he appears to hold a "picture theory of meaning"; the theory is discussed (and refuted) by E. Daitz, "The Picture Theory of Meaning," 53–74.

[280] Matthew 4:1–11 (= Luke 4:1–13).

[281] Used in *Antirrheticus* II, 56 (Frankenberg ed., 492–493).

[282] Evagrius Ponticus, *Rerum monachalium rationes* 5 (*PG* 40, 1257).

[283] Used in *Antirrheticus* I, 7 (Frankenberg ed., 474–475), on the necessity of the monk to fast.

[284] Evagrius Ponticus, *Rerum monachalium rationes* 1 (*PG* 40, 1252–1253).

[285] Evagrius Ponticus, *Antirrheticus* I, 67 (Frankenberg ed., 484–485).

[286] A "scientific" theory accompanies the

about himself that he ate once a day.)[288] The "Nazirite's" (i.e., the monk's) way of life, according to Evagrius, requires that he never take to fullness bread, water, or sleep.[289] Restriction of eating and drinking contributes to the monk's reduced sexual desire[290] and to fewer "evil dreams" that plague him while he sleeps.[291] Evagrius was following medical theory of his day when he counseled that the limitation of liquids dried up the arteries, thus helping to prevent "accidents of the night," but he gives the theory a religious interpretation: excessive moisture provides Satan with the occasion to excite sexual thoughts by day and dreams by night so as to deprive the monk of "the light of purity."[292] Cassian likewise emphasizes the limitation of water as a key to preventing nocturnal emissions,[293] a teaching he may have derived from Evagrius. Restriction on food also has another "medico-moral" benefit: by preventing the accumulation of bile, it helps the monk to control anger.[294] In addition to the limitation of food and water, toil, solitude,[295] and vigils[296] are also recommended for the quenching of desire. Evagrius himself employed a more drastic measure to foil the demon of *porneia*: standing naked in a well on a winter night.[297]

The monk must also learn to cut off the *logismoi* as soon as they arise: *askēsis* means resisting immediately any *logismos* that appears.[298] We must be like "gate-keepers" who question each thought to find out if it is friend or foe;[299] the contemplative mind, Evagrius suggests, serves as a watchdog, chasing away any impassioned *logismoi*.[300] If, however, the monk dwells on the thought, turning the image around in his mind, then he is culpable for his resulting excitement. Evagrius's friend Dioscorus, one of the Tall

---

latter: demons gravitate to water. See *Antirrheticus* II, 22 (Frankenberg ed., 488–489); cf. Evagrius's teaching in *Historia monachorum* 20, 16 (Festugière ed., 123). On these topics see Aline Rousselle, *Porneia: On Desire and the Body in Antiquity*, chap. 10 ("From Abstinence to Impotence").

[287] Evagrius Ponticus, *De humilitate* (Muyldermans ed., tr., *Evagriana Syriaca*, Syriac, 112; French, 148).

[288] Evagrius Ponticus, *Ep. ad Melaniam* 7 (Parmentier tr., 14).

[289] Evagrius Ponticus, *De jejunio* 8 (Muyldermans ed., tr., *Evagriana Syriaca*, Syriac, 116; French, 151).

[290] That one passion leads to another is a central aspect of Evagrius's teaching on the passions: *De diversis malignis cogitationibus* 1 (PG 79, 1200).

[291] Evagrius Ponticus, *Sententiae ad monachos* 11 (Gressman ed., 154).

[292] *Apophthegmata patrum* (Syriac) II, 655 (Budge tr., 416–417).

[293] John Cassian, *Conlationes* XII, 11 (SC

54, 139); cf. *Historia monachorum* 20,3 (Festugière ed., 119).

[294] Evagrius Ponticus, *De perfectione* 14 (Muyldermans ed., "Les *Capita cognoscitiva*," Syriac, 105; French, 105).

[295] Evagrius Ponticus, *Practicus* 15 (SC 171, 536).

[296] Evagrius Ponticus, *Ep.* 55, 3 (Frankenberg ed., 602–603; Bunge tr., 270).

[297] Palladius, *Historia Lausiaca* 38, 11 (Butler ed., vol. 2: 121); the Coptic version gives the fuller details (Amélineau ed., 116).

[298] Evagrius Ponticus, *De tutelis* 4 (Muyldermans ed., tr., *Evagriana Syriaca*, Syriac, 126; French, 158). Although we cannot control whether "thoughts" come to us, we *can* control whether we linger over them or cut them off: *Practicus* 6 (SC 171, 508).

[299] Evagrius Ponticus, *Ep.* 11, 3 (Frankenberg ed., 574–575; Bunge tr., 224).

[300] Evagrius Ponticus, *Kephalaia gnostica supplementum* 10 (Frankenberg ed., 430–431) (= Cod. Barb. Gr. 515, #5 [Muyldermans ed., "Evagriana" (1931), 51]).

Brothers, differentiated culpable and nonculpable night fantasies on just this basis: if the monk had deliberately pondered the images, turning them around in his mind, then he was responsible for his resulting "pollution"; if, however, he had not dwelt on the "thought," he was innocent.[301] As Evagrius put it, vividly imagining the pictures presented to the mind increases rather than excises passions:[302] the monk becomes troubled when he gives his assent to the "evil thoughts" aroused by *thumos* and *epithumia* and imprinted on his mind.[303] The issue, then—as in Stoic epistemology and ethics—is one of consent: although we do not have the power to eradicate "unclean thoughts" completely, we can withhold our assent to them.[304]

Most desirable is the state of *apatheia*,[305] in which the monk can no longer be tempted by demonic illusions: nothing on earth, Evagrius claims, can stain this impassible soul.[306] A noteworthy aspect of Evagrius's teaching on *apatheia* is its low rank on his scale of monastic virtues; it is not the *telos* of the monk's life, but a mere preparation for contemplation. Thus for Evagrius, *apatheia* lies in the realm of the *praktikos*, not in the higher realms of knowledge and contemplation.[307] The homely measures he advocates—a dry diet and the practice of love—should, he thinks, readily bring the monk to that state.[308] Evagrius distinguishes between a "small" or "imperfect" impassibility and a "larger," more "perfect" one: "imperfect" impassibility means that the monk has conquered the passions prompted by *epithumia* and is proceeding on to conquer those stimulated by *thumos*;[309] "perfect" impassibility is attained when all the passions have been extirpated.[310] When the monk no longer "feels," then he is truly free from passion.[311] He no longer receives the *eidōla* that come from the senses:[312] he has broken his mind's receptivity to images. He can judge

[301] *Historia monachorum* 20, 1–2 (Festugière ed., 118–119).

[302] Evagrius Ponticus, *Practicus* 23 (*SC* 171, 554).

[303] Evagrius Ponticus, *Ep.* 55, 2 (Frankenberg ed., 602–603; Bunge tr., 269).

[304] Evagrius Ponticus, "Letter of Advice," (157bB), (Frankenberg ed., 560–561); cf. *Practicus* 6 (*SC* 171, 508).

[305] For a discussion of Evagrius's teaching on *apatheia*, see R. Draguet, " 'L'Histoire Lausiaque': Une oeuvre écrite dans l'esprit d'Evagre," 329–333; Antoine and Claire Guillaumont, *Evagre le Pontique, Traité Pratique* (*SC* 170, 98–112).

[306] Evagrius Ponticus, *Kephalaia gnostica* V, 64 (*PO* 28, 203).

[307] Evagrius Ponticus, in Cod. Paris. Graec. 913, #16 (Muyldermans ed., "Evagriana: Note Additionelle A," 375); *Kephalaia gnostica* II, 4 (*PO* 28, 61, 63); cf. *Kephalaia gnostica* II, 6 (*PO* 28, 63). See discussion in Antoine Guillaumont, "Un philosophe du désert: Evagre le Pontique," 42–43, also citing *De diversis malignis cogitationibus* 15 and *Practicus* 60.

[308] Evagrius Ponticus, *Practicus* 91 (*SC* 171, 692, 694), cf. Socrates, *HE* IV, 23 (*PG* 67, 516).

[309] Evagrius Ponticus, *De diversis malignis cogitationibus* 15 (*PG* 79, 1217).

[310] Evagrius Ponticus, *Practicus* 60 (*SC* 171, 640).

[311] Evagrius Ponticus, *Practicus* 4 (*SC* 171, 502). John Bamberger reminds readers of Evagrius that Evagrius also had a more positive approach to *aisthēsis* in some other discussions (see Bamberger's translation of *The Praktikos*, 16n.23).

[312] Evagrius Ponticus, *Kephalaia gnostica* V, 12 (*PO* 28, 181).

whether or not the apathetic state has been reached by examining his thoughts by day and his dreams by night.[313]

Perfection is achieved when there is no more struggle, when there are no more disturbing impulses against which the monk must contend,[314] when neither present experience nor past memory can move him.[315] Then his prayer will be "pure,"[316] and to him will the Holy Trinity reveal itself.[317] Stripped of the passions, his *nous* becomes "like light,"[318] that is, like God. Thus does *apatheia* guide the monk to the highest state available to humans in this corporeal world: the intense and formless contemplation of the Godhead that suggests no images to the mind and renders it one with the Divine. Representation has been vanquished. The words framed by W.J.T. Mitchell to summarize the development of an iconoclastic rhetoric that repudiates "false images" while attempting to locate "true" ones can be applied to no one better than Evagrius:

> In this scenario of intellectual history, the worship of graven images in the dark groves and caves of heathen superstition has given way to a superstitious belief in the power of graven mental images that reside in the dark cave of the skull. And the urge to enlighten the savage idolator gives way to the project of enlightening all the benighted worshipers of "idols of the mind."[319]

Evagrius is, then, the quintessential iconoclast, radicalizing and internalizing the historical anti-idolatry campaign waged by Theophilus in the last decade of the fourth century. Before 399, Theophilus's iconoclastic moves against Egyptian paganism formed a seamless whole with a theology that set itself against "imaging" God. The illogic that attends the rendering of this unity of theory and praxis suggests, once again, that factors other than religion motivated Theophilus's behavior. By the time Theophilus conducted his rampage against the Nitrian monks on the grounds of their alleged Origenism, however, Evagrius was dead. Although Theophilus accorded Evagrius no explicit recognition, his silence may constitute an effective *damnatio memoriae*, for the Origenism that Theophilus condemned in the years after 399 was not simply that of the third-century Alexandrian father of speculative theology: it was an Origenism marked by both the controversies of the 390s and the themes of Evagrian piety. We next turn to the changing charges against Origenism.

---

[313] Evagrius Ponticus, *Practicus* 56; cf. 64 (*SC* 171, 630, 648).

[314] Evagrius Ponticus, *Practicus* 68 (*SC* 171, 652).

[315] Evagrius Ponticus, *Practicus* 67 (*SC* 171, 652).

[316] Evagrius Ponticus, *Ep.* 1, 2; 4 (Frankenberg ed., 566–567; Bunge tr., 211, 212).

[317] Evagrius Ponticus, *Ep.* 61, 3; cf. *Ep.*

58, 4 (Frankenberg ed., 610–611, 606–609; Bunge tr., 282, 277).

[318] Evagrius Ponticus, *Kephalaia gnostica* V, 15 (*PO* 28, 183).

[319] Mitchell, *Iconology*, 165. Mitchell himself highlights the futility of the enterprise, given the contamination by language of all pictorial imagery (cf. 42).

CHAPTER THREE

The Charges against Origenism

Shifts in the assault upon Origenism in the writings of Epiphanius, Theophilus, Jerome, and Shenute reveal the changing complexion of Origenism's perceived dangers in the later fourth and fifth centuries. Although texts of Origen are frequently quoted in these assaults, the attacks center so firmly on issues of concern to the critics' own era that they frequently either underestimate or miss entirely the theological problems with which Origen himself grappled.

Thus Epiphanius's early critiques of the 370s, recorded in his *Ancoratus* and *Panarion* 64, were supplemented by arguments designed to combat the Origenism flourishing in the Egyptian desert by the closing years of the century, as is evident from the changed perspective of his letter in 394 to John of Jerusalem: the heightened debate over asceticism colored both his and his successors' attacks on Origenism from this period onwards. A few years later, the polemics of Theophilus—some points of which hint at a knowledge of Evagrian Origenism—likewise engaged contemporary concern over "the body" as well as the texts of Origen. In the opening years of the fifth century, Jerome, exploiting his own extensive study of Origen as well as appropriating his predecessors' arguments, manipulated the charge of Origenism to assail his personal enemies and to defend himself from accusations of heresy. His central theological point, however, was one he had forged not in the Origenist controversy but in the passionate debates over asceticism and moral hierarchy a decade or more earlier. Last, the Origenism that Shenute confronted in the Thebaid thirty years or more after the controversy's alleged demise reveals the continued progress of "Evagrianization" in the Egyptian wing of the movement. Although the end of the Evagrian trajectory takes us beyond the purview of this study to the sixth century, we can nonetheless recall that Justinian's anathemas against Origen and his supporters not only name Evagrius as an Origenist heretic, but also cite the teachings of Evagrius as if they were Origen's.[1]

In tracing the course of these allegations from Epiphanius to Shenute, we shall see how the charge of Origenism proved sufficiently malleable to serve as a reflex for changing religious concerns. Indeed, at times, it was *so* malleable that Origen's theology was often obscured in the clamor of contemporary debate. A chronological tour through the writings of Epiphanius, Theophilus, Jerome, and Shenute that pertain to Origenism will provide a surprisingly close index of how themes of Origen's theology intersected with religious issues that engaged these writers in their own times. Of these, concerns that arose over "the body" in the late fourth century stand at the forefront of the discussion: contemporary discourse on "the body" has marked the understandings of Origen's theology. By examining each author's writings in the order of their composition, we can note the exact points at which such new concerns emerge and posit some hypotheses about the reasons for their emergence.

EPIPHANIUS'S VERSION OF ORIGENISM AND HIS ANTI-ORIGENIST CHARGES

We begin our investigation with an examination of Epiphanius's anti-Origenist charges in the *Ancoratus*, dated to 374, and in *Panarion* 64, dated to 376,[2] indictments that proved central to both Theophilus's and Jerome's polemical constructions. Moreover, if (as has been argued) Epiphanius's *Ancoratus* was translated into Sahidic in 399 or 400—at the very height of the controversy—even those monks of the Egyptian desert unlettered in Greek could have become familiar with such points of the Origenist debate as the resurrection or nonresurrection of the body.[3] Epiphanius's understanding of Origenism thus was a base for later discussions of the topic among both the learned and the less-than-learned.

---

[1] Guillaumont, *Les "Kephalaia Gnostica,"* 156–158. The implications of this point were readily seen by Gustave Bardy, who as early as 1923 denounced Koetschau's use of the sixth-century anathemas in constructing his edition of Origen's *De principiis* (*Recherches*, 69, 204–205).

[2] Dechow, *Dogma*, 13–14. I wish to acknowledge my large debt to Dechow's intelligent explication of Epiphanius.

[3] Dechow, *Dogma*, 104, posits that the Pachomian stories revealing an anti-Origen-ist bias may have been inserted into the Pachomian corpus in the wake of the Sahidic translation of the *Ancoratus*. He also posits that the interest that Shenute and the Theban/Pachomian monks displayed in a "this flesh" theory of the resurrection body may be related to the appearance of the Sahidic translation of the *Ancoratus* (230–239, 218). Shenute himself could have read Epiphanius in the original Greek, but not all the Pachomian monks could have done so.

In the *Ancoratus* of 374, Epiphanius's *announced* target, however, is Trinitarian heresy: the "Ariomaniacs" surpass all other heretics in their impiety, he declares.[4] It comes as no surprise, then, that one of the complaints he registers against the "disgraceful" Origenists[5] is that Origen in *On First Principles* taught that the Son is "less" than the Father.[6] Likewise, in the explication of the Creed that rounds out the *Ancoratus*, Epiphanius stresses that Christians must affirm the Son and Holy Spirit to be of the same "*hypostasis* or *ousia*" as the Father.[7] Epiphanius does not in this work, however, press the charge of "idolatry" (identified with "worshiping a creature") against Origen for his subordinationism, even though "idolatry" is counted among the worst sins at several points in the *Ancoratus*.[8]

Epiphanius's true complaint against Origen and the Origenists, nonetheless, even in his work of 374, is focused elsewhere than on his alleged target, Trinitarian dogma: as Jon Dechow has suggested, the Trinitarian issues central to the earlier attacks upon Origen cited in Pamphilus/Eusebius's *Defense of Origen* and to the anonymous apology for Origen cited in Photius's *Bibliotheca* Codex 117 have to some degree—although not completely—faded in importance by Epiphanius's day.[9] Already in the *Ancoratus*, the major line of assault against Origen pertains to issues of "materiality" as they manifest themselves in discussions of the body and of allegorical exegesis. Woven into Epiphanius's arguments is a consideration of the "image of God,"[10] a topic that two decades later would occasion great dispute, especially the question (posed as early as the *Ancoratus*) of how the "image of God" relates to the presence of Christ in the Eucharist.[11] Thus themes of the later debate are foreshadowed in Epiphanius's early work.

In the *Ancoratus*, Epiphanius's criticism both of Origen's allegorical exegesis and of his teaching on the resurrection focuses on "bodiliness."[12] The events described in the Genesis creation story are to be taken literally,

---

[4] Epiphanius, *Ancoratus* 116 (*GCS* 25, 144). A target less extensively discussed but nonetheless prominent in the *Ancoratus* is Apollinarianism. Epiphanius wants to assure his readers that Jesus possessed all the constitutive elements of humanity (body, soul, and mind); only sin is excluded (*Ancoratus* 35; 76; 119 [*GCS* 25, 44–45, 95–96, 148]).

[5] Epiphanius, *Ancoratus* 13 (*GCS* 25, 21).

[6] Epiphanius, *Ancoratus* 63 (*GCS* 25, 75–76).

[7] Epiphanius, *Ancoratus* 119 (*GCS* 25, 149). We find the same confusion of *ousia* and *hypostasis* in Jerome, *Ep.* 15, 4–5 (*CSEL* 54, 65–67). Epiphanius wrote the *Ancoratus* seven years before the Council of Constantinople made formal the distinction of the terms.

[8] Epiphanius, *Ancoratus* 87; 102 (*GCS* 25, 108, 122) and especially 103 (*GCS* 25, 123–124), where Egyptian theriomorphism is singled out as the worst form of idolatry.

[9] Dechow, *Dogma*, 248–251, 265–270. I see them as still, in the 370s, retaining some importance. By the 390s, the subordinationist charges against Origen definitely are part of an "archaizing" motif.

[10] Epiphanius, *Ancoratus* 56–57 (*GCS* 25, 65–67).

[11] Epiphanius, *Ancoratus* 57 (*GCS* 25, 66–67).

[12] For discussion, see Calogerro Riggi, "La forma del corpo risorto secondo Metodio in Epifanio (Haer. 64)," 75–92.

Epiphanius assures the monks to whom he writes.[13] Eden was a real place situated on the earth, not in the heavens.[14] The names of Eden's rivers are likewise authentic: Epiphanius obligingly supplies the geographical details.[15] His attack upon allegorical readings centers on Origen's exegesis of the "tunics of skins" with which God furnished the naked Adam and Eve after the first sin (Genesis 3:21). Epiphanius is appalled at Origen's flippancy in discounting a literal interpretation of the leather clothing: "Is God a tanner?" Epiphanius's response is rhetorical, although beside the point: Which is easier, for God to make heaven and earth from nothing, or to make tunics of skins? That Adam and Eve are here supplied with real clothing is bolstered by an appeal to Jesus's wearing of clothes even in his resurrection state ("I think that he was not nude," Epiphanius muses).[16] Epiphanius is clearly more interested in pressing a literal reading of the Bible than in engaging in philosophical debate about the status of materiality.

Against those who claim that only souls, not bodies, are resurrected, Epiphanius has a ready argument: how can a soul be "resurrected" when it never dies? It is not souls but bodies that we place in sepulchres.[17] The followers of Origen should confess not just that the dead are raised, but that they are raised with "this flesh"—the very kind of flesh that Jesus took for his own body from the Virgin Mary.[18] Epiphanius associates the denial of a "this flesh" resurrection teaching both with the Hieracites, now stirring up the Egyptian monks,[19] and with Origenists, who on this point, he claims, fall into worse error than even the pagans.[20] Yet having made a strong stand for a "this flesh" resurrection body, Epiphanius continues—somewhat unreflectively—to contrast the thick, coarse, corruptible, and mortal bodies we presently possess with the delicate, light, incorruptible, and immortal ones we will acquire in the resurrection.[21] Assuring his readers that all parts of the body will rise, Epiphanius appeals to a host of Bib-

---

[13] Epiphanius, *Ancoratus* 55 (*GCS* 25, 64–65).

[14] Epiphanius, *Ancoratus* 58 (*GCS* 25, 67).

[15] Epiphanius, *Ancoratus* 58 (*GCS* 25, 67–68).

[16] Epiphanius, *Ancoratus* 62 (*GCS* 25, 74–75). The form of argumentation is duplicated in Theophilus's Twenty-First Festal Letter of 406: "What is easier, for a man to be made from the earth without parents, or for Christ our Savior to be born from a virgin with flesh and with a soul capable of sensation?" This fragment is preserved in Zacharias Rhetor's *Church History* (*CSCO* 83, Syriac, 198; *CSCO* 87, Latin, 137). Origen's fullest discussion of the "tunics of skins" comes in his *Commentary on Genesis*, on verse 3:21 (*PG* 12, 101). For an English translation of this important passage, see Dechow, *Dogma*, 316–317. Epiphanius implies that Origenists teach a nonbodily resurrection doctrine by arguing that Christ left his "clothes" in the sepulchre when he rose (*Ancoratus* 62 [*GCS* 25, 75]).

[17] Epiphanius, *Ancoratus* 86 (*GCS* 25, 106).

[18] Epiphanius, *Ancoratus* 87 (*GCS* 25, 107–108).

[19] Epiphanius, *Ancoratus* 82 (*GCS* 25, 103).

[20] Epiphanius, *Ancoratus* 87 (*GCS* 25, 107–108).

[21] Epiphanius, *Ancoratus* 90–91 (*GCS* 25, 111-112), citing I Corinthians 15:53.

lical examples that could be called prefigurations to the resurrection: the son of the widow of Zarephath (I Kings 17:22), Enoch (Genesis 5:24), and the people whom Jesus is represented as returning to life (John 11:43; Luke 7:14; Mark 5:41; Matthew 8:13).[22] Likewise, he claims that those who went down to Hades were not separated from their bodies.[23]

One of Epiphanius's main objections to an anthropology that separates soul and body, either here or in the hereafter, is moral: if the "I" is not identified with the body, we might attempt to exonerate ourselves from our commission of fornication, adultery, theft, idolatry, and other sins by claiming that it was not "I" but only "the body" that was responsible for such wrongdoing.[24] Body and soul stand together before God's judgment, Epiphanius insists;[25] together they constitute the "self." Origen's treatment of the resurrection body, in his view, endangers the Christian injunction to upright behavior.

In the *Ancoratus*, however, Epiphanius does not (as he will in *Panarion* 64) appropriate Methodius's critique of Origen's teaching on the resurrection body. Modern scholars will see this absence as an advantage, not as a deficiency, since Methodius misunderstood Origen's teaching on the body's "form" and constant flux that renders impossible the identification of "this flesh."[26] By condensing and further confusing Methodius's rendition of Origen's teaching,[27] Epiphanius in *Panarion* 64 provided little help for later readers struggling to comprehend the "heretical" aspects of Origen's theology of the resurrection. Whatever the inadequacies of Epiphanius's presentation in the *Ancoratus*, he at least does not further compromise his argument by citing Methodius's *De resurrectione*.

Although in the *Ancoratus* Epiphanius does not implicate Origenism in particular on this point, his treatment of the "image of God" should be briefly noted. Ruling out the identification of the "image" with the soul, the mind, the body, and the virtues,[28] he states that possession of the "image" does not make us equals with God, for God can in no way be comprehended. Interestingly, Epiphanius illustrates our dissimilarity to God with an analogy taken from Jesus's words at the Last Supper: even though

---

[22] Epiphanius, *Ancoratus* 98 (*GCS* 25, 118–119).

[23] Epiphanius, *Ancoratus* 99 (*GCS* 25, 119).

[24] Epiphanius, *Ancoratus* 87 (*GCS* 25, 108).

[25] Epiphanius, *Ancoratus* 88 (*GCS* 25, 109–110); cf. his explication of the Creed, in which Epiphanius insists that judgment shall be for *both* souls and bodies (*Ancoratus* 119 [*GCS* 25, 149]).

[26] See discussion below, pp. 93–94.

[27] See Henri Crouzel, "Les Critiques ad-ressées par Méthode et ses contemporains à la doctrine origénienne du corps ressuscité," 711; "La Doctrine origénienne du corps ressucité," 257; L. G. Patterson, "Who Are the Opponents in Methodius' *De Resurrectione?*" 223–224; Dechow, *Dogma*, 357–361, 384–388; "Origen and Christian Pluralism: The Context of His Eschatology," 337–356; "Third-Century Resurrection Controversy: Methodius, *On the Resurrection*."

[28] Epiphanius, *Ancoratus* 56 (*GCS* 25, 65–66).

Jesus says "This is my body," we can see that the two entities, bread and Jesus, are not "equal" or alike, for divinity is not capable of being seen.[29] Epiphanius, like the later Iconodules, implies that a lack of exact "likeness" between archetype and image in no way damages the power of an image to represent its model.[30] The attentive reader will note, however, that although Epiphanius has not revealed in what the "image of God" consists, he nevertheless insists on the basis of Genesis 1:26–27 that we confess that humans remain "in God's image."

In *Panarion* 64, composed in 376, two charges against Origen stand at the forefront of Epiphanius's argument. The first pertains to Trinitarian issues: here, Origen's alleged subordinationism is at the center of the attack. The second turns on notions of the body and treats God's original creation of human flesh and the final resurrection (or nonresurrection) of the body. The importance of the first charge faded in the course of the controversy: although in the 370s, Arians of various persuasions had developed ever more refined ways of distinguishing the Father from the Son, by the turn to the fifth century, subordinationism would appear more an archaizing motif than an issue of contemporary concern. Issues about bodiliness, in contrast, will have acquired even greater importance, following the heated debates over asceticism in the 380s and 390s.

According to Epiphanius in *Panarion* 64, Origen's subordinationism stimulated the development of Arianism:[31] he singles out as case-in-point Origen's statement that the Son cannot "see" the Father, nor the Holy Spirit the Son.[32] For Origen, of course, this assertion was the logical consequence of the incorporeality of the Godhead[33]—a point that is lost on Epiphanius, for whom the Son's inability to "see" the Father signals only Arian subordinationism. Even though Epiphanius acknowledges that Origen held the Son to be "of the *ousia* of the Father," he also reports that Origen called the Son "created" (*ktiston*).[34] Faulting Origen's reference to the Savior as a "made God" (*gennētos theos*),[35] Epiphanius expounds the difference between *genētos* and *gennētos*,[36] a distinction that had not achieved doctrinal importance until the formula "begotten not made" was proclaimed at the Council of Nicaea in 325.[37] Epiphanius turns to the Gos-

---

[29] Epiphanius, *Ancoratus* 57 (*GCS* 25, 66–67). Cf. the argument reported in the *Apophthegmata patrum*; see above, pp. 64–65.
[30] See above, p. 59.
[31] Epiphanius, *Panarion* 64, 4 (*GCS* 31², 409–410).
[32] Epiphanius, *Panarion* 64, 4 (*GCS* 31², 410).
[33] Origen, *De principiis* I, 1, 1; 1, 6; 1, 8; 2, 6 (*GCS* 22, 16–17, 20–23, 24–26, 34–37).
[34] Epiphanius, *Panarion* 64, 4; 5 (*GCS*

31², 410, 415). On Origen's use and understanding of *ktisma*, see Dechow, *Dogma*, 281–284.
[35] Epiphanius, *Panarion* 64, 7 (*GCS* 31², 416–417).
[36] Epiphanius, *Panarion* 64, 8 (*GCS* 31², 417). For Epiphanius's confusion of *ousia* and *hypostasis*, see above, p. 87.
[37] On the distinction, see, for example, J.N.D. Kelly, *Early Christian Doctrines*, 46, 232; Dechow, *Dogma*, 291–294.

pels to bolster his case against the word "created" as applicable to the Son: we do not, he says, find the phrase "My Father created me," or "I create the Son," but rather, "I and the Father are one" (John 10:30), "He who has seen me has seen the Father" (John 14:9), and "No one knows the Father except the Son and anyone to whom the Son chooses to reveal him" (Matthew 11:27).[38] For Epiphanius, it is impossible for Christians to adore a god that is "made." Worshiping any created thing, even a "created" Son of God, leads to the worship of another creature—and it is against such pagan "creature worship" that Paul warns in Romans 1:25.[39] For Epiphanius, Origen's subordinationism thus entails a form of idolatry, which he attempts to document by repeating the rumor that Origen denied the faith by offering sacrifice to pagan gods.[40]

A second broad set of problems in *Panarion* 64 deals with Origen's teaching on the body. According to Epiphanius, Origen believed that souls of men preexisted their bodies as "angels" or "powers," and that because of sins committed in their preexistent state, they were enclosed in bodies. On this reading, Epiphanius protests, the body would be a prison, a chain. Falling from the heavenly heights, the souls according to Origen are said to "cool down": Epiphanius repeats the wordplay that *psychē* (soul) is derived from *psychesthai* (to become cold). Again, as in the *Ancoratus*, Origen is faulted for an allegorical understanding of the "tunics of skins."[41]

All these interpretations Epiphanius disputes. Humans were created as bodies and souls together;[42] the "tunics of skins" cannot be bodies (as Origen is alleged to have taught) because Adam and Eve acquired these tunics only after the first sin, and they surely had bodies before then.[43] What would it mean for Adam to say, "bone of my bone and flesh of my flesh" (Genesis 2:23) if he and Eve did not have bodies? They certainly didn't cover their "souls" with fig leaves, Epiphanius scoffs.[44] Again he notes Origen's reprehensible response to the proposition that God furnished the couple with leather clothes: "God is not a tanner." According to Epiphanius, we should adhere literally to the Genesis story that God made the first human from the earth, not from "skins."[45] Such verses as Romans 7:9 ("I was once alive apart from the law") cannot be used by Origenists to argue

[38] Epiphanius, *Panarion* 64, 9 (*GCS* 31², 418).

[39] Epiphanius, *Panarion* 64, 8 (*GCS* 31², 417–418).

[40] Epiphanius, *Panarion* 64, 2 (*GCS* 31², 404): according to Epiphanius, Origen was given a choice between sacrificing to a pagan idol or committing a sexual act with an Ethiopian male; for his choice of sacrifice, Origen was expelled from the church and lost the glory of martyrdom that might have been his. One wonders what the penalty for the other choice might have been?

[41] Epiphanius, *Panarion* 64, 4 (*GCS* 31², 411–412). See Dechow, *Dogma*, 297–301.

[42] Epiphanius, *Panarion* 64, 26 (*GCS* 31², 442); Methodius is the source.

[43] Epiphanius, *Panarion* 64, 25; 31 (*GCS* 31², 441, 449); Methodius is the source.

[44] Epiphanius, *Panarion* 64, 65 (*GCS* 31², 506); Methodius is the source.

[45] Epiphanius, *Panarion* 64, 63 (*GCS* 31², 500–501).

for a preexistence of souls before bodies.[46] For Epiphanius, Origen's allegorical interpretation led him astray on these and other issues pertaining to the body: Paradise and its rivers are again used as cases-in-point.[47]

One new motif that emerges in *Panarion* 64 is that the discussion of the "image of God"—more precisely, the discussion of humans' *loss* of the "image"—is now explicitly linked to Origen.[48] For Epiphanius, man was (and still remains) in God's "image" and was meant to be the "ornament of the world" (*ton kosmon tou kosmou*).[49] As Jon Dechow and others have argued, Epiphanius, who here borrows from Methodius's earlier attack, paints Origen's view too negatively. Where, on his reading of Origen, would there be any possibility for human improvement? How could one even imagine human perfection, if the image were totally obscured? Origen's optimistic view that the world provides a training ground by which we develop our religious and moral strength has been discounted by Epiphanius's claim that for Origen the "image" is obliterated.[50] To this topic we shall return below.

The main issue concerning bodily nature on which Epiphanius wishes to fault Origen in *Panarion* 64 concerns the resurrection state. Here, Epiphanius turns to Methodius's treatise *On the Resurrection* for assistance.[51] Both in his own arguments and in the passages he cites from Methodius, Origen's *Commentary on Psalm 1* serves as an important source.[52]

Of the arguments pertaining to the resurrection body that Epiphanius used in the *Ancoratus*, several are repeated in *Panarion* 64. Since souls (unlike bodies) neither die nor are buried, they cannot strictly speaking be said to be "resurrected."[53] Various resuscitations mentioned in Scripture are adduced as evidence that bodies can be raised.[54] Epiphanius also in *Panarion* 64 appeals to the argument concerning the fairness of God's judgment on human behavior: if the body has endured human labors, has allowed itself to be tamed in holiness, then it should not be deprived of a reward along with its soul, for "God is not unjust as to overlook your work" (Hebrews

---

[46] Epiphanius, *Panarion* 64, 49 (*GCS* 31², 476): the argument is from Methodius, whom Epiphanius here cites; cf. *Panarion* 64, 55 (*GCS* 31², 486).

[47] Epiphanius, *Panarion* 64, 4 (*GCS* 31², 413); cf. *Ancoratus* 58 (*GCS* 25, 67–68). See Dechow, *Dogma*, 333–346.

[48] Epiphanius, *Panarion* 64, 4 (*GCS* 31², 412). For Methodius, too, it is impossible for "the image" to be lost: Epiphanius cites him in *Panarion* 64, 27 (*GCS* 31², 444).

[49] Epiphanius, *Panarion* 64, 27 (*GCS* 31², 444–445).

[50] Dechow, *Dogma*, 305–307. See also pp. 101–102 and nn. 121 and 123 below.

[51] The original Greek of Methodius's treatise is not extant; chapters 12–62 of Epiphanius's *Panarion* 64 constitute direct citations from this work. An old Slavonic translation of Methodius's *De resurrectione* has been preserved. It is edited and translated, with the Greek remains, by G. Nathanael Bonwetsch in *GCS* 27, 217–424.

[52] See, e.g., *Panarion* 64, 6–7; 12–16 (*GCS* 31², 415–416, 421–427).

[53] Epiphanius, *Panarion* 64, 63 (*GCS* 31², 502).

[54] Epiphanius, *Panarion* 64, 64; 67–71 (*GCS* 31², 503–504, 509–521); citing Genesis 5:24; II Kings 2:11; I Corinthians 15, among other passages.

6:10).[55] And conversely, bodies that participated in adultery, fornication, and idol worship should not be able to blame souls alone for these misdeeds at the Last Judgment.[56]

The most extensive teaching of *Panarion* 64 on the resurrection body, however, is derived from Methodius: sections 12–62 of the chapter are borrowed directly from Methodius's *De resurrectione*. Epiphanius begins his discussion with a reference to Origen's explication of Psalm 1:5 in his *Commentary on Psalm 1*, here given in its Septuagint reading, "Thus the wicked shall not rise in judgment."[57] He cites Origen's question as to what aspect of the body shall be raised: do we get back the full head of hair from our youth, or will aged domes present themselves as balding? The problem that Origen here addresses pertains to the flux of the body: even if we *were* to affirm the resurrection of "the body," what precisely are we affirming, since the body is in a constant state of change?[58] Epiphanius responds witheringly that such queries are mere "syllogisms" that detract from the certainty of Christian faith in the resurrection.[59] Yet rather than answer Origen's question, which does not seem so trivial to modern commentators, Epiphanius turns to Methodius's treatise *On the Resurrection* for assistance. Given Methodius's flawed interpretation of Origen, we might prefer that Epiphanius had cast this source aside and relied on his own readings.

That Origen had a subtle and often unappreciated understanding of the "spiritual body" has been vigorously argued in recent years by several scholars.[60] In his *Commentary on Psalm 1*, Origen tried to explain how one could account for a constant human identity when the physical aspects of the body were in a state of daily flux. The most cogent modern scholarship on the subject singles out Origen's notion that there is a "corporeal form" that provides this identity, an *eidos* that will "ensure the substantial identity between the earthly body and the glorious body."[61] It seems likely that this teaching could be taken as an "orthodox" interpretation of the resurrection body—if commentators had so wished to interpret it.

---

[55] Epiphanius, *Panarion* 64, 71 (GCS 31², 519). According to Pamphilus, the very same argument was used by Origen himself: see p. 162 below for discussion and references.

[56] Epiphanius, *Panarion* 64, 71 (GCS 31², 520).

[57] Epiphanius, *Panarion* 64, 10 (GCS 31², 419).

[58] Epiphanius, *Panarion* 64, 10 (GSC 31², 419).

[59] Epiphanius, *Panarion* 64, 11 (GCS 31², 420).

[60] Most notably, Henri Crouzel, "La Doctrine origénienne," 241–257; "Les Critiques adressées," 690–691; followed by Dechow,

Dogma, 373–384. H. Cornélis concludes a detailed study of the relationship of the incorporeal and the corporeal in Origen's thought with the claim that it is in perfect keeping with Origen's notion of the *logikoi* as occupying a "median" position that they should be attached to matter of some sort: "Les Fondements cosmologiques de l'eschatologie d'Origène," 32–80, 201–247; esp. 247. For an illuminating discussion of the corporeal *eidos* in Greek philosophy and in Origen, see Alain LeBoulluec, "De la Croissance selon les Stoïciens à la résurrection selon Origène," 143–155.

[61] Crouzel, "La Doctrine origénienne," 256; translation from Dechow, *Dogma*, 382.

Methodius, it appears, did not—nor, for that matter, did he even understand Origen's teaching. He interprets Origen's "*eidos*" to mean "outward appearance," as if *eidos* were identical with *morphē* and consisted in the visible characteristics of the body.[62] In Methodius's dialogue, even Proclus, the character casted to support Origen's position, claims that the spiritual body in the resurrection will have the same *morphē* (not *eidos*, as he should have said) as it did on earth, even though the "matter" of the corporeal body is in a state of constant flux.[63] In fragments of the same treatise preserved in Photius (Codex 234), Methodius accuses Origen of teaching that the human form is "useless" and will completely disappear,[64] and that the "spiritual body" is only a body "in appearance."[65] Despite his less than lucid argumentation, Methodius clearly denies that an uncorrupted "form" could be resurrected while the body on which the "form" was "stamped" was destroyed. When you melt down a statue, he argues, the "form" of a man or a horse disappears, but the "material" of the statue remains.[66] Methodius's analogy shows that for him—in contrast to Origen—"form" is a property of outward, physical appearance.

Epiphanius apparently believes that Methodius's critique constitutes a compelling refutation of Origen's views. He adds that he himself rejects any distinction between the *physikos* body and the *pneumatikos* body.[67] Yet having again claimed a "this flesh" resurrection theory, Epiphanius undercuts his own argument by conceding that *some* fleshly particles may not rise with the rest of the body.[68] Moreover, although he affirms that the body of Christ on the cross was the same body as that which rose, he nonetheless believes that the body that passed through the closed door (John 20:26) was a "subtle" body, not a "coarse" one.[69] Thus Epiphanius in *Panarion* 64 confuses Origen's teaching on the resurrection body both by his dependence upon Methodius and by the seeming inconsistencies in his own position.

By 394, eighteen years after the *Panarion* was written, a shift concerning the charges against Origenism is noticeable in Epiphanius's attack—and this at the very moment when the controversy pertaining to Origen had erupted in Palestine. In Epiphanius's letter to John of Jerusalem that constitutes our main evidence for his views on Origenism in 394, he first at-

---

[62] Crouzel, "Les Critiques," 693–694, 697, 711; Patterson, "Who Are the Opponents," 223–224. Patterson argues that Origen may not be the sole opponent; in fact, Methodius may be more concerned with Gnostic teaching than with Origen's views (224–225, 228–229). Also see Dechow, *Dogma*, 354–366.

[63] Epiphanius, *Panarion* 64, 17 (*GCS* 31², 428–429).

[64] Methodius, cited in Photius, *Bibliotheca*

codex 234 (*PG* 103, 1129).

[65] Methodius, cited in Photius, *Bibliotheca* codex 234 (*PG* 103, 1132).

[66] Methodius, cited in Photius, *Bibliotheca* codex 234 (*PG* 103, 1133).

[67] Epiphanius, *Panarion* 64, 63 (*GCS* 31², 502).

[68] Epiphanius, *Panarion* 64, 67 (*GCS* 31², 509–510).

[69] Epiphanius, *Panarion* 64, 64 (*GCS* 31², 503–504).

tempts to explain why his ordination in Palestine of Jerome's brother to the priesthood was not a violation of John of Jerusalem's episcopal jurisdiction.[70] After vigorously defending his behavior, Epiphanius tells John in what respects Origen's teaching is erroneous and why John must protect his flock from its evils.

The first charge that Epiphanius raises in the letter of 394 is one familiar from *Panarion* 64: Origen had written that the Son cannot see the Father and the Holy Spirit cannot see the Son.[71] Next, Epiphanius rapidly skims through many of the charges that he had raised against Origen in his previous works: that souls preexisted in heaven and were cast down into bodies as tombs as a penalty; that souls "cooled off" and that bodies are "chains" or "funeral monuments" for the fallen souls.[72] Psalm 119:67 ("Before you humbled me for my wickedness, I went wrong") and Psalm 116:7 ("Return unto thy rest, O my soul") are again, as in *Panarion* 64,[73] cited as Scriptural verses that Origen misappropriated to argue for a heavenly preexistence of souls before their descent into bodies.[74] That Origen believes that the "tunics of skins" are human bodies, first given after the Fall, is again mentioned, and Origen's famous question, "Is God a tanner?", repeated. Once more, Epiphanius defends the notion that bodies existed before the Fall by an appeal to Genesis 2:23, that Eve was "bone of my bone and flesh of my flesh" to Adam. That it was real bodies that were covered with fig leaves is again asserted.[75] Origen's treatment of Psalm 1 is again singled out for its alleged denial of the resurrection body as "this flesh."[76] Once more, Epiphanius rejects the allegorical interpretation of Paradise: Paradise was on this earth, and its rivers were real.[77] Last, he returns to Origen's alleged teaching on the human loss of "the image of God"—but here he will develop the point further than he did in the *Ancoratus* or in *Panarion* 64.[78] These criticisms are, by 394, stock charges in Epiphanius's attack on Origen.

There are, however, three charges against Origen that Epiphanius in his letter of 394 either adds to (or greatly expands beyond) those in the *Panarion*: (1) that the original bodiless condition of humans, and their sub-

---

[70] Epiphanius, *Ep. ad Iohannem Episcopum* (= Jerome, *Ep.* 51) 1–2 (*CSEL* 54, 396–399).

[71] Epiphanius, *Ep. ad Iohannem Episcopum* (= Jerome, *Ep.* 51) 4 (*CSEL* 54, 401).

[72] Epiphanius, *Ep. ad Iohannem Episcopum* (= Jerome, *Ep.* 51) 4 (*CSEL* 54, 401–402).

[73] Epiphanius, *Panarion* 64, 4 (*GCS* 31², 412).

[74] Epiphanius, *Ep. ad Iohannem Episcopum* (= Jerome, *Ep.* 51) 4 (*CSEL* 54, 402).

[75] Epiphanius, *Ep. ad Iohannem Episcopum*

(= Jerome, *Ep.* 51) 5 (*CSEL* 54, 403–404).

[76] Epiphanius, *Ep. ad Iohannem Episcopum* (= Jerome, *Ep.* 51) 5 (*CSEL* 54, 404); cf. *Panarion* 64, 12–16 (*GCS* 31², 421–427).

[77] Epiphanius, *Ep. ad Iohannem Episcopum* (= Jerome, *Ep.* 51) 5 (*CSEL* 54, 404–405); cf. *Panarion* 64, 4 (*GCS* 31², 413).

[78] Epiphanius, *Ep. ad Iohannem Episcopum* (= Jerome, *Ep.* 51) 6–7 (*CSEL* 54, 407–410); cf. *Ancoratus* 56–57 (*GCS* 25, 65–67); *Panarion* 64, 4 (*GCS* 31², 412).

sequent "fall" into bodies, implies a deprecation of reproduction;[79] (2) that
the devil will be saved, so that he will be a coheir with the righteous men
of the Bible in heaven;[80] and (3) that Adam lost the "image of God."[81] In
addition, Epiphanius reports to John of Jerusalem on an iconoclastic activity in which he had engaged: tearing down a curtain in a Palestinian church
that was decorated with an image of either Christ or one of the saints.[82]
This image demolition correlates precisely with themes in Epiphanius's
iconoclastic writings of the 390s, to which we return below. Last, and significantly, Epiphanius closes his letter to John of Jerusalem with a warning
against Palladius, depicted as a heretic who at that very moment is spreading the evil teaching of Origen throughout Palestine.[83] On each of these
points, Epiphanius engages issues of Origenist discussion of the 390s, not
issues of special concern in Origen's own day. Gone now is his retreat to
Methodius's confused argumentation, or to warring words against Arian
heretics. The topics he discusses here are burning issues of his own time;
we explore below why they came to prominence in the 390s.

The first of these new issues raised in Epiphanius's letter to John of Jerusalem concerns the deprecation of reproduction that Origen's view of an
original nonbodily condition allegedly entails: if the soul is shut up in the
body as in a tomb, what would become of the blessing to Adam, to Noah,
and to their offspring, "Be fruitful, multiply, and fill the earth" (Genesis
1:28; 9:7)? Are we to think that God was incapable "through the action
of his blessing" to provide souls for human beings? Did God have to wait
for the angels to sin in order for there to be human births on earth? (The
latter questions also reveal Epiphanius's entry into the unresolved debate
on the origin of the soul.) Those who agree with Origen on this point
should join the Origenists who refuse to pray for an ascent to heaven for
fear that through another sin they might be cast down to earth once
more.[84]

We may indeed question if *only* the views of the historical Origen here
occupy Epiphanius's thoughts: given the controversies over asceticism that
beset the 380s and 390s, it is likely that more than Origen's teaching pure
and simple is at stake. But what debate in particular did Epiphanius have
in mind? Was he, for example, recalling the attacks upon reproduction and/
or marriage made by Manicheans and Hieracites? Does his assault on Ori-

---

[79] Epiphanius, *Ep. ad Iohannem Episcopum*
(= Jerome, *Ep.* 51) 4 (*CSEL* 54, 402).

[80] Epiphanius, *Ep. ad Iohannem Episcopum*
(= Jerome, *Ep.* 51) 5 (*CSEL* 54, 403).

[81] Epiphanius, *Ep. ad Iohannem Episcopum*
(= Jerome, *Ep.* 51) 6–7 (*CSEL* 54, 407–
410).

[82] Epiphanius, *Ep. ad Iohannem Episcopum*
(= Jerome, *Ep.* 51) 9 (*CSEL* 54, 411).

[83] Epiphanius, *Ep. ad Iohannem Episcopum*
(= Jerome, *Ep.* 51) 9 (*CSEL* 54, 412).

[84] Epiphanius, *Ep. ad Iohannem Episcopum*
(= Jerome, *Ep.* 51) 4 (*CSEL* 54, 402). Although Epiphanius cites Genesis 1:28 in
Panarion 64, 31 (*GCS* 31², 450), he uses it
only to stress the bodily nature of humans at
creation, not as part of a debate over marriage and reproduction.

genist theory in 394 reflect his fear that Manichean or Hieracite views on these subjects might infiltrate "orthodox" Christianity? His discussion of these groups in *Panarion* 66 and 67, respectively, does not provide convincing evidence for this hypothesis: when we turn to Epiphanius's treatment (circa 376) of Hieracite and Manichean views on marriage, we find that he does not enlist either Genesis 1:28 or 9:7 against them. Moreover, despite the extraordinary length of Epiphanius's chapter on Manicheanism, he devotes—astonishingly—almost no attention to the Manichean attack on reproduction; in the one section in which he even mentions the issue of marriage, he merely cites Jesus' response to the Pharisees on the question of divorce (Matthew 19:3–9) and the Ephesians 5 analogy that links husband and wife to Christ and the Church.[85] Nowhere do we find the Genesis creation story brought forward as a retort to Manichean deprecations of reproduction. Despite Epiphanius's long and detailed attack upon Manichean theology, the issue of procreation receives almost no attention. It was not the denigration of Manichean reproduction, we infer, that occupied his mind when he wrote to John of Jerusalem.

We are on no firmer ground in positing that fear of Hieracite teaching stood behind Epiphanius's concern in 394 to uphold the goodness of procreation through an appeal to Genesis. Although Epiphanius reports in *Panarion* 67 that Hieracas' teaching was especially popular among the Egyptian monks,[86] he does not appeal to Genesis 1:28 or 9:7 against their views on marriage. This omission may have been for a good reason: according to Epiphanius, Hieracas did not dispute the appropriateness of marriage and reproduction for the ancient Hebrews but only for Christians.[87] Thus to counter the Hieracite appeal to such New Testament passages as I Corinthians 7:7 and 34, and Matthew 19:12 and 25:1–2,[88] Epiphanius could not resort to Old Testament proof-texts. Rather, he cites the Gospel of John (Jesus performs his first miracle at a wedding)[89] and I Timothy's advocacy of remarriage and childbearing for widows[90] to rebut Hieracas' claim that only ascetics could be Christians.[91] Thus we may conclude that neither fear of Manicheans nor of Hieracites stood behind Epiphanius's appeal in his letter of 394 to the "Reproduce and multiply" text to refute the alleged degradation of reproduction by Origenists. What then *had* prompted Epiphanius's newfound concern—a concern not evident in either the *Ancoratus* or in *Panarion* 64—over the implications of Origenist theology for reproduction?

---

[85] Epiphanius, *Panarion* 66, 56 (*GCS* 37², 92).

[86] Epiphanius, *Panarion* 67, 1 (*GCS* 37², 133).

[87] Epiphanius, *Panarion* 67, 1 (*GCS* 37², 133–134).

[88] Epiphanius, *Panarion* 67, 2 (*GCS* 37², 134).

[89] Epiphanius, *Panarion* 67, 6 (*GCS* 37², 138).

[90] Epiphanius, *Panarion* 67, 6 (*GCS* 37², 138).

[91] Epiphanius, *Panarion* 67, 2 (*GCS* 37², 134).

A more probable source for Epiphanius's new praise of reproduction in 394 was, I posit, Jerome, or more precisely, the controversies in which Jerome had been involved over this issue. Recall that in the previous year, Jerome had engaged in an ardent battle with Jovinian on questions of asceticism.[92] The central Scriptural quotations that framed their long literary debate were Genesis 2:24 (that the two shall become "one flesh," ratified by Jesus in Matthew 19:5), and Genesis 1:28 and 9:1 ("Reproduce and multiply"). Jovinian had argued that God's blessing not only on Adam and Eve at creation, but also on Noah, his wife, his sons, and their wives after the Flood, showed that not even human sinfulness could eradicate the goodness of reproduction.[93]

These verses are precisely the ones that Epiphanius lists as effective polemic against Origen in his letter to John of Jerusalem.[94] Yet we must ask how likely it is that Epiphanius knew about Jerome's debate with Jovinian. Unfortunately, all of Jerome's letters written between 387 and 393 are lost—the very years in which he might have complained to Epiphanius and other friends about Jovinian's views. Hence we have no epistolary evidence for this period. We do know, however, that Epiphanius was in Palestine in 394 and that he then had contact with Jerome's monastery: recall that he had ordained Jerome's brother Paulinianus, who was a monk in Jerome's Bethlehem establishment.[95] That Epiphanius knew about the debate that had recently raged between Jerome and Jovinian thus appears highly probable.

Jerome had been hot with anger at Jovinian's insinuations that his ascetic fervor, with its alleged degradation of reproduction, verged on "Manicheanism." He stormed in reply, "I am no Marcionite, Manichean, or Encratite. I know that God's first commandment was 'Be fruitful, multiply, and fill the earth' "—an assertion that he then undercuts by arguing the superiority of virginity to even "honorable marriage."[96] Yet Jerome as well as Jovinian could manipulate Genesis for his own purposes: he points out to his readers that Adam and Eve were virgins in Paradise before the Fall and that marriage entered human life only when they were expelled from Eden.[97] It is likely, I think, that Epiphanius had registered, via Jerome's debate, that the Genesis texts must be used as central exegetical strategies

---

[92] Jerome, *Ep.* 54, 18 (*CSEL* 54, 485): in this letter to Furia, dated to 394, Jerome says that he published his book against Jovinian "about two years ago."

[93] Jerome, *Adversus Jovinianum* I, 5 (*PL* 23, 225–226).

[94] Epiphanius, *Ep. ad Iohannem Episcopum* (= Jerome, *Ep.* 51) 4 (*CSEL* 54, 402).

[95] Epiphanius, *Ep. ad Iohannem Episcopum* (= Jerome, *Ep.* 51) 1 (*CSEL* 54, 396–397).

[96] Jerome, *Adversus Jovinianum* I, 3 (*PL* 23, 223). How quickly Jerome forgot that he as a Christian intended to champion Genesis 1:28 is suggested by his *Epistle* 52, 10, dated to 394: there, "be fruitful and multiply" is relegated to the status of the "old law" and mocked (*CSEL* 54, 432).

[97] Jerome, *Adversus Jovinianum* I, 16 (*PL* 23, 246).

for any argument about embodiment and reproduction. Epiphanius's appeal to Genesis stems not from antiquarian interests, but from the religious concerns of his own day.

A second new point that had come to prominence in Origenist (and anti-Origenist) discussion since Epiphanius's writing of the *Panarion* was the theme of the restoration of the devil to his "pre-Fall" position. In Origen's scheme, this assertion expressed both his passionate conviction that the power of God's goodness is such that it will eventually overcome even entrenched evil,[98] and his claim that *all* rational beings will be restored to their original status as minds.[99] While Origen's motivation for his thesis on the restoration of the devil focuses on theology and "anthropology," Epiphanius's objection to the teaching, in contrast, is moral: all differentiation on the basis of merit would be eradicated if the devil were to be made equal to the blessed saints. If John the Baptist, John the apostle and evangelist, Peter, Isaiah, Jeremiah, and the other prophets are to be *coheredes* with the devil,[100] the hope of reward for righteous living is rendered meaningless.

Epiphanius's second new argument also carries a resonance from the debate between Jerome and Jovinian. As I have argued elsewhere,[101] early in his career Jerome had rehearsed Origen's opinions on the *apokatastasis* in general and on the restoration of the devil in particular without indicating any disapproval of these views[102]—a point that Rufinus was quick to note.[103] In the course of the 390s, however, Jerome retreated from any association with this theory, no doubt in part because its implication played to Jovinian's argument that there is only one reward in heaven, that there will be no "ranks" of the more or less virtuous on the basis of ascetic fervor.[104] In response to Jovinian, Jerome affirmed differentiation: it is not merely a question of dividing the sheep from the goats, but there will be a further division among the sheep themselves.[105] Since God does not act unjustly, he cannot be imagined to "assign equal rewards for unequal de-

[98] Origen, *De principiis* I, 6, 1; 6, 4; III, 6 (*GCS* 22, 78–79, 84–85, 279–291). See also Joseph Wilson Trigg, *Origen: The Bible and Philosophy in the Third-century Church*, esp. 110–111.

[99] Origen, *De principiis* I, 7, 5; II, 11, 6; III, 6, 1–4 (*GCS* 22, 91–94, 189–191, 279–286).

[100] Epiphanius, *Ep. ad Iohannem Episcopum* (= Jerome, *Ep.* 51) 5 (*CSEL* 54, 403). In Romans 8:17, the *sunklēronomoi*/*coheredes* language is used to designate humans as "fellow heirs with Christ"; in Ephesians 3:6, it is used to indicate that Gentiles who convert to Christianity will be "fellow heirs" with converted Jews.

[101] Elizabeth A. Clark, "The Place of Jerome's Commentary on Ephesians in the Origenist Controversy: The Apokatastasis and Ascetic Ideals," 154–171.

[102] Jerome, *Comm. in Ep. ad Ephesios* II (on Ephesians 4:16) (*PL* 26, 535); cf. on Ephesians 4:3–4 (*PL* 26, 527). On "*apokatastasis*," see *RAC* 4 (1950), cols. 510–516.

[103] Rufinus, *Apologia contra Hieronymum* I, 35–36; 44–45 (*CCL* 20, 69–70, 79–82).

[104] For the arguments from Scripture, see Jerome, *Adversus Jovinianum* I, 3; II, 18–20 (*PL* 23, 223–224, 326–329).

[105] Jerome, *Adversus Jovinianum* II, 22 (*PL* 23, 330).

serts."[106] Thus Jerome argues that although Noah and his sons were all delivered in the Flood, Ham was not of the same merit as Noah; likewise, although both Peter and Caiaphas denied Jesus, they were not equally wicked.[107] Stratification of both the saved and the condemned is essential in order to "fine-tune" moral judgment.

Epiphanius's objection to the Origenist thesis concerning the restoration of the devil rehearses precisely the same rhetorical pattern: differentiation on the basis of personal merit must be preserved at all costs. If the less good are admitted on the same basis as the very good, the "slippery slope" has been uncovered that (in Jerome's phrase) would result in whoremongers being rated equal to virgins[108] or (in the *apokatastasis* discussion of Epiphanius) the devil to John the Baptist, Peter, and the prophets.[109]

There was, however, a second probable stimulus to Epiphanius's discussion of the *apokatastasis*: the Evagrian theology of the 390s that was fuelling Origenist discussion in the Egyptian desert. The particular clue comes in Epiphanius's critique of language about the "coinheritance" of the devil with the saints. This terminology permeates the writings of Evagrius, who borrowed it from Romans 8:17 and Ephesians 3:6 to express the spiritual state to which believers will be assumed along with Christ. He also uses the terms to differentiate between ranks of believers, between the person who will know the intellections of all beings after the first judgment (the "inheritor")[110] and the one who, achieving the final Unity, will delight in the contemplation of Christ (the "coinheritor").[111] Moreover, he employs the language of "inheritance" and "coinheritance" to contrast the divine nature of the Word with the human Jesus: the Word, he says, does not "inherit"; rather, Christ "inherits" the Word.[112] And, contrasting Christ with the Father, Evagrius posits that "Christ is inherited and inherits, but the Father is only inherited."[113] Thus we can assert that the "inheriting" and "coinheriting" language to which Epiphanius objects was used by the very Origenist monks whose views on a restoration to unity he wishes to combat.

More precisely, we know that the *apokatastasis*, the final restoration of all rational beings to unity, was a favorite theme of Evagrius. That this was considered to be an especially dangerous aspect of his theology is suggested by the fact that the bowdlerized second Syriac translation of his

[106] Jerome, *Adversus Jovinianum* II, 23 (*PL* 23, 333).
[107] Jerome, *Adversus Jovinianum* II, 25 (*PL* 23, 336).
[108] Jerome, *Adversus Jovinianum* I, 4 (*PL* 23, 225).
[109] Epiphanius, *Ep. ad Iohannem Episcopum* (= Jerome, *Ep.* 51) 5 (*CSEL* 54, 403).
[110] Evagrius Ponticus, *Kephalaia gnostica* IV, 4 (*PO* 28, 137).
[111] Evagrius Ponticus, *Kephalaia gnostica* IV, 8 (*PO* 28, 139).
[112] Evagrius Ponticus, *Kephalaia gnostica* IV, 9 (*PO* 28, 139); the S₁ translator changes this "suspicious" Christology: it is not Christ who inherits, but the *logikoi* (138).
[113] Evagrius Ponticus, *Kephalaia gnostica* IV, 78 (*PO* 28, 171).

Kephalaia gnostica (Guillaumont's "S_1" translation)[114] eliminates the *apokatastasis* teaching whenever possible, or at the very least modifies it to render it more "orthodox." The original Syriac translation that seems to preserve Evagrius's own teaching more accurately,[115] however, clearly indicates that the devil, too, will be included in the restoration to the original unity. Thus Evagrius over and again writes that "all" rational creatures will participate in the blessed end,[116] when no more "evil body" shall exist.[117] Then, "all" will come to know and contemplate Christ;[118] "every rational nature" will come to adore the name of the Lord.[119] Far from differentiating the sheep from the goats, or even among the ranks of "sheep," on which Jerome and Epiphanius insist, Evagrius has put the edge on Origen's point that God's goodness is so powerful that even the devil's malice will be overcome. Epiphanius's attack upon the Origenist notion of the restoration of the devil thus acquires an immediacy from debates of the 390s.

A third point in Epiphanius's letter to John of Jerusalem—expanded from its original mention in *Panarion* 64[120]—concerns the charge that Origen taught that Adam had lost the "image of God" in which he had been created. Here, as Henri Crouzel and Jon Dechow have argued,[121] Epiphanius exaggerates Origen's view. One interpretation of Origen's position on the "loss of the image" is that since God is incorporeal, his "image" must also be, and that with the precosmic fall of the rational beings into bodies, this incorporeality was lost.[122] Moreover, Crouzel notes, there are varying statements regarding the "image of God" and its fate within Origen's writing themselves: some passages point in the direction of affirming the loss of God's "image" through sin, while others suggest that humans retain the "image" despite their waywardness.[123] Thus there is no consistent position to be found in Origen's remarks on "the image" on which to base a definitive judgment; perhaps the concept was not of central concern

[114] Guillaumont, *Les "Kephalaia Gnostica,"* 236–238; also see Antoine and Claire Guillaumont, "Le Texte véritable," 198–201.

[115] Guillaumont, *Les "Kephalaia Gnostica,"* 25–30, 236–239; Antoine and Claire Guillaumont, "Le Texte véritable," esp. 198–203.

[116] Evagrius Ponticus, *Kephalaia gnostica* III, 51 (*PO* 28, 119); the S_1 translator emends Evagrius to state that there will be two groups, one of which will receive joy and the other, torment (118).

[117] Evagrius Ponticus, *Kephalaia gnostica* III, 40 (*PO* 28, 113); S_1 changes this to read that it is in accordance with the state of their conduct that God clothes the *logikoi* with bodies (112).

[118] Evagrius Ponticus, *Kephalaia gnostica* VI, 15 (*PO* 28, 223); S_1 reduces the contemplators of Christ to "those who obey him" (222).

[119] Evagrius Ponticus, *Kephalaia gnostica* VI, 27 (*PO* 28, 229). For Evagrius on the restoration of the devil, also see his *Scholia ad Proverbia* 95; 143 (*SC* 340, 194, 238).

[120] Epiphanius, *Panarion* 64, 4 (*GCS* 31², 412).

[121] Henri Crouzel, *Théologie de l'image de Dieu chez Origène*, 206–211; Dechow, *Dogma*, 307.

[122] Dechow, *Dogma*, 305.

[123] Crouzel, *Théologie*, 206–211, with full references.

to Origen, who emphasized more strongly the restoration of rational beings to their original condition.

Epiphanius, however, was of no mind to take a generous approach to Origen's teaching: on the point of humans' loss of "the image," he interprets Origen through the teachings of more radical Origenists of his own day, such as Evagrius, who clearly stated that humans had lost the "image of God." Epiphanius appeals directly to Scripture: since the Bible nowhere states that Adam lost "the image," we should not believe that either he or his descendants did. He lists a battery of Biblical texts to support his view. The fact, for example, that animals are subject to Adam's descendants even after the Fall is proof that humans still retain "the image." Adam's own son Seth is explicitly said to have possessed "the image": Genesis 4:25 and 5:3 are cited. God himself adduces as a justification for not shedding blood the fact that we have "the image" (Genesis 9:6). And Paul appeals (albeit somewhat confusedly) to the possession of "the image" by males as a reason for keeping their hair short (I Corinthians 11:7). With these and other Scriptural verses, Epiphanius thinks that he has bested the Origenists.[124]

Despite Epiphanius's location of seven Scriptural passages pertaining to the "image"—not the mere three for which John had apparently asked[125]—Epiphanius nowhere indicates *why* championing the retention of the "image of God" is such an important point. In fact, here, as in the *Ancoratus*,[126] he explicitly *rejects* defining in what "the image" consists. Although others, he reports, have conjectured that it was Christ's body, or the soul, or sensation, or virtue, or baptism, or human rulership, the speculators would have done better to stop their mouths and left the definition of "the image" as one of God's mysteries. Since they did not so refrain, they have plunged themselves into "a mire of sin."[127] Yet Epiphanius never states *why* their views are sinful: his adamance on this point appears simply as a reflex of his Biblical literalism.

As I argued in the previous chapter, late fourth-century discussion of the "image of God" was tied to a particular constellation of anti-imagistic teachings that ranged from Evagrius Ponticus's views on the *logismoi* to the anti-idolatry campaign waged by Christian churchmen in Egypt during the 390s. The tight association of "image of God" language with the discus-

---

[124] Epiphanius, *Ep. ad Iohannem Episcopum* (= Jerome, *Ep.* 51) 6 (*CSEL* 54, 407–409), also citing James 3:7–9; Genesis 9:4–6; Psalm 38:7; Wisdom 2:23. For discussion of these passages in Epiphanius's argumentation, see Dechow, *Dogma*, 429–433.

[125] Epiphanius, *Ep. ad Iohannem Episcopum* (= Jerome, *Ep.* 51) 7 (*CSEL* 54, 409).

[126] Epiphanius, *Ancoratus* 55 (*GCS* 25, 64–65). In his discussion of the Audians in *Panarion* 70, 2 (*GCS* 37², 234), Epiphanius

faults this group for holding that the "image" lies in the human body: this of course implies that God is corporeal and visible.

[127] Epiphanius, *Ep. ad Iohannem Episcopum* (= Jerome, *Ep.* 51) 7 (*CSEL* 54, 409–410). Epiphanius's view that human dominance over the earth is the central characteristic of "the image of God" suggests that he may have thought the human copying of God's rulership was the central issue at stake.

sion (and practice) of iconoclasm also occurs in Epiphanius, but here in a different combination. Having devoted two sections of his letter to John of Jerusalem to the claim that humans have retained "the image of God" despite sinfulness[128] (and having warned John to guard his own soul and not to "murmur" against him[129]), Epiphanius describes his own iconoclastic activity at the town of Anablatha: seeing in the local church a curtain with an image "either of Christ or of one of the saints," he ripped it to shreds as a blasphemous object. When the church custodians protested the loss of their property, Epiphanius offered to send them a new curtain from Cyprus.[130]

Beginning with Karl Holl in 1916,[131] scholars have extracted fragments of three iconoclastic writings now accepted as Epiphanius's from the writings of the ninth-century Byzantine patriarch Nicephorus that pertain to the Iconoclastic controversy. Surprisingly, the sentiments contained therein seem much closer to Evagrius's position on images than we might have expected, given Epiphanius's anti-Origenist stance. In a pamphlet against images and in a letter to Theodosius I (both probably written in 393–394,[132] the precise time of Epiphanius's letter to John of Jerusalem), and in a testament to his community dating from some years later,[133] Epiphanius repeatedly sounds the theme that having pictures of Christ, Mary, and the martyrs is, at root, idolatry[134]—a theme earlier expressed in the *Ancoratus* when he argued that to represent spiritual things through an image is a stage on the way to worshiping pagan gods.[135] From the viewpoint of the 390s, Epiphanius fears that the devil is again on the prowl to lead Christians back into idolatry.[136] Epiphanius marshalls a variety of arguments to prove his point.

For one, he alleges that pictures are basically deceptive: they confuse truth and falsity by depicting something as present when it is not.[137] Image makers rely on their fantasies to represent things that they cannot possibly have known.[138] The Bible correctly rules out images,[139] for God is incom-

---

[128] Epiphanius, *Ep. ad Iohannem Episcopum* (= Jerome, *Ep.* 51) 6–7 (*CSEL* 54, 407–410).

[129] Epiphanius, *Ep. ad Iohannem Episcopum* (= Jerome, *Ep.* 51) 8 (*CSEL* 54, 410–411).

[130] Epiphanius, *Ep. ad Iohannem Episcopum* (= Jerome, *Ep.* 51) 9 (*CSEL* 54, 411).

[131] Karl Holl, "Die Schriften des Epiphanius gegen die Bilderverehrung," 351–387. Georg Ostrogorsky's doubts about the attribution of the fragments to Epiphanius have not found favor with other scholars: see Ostrogorsky, *Studien zur Geschichte des byzantinischen Bilderstreites.*

[132] Holl, "Die Schriften," 382.

[133] Hans Georg Thümmel, "Die bilderfeindlichen Schriften des Epiphanios von Salamis," 171.

[134] Epiphanius, Fragment 1 (Holl, "Die Schriften," 356).

[135] Epiphanius, *Ancoratus* 102 (*GCS* 25, 122–123).

[136] Epiphanius, Fragment 19 (Holl, "Die Schriften," 360).

[137] Epiphanius, Fragment 3 (Holl, "Die Schriften," 357).

[138] Epiphanius, Fragments 24; 26 (Holl, "Die Schriften," 361–362).

[139] Epiphanius, Fragment 18 (Holl, "Die Schriften," 359).

prehensible and inexpressible;[140] the only memorial we should have to God is one we bear, incorporeally, in our hearts.[141] Epiphanius knows that some of his opponents argue that since Christ became a human, we can legitimately depict him as a human: they forget, Epiphanius retorts, that even when Christ was a man, he still retained his similarity (*homoios*) to God the Father.[142] The image makers thus inappropriately use dead matter to represent the eternally living Christ.[143] Last, in an argument startlingly like Evagrius's, Epiphanius adds that it is unseemly to let what we see through our eyes excite us, stirring our minds to wander unsteadily.[144]

Given this strong anti-imagistic correspondence with Evagrius's teaching, Epiphanius's failure to produce an explanation for *why* Christians must affirm the permanent retention of the "image of God" in humans is striking: that the language of "image" is used in Genesis seems to be the only basis for his position. We are reminded that Origenist sympathizers in Palestine, such as Rufinus, had labelled Epiphanius an "Anthropomorphite,"[145] and that the so-called Anthropomorphite contingent in Egypt had allegedly insisted that God's "image" was visibly present in humans, as detailed in the last chapter. Yet the allegation of Anthropomorphitism flies in the face of Epiphanius's own affirmation of God's incorporeality and of the strong anti-imagistic stance he adopted in his iconoclastic writings. Perhaps he, like the later Iconodules, would stress that it is permissible to affirm an "image" even though great differences exist between it and its model.[146] A less charitable explanation of Epiphanius's position might posit that it is characterized by the inconsistency that marks other aspects of his theology.

Epiphanius's opposition to Origenism thus appears less compelling than one might originally have predicted. His failure to argue points or to explain his insistence that certain teachings must be upheld, in addition to his inconsistent position on the resurrection body, weakens the force of his critique. Nonetheless, Epiphanius's version of the charges against Origen was to influence his successors, Theophilus and Jerome, even though each made independent readings of Origen's works and each had different experiences of contemporary Origenism.

---

[140] Epiphanius, Fragment 12 (Holl, "Die Schriften," 359).

[141] Epiphanius, Fragment 33 (Holl, "Die Schriften," 363).

[142] Epiphanius, Fragments 13; 15 (Holl, "Die Schriften," 359).

[143] Epiphanius, Fragment 7 (Holl, "Die Schriften," 358).

[144] Epiphanius, Fragment 33 (Holl, "Die Schriften," 363).

[145] Jerome, *Apologia contra Rufinum* III,

23 (*SC* 303, 274, 276); but cf. Jerome, *Contra Ioannem* 11 (*PL* 23, 380), in which Epiphanius is said to have declared himself to be an anti-Anthropomorphite. In any event, it is of interest that "Joseph's" *Hypomnestikon* 62 (*PG* 106, 157) associates Anthropomorphism with Eleutheropolis, Epiphanius's home town. I thank Stephen Goranson for this point.

[146] For a discussion of the arguments, see above, p. 59.

THEOPHILUS'S VERSION OF
ORIGENISM AND HIS ANTI-ORIGENIST
CHARGES

Although Theophilus intervened in
the Origenist dispute in Palestine in 396, his letter that attempts in that
year to reconcile John of Jerusalem and Jerome is not extant.[147] The first
anti-Origenist statement outlining his program of attack dates from four
years later. In the spring or summer of A.D. 400, Theophilus reports to
Jerome[148] and to Epiphanius[149] that he has struck down the *furiosi homines*
who had sown the Origenist heresy in the Nitrian monasteries.[150] Nitrian
monasticism has, thanks to his efforts, been restored to its former "modest
and sweet" condition.[151] The holy monks have been freed from "the serpents of Origen" who abandoned their caves—by which Theophilus appears to mean that the Tall Brothers, "raving with bacchantic fury on behalf of the new heresy," had departed for Constantinople.[152] Theophilus's
two letters aim to enlist Jerome's literary support against Origenism[153] and
to urge Epiphanius to summon a council of bishops on Cyprus to condemn Origen. In addition, he urges the participants in the proposed council to send their statement of condemnation to churches in Constantinople
and in Asia Minor, so that other bishops may be duly warned of the Origenist threat.[154] Also in 400 or shortly after, Theophilus wrote both to
"Origenist monks" and to "the saints in Scete,"[155] but of these letters there
remain only fragments listing a single error of Origen: that he mocked the
resurrection from the dead.[156]

Thus the first detailed statement of Theophilus's charges against Origenism now extant is the synodal letter to the bishops of Palestine and Cyprus
that he appended to his private epistle to Epiphanius.[157] We owe the preservation of the synodal letter to Jerome's translation of the copy sent him
by Epiphanius, probably in the fall of 400,[158] the first of four letters by

---

[147] Pierre Nautin, "La Lettre de Théophile
d'Alexandrie à l'église de Jérusalem et la réponse de Jean de Jérusalem (juin-juillet
396)," esp. 392: the general themes of Theophilus's letter can be reconstructed from Jerome's *Against John of Jerusalem* and his Epistle 82 to Theophilus.

[148] Theophilus, *Epp. ad Hieronymum* (=
Jerome, *Epp.* 87 and 89) (*CSEL* 55, 140,
142–143).

[149] Theophilus, *Ep. ad Epiphanium* (= Jerome, *Ep.* 90) (*CSEL* 55, 143–145).

[150] Theophilus, *Ep. ad Hieronymum* (= Jerome, *Ep.* 87) (*CSEL* 55, 140).

[151] Theophilus, *Ep. ad Hieronymum* (= Jerome, *Ep.* 89) (*CSEL* 55, 143).

[152] Theophilus, *Ep. ad Epiphanium* (= Jerome, *Ep.* 90) (*CSEL* 55, 144).

[153] Theophilus, *Ep. ad Hieronymum* (= Jerome, *Ep.* 87) (*CSEL* 55, 140).

[154] Theophilus, *Ep. ad Epiphanium* (= Jerome, *Ep.* 90) (*CSEL* 55, 144–145).

[155] *CPG* II, 2602, 2603.

[156] See the fragment in Justinian, *Liber adversus Origenem* (*PG* 86, 967).

[157] Theophilus, *Ep. ad Epiphanium* (= Jerome, *Ep.* 90) (*CSEL* 55, 143–145).

[158] Theophilus, *Synodica ep.* (= Jerome,
Ep. 92) (*CSEL* 55, 147–155); Epiphanius's
accompanying letter to Jerome is *Epistle* 91
in the letters of Jerome (*CSEL* 55, 145–
146). Favale (*Teofilo*, 112) thinks that The-

Theophilus detailing the errors of Origen that Jerome translated into Latin. The synodal letter of 400 is preserved as Epistle 92 of Jerome; the festal letter of 401 as Epistle 96, that of 402 as Epistle 98, and that of 404 as Epistle 100. These letters contain by far the most extensive discussions extant of Theophilus's anti-Origenist argument. They can be supplemented by material derived from Theophilus's sermons and from fragments of his letters preserved either in Greek or in translation.[159] We thus can trace Theophilus's anti-Origenist argumentation over a four-year period. Surprisingly, the shortness of the time span in no way diminishes our ability to track his shifts in emphasis: we shall see how quickly he lost interest in combatting Origenism, a point also noted by his own contemporaries.[160]

In his synodal letter of 400, Theophilus first explains to the bishops of Palestine and Cyprus his activities against Origenists in the Nitrian monasteries. He claims that he was "forced" to his actions by the prayers and requests of the abbots and priests who presided over the (unspecified) monasteries.[161] His appeal to the rhetoric of compulsion, however, may well be overstated: we now know from recently published fragments of Theophilus's letters that he had agents positioned in the Egyptian desert to inquire about the monks' theological views. The agents apparently had reported to the bishop that the monks seemed orthodox on Trinitarian issues, and were willing to anathematize both Origen's view that prayer should not be offered to Jesus and his "blasphemies" about the Son and the Holy Spirit. For Theophilus, this was hardly enough: he instructs the agents that they must press the monks further to uncover their opinions on how souls and bodies come together, on the restoration of the devil and of sinners to an original purity.[162] The import of this fragment is to suggest that Theophilus may not have waited for the "prayers and requests" of churchmen to launch his campaign against Origenism in the monasteries. He may rather have taken the situation into his own hands, as the narrations of Palladius and the ecclesiastical historians suggest.[163]

We also learn the exact targets of Theophilus's wrath from the opening section of his synodal letter: someone who had cut off his ear, someone

---

ophilus's Synodal Letter dates from August or early September 400, since the bishops gathered in Jerusalem were there for the Feast of the Dedication, which was observed September 14–21.

[159] On the state of the Theophilan corpus, see *CPG* II, 112–134; Favale, *Teofilo*, pt. I; H.-G. Opitz, "Theophilus von Alexandrien," cols. 2159–2165; Marcel Richard, "Les Ecrits de Théophile d'Alexandrie," 33–50; Tito Orlandi, "Theophilus of Alexandria in Coptic Literature," 100–104.

[160] Socrates, *HE* VI, 17 (*PG* 67, 716).

[161] Theophilus, *Synodica ep.* 2 (= Jerome, *Ep.* 92) 1 (*CSEL* 55, 147).

[162] Theophilus, Fragment 1, in Marcel Richard, "Nouveaux Fragments de Théophile d'Alexandrie," 61; cf. Richard's commentary, 58.

[163] See references and discussion above, pp. 44–49.

(else) who cut out his tongue, and "certain foreigners" who had lived in Egypt "for a short while," but who now had departed for Palestine ("your province"); the latter are described as "poor in grace but rich in money."[164] The first, earless target can be readily identified as Ammonius, one of the Tall Brothers, who cut off his left ear to prevent forcible ordination to the priesthood or bishopric.[165] When Timothy of Alexandria (bishop from 381–385) threatened to ordain him anyway, Ammonius allegedly swore that he would cut out his tongue as well, if necessary, to prevent ordination.[166] Thus we also have a possible candidate for Theophilus's second referent.

We may, however, have an even better candidate. Evagrius Ponticus. In his description of the Egyptian monks that includes a section of extracts by and about Evagrius,[167] the church historian Socrates reports the story of Ammonius's cutting off his ear to avoid episcopal ordination. Socrates continues:

> A long time after this, Evagrius, when Theophilus, bishop of the city of Alexandria, wished to carry him off to be a bishop, escaped without any part of his body mutilated. Evagrius happened to meet up with Ammonius and said somewhat jokingly to him that he had acted badly in cutting off his ear; by doing so he had made himself guilty before God. Ammonius replied to him, "And what about you, Evagrius: do you think that you will escape punishment when you have cut off your tongue? From love of self you have not wanted to use that gift which has been given you."[168]

Although Ammonius's charge is metaphorical—that by refusing to use his gift of speech for priestly service in the church, as Theophilus wished, Evagrius had in effect "cut off his tongue"—the suggestion that we may here have a hidden reference to Evagrius is intriguing. This is the first of several hints prompting us to suspect that although Evagrius is never directly named by Theophilus in his extant letters, his theology forms a backdrop for Theophilus's charges against Origenism.

As for the "foreigners" who had now fled to Palestine, this could not include Evagrius, who had died in 399, and perhaps not the Tall Brothers, who were from Egypt, but may possibly include monks who fled The-

---

[164] Theophilus, *Synodica ep.* (= Jerome, *Ep.* 92) 1 (*CSEL* 55, 148).

[165] Palladius, *Historia Lausiaca* 11, 1–2 (Butler ed., vol. 2: 33).

[166] Palladius, *Historia Lausiaca* 11, 3 (Butler ed., vol. 2: 33).

[167] Socrates, *HE* IV, 23 (*PG* 67, 516–521).

[168] Socrates, *HE* IV, 23 (*PG* 67, 521). The reference to Theophilus's attempt to lure Evagrius into ecclesiastical service correlates well with the sentiment of Epistle 13 of Evagrius, whose addressee may well be Theophilus. In the letter, Evagrius protests that since the monk's duty is to rid himself of the passions and of the *eidōla* of the world, he cannot in good faith leave the monastery for the secular world. See Bunge, *Evagrios Pontikos, Briefe*, 187, 225–226.

ophilus's attack such as Palladius or John Cassian.[169] That they are called "rich" points directly to Isidore and his circle, whose wealth paid for the expenses of the fleeing monks, according to Theophilus.[170] Having noted the main targets of his anti-Origenist campaign, Theophilus begins a statement of the charges.

Theophilus reports in the synodal letter that he had assembled the other Egyptian bishops for a seminar, in effect, on the books of Origen.[171] In the course of his letter, he mentions three of the works they read: *On First Principles*,[172] *On Prayer*,[173] and *On the Resurrection*.[174] Thus even though Theophilus knew Epiphanius's anti-Origenist polemic, he also had made an independent survey of Origen's writings on his own.

Theophilus's charges against Origen commence with an attack on his subordinationism, already targeted by Epiphanius. Theophilus reports that Origen in the *On First Principles* taught that although the Son is truth when compared to us, he is a "lie" when compared to the Father; that Christ's reign will one day end; and that "to the extent that Peter and Paul differ from the Savior, to that extent is the Savior less than the Father."[175]

Next, Theophilus rapidly skims through Origen's other errors: he teaches that the devil will be restored and submitted to God along with Christ;[176] he proclaims that prayer should be directed to the Father alone, not to the Son nor even to the Father and Son together;[177] he denies the resurrection from the dead, holding instead that "after many ages" our bodies will be reduced to nothing and dissolve into thin air—but that in the meantime, resuscitated bodies will be both corruptible and mortal.[178]

---

[169] See above, pp. 37–38, and below, pp. 189, 249.

[170] Theophilus, *Synodica ep.* (= Jerome, *Ep.* 92) 3 (*CSEL* 55, 151). Palladius also describes Isidore as "very rich and exceedingly generous" (*Historia Lausiaca* 1, 4 [Butler ed., vol. 2: 15]).

[171] Theophilus, *Synodica ep.* (= Jerome, *Ep.* 92) 1 (*CSEL* 55, 148).

[172] Theophilus, *Synodica ep.* (= Jerome, *Ep.* 92) 2; 4 (*CSEL* 55, 148, 152).

[173] Theophilus, *Synodica ep.* (= Jerome, *Ep.* 92) 2 (*CSEL* 55, 148–149); Theophilus cites from *De oratione* 15.

[174] Theophilus, *Synodica ep.* (= Jerome, *Ep.* 92) 4 (*CSEL* 55, 152).

[175] Theophilus, *Synodica ep.* (= Jerome, *Ep.* 92) 2 (*CSEL* 55, 149). Henri Crouzel disputes the allegation that Origen taught that Christ's reign would come to an end: see his article, "Origène a-t-il tenu que la regne du Christ prendrait fin?", 51–61. Interestingly, Crouzel does not wish to pin the charge on Evagrius Ponticus, either (56–59, 61)—but Crouzel gives Evagrius a very "or-

thodox" interpretation (61). In this, his assessment of Evagrius seems closer to Bunge's and further from Guillaumont's.

[176] Theophilus, *Synodica ep.* (= Jerome, *Ep.* 92) 2 (*CSEL* 55, 149). That from the eternity of hell, no one is delivered, is also stressed in his "Homily on Repentance and Continence," in E. A. Wallis Budge, ed., tr., *Coptic Homilies in the Dialect of Upper Egypt, Edited from the Papyrus Codex Oriental 5001 in the British Museum*, Coptic, 66–79; English, 215–225. The eternity of hellfire is also affirmed in Theophilus's "Homily on Death and Judgment" (see *CPG* II, 2618); see the Syriac text and translation in Maurice Brière, "Un Homélie inédite de Théophile d'Alexandrie," 79–83.

[177] Theophilus, *Synodica ep.* (= Jerome, *Ep.* 92) 2 (*CSEL* 55, 149), citing *De oratione* 15.

[178] Theophilus, *Synodica ep.* (= Jerome, *Ep.* 92) 2 (*CSEL* 55, 149). Theophilus asks, how can this view represent the destruction of the devil and his empire of death?

As for the heavenly powers, Origen thinks that they receive their ranks, names, and duties through a precosmic fall.[179] He blasphemously posits that the angels gathered around Israel's sacrificial altar[180] and that Christ's foreknowledge was based on the movement of the stars.[181] Theophilus twice notes that Origen's teaching is mingled with "idolatry,"[182] a point he reinforces by claiming that Origenists in Alexandria had spoken against the destruction of the Serapeum "and other idols."[183] Origen is also faulted for his alleged tolerance toward magic.[184] From *On First Principles*, Theophilus derives the charge that for Origen Christ was not the Word of God incarnate but a soul who descended from the heavenly regions.[185] Also offensive to Theophilus is Origen's alleged thesis that Jesus will one day be crucified for the demons and evil spirits.[186] This list constitutes Theophilus's first summary of the errors in Origen's theology.

Other documents help to illuminate this early stage of Theophilus's attack upon Origen. José Declerck has argued that Greek fragments found in Codex Athos, Vatopédi 236 are from the proceedings of the synod of Alexandria that Theophilus convened in 399 or 400.[187] If so—and Declerck's case seems strong—these fragments supplement what we know from his synodal letter and from fragments regarding the synod preserved in Justinian's work against Origenism.[188]

The first fragment of the synodal report published by Declerck describes Origen's expulsion from the church of Alexandria by bishop Heraclas, described as a good doctor who feared the "abscess," the "ulcerous evil" of Origen and his teaching. After his expulsion from Alexandria, Origen settled in Caesarea, where "like a Jewish merchant" who appears outwardly honest, he mixed the bitter with the sweet. Among his several "senseless" teachings were that souls sinned in heaven and were shut in the prisons of bodies by God for purification and correction of the sins committed above.[189] Declerck identifies this fragment as from Theophilus's *Against Origen*, which Gennadius says contained a report of Heraclas' expulsion of Origen from the Alexandrian church.[190]

---

[179] Theophilus, *Synodica ep.* (= Jerome, *Ep.* 92) 2 (*CSEL* 55, 149).

[180] Theophilus, *Synodica ep.* (= Jerome, *Ep.* 92) 2 (*CSEL* 55, 149–150).

[181] Theophilus, *Synodica ep.* (= Jerome, *Ep.* 92) 2 (*CSEL* 55, 150).

[182] Theophilus, *Synodica ep.* (= Jerome, *Ep.* 92) 2; 5 (*CSEL* 55, 150, 153).

[183] Theophilus, *Synodica ep.* (= Jerome, *Ep.* 92) 3 (*CSEL* 55, 150).

[184] Theophilus, *Synodica ep.* (= Jerome, *Ep.* 92) 4 (*CSEL* 55, 152).

[185] Theophilus, *Synodica ep.* (= Jerome, *Ep.* 92) 4 (*CSEL* 55, 152).

[186] Theophilus, *Synodica ep.* (= Jerome, *Ep.* 92) 4 (*CSEL* 55, 152).

[187] José Declerck, "Théophile d'Alexandrie contre Origène: Nouveaux fragments de l'*Epistula Synodalis Prima* (*CPG* 2595)," 495–507.

[188] Justinian, *Liber adversus Origenem* (*PG* 86, 969–971); see *CPG* II, 2595. The fragment concerns Origen's expulsion from the Alexandrian church and his teaching on the preexistence of souls.

[189] Theophilus, Fragment 1, *Ep. synodalis prima* (Declerck ed., tr., "Théophile," Greek, 503–504; French, 504–505).

[190] Declerck, "Théophile," 507; cf. Gennadius, *De viris inlustribus* 34 (*TU* 14,1, 73–74); cf. note 187.

The second Greek fragment from the synodal letter expounds more fully the argument against the preexistence and fall of souls. Theophilus here argues that if preexistent souls fell, as Origen held, then the prophet Zechariah should not have written that the Lord "formed the spirit of man within him" (Zechariah 12:1): he rather should have said that God "enclosed" or "cast down" the spirit. Since, however, this is not Zechariah's wording, we must believe with the prophet that it is God who made man's spirit and placed it within him. Theophilus then mocks Origen's pretentious claim to know what happened in the heavens.[191]

To these fragments, we can add still another testimony that Marcel Richard thinks can be precisely pinpointed to Holy Thursday (March 29) of the year 400:[192] Theophilus's "Homily on the Mystical Meal."[193] Richard notes that the two "crimes" attributed to Theophilus's opponents in this Homily—that they think badly of Christ and that they profane the resurrection of Christ—are nearly identical with the charges in the festal letter of 401, and suggest that the Homily should be dated to the early stage of Theophilus's attack on Origenism. Although Origen is not directly named, the target is clearly Origenism. Theophilus first locates the enemy that he urges his congregation to flee: the desert monks who clothe themselves in "tunics without sleeves." Although they wear the signs of the monastic life, they do not embody its requisite virtues. We should guard against these men with their "garments of skins."[194] This witticism leads us directly to the Origenist exegesis of Genesis 3:21, which, as we have seen, had become a central issue in the debate over the creation or acquisition of bodies. These monks are said to have caused a disorder in "our city"—that is, Alexandria.[195]

What stumbling blocks do these monks set to trip up believers? According to Theophilus, they shatter faith in the resurrection. Moreover, they deny the likeness of Christ to the Father on the grounds that the Incarnation differentiated a human being from the Godhead, a hint that the later Christological errors associated with Evagrian Origenism as developed in the fifth and sixth centuries may already have been noticeable among the formulations of the Egyptian monks in the 390s.[196] Against this view, Theophilus argues that if we confess that it is the body of God that is distributed in the Eucharist, then we must affirm that Christ is truly God. In drinking the "blood of God" in the Eucharist, we do not take the "naked God" (*theos gymnos*)—that is, one of the Trinity—but the Word of God

---

[191] Theophilus, Fragment 2, *Ep. synodalis prima* (Declerck ed., tr., "Théophile," Greek, 505–506; French, 506–507; cf. n.189 above.

[192] Marcel Richard, "Une Homélie de Théophile d'Alexandrie sur l'institution de l'Eucharistie," 52–54.

[193] *CPG* II, 2617; text of *In mysticam*

coenam in *PG* 77, 1016–1029.

[194] Theophilus, *In mysticam coenam* (PG 77, 1028).

[195] Theophilus, *In mysticam coenam* (PG 77, 1028).

[196] See especially Guillaumont, *Les "Kephalaia Gnostica,"* 147–159.

made flesh. If Christ were only human, the holy table would not be able to provide communicants with life eternal.[197]

In these brief lines, I think, we encounter not so much a criticism of Origen's own teachings, but of the Origenism then flourishing in the Egyptian desert, for which the Eucharistic debate had acquired central importance."[198] Most dramatically, the comparison between the "naked God" and God "enfleshed" in Christ carries strong Evagrian associations: recall Evagrius's phrase in his *Epistula fidei*, that the original Godhead was "naked" (*gymnos*) and received "clothing" only with the Incarnation, a view Evagrius supports by quoting Matthew 25:36, "I was naked and you clothed me."[199] Thus if Richard's dating of the "Homily on the Mystical Meal" to the year 400 is correct, Theophilus gives evidence that he already knows some of the distinctive issues and language of the Origenist debate that were occupying the desert monks. He had, it appears, done more than conduct a study group with his fellow bishops on writings of Origen himself. Origen is here interpreted through the lens of Evagrian Origenism.

We have not only Theophilus's letter of 400 to the bishops of Palestine and Cyprus, gathered in Jerusalem for the Feast of the Dedication, but also his addressees' response. From it we infer either that Origenism was not nearly so far-flung in its reach as Theophilus had feared, or that the Palestinian bishops were discreetly refusing to lend him any ammunition for his anti-Origenist cause: the bishop of Jerusalem himself, John, was an Origenist sympathizer.[200] Never, they replied, had they heard anyone teaching the points that Theophilus had identified as Origenist: that Christ's kingdom will come to an end,[201] that the devil will be restored, or that the Son is not the truth when compared to the Father. Rather, the only heresy that had caused recent problems in Palestine was Apollinarianism, and only "a few" heretics of this stripe remained.[202] The sincerity of the bishops' testimony might well be questioned from the one other response we have to Theophilus's synodal letter: a private letter to Theophilus from Dionysius, bishop of Lydda (Diospolis), who warmly congratulates Theophilus for expelling the dreadful Origenist heretics and urges him to keep up his campaign.[203] *Someone* in Palestine knew about Origenists and thought they should be rooted out.

In his festal letter of 401 (= Jerome, *Epistle* 96),[204] Theophilus returns

---

[197] Theophilus, *In mysticam coenam* (*PG* 77, 1028–1029).

[198] See above, pp. 63–66.

[199] Evagrius Ponticus, *Ep. fidei* 8 (*PG* 32, 261); see the discussion above, p. 62nn. 102–103, for the ascription of this work to Evagrius.

[200] See Jerome, *Contra Ioannem* 4; 6; 18 (*PL* 23, 374–376, 386).

[201] *Responsum synodi Hierosolymitanae ad*

superiorem Theophili synodicam ep. (= Jerome, *Ep.* 93) (*CSEL* 55, 155); cf. Crouzel, "Origène a-t-il tenu," 52.

[202] *Responsum synodi Hierosolymitanae* (= Jerome, *Ep.* 93) (*CSEL* 55, 155).

[203] Dionysius, *Ep. ad Theophilum* (= Jerome, *Ep.* 94) (*CSEL* 55, 156–157).

[204] Some Greek fragments of this Sixteenth Festal Letter are preserved in F. Diekamp, *Doctrina Patrum De Incarnatione*

to many of the same themes. The angelic city above is free (Galatians 4:26) and knows no sin, no dissensions, no ruins, no transmigrations; and any who do not confess Christ (such as the Jews) are not worthy to be its citizens.[205] After repeating errors that others—not Origen—hold regarding Christ, Theophilus attacks the Origenist theme that Christ's reign will someday come to an end.[206] To Theophilus, this view sounds subordinationist: if Christ's reign were to end, so would his divinity, and then he would cease to be one with God.[207] The restoration of the devil is also said to be one-of-a-piece with subordinationism: as Jesus is demoted, the devil is promoted. For Theophilus, such a denigration of Christ is blasphemy.[208] While even the Magi[209] and Pilate[210] confess that Christ is King of the Jews, Origen repudiates their pious confession when he asserts that Christ's kingdom is not eternal.[211]

The lack of security for believers that attends Origen's scheme shocks Theophilus: souls may fall again, innumerable times, suggesting that Christ's Passion was to no avail.[212] As for the alleged Origenist notion that Christ will suffer for the demons, the claim entails the consequence that Christ will actually *become* one of the demons:[213] are we to imagine that Christ took up a "temple of demons" after he left the "temple of his body," Theophilus scoffs?[214] Once more, Origen is charged with holding that our bodies will be subject to corruption and death when they are raised[215]—yet if the body is reduced to nothing, as Origen is also alleged to have taught, the souls that fall once more will have to be furnished with new bodies.[216] The Origenist teaching on the fall of the rational creatures is again criticised,[217] especially that this fall accounts for the creation of the sun, the moon, and the stars.[218] On Origen's belief, we would have to think that there would have been no visible creatures unless the invisible

---

Verbi: Ein griechisches Florilegium aus der Wende des siebenten und achten Jahrhunderts, chap. 25, 180–183.

[205] Theophilus, *Ep. paschalis* (401) (= Jerome, *Ep.* 96) 2 (*CSEL* 55, 160): the teaching is not here ascribed to Origen.

[206] Theophilus, *Ep. paschalis* (401) (= Jerome, *Ep.* 96) 5 (*CSEL* 55, 162–163).

[207] Theophilus, *Ep. paschalis* (401) (= Jerome, *Ep.* 96) 7 (*CSEL* 55, 164–165).

[208] Theophilus, *Ep. paschalis* (401) (= Jerome, *Ep.* 96) 8 (*CSEL* 55, 165); Jeremiah 2:12–13 is cited as an appropriate sentiment against Origen's "blasphemy."

[209] Theophilus, *Ep. paschalis* (401) (= Jerome, *Ep.* 96) 8 (*CSEL* 55, 166).

[210] Theophilus, *Ep. paschalis* (401) (= Jerome, *Ep.* 96) 9 (*CSEL* 55, 166–167).

[211] Theophilus, *Ep. paschalis* (401) (= Jerome, *Ep.* 96) 8; 9 (*CSEL* 55, 166–167).

[212] Theophilus, *Ep. paschalis* (401) (= Jerome, *Ep.* 96) 9 (*CSEL* 55, 167).

[213] Theophilus, *Ep. paschalis* (401) (= Jerome, *Ep.* 96) 10 (*CSEL* 55, 168).

[214] Theophilus, *Ep. paschalis* (401) (= Jerome, *Ep.* 96) 12 (*CSEL* 55, 171–172).

[215] Theophilus, *Ep. paschalis* (401) (= Jerome, *Ep.* 96) 13 (*CSEL* 55, 172): how is this to conquer the empire of death, Theophilus asks?

[216] Theophilus, *Ep. paschalis* (401) (= Jerome, *Ep.* 96) 15 (*CSEL* 55, 174); on possible states of the resurrection body in Origen, see Crouzel, "La Doctrine origènienne," esp. 192–194, 257–258.

[217] Theophilus, *Ep. paschalis* (401) (= Jerome, *Ep.* 96) 17 (*CSEL* 55, 177).

[218] Theophilus, *Ep. paschalis* (401) (= Jerome, *Ep.* 96) 17 (*CSEL* 55, 177).

ones fell![219] Once more, Origen is blamed for lending his *patrocinium* to the magic arts[220]—and Theophilus implies that anyone who tolerates magic must also allow idolatry.[221]

Two new points surface in the festal letter of 401 that seemingly relate more to the Origenist debates of Theophilus's own day than to Origen's texts themselves. The first concerns the Eucharist and is used as an argument for why the demons cannot be saved: since we gain salvation by participating in Christ's body and blood in the Eucharist, as the words of institution indicate ("Take, eat . . ."), and since demons cannot share in his body and blood, they have no hope. Theophilus cites I Corinthians 10:20–21, that we should not "communicate with demons."[222] He may also hint at the unexpressed point that demons have no proper bodily substance that could allow them to share in Christ's body and blood: the "food" of the demons, Theophilus explains, is rather "those who deny God." Alternatively, the devil himself is said to be the "food" of the impious.[223] Likewise, the Eucharist is brought forward as an argument for the reality and meaningfulness of corporeal nature. Theophilus discounts the views of "Manicheans" like Origen, for Christ showed that the body is not submitted to "vanity" when he proclaimed in John 6:54, "Whoever does not eat my flesh and drink my blood will have no part with me."[224]

A second new issue for Theophilus in 401 is the implication of Origen's teaching for marriage and reproduction. If bodies could not have existed without souls first sinning in heaven and being cast down, chained to the "peniteniary" (*ergastulum*) of the body, marriage must be condemned. How could marriage be "honorable" and "immaculate" (Hebrews 13:4) if the soul becomes enclosed in a body only after it is stained with sin? Hannah, the mother of Samuel, would be guilty for desiring a child (I Samuel 1:10–11) if it were necessary for a soul to leave its beatitude, be weighted down by sin, and fall to earth in order for her to bear her son. When "Moses" foretold that God would multiply the Israelites a thousand times (Deuteronomy 1:10–11), are we to imagine that "crowds of souls in the heavens" were obliged to sin in order for the Israelite race to be established? How could David have said that to see your children's children is a blessing (Psalm 128:5–6) if souls must sin in order to increase the family line?[225]

Theophilus then turns to the argument that Epiphanius had mentioned

---

[219] Theophilus, *Ep. paschalis* (401) (= Jerome, *Ep.* 96) 17 (*CSEL* 55, 177).
[220] Theophilus, *Ep. paschalis* (401) (= Jerome, *Ep.* 96) 16 (*CSEL* 55, 176).
[221] Theophilus, *Ep. paschalis* (401) (= Jerome, *Ep.* 96) 16 (*CSEL* 55, 176).
[222] Theophilus, *Ep. paschalis* (401) (= Jerome, *Ep.* 96) 11 (*CSEL* 55, 169).

[223] Theophilus, *Ep. paschalis* (401) (= Jerome, *Ep.* 96) 11 (*CSEL* 55, 170), citing Habbakuk 1:16 and Psalm 74:14.
[224] Theophilus, *Ep. paschalis* (401) (= Jerome, *Ep.* 96) 17 (*CSEL* 55, 177).
[225] Theophilus, *Ep. paschalis* (401) (= Jerome, *Ep.* 96) 18 (*CSEL* 55, 177–179).

in his letter to John of Jerusalem in 394: the "reproduce, multiply, and fill the earth" commandment that God gave to Adam and Eve (Genesis 1:28) would be no *blessing* if souls had to sin and be sent down to earth in order for bodies to be born. Instead, the command would entail a curse—yet, Theophilus argues, the "curse" upon humans came only after they sinned in Eden by their own volition. God has constituted the nature of the human body directly; it does not originate through the sin of souls.[226] Origen and all "apocryphal Scriptures," Theophilus concludes, are to be rejected by believing Christians.[227]

When he compiled his next festal letter, of 402, Theophilus was not concerned attacking the Origenists until he had devoted seven sections to other matters, especially to the Apollinarian heresy.[228] Weaving his path from the Apollinarians' alleged teaching that Christ took his flesh from heaven, Theophilus remarks that neither did Christ have a preexistent soul in the heavens: such would not have been "his" soul.[229] Warning his audience against clothing themselves in "the tattered rags of the philosophers" (as did Origen) rather than "the new and most solid vestments of the Church,"[230] Theophilus excoriates Origen's teaching on the fall of souls. Most interesting, here for the first time, this precosmic fall of souls is described (in Jerome's Latin translation) as a *motus*:[231] assuming that *motus* is a translation of *kinēsis*, we are in the world of Evagrius, for whom *kinēsis* became the distinctive word used to denote the precosmic disruption that brought the process of physical creation in its train.[232] Here is yet another hint that Theophilus knew the language and concepts of Evagrian Origenism. He did not, however, openly share this knowledge with the recipients of his letter, a point that renders understandable Jerome's apparently complete ignorance of Evagrian theology until well after the controversy was supposedly over.

Just such a view of the origins of physicality is what Theophilus wants to challenge. The very beauty of the world (*kosmos*) depends upon its or-

[226] Theophilus, *Ep. paschalis* (401) (= Jerome, *Ep.* 96) 19 (*CSEL* 55, 179).

[227] Theophilus, *Ep. paschalis* (401) (= Jerome, *Ep.* 96) 20 (*CSEL* 55, 180). Whether or not the Greek fragment of Theophilus found in Codex Vat. Barber. gr. 569, which covers these identical themes on procreation, comes from this Sixteenth Festal Letter of 401 is unclear: see discussion in Marcel Richard, "Les Fragments exégétiques de Théophile d'Alexandrie et de Théophile d'Antioche," 388–389, esp. n.1.

[228] Theophilus, *Ep. paschalis* (402) (= Jerome, *Ep.* 98) (*CSEL* 55, 185–211): Apollinarians are chastized in sections 4–7 before

the Origenists are arrived at in section 8. Apollinaris is congratulated for attacking Origen, along with Arians and Eunomians— but this does not excuse Apollinaris' other errors (sec. 6, 191).

[229] Theophilus, *Ep. paschalis* (402) (= Jerome, *Ep.* 98) 8 (*CSEL* 55, 192–193).

[230] Theophilus, *Ep. paschalis* (402) (= Jerome, *Ep.* 98) 9 (*CSEL* 55, 193–194).

[231] Theophilus, *Ep. paschalis* (402) (= Jerome, *Ep.* 98) 10 (*CSEL* 55, 194).

[232] Evagrius Ponticus, *Kephalaia gnostica* I, 49; 51; III, 22; VI, 85 (*PO* 28,1, 41, 107, 253), and Guillaumont, *Les "Kephalaia Gnostica,"* 37–39, 244.

namentation with creatures. If the body is negatively evaluated, Christ should have freed our souls from our bodies rather than assumed a body himself. Likewise, he should not have promised a resurrection: how much better for souls to fly up to heaven than to be weighted down with corporeality.[233] On Origen's understanding of creation, there could be no ranking among the principalities, powers, thrones, and dominions without a precosmic fall:[234] that is, the hierarchy of celestial powers would be the product of sin.

Moreover, Theophilus writes, Origen's teaching implicates him in very dubious propositions about the Son of God. Theophilus believes that Origen's interpretation of Philippians 2:5–7 (the "self-emptying" of God in Christ) does not refer to the Son "himself," but only to his soul. Does this not mean that Origen thinks that the Savior's soul is divine? If he does, he has involved himself in idolatry, exchanging the image of the incorruptible God for that of a corruptible man (Romans 1:22–23).[235] Yet, on the other hand, if we hold (as Origen's theory might suggest) that Christ's soul was originally a mind (*mens*) that "cooled off," wouldn't this "cooling" stand against the Gospel affirmations of Christ's constancy in love?[236] Worse, Origen compares the unity of the Father and the Son to the unity existing between the Son of God and the soul he assumes.[237] For Theophilus, this comparison implies the erroneous view that the nature of soul and the nature of divinity are one; rather, the "soul" should be understood as a substance made by the Son[238] in his role as creating Word.

According to Theophilus in this festal letter of 402, Origen slanderously limits God's power by positing that God made only as many creatures as he could control. Rather, Christians should believe that God made the number of creatures that "ought to have been made,"[239] since God is not controlled by matter.[240]

Once again, the Magi are enlisted to show up the errors of Origen: he should rather have behaved as they did, abandoning their unbelief and ignorance to acknowledge the King of the Jews and to bring him gifts. Theophilus now indulges in a bit of allegorical exegesis regarding the significance of the gifts: the gold represents the splendor with which the true faith shines forth; the frankincense signifies the perfume of "sweet-smelling

---

[233] Theophilus, *Ep. paschalis* (402) (= Jerome, *Ep.* 98) 10 (*CSEL* 55, 195).

[234] Theophilus, *Ep. paschalis* (402) (= Jerome, *Ep.* 98) 12 (*CSEL* 55, 195).

[235] Theophilus, *Ep. paschalis* (402) (= Jerome, *Ep.* 98) 14 (*CSEL* 55, 198–199).

[236] Theophilus, *Ep. paschalis* (402) (= Jerome, *Ep.* 98) 15 (*CSEL* 55, 199–200).

[237] Theophilus, *Ep. paschalis* (402) (= Jerome, *Ep.* 98) 16 (*CSEL* 55, 200); cf. Ori-

gen, *De principiis* IV, 4, 4 (*GCS* 22, 354); the text is taken from Theodoret, *Dialogus* II (*PG* 83, 197).

[238] Theophilus, *Ep. paschalis* (402) (= Jerome, *Ep.* 98) 16 (*CSEL* 55, 200).

[239] Theophilus, *Ep. paschalis* (402) (= Jerome, *Ep.* 98) 17 (*CSEL* 55, 201–202).

[240] Theophilus, *Ep. paschalis* (402) (= Jerome, *Ep.* 98) 18 (*CSEL* 55, 203).

conduct"; and the myrrh is the continence that dries up excessive *voluptas* and the flowing *incentiva* of the flesh.[241]

One new point in this festal letter of 402 pertains to Eucharistic teaching: Theophilus decries Origen's alleged limitation of the Holy Spirit's field of operation to rational entities alone. For Theophilus, the objectionable aspect of this view is that it excludes the Spirit's operation on the waters of baptism[242] and on the bread and wine in the Eucharist. Bread and wine, when placed on the table, are surely inanimate entities, but they are sanctified by the invocation (perhaps the *epiklēsis*, in the Greek original) and by the coming of the Spirit. Moreover, Scripture itself testifies to the Spirit's presence everywhere on earth: Psalm 139:7 and Wisdom 1:7 are adduced as evidence.[243] Theophilus thus fears that the sacramental life of the Church, the very power of the sacramental elements, is shattered by Origen's teaching on the Holy Spirit.

In the last of Theophilus's letters translated by Jerome, dated to 404, Origenism has faded even further as a target for Theophilus's attack. Just as in 402, Theophilus devoted seven chapters to his attack on Apollinarians before he shifted to Origenists, so now, in 404, it takes him ten chapters before he strikes at Origen. Two events of Theophilus's own time suggest to him that Christ truly is God: "the temples of demons" have been overturned (Theophilus probably thinks especially of the Serapeum) and the Origenists have been conquered.[244] Although Theophilus here again resumes his attack on Origen's notion of the fall of minds into bodies, in the letter of 404 the *entire* argument on the precosmic fall and its subsequent effects revolves around the issue of marriage and reproduction: there is *no* other issue that Theophilus chooses to debate. The field of attack on Origenism is centered squarely on the status of the body. The progression of his argument against Origenism from 400 to 404 thus parallels the narrowing concern of Epiphanius's attack.

---

[241] Theophilus, *Ep. paschalis* (402) (= Jerome, *Ep.* 98) 19 (*CSEL* 55, 204).

[242] Whether or not we accept the authenticity of the letter of Theophilus to Horsiesius, the text testifies to the notion that the Spirit was expected to act upon the baptismal waters by manifesting itself as a rod of light (or, alternatively, as a sword of fire). For the Coptic text, see W. E. Crum, ed., tr., *Der Papyruscodex saec. VI–VII der Phillippsbibliothek in Cheltenham: Koptische Theologische Schriften*, Coptic, 12–17; German, 65–72; for a French translation of the letter, see L. Theodore Lefort, tr., *Les Vies coptes de Saint Pachôme et de ses premiers successeurs*, 389–395. For a discussion of the letter's authenticity, see Wilhelm Hengstenberg,

"Pachomiana mit einem Anhang über die Liturgie von Alexandrien," 228–252. The main point of the letter concerns the dating of Easter, which the Alexandrian church was celebrating on a different day from Rome. For Theophilus's concern that the day of Easter be fixed, see his letter to Theodosius I in Bruno Krusch, *Studien zur Christlich-Mittelalterlichen Chronologie: Der 84Jährige Ostercyclus und seine Quellen*, 221.

[243] Theophilus, *Ep. festalis* (402) (= Jerome, *Ep.* 98) 13 (*CSEL* 55, 196–197). Cf. the discussion in the dialogue between Theophilus and Aphou, described above, p. 64.

[244] Theophilus, *Ep. paschalis* (404) (= Jerome, *Ep.* 100) 11 (*CSEL* 55, 225).

Theophilus's argument in 404 proceeds from a consideration of Biblical passages. Why would "Paul" have urged young people to marry and procreate (I Timothy 5:14) if bodies are prisons for "angels" (i.e., souls) who fell from heaven? Marriage would be the result of the punishment of souls, not for the sake of the creation of bodies. "Reproduce and multiply" (Genesis 1:28) was meant as a blessing and was reinforced by "Paul" in Hebrews 13:4 ("Marriage is honorable and the nuptial bed without stain"). The purpose of bodily reproduction is to compensate for death by a succession of births. If the souls sinned in heaven, they certainly did not deserve a blessing, but rather a punishment. When the prophet Isaiah (60:22) wrote, "The least shall be in the thousands and the smallest, a great nation," his prediction of an increase of population was meant to stand as a blessing.[245] Theophilus concludes his one-issue attack with a jibe at "the idols of Origen": his teachings are compared to pagan idolatry that lends God a form and even supplies him with genital organs, sometimes male, sometimes female.[246] The dubiousness of such a charge in light of Origen's teaching on the absolute incorporeality of God will strike the reader immediately. Theophilus clearly is interested not so much in historical accuracy as in aligning his cause with the anti-pagan compaign, while branding Origenists with "idolatry."

One phrase in Theophilus's discussion of the theology of reproduction in the letter of 404 hints that we are perhaps glimpsing an Evagrian form of Origenism. Theophilus writes that the first humans should not be imagined as "naked souls" (*nudae animae*), but should be ascribed bodies—and sexually differentiated ones, at that—from the very start.[247] This phrase, the first time used by Theophilus in the letters translated by Jerome, appears to be the Latin rendition of Evagrius's teaching that the rational creatures, the minds, were originally *gymnos*;[248] Origen does not in *De principiis* or in his exegetical writings himself use this terminology.[249] Theophilus continues his argument with the point that the souls did not become "clothed with bodies" as a punishment for sin:[250] this phrase, too, is Evagrian, but since it also has resonances with Origen's interpretation of the "tunics of skins," we probably cannot claim it as a distinctively Evagrian contribution to religious language,[251] as with justification we can claim the phrase "naked minds."

[245] Theophilus, *Ep. paschalis* (404) (= Jerome, *Ep.* 100) 12 (*CSEL* 55, 225–226).

[246] Theophilus, *Ep. paschalis* (404) (= Jerome, *Ep.* 100) 13 (*CSEL* 55, 226–227).

[247] Theophilus, *Ep. paschalis* (404) (= Jerome, *Ep.* 100) 12 (*CSEL* 55, 226).

[248] Evagrius Ponticus, *Kephalaia gnostica* III, 6; III, 70 (*PO* 28, 101, 127); *Ep. ad Melaniam* 6 (Frankenberg ed., 618; Parmentier

tr., 12).

[249] My conclusion on this point has been confirmed in a conversation with Henri Crouzel.

[250] Theophilus, *Ep. paschalis* (404) (= Jerome, *Ep.* 100) 12 (*CSEL* 55, 225): "*corporibus animae vestiuntur.*"

[251] For Origen's language of "clothing," see, e.g., *De principiis* I, 7, 5; II, 3, 2–3; II, 9,

A question that might well be raised concerning Theophilus's four letters here described is whether Jerome has faithfully translated the original Greek. The recovery of fourteen Greek fragments of Theophilus's letters—only one of which was previously known—has greatly confirmed our faith in Jerome's rendition of Theophilus's arguments.[252] The fragments derive from six letters of Theophilus and are cited in an anti-Origenist florilegium that Marcel Richard believes was composed in the second quarter of the sixth century during the eruption of the Origenist controversy's later phase in Palestine.[253] In them we find confirmation that Theophilus had indeed read Origen's *On First Principles*[254] and the *Treatise on Prayer*.[255] Especially important for our purposes are fragments 3–11, taken from a letter that Theophilus wrote against Origenists when he visited Constantinople in 403[256] to engineer the ouster of John Chrysostom from the bishopric of that city. From fragment 3, we learn that Theophilus believed Origen to be guilty of two principal errors: the subordination of the Son and the doctrine of the resurrection.[257]

On the first point, Theophilus charges Origen along with Arius with teaching that the Son and the Holy Spirit are "creatures" (*ktisma*).[258] He also repeats Origen's claim that although the Son is truth to us, he is not truth when compared to the Father.[259] The view that the seraphim of Isaiah might be the Son and Holy Spirit is also disputed by Theophilus.[260]

---

3 (*GCS* 22, 92, 115–118, 166); on the "tunics of skins," see the *Selecta in Genesim* (on Genesis 3:21) (*PG* 12, 101); cf. Evagrius Ponticus, *Kephalaia gnostica* III, 8 (*PO* 28, 101).

[252] Richard, "Nouveaux Fragments"; the one fragment previously known is #2, cited by Justinian in his *Liber adversus Origenem* (*PG* 86, 967). The florilegium is found in Codex Athos, Vatopédi 236.

[253] Richard, "Nouveaux Fragments," 57.

[254] Theophilus, Fragment 5 (Richard ed., "Nouveaux Fragments," 62).

[255] Theophilus, Fragment 12 (Richard ed., "Nouveaux Fragments," 65).

[256] Richard, "Nouveaux Fragments," 58.

[257] Theophilus, Fragment 3 (Richard ed., "Nouveaux Fragments," 61).

[258] Theophilus, Fragment 4 (Richard ed., "Nouveaux Fragments," 62).

[259] Theophilus, Fragment 5 (Richard ed., "Nouveaux Fragments," 62). Note that this wording is softer than the version given in Theophilus, *Synodica epistula* (= Jerome, *Ep.* 92) 2 (*CSEL* 55, 148–149) that the Son when compared to the Father is a "lie."

[260] Theophilus, Fragment 5 (Richard ed.,

"Nouveaux Fragments," 63). If Theophilus is indeed the author of *Tractatus contra Origenem de visione Isaiae* (see *CPG* II, 2683), the rebuttal of Origen's interpretation of the seraphim of Isaiah 6 as the Son and the Holy Spirit is connected to an idolatry charge: Origen designates the Son and the Holy Spirit as the seraphim "as if he were some sculptor of idols and maker of new images" (*In Isaiam* VI, 1–7, in G. Morin ed., *Anecdota Maredsolana* 3, 3 [1903], 119). Theophilus here even manages to turn Origen into an Anthropomorphite. According to Theophilus, Origen depicts the wings of the seraphim as covering not their *own* faces and feet, but God's. Theophilus then can launch into an anti-Anthropomorphite diatribe: no one can see God; Exodus 33 stands against God's visibility (107–108). For discussion of the authorship of this treatise, see Berthold Altaner, "Wer ist der Verfasser des Tractatus in Isaiam VI, 1–7?" 147–151; Favale, *Teofilo*, 23–24; and Lucien Chavoutier, "Querelle Origèniste et controverses Trinitaires a propos du Tractatus Contra Origenem de Visione Isaiae," 9–14.

He cites John 10:30 ("I and the Father are one") as a refutation of Origen's teaching that to the degree that the Son is superior to created things, the Father surpasses the Son.[261] Origen's teaching in *De oratione* on the inappropriateness of praying to Christ is mentioned by Theophilus in fragments from letters to Atticus, a priest (and future bishop) of Constantinople[262] and to the deacon Serapion,[263] both of which letters Richard believes were also written in 403 in Constantinople.[264] None of these brief allegations is elaborated, however, and the charge of subordinationism actually constitutes a small proportion of Theophilus's discussion in these fragments. More significant is the observation that the charge of subordinationism is here ascribed *only* to Origen himself, not to his followers:[265] there is no railing against "Origenists" who subordinate the Son to the Father.

Much fuller, by contrast, is Theophilus's discussion of issues concerning the resurrection. He covers a variety of points and makes clear that he aims not just at Origen himself, but at "his disciples," explicitly so called;[266] "they" and "the Origenists" now become his major targets.[267] According to Theophilus, Origen's teaching on the resurrection is duplicitous: although Origen pretends that he believes in the resurrection, his wording in fact belies his claim, for he fails to affirm the resurrection of *bodies*. Rather, Origen is alleged to teach that souls return to immateriality or to "mind." If this were so, Theophilus responds, Christ's work would serve to confirm death, not overcome it.[268] Does Origen, who imagines only a "corruptible" body, think that Paul was simpleminded when he wrote of the body, "It shall be raised imperishable" (I Corinthians 15:42),[269] Theophilus asks? Origenists are also accused of saying that the resurrection of the body has no worthy *eidos*, but rather has the *schēma* of a sphere:[270] here we have clear proof that Theophilus accepted Epiphanius's (and through him, Methodius's) erroneous interpretation that Origen identified *eidos* with *schēma* and construed them as outwardly visible entities.[271] To this allegation borrowed from his predecessors, Theophilus appends his own view: at the end, each will have his *own* body. Just as one form is appropriate for the beasts and another for the birds, so humans will receive their own *eidos* in the resurrection.[272] The latter point, as we have seen, would

---

[261] Theophilus, Fragment 10 (Richard ed., "Nouveaux Fragments," 64).

[262] Theophilus, Fragment 12 (Richard ed., "Nouveaux Fragments," 65).

[263] Theophilus, Fragment 13 (Richard ed., "Nouveaux Fragments," 65).

[264] Richard, "Nouveaux Fragments," 58.

[265] This is the case for all the subordinationist charges listed in nn.258–263 above.

[266] "Disciples" in Fragment 5 (Richard ed., "Nouveaux Fragments," 63).

[267] Theophilus, Fragments 8; 5 (Richard ed., "Nouveaux Fragments," 63–64, 62).

[268] Theophilus, Fragment 4 (Richard ed., "Nouveaux Fragments," 61–62).

[269] Theophilus, Fragment 5 (Richard ed., "Nouveaux Fragments," 63).

[270] Theophilus, Fragment 8 (Richard ed., "Nouveaux Fragments," 63–64).

[271] See discussion above, pp. 89, 94.

[272] Theophilus, Fragment 8 (Richard ed., "Nouveaux Fragments," 64). To this can be

not have been disputed by Origen—although for him, the surviving *eidos* was not a fleshly entity.[273]

To his major attack on Origen's resurrection teaching in the Greek fragments of these letters, Theophilus adds the charges that Origen believed that Christ would be crucified on behalf of the demons;[274] that minds or souls fell from heaven;[275] and that there could not have been ranks among the heavenly powers unless some sunk to lower positions through sin.[276] Last, Theophilus repeats the charge, apparently derived from Epiphanius, that Origen was an idolator: in Theophilus's version, Origen was condemned for pouring out a libation to idols.[277] Thus it is clear that in these Greek fragments of Theophilus's writings, the same charges are leveled against Origen and the Origenists as are raised in Jerome's Latin translations of four letters of Theophilus.

Most significant for our purposes, two issues are singled out as causing grave disturbances among the present inhabitants of the monasteries: thus we can pinpoint the issues of *contemporary* Origenist concern. The first issue, predictably, concerns the Anthropomorphite controversy. Theophilus's brief description is interesting in that he distinguishes the Origenist debate from the anti-Anthropomorphite debate, and the reason for his distinction becomes immediately evident: he aligns himself against the Origenists and with the anti-Anthropomorphites, a shrewd move that signals the conflation of his political and theological astuteness. Theophilus no doubt so differentiates Origenists from anti-Anthropomorphites in order to fault the former while applauding the latter. Describing the Anthropomorphites as "uncultivated and simpleminded," he nonetheless judges them heretical.[278] Thus it appears that as early as 403, Theophilus had again assumed his earlier anti-Anthropomorphite stance after a brief flirtation with the Anthropomorphite monks when he needed them as political allies. Did the author of the dialogue between Aphou and Theophilus not know how ephemeral Theophilus's conversion to Anthropomorphism had been[279]—or did Theophilus's backsliding prove too inconvenient for his argument and hence remain unmentioned?

---

added Theophilus's affirmation in his exegesis of Psalm 93:1, that Christ took "his own body" when he rose again: see the Greek fragment given in Richard, "Les Fragments exégétiques," 391.

[273] See above, p. 93.

[274] Theophilus, Fragment 5 (Richard ed., "Nouveaux Fragments," 62). Theophilus bristles at the notion that Christ would have to enter into a "likeness" with the demons to be crucified on their behalf, since the efficacy of his crucifixion on behalf of humans rested on his having entered into the *homoiōsin* with them.

[275] Theophilus, Fragment 9 (Richard ed., "Nouveaux Fragments," 64).

[276] Theophilus, Fragment 6 (Richard ed., "Nouveaux Fragments," 63).

[277] Theophilus, Fragment 13 (Richard ed., "Nouveaux Fragments," 65). See Epiphanius, *Panarion* 64, 2 (*GCS* 31[2], 404) and discussion p. 87 above.

[278] Theophilus, Fragment 7 (Richard ed., "Nouveaux Fragments," 63).

[279] See above, pp. 37–38.

Another Origenist opinion now disturbing the inhabitants of monasteries, Theophilus writes in these previously unknown letters, concerns the original incorporeal state of humans and their "fall" into bodies. According to Theophilus, not only does this teaching go against Genesis 2:7, that God made human bodies from the earth, it also has deeply disturbing implications for our understanding of marriage and reproduction. Why would woman have been made and how, on this thesis, could there have been reproduction if the souls had not erred? To the contrary, Genesis teaches us that God "made them male and female, and blessed them, saying, 'Reproduce, multiply, and fill the earth' " (Genesis 1:28). How could these words have been a blessing if the manner of production of bodies involved a fall of sinful souls from heaven?[280] This is, of course, the same charge that rose to prominence in Theophilus's argumentation in 401 and thereafter, assuming central importance in his letter of 404.[281] The Greek fragments of Theophilus's letters preserved in Codex Athos, Vatopédi 236 thus confirm the thesis that the charges against Origen of Trinitarian error recede while contemporary Origenist issues being discussed in the Egyptian desert—especially those pertaining to the body—gain importance in Theophilus's polemic, even within the brief time that elapsed between 400 and 404. As with Epiphanius, so with Theophilus: issues pertaining to the body have upstaged earlier concerns, and the villain's role has been assigned to Origenists rather than to Origen alone.

JEROME'S VERSION OF ORIGENISM
AND HIS ANTI-ORIGENIST CHARGES

Although Georg Grützmacher's description of the Origenist controversy has been emended at several points,[282] his judgment that Theophilus of Alexandria's critique of Origen was conceptually sharper than Jerome's[283] still seems apt. Indeed, we can hypothesize one reason why this might have been the case: Theophilus was familiar with a more radical form of Origenism circulating in the Egyptian desert, of which Jerome seems largely unaware. Jerome, to be sure, was an avid student of Origen's writings, yet his grasp of Origenism's coherence as a theological system appears limited. Rather, Jerome seems to have espoused the anti-Origenist cause for personal rather than intellectual reasons, to rescue his own reputation from the taint of heretical association. To save his own skin while lacerating that of Rufinus appears his primary

---

[280] Theophilus, Fragment 11 (Richard ed., "Nouveaux Fragments," 65).
[281] Theophilus, *Ep. paschalis* (401) (= Jerome, *Ep.* 96) 18 and *Ep. paschalis* (404) (= Jerome, *Ep.* 100) 12 (*CSEL* 55, 177–

179, 225–226).
[282] Grützmacher, *Hieronymus*, vol. 3, chap. 10.
[283] Grützmacher, *Hieronymus*, vol. 3: 91.

mission. Secondarily, and as his central religious concern, Jerome was determined to preserve the notion of moral hierarchy (based largely on degrees of ascetic renunciation) both in this life and in the next. Jerome's concern for moral hierarchy lends a rather different coloration to his version of Origenism than is found in the polemics of Epiphanius and Theophilus, despite his dependence upon their writings.

A reading of Jerome's works in chronological order reveals that until 396, he made little or no effort to distance himself from Origen or Origenist opinions. When in that year he finally moved to attack Origen's theology, his motivation seemingly stems as much from his own recent encounter with Jovinian as from a perception of the dangers Origenism posed. Jerome's earliest critiques of Origen, such as that contained in his polemic *Against John of Jerusalem*, are borrowed almost entirely from those of his predecessors, especially from Epiphanius. Only with Rufinus's publication of a Latin translation of Origen's *On First Principles* and his *Apology against Jerome* did Jerome understand that he himself was in serious danger of being pronounced an Origenist. He responded to this threat by explaining away as convincingly as he could his earlier use of Origen's works. Yet it is striking how small a space the analysis of Origen's heterodox opinions actually occupies in Jerome's response to Rufinus, the *Apologia contra Rufinum*, his major writing that pertains to the Origenist controversy. Only later, in 409–410, when the controversy was ostensibly over, did he provide a detailed list of the errors found in *On First Principles*. And five more years passed before Jerome suddenly—and most belatedly—recognized the role that Palladius and Evagrius Ponticus had played in the dispute. Jerome's controversy, in other words, is differently constructed from Theophilus's.

Although from the standpoint of 402 or 403, Jerome pretended that even during his visit to Egypt in 386 he had noticed Origenist "serpents" hissing in the monasteries of Nitria,[284] there is no evidence from Jerome's early writings that suggests he found Origenist interpretation alarming and much that suggests he considered Origen's exegesis acceptable to Christian orthodoxy. In some respects, Jerome proved to be his own worst enemy, for by his repeated urging of readers to examine for themselves his treatment of Origen in his early writings, especially in his *Commentaries on Ephesians* and *on Ecclesiastes*, written in the late 380s,[285] he sowed the seeds for accusations of Origenism against himself. Although some modern commentators have denied the strong Origenist coloration of these early

---

[284] Jerome, *Apologia* III, 22 (*CCL* 79, 94).
[285] Jerome, *Epp.* 61, 2; 84, 2 (*CSEL* 54, 578; *CSEL* 55, 122). The *Commentary on Ephesians* is dated to 386–387, and the *Commentary on Ecclesiastes* to 389–390, by Grütz-

macher (vol. 1: 101). Cavallera places the *Ecclesiastes Commentary* in 388–389, following Jerome's *Commentaries* on the Pauline Letters: *Saint Jérôme*, vol. 1: 2, 27.

commentaries,[286] and have downplayed the frequency with which Jerome either incorporated questionable Origenist opinions or failed to distance himself sufficiently from Origenist views,[287] such assessments appear to be grounded more in apologetic motives than in a close reading of Jerome's early works. Jerome's *Commentary on Ephesians* provides a good illustration of his early cavalier approach to Origen.

Only in the prologue to the *Commentary*, not in the body of the work, does Jerome inform his readers that he has borrowed from Origen's three volumes on Ephesians as well as from commentaries by Apollinaris and Didymus. Although Jerome claims that he has added to and subtracted from these books, he asks the "attentive reader" to note at the outset that his *Commentary* comes partly from Origen, Apollinaris, and Didymus, and partly from himself.[288] Nowhere, however, in his own three-book *Commentary* does Jerome explicitly identify any opinion as Origen's, and in only two places does he dissent from the Origenist view he presents.[289] Jerome's practice prompted Rufinus's complaint that Jerome constantly cited an "other" commentator without either identifying the unnamed interpreter as Origen or dissociating himself from the interpretation presented. Rufinus thus faults Jerome for allowing readers to assume that the Origenist interpretation is acceptable.[290] In his *Apology against Jerome*, Rufinus selects fifteen passages from the *Ephesians Commentary* for attack; Jerome in his *Apology against Rufinus* responds to six of them.[291] By my count, however, there are at least twenty-one passages in the *Ephesians Commentary* in which Jerome cites an interpretation that can reasonably be considered Origen's.[292]

Among the points of Origenist exegesis that Jerome mentions (without apparent disapproval) in the *Ephesians Commentary* are that sexual differ-

---

[286] Brochet, *Saint Jérôme*, 283–284.

[287] Grützmacher makes little reference to the centrality of the *Ephesians Commentary* for the controversy: *Hieronymus*, vol. 2: 37–44; vol. 3, chap. 10. Cavallera, by contrast, gives greater scope to Origen's influence on this book: *Saint Jérôme*, vol. 1: 2, 99. Also see Kelly, *Jerome*, 251, 253–254.

[288] Jerome, *Comm. in Ep. ad Ephesios, prologus* (PL 26, 472).

[289] Jerome rejects an Origenist interpretation when commenting on Ephesians 4:16 and 5:6.

[290] E.g., Rufinus, *Apologia* I, 28; 32; 40; 43 (CCL 20, 62–63, 66–67, 74–75, 78). Rufinus notes that Jerome sometimes takes a position contrary to the "other" whom he cites: are we to think that he is then condemning Origen? (*Apologia* I, 33; 34; 36 [CCL 20, 67, 68–69, 70]). Latin chapter numbers are used throughout for Rufinus's *Apology*.

[291] The verses in Ephesians for which Rufinus notes Jerome's Origenist interpretations, and the places in Rufinus's *Apologia* where they are discussed, are as follows: Ephesians 1:4 in I, 26–27; 1:5 in I, 29; 1:12 in I, 32, 34; 1:17 in I, 39; 1:20–21 in I, 38; 1:22 in I, 40; 2:3 in I, 40; 2:7 in I, 37; 2:15 in I, 41; 2:17 in I, 40–41; 4:4 in I, 43; 4:16 in I, 44; 4:25 in II, 1-2; 5:28 in I, 24–25; 6:20 (cf. 3:l), in I, 42. Jerome responds to the criticisms of his interpretation of the following verses in his *Apology*: Ephesians 1:4 in I, 22; 1:20–21 in I, 23; 2:7 in I, 24; 4:16 in I, 26–27; 5:28–29 in I, 28–29; 6:20 (cf. 3:10 and 4:1) in I, 25.

[292] Passages with an Origenist cast that are not dealt with by Rufinus: Jerome's remarks on Ephesians 1:10; 2:1ff., 19; 5:5; 6:1, 13.

entiation will at the end be erased;[293] that souls were cast down from heaven into bodies;[294] that holy saints have been sent to earth to recall fallen, now-embodied souls to their original state;[295] that humans will later acquire an "angelic" nature;[296] that the devil, as well as sinners and unbelievers, will eventually be saved;[297] that our condition in this life depends upon our preexistent merit or lack of merit in the heavens;[298] and that in the age to come, ascents and descents, increases and decreases will continue among the principalities and powers.[299]

To be sure, at a few points in the *Ephesians Commentary* Jerome pulls back from associating himself too closely with such ideas. Thus he rejects the notion that there will be only *one* angelic condition in the final consummation[300] and that future punishment consists simply in mental anguish rather than in physical torment.[301] Moreover, Jerome does not always furnish an Origenist exegesis of passages that seemingly cry out for one: for example, he fails to note Origen's exegesis of Job 15:14–15, that not even the stars are clean in God's sight.[302] He also sometimes provides a moral interpretation of a verse rather than the cosmological or ontological exegesis of *On First Principles*.[303] Despite these qualifications, however, Rufinus's charge that Jerome was a not-so-covert Origenist receives sufficient support from the *Ephesians Commentary* to make Jerome's protests of innocence ring hollow.

In his exegesis of Biblical books in the early 390s, Jerome also shows

---

[293] Rufinus, *Apologia* I, 24; 45; 41 (*CCL* 20, 58, 81–82, 76); see also I, 27–29; 31–32 (*CCL* 20, 61–64, 66–67); cf. Jerome, *Comm. ad Eph.* III (*PL* 26, 567).

[294] Rufinus, *Apologia* I, 39; 40; 42 (*CCL* 20, 73–75, 77–78); cf. Jerome, *Comm. ad Eph.* I (*PL* 26, 497, on Ephesians 2:1ff.); III (*PL* 26, 587, on Ephesians 6:20).

[295] Rufinus, *Apologia* I, 27–28 (*CCL* 20, 61–63; cf. Jerome, *Comm. ad Eph.* I (*PL* 26, 476–477, on Ephesians 1:4).

[296] Rufinus, *Apologia* I, 44 (*CCL* 20, 75–76). Rufinus cites Jerome's remarks on Ephesians 2:17 in *Comm. ad Eph.* I (*PL* 26, 505–506). Also see Jerome's comments on Ephesians 2:19ff., (*Comm. ad Eph.* I [*PL* 26, 507–508]), on the unity of the angelic and the human natures in the afterlife. The nature will be incorporeal; angels do not have "knees" to bow to their Master; see Jerome's comments on Ephesians 3:14 in *Comm. ad Eph.* II (*PL* 26, 518).

[297] Rufinus, *Apologia* I, 34–35; 36; 37; 43; 44; 45 (*CCL* 20, 69–70, 71–72, 78–81); cf. Jerome, *Comm. ad Eph.* I (*PL* 26, 485–486, 500, on Ephesians 1:12 and 2:7).

[298] Rufinus, *Apologia* I, 27 (*CCL* 20, 61–62); cf. Jerome, *Comm. ad Eph.* I (*PL* 26, 479, on Ephesians 1:5).

[299] Jerome, *Comm. ad Eph.* I (*PL* 26, 491–492, on Ephesians 1:21). Although Kasimierz Romaniuk believes that there is little in the *Ephesians Commentary* that is Origenistic, he does concede that this passage has a somewhat Origenistic tone ("Une Controverse entre saint Jérôme et Rufin d'Aquilée à propos de l'épître de saint Paul aux Éphésiens," 95–97). See Rufinus, *Apologia* I, 38 (*CCL* 20, 72) and Jerome's reply, *Apologia* I, 23 (*CSEL* 79, 23).

[300] Jerome, *Comm. ad Eph.* II (*PL* 26, 535, on Ephesians 4:16).

[301] Jerome, *Comm. ad Eph.* III (*PL* 26, 522, on Ephesians 5:6). See Origen, *De principiis* II, 10, 4; 10, 8 (*GCS* 22, 177–178, 181–183).

[302] Jerome, *Comm. ad Eph.* I (*PL* 26, 493, on Ephesians 1:22–23).

[303] E.g., Jerome, *Comm. ad Eph.* I (*PL* 26, 477–478, on Ephesians 1:4); II (*PL* 26, 524–525 on Ephesians 4:1); III (*PL* 26, 587, on Ephesians 6:20).

himself undisturbed by Origenist interpretation. Although *The Hebrew Questions on Genesis*, usually dated to around 390, contains nothing on heresy of any sort, it does show that Jerome was already piqued by criticisms of his use of the Hebrew text of the Old Testament, a practice that Origen before him had employed. He responds by scoffing that he is no frightened baby who trembles when he hears Origen accused for his reliance on the Hebrew text.[304]

Jerome's *Commentarioli on Psalms*, dated to 390 or 391,[305] openly claims Origen's exposition of Psalms as a base[306] and Origen is explicitly named as a source at two points.[307] In this work, Jerome frequently mentions Origenist interpretations, or refutes their opposites, without labelling them as Origen's. Thus he sets himself firmly against a traducianist explanation of the soul's origin;[308] suggests that there will be a time when sin, identified with the devil, will be no more;[309] and informs his readers (without demurrer) that "some think" that the soul descends into the body,[310] and that the "valley of tears" of Psalm 84:6 means "the present world."[311] Last, Jerome faults the Novatianists, who espoused a highly rigorous view of who deserved salvation, with an appeal to Psalm 145:9 ("The Lord is good to all and his pity is on all his works") and his position rests on the Origenist principle that nothing and no one can be outside the possibility of salvation.[312] Within a decade, Jerome will have learned to his regret that he could not with impunity set forth such positions without distancing himself from them.

Before 392 or 393, Jerome wrote commentaries on the books of Zephaniah, Haggai, and Nahum.[313] While the first two of these contain nothing of interest for our purposes, with the *Nahum Commentary*, Jerome begins a practice that he will employ throughout the Origenist controversy: he assails the teachings of past, long-dead heretics, a practice that undoubtedly serves to advertise his own orthodoxy. Thus in the relatively short compass of the *Nahum Commentary*, Jerome levels jibes at Montanus, Prisca, Maximilla, Valentinus, Marcion, Bardesanes, Tatian, Basilides, Eunomius, Mani, and Novatian.[314]

---

[304] Jerome, *Hebraicae quaestiones in Libro Geneseos*, prologus (*CCL* 72, 2); for dating to approximately 389–391, see *CCL* 72, vii; cf. Cavallera, *Saint Jérôme*, vol. 1: 2, 27–28.

[305] For dating to about 391, see *CCL* 72, viii.

[306] Jerome, *Commentarioli in Psalmos, prologus* (*CCL* 72, 177).

[307] Jerome, *Commentarioli in Psalmos* 1:4; 4:7 (*CCL* 72, 180, 185). I use the modern numbering of chapters in the book of Psalms.

[308] Jerome, *Commentarioli in Psalmos* 33:15 (*CCL* 72, 204).

[309] Jerome, *Commentarioli in Psalmos* 37:10 (*CCL* 72, 206).

[310] Jerome, *Commentarioli in Psalmos* 58:4 (*CCL* 72, 211).

[311] Jerome, *Commentarioli in Psalmos* 84:6 (*CCL* 72, 220).

[312] Jerome, *Commentarioli in Psalmos* 145:9 (*CCL* 72, 244).

[313] These *Commentaries* are dated to 393 following; see the listing in *De viris inlustribus* 135 and *CCL* 76, v.

[314] Jerome, *In Naum* (*CCL* 76A, 526, 530, 533, 536, 574).

In commentaries written after *Nahum* but before those completed in 406[315] Jerome turned to Habbakuk and Micah. In his commentaries on both of these prophets, he continues to name specific heretics of the past: in the *Commentary on Habakkuk*, he attacks Montanists, Mani, Arius, and Eunomius;[316] in the *Micah Commentary*, which we know postdates his work on Nahum,[317] Jerome singles out Marcion, Mani, Basilides, Arius, and Eunomius.[318] Probably these heresies—Manicheanism and Marcionism excepted—posed little serious threat by the 390s either in Rome or in Palestine. Was Jerome's attack upon these long-dead figures simply a convenient means for him to announce his own theological correctness?

The commentaries on Habakkuk and on Micah also provide our first indications that an indictment of Origen was in the wind. In the *Habakkuk Commentary* Jerome writes—without further elaboration—that "the snake hisses and Sardanapalus reviles,"[319] code names that he will later use when he accuses Rufinus of Origenism: does he already intend the same referent? And in the *Micah Commentary*, Jerome reports that he is being slandered: people are alleging that his works are actually composed out of the writings of Origen. Jerome does not, interestingly, deny the truth of the accusation, but asks what crime there is in transferring the "blessing" (*benedicta*) of the Greeks to the Romans? After all, many famous Latin writers of earlier centuries used Greek works as their base, and Latin church writers before him have mined the Greek theologians, most notably Origen.[320] Given these intriguing references to the beginning of the Origenist controversy, it is unfortunate that we are not able to date these two commentaries more precisely.

In the 390s, other disputes had developed that would prove decisive for Jerome's approach to Origenism. In probably 393, Jerome received Jovinian's attack upon his ascetic theology that led to his outraged response, the *Adversus Jovinianum*.[321] And in the next year, Jerome was sent a copy of Epiphanius's accusatory letter to John of Jerusalem on Origenism that, three years later, would prompt his diatribe, *Against John of Jerusalem*.[322] Yet that even in 394 and beyond, Jerome was not attuned either to confront or deny possible Origenist interpretations is suggested by *Epistle*

---

[315] The *Commentaries* of 406 are on Zechariah, Malachi, Hosea, Joel, and Amos; see *CCL* 76, v.

[316] Jerome, *In Ababuc* I (*CCL* 76A, 580, 606, 614).

[317] In the prologue to Book III of his *Amos Commentary* of 406, Jerome lists the *Micah Commentary* after the *Nahum Commentary* (see *CCL* 76, 300).

[318] Jerome, *In Michaeam* I; II (*CCL* 76, 435, 504).

[319] Jerome, *In Ababuc* II, *prologus* (*CCL* 76A, 618).

[320] Jerome, *In Michaeam* II, *prologus* (*CCL* 76, 473).

[321] Pierre Nautin, "Etudes de chronologie hiéronymienne (393–397)," *Revue des Etudes Augustiniennes* 20 (1974): 253–255, 277.

[322] Pierre Nautin, "Etudes de chronologie hiéronymienne (393–397)," *Revue des Etudes Augustiniennes* 18 (1972): 211–213; 20 (1974), 277–279.

55.[323] In this letter, Jerome replies to a query regarding the meaning of I Corinthians 15:25–28 (that in the end, the Son will subject himself to the Father and God will be "all in all"). That this verse, so ripe for Origenist exegesis—or for its denial—is not considered at all within the Origenist framework of discussion even in passing is striking: Jerome's interpretation is grounded squarely in an anti-Arian polemic that denies the Son's subordination.[324] The Origenist teaching on the *apokatastasis*, the restitution of all things to their original heavenly condition, seems completely absent from Jerome's mind.

Only in 396, it appears, did Jerome begin to comprehend that he must take a public stand on Origen's teaching. In late 395 or early 396,[325] writing to Vigilantius, Jerome posits that four errors mar the works of Origen: his teachings on the resurrection body, on the condition of souls, on the repentance of the devil, and on the identification of the seraphim of Isaiah 6:2 with the Son and the Holy Spirit. It is astonishing that Jerome here deems the error regarding the seraphim the most significant of the four.[326] He informs Vigilantius that he anathematizes Origen daily—although he also claims that he can separate the good from the evil in Origen's teaching, the good pertaining solely to Origen's massive knowledge of Scripture. "Read what I wrote in my *Commentaries on Ephesians* and *on Ecclesiastes*," he invites his correspondent.[327]

In the late 390s, Jerome with ever-increasing eagerness announced his separation from Origen's views. In *Epistle* 62,[328] written to his friend Tranquillinus who had reported to Jerome on Origenist activities at Rome, Jerome again insists that he always knew how to differentiate the bad from the good in Origen's writings. Yet in Jerome's opinion, those who manifest too much aversion to the Alexandrian theologian are as "perverse" as those who favor his teachings indiscriminately. He again recommends Origen's Biblical commentaries as useful readings for Christians. Although Jerome asserts that he does not want to take sides in the growing debate over Origen, he confesses that if pressed to do so, he will opt for simple piety over speculative "blasphemy."[329]

Jerome's Biblical commentaries from the late 390s, as well as his letters from the period, reveal his new-found need to reject publicly certain aspects of Origen's teachings. Two writings in which these criticisms of Or-

---

[323] Epistle 55 is dated between 393–397 (Cavallera, *Saint Jérôme*, vol. 1: 2, 44); it is mentioned in the *Commentary on Matthew*, dated to 398.

[324] Jerome, *Ep.* 55, 3 (5) (*CSEL* 54, 491).

[325] Cavallera, *Saint Jérôme*, vol. 1: 2, 45.

[326] Jerome, *Ep.* 61, 2 (*CSEL* 54, 577). Grützmacher, *Hieronymus*, vol. 1: 100, dates the letter to 399–403; Cavallera, *Saint Jérôme*,

vol. 1: 2, 45, to late 395–early 396; Kelly, *Jerome*, 206–207, to 396.

[327] Jerome, *Ep.* 61, 2 (*CSEL* 54, 577).

[328] Jerome, *Ep.* 62 to Tranquillinus, dated to 396 by Vallarsi and to 399–403 by Grützmacher; see Grützmacher, *Hieronymus*, vol. 1: 100; Cavallera, *Saint Jérôme*, vol. 1: 2, 45.

[329] Jerome, *Ep.* 62, 2 (*CSEL* 54, 584).

igen appear are the *Commentary on Jonah*, dated to 396,[330] and the *Commentary on Matthew*, dated to 398.[331] Jonah 3:6–9, describing the repentance of the king of Nineveh, excites Jerome's anti-Origenist ire: Origenists had identified the king with the devil,[332] following Origen's interpretation in *On First Principles* I, 6, 2–3.[333] Jerome reports that "some" hold that the king of Nineveh is the devil who at the end of the world repents and is restored to his former position: as a rational creature formed by God, not even the devil will perish. Jerome rejects this interpretation on more than one ground. Most simply, the interpretation is not found in Scripture. More important, it encourages moral laxity by suggesting that humans will be saved despite their vices: if even the devil is to be restored, why shouldn't sinners be? Although God is a most merciful deity, Jerome assures his readers, he has nonetheless prepared eternal hellfire for the devil and for unrepentant sinners. If all "rational creatures" including the devil are to be raised to the same heavenly dignity, what grounds for distinction will there be between virgins and prostitutes, between the mother of Jesus and "the victims of public lust"? "Will Gabriel be like the devil? will the apostles be the same as demons? prophets and false prophets? martyrs and persecutors?" Even if the proponents of this exegesis (i.e., Origenists) argue that it will take infinite ages for the final restitution to equality to occur, according to them the end is eventually the same for all—and if so, our actions here and now do not count. A Biblical commentary is not the place to argue at length against this "perverse teaching," Jerome claims. Nonetheless, he is enraged against those (John of Jerusalem? Rufinus?) who affirm such beliefs in private but who deny them in public.[334]

The restoration of the devil is also the point of Origen's theology that Jerome attacks in his *Commentary on Matthew* when he interprets Matthew 18:24, the parable of the ungrateful servant. Origen's comment on this passage[335] implied that the servant who is forgiven the huge debt of ten thousand talents by the master (= God) is the devil. Jerome rejects this interpretation: why then is the servant who owed much less, only one hundred denarii, not forgiven by the master? If the greater debt is forgiven, so

---

[330] See *CCL* 76, v; Cavallera, *Saint Jérôme*, vol. 1: 2, 44; Grützmacher, *Hieronymus*, vol. 1: 101 (dating to 395–396).

[331] See *SC* 242, 9; Cavallera, *Saint Jérôme*, vol. 1: 2, 46; Grützmacher, *Hieronymus*, vol. 1: 101.

[332] Jerome, *In Ionam* (*CCL* 76, 406–408, on Jonah 3:6–9).

[333] Origen, *De principiis* (*GCS* 22, 79–84); cf. Jerome, *In Danielem* I (*CCL* 75A, 808–809, on Daniel 3:29). For Origen's exegesis of Jonah, see Yves-Marie Duval, *Le Livre de Jonas dans la littérature chrétienne grecque et*

latine: Sources et influence du Commentaire sur Jonas de saint Jérôme, 191–209.

[334] Jerome, *In Ionam* (*CCL* 76, 407–408, on Jonah 3:6–9). See also Duval, *Le Livre*, 325–358, and "Saint Cyprien et le roi de Ninive dans l'*In Ionam* de Jérôme: La conversion des lettrés à la fin du IVᵉ siècle," 551–570.

[335] Origen, *In Matheum* XIV, 10 (*GCS* 40, 299). In his preface to his *Commentary on Matthew*, Jerome reports that he has read and used Origen's twenty-five volume *Commentary*, as well as his *Homilies* (*CCL* 77, 4).

should the lesser. To Jerome, the interpretation of the passage given by Origenists is inconsistent.[336] Jerome overlooks the fact that according to the parable, the one hundred denarii were not owed to the master, but to the first servant—although the implications of this reading for the Origenist interpretation would suggest that humans are indebted to the devil, a point likewise anathema to Jerome.

It is highly significant that the central issue so exercising Jerome in these two commentaries is one with deep resonances in his recent fight against Jovinian.[337] It was, indeed, in the Jovinianist controversy that Jerome had adamantly affirmed a hierarchy in the afterlife based on the degrees of merit accumulated by humans in this life—a merit calculated by the stringency of ascetic renunciation.

As early as his *Commentary on Ephesians*, Jerome had pulled back from the implications of Origen's view that there will eventually be, in the final restitution of all things, a simple unity. In that early work, Jerome hints that the "oneness" of the future restoration in the heavenly afterlife will leave room for gradation on the basis of moral rank. Thus although the devil and his angels will be part of Christ's future reign, they will not receive "the praise of his glory," for they followed God only out of necessity, not voluntarily, and Jerome insists that "for diversity of hopes, diverse rewards will be received."[338] His concern for hierarchy in heaven is further revealed in his statement that the "governments, authorities, powers, and dominions" will be ranked in the future life just as officers within a government: surely God, the King of kings, will not be satisfied with a single order of servants when mere human kings are not?[339]

The problem of unity and diversity in heaven is again broached by Jerome in his comments on Ephesians 4:4 (the injunction to be of one body and one spirit, in accord with "the one hope of your calling"). Jerome puts a question to the text: How can there be only "one hope of your calling" when John 14:2 states that in the Father's house there are many mansions? He answers: The Kingdom of Heaven in general is the "one hope of your calling," but *within* the one house there are "many mansions." Jerome then notes the theory that posits the future restoration of all things to their primitive condition, when we shall all become one in the Father and the

---

[336] Jerome, *In Matheum* III (*CCL* 77, 164, on Matt. 18:24). A second passage in which Jerome attacks Origenist interpretation in the *Commentary on Matthew* is his exegesis of Matthew 6:10, where he faults the notion that "falls" and sins can be found in heaven (*CCL* 77, 36–37).

[337] Jovinian's treatise and Jerome's response, the *Adversus Jovinianum*, are most

probably to be dated to 393: Kelly, *Jerome*, 182; cf. Cavallera, *Saint Jérôme*, vol. 1: 2, 43–44; Grützmacher, *Hieronymus*, vol. 1: 101 (to 392–393).

[338] Jerome, *Comm. ad Eph.* I (*PL* 26, 485–486, on Ephesians 1:12).

[339] Jerome, *Comm. ad Eph.* I (*PL* 26, 491–492, on Ephesians 1:21).

Son, as John 17:21 states.[340] Here, the *apokatastasis* and gradation of rank are held in concert.

Jerome's interest in preserving a hierarchy in heaven had been developed in his other writings of the 380s as well. Even in the mid-380s, he had ranked virgins, widows, and the married in a scheme derived from the parable of the sower: 100-fold, 60-fold, 30-fold.[341] Yet it was during his controversy with Jovinian that the theme of hierarchy among Christians, and consequently a hierarchy of rewards in heaven, became crucial to him. Although Jerome and Jovinian *agreed* that all sins are forgiven in the baptismal laver, Jovinian opposed the notion of rank among Christians, both here and hereafter.[342]

Thus we find that the letters of Jerome from 393 on (i.e., after the controversy with Jovinian) make abundant use of hierarchical imagery. Jerome devises endless comparisons: people are likened to vessels of gold, silver, wood, and earth, as in II Timothy 2:20; to those who build with gold, silver, and gems, as compared to hay, wood, and stubble, as in I Corinthians 3:10–12; to the 100-fold, 60-fold, and 30-fold harvests;[343] and to the varying lights of the sun, moon, stars, lamps, and lanterns.[344] Defending the seeming violence of his treatise *Against Jovinian*, Jerome confesses that he cannot bear to believe that there is only one reward for hunger and for surfeit, for filth and for finery, for sackcloth and for silk.[345]

The *Adversus Jovinianum* itself provides the fullest explication of these views. Recall Jovinian's position: that all the baptized are of equal merit whether they be virgins, widows, or the married, if they are equal in other respects, and that there is only one reward in heaven for those who keep their baptismal vows.[346] Against Jovinian, Jerome piles up his metaphors of gold, silver, and hay; of grain, stalk, and ears; of 100-fold, 60-fold, 30-fold harvests.[347] On Jovinian's premise, says Jerome, whoremongers would be equal in heaven to virgins,[348] a view Jerome finds shocking *despite* his continued assertion that the church pardons not just fornicators and the incestuous,[349] but penitent whoremongers themselves.[350] Pardon, however, does not mean that all will have the same reward. Paul's claim that different "gifts" will have their different "rewards" (cf. I Corinthians 7:7,

---

[340] Jerome, *Comm. ad Eph.* II (*PL* 26, 526–527, on Ephesians 4:3–4).

[341] Jerome, *Ep.* 22, 15 (*CSEL* 54, 163); see also *Epp.* 24, 1; 39, 8 (*CSEL* 54, 214, 308).

[342] Jerome, *Adversus Jovinianum* I, 3 (*PL* 23, 224).

[343] Jerome, *Epp.* 49, 2 (*CSEL* 54, 353); 66, 2 (*CSEL* 54, 648); 123, 8 (*CSEL* 56, 82).

[344] Jerome, *Ep.* 49, 14 (*CSEL* 54, 372).

[345] Jerome, *Ep.* 49, 21 (*CSEL* 54, 387).

[346] Jerome, *Adversus Jovinianum* I, 3 (*PL* 23, 224).

[347] Jerome, *Adversus Jovinianum* I, 3 (*PL* 23, 223).

[348] Jerome, *Adversus Jovinianum* I, 4 (*PL* 23, 225).

[349] Jerome, *Adversus Jovinianum* I, 8 (*PL* 23, 231).

[350] Jerome, *Adversus Jovinianum* I, 15 (*PL* 23, 245).

12:4ff.) is applied to the differing ascetic statuses of Christians.[351] Baptism does not wipe out the difference between virgins and harlots, despite the Christian belief that we all become "new men" in baptism.[352] Jovinian's opinion should be faulted, for on it the telling of an ordinary fib would send one to the same "outer darkness" inhabited by those guilty of parricide.[353]

Jovinian's view, that there are only two categories, the saved and the damned,[354] is assessed by Jerome as more akin to the philosophy of the Old Stoics than to that of Christians.[355] Jerome devotes most of Book II of the *Adversus Jovinianum* to the refutation of this view. Although Jovinian quotes Matthew 25 on the twofold division between sheep and the goats,[356] Jerome reminds him (and us) that there is a great difference between one sheep and another. In fact, Jerome takes gradation in the afterlife as a necessary proposition for the defense of God's justice, since it would be unfair to assign the same reward for unequal merits.[357] The *whole* truth is not taught by the passage on the sheep and the goats, or on that concerning the wise and the foolish virgins.[358] Other Biblical references need to be recalled. Jerome offers suggestions: Jesus' words on the greatest and the least in the Kingdom of Heaven (Matthew 20:26–27) or on the diverse number of talents that the master gave his three servants (Matthew 25:14–30)[359] provide fitting examples of gradations among the ranks of Christians.

Two Biblical passages Jerome uses against Jovinian are particularly revealing, since they concern the same issues he faced during the Origenist controversy. His interpretation of these passages, *contra* Jovinian, solidifies the argument he will use against Origenism a few years later. One passage is the parable of the laborers in the vineyard. Jovinian had noted that all the laborers received the same reward, one penny; no differentiation was made, despite the different lengths of time they had worked. Jerome interprets the parable differently: the one penny means only that the laborers will all arrive at one heaven, but the emphasis of the parable lies in their varying calls.[360] Here Jerome posits the theme of one afterlife, but gradation within it, the same view he will later press against a simple acceptance of the *apokatastasis*.

---

[351] Jerome, *Adversus Jovinianum* I, 8 (*PL* 23, 232).

[352] Jerome, *Adversus Jovinianum* I, 33 (*PL* 23, 267).

[353] Jerome, *Adversus Jovinianum* II, 31 (*PL* 23, 342–343).

[354] Jerome, *Adversus Jovinianum* II, 18 (*PL* 23, 326–327).

[355] Jerome, *Adversus Jovinianum* II, 21; 33; 35 (*PL* 23, 329, 345, 349).

[356] Jerome, *Adversus Jovinianum* II, 18 (*PL* 23, 326).

[357] Jerome, *Adversus Jovinianum* II, 23 (*PL* 23, 333).

[358] Jerome, *Adversus Jovinianum* II, 25 (*PL* 23, 336).

[359] Jerome, *Adversus Jovinianum* II, 33 (*PL* 23, 344).

[360] Jerome, *Adversus Jovinianum* II, 32 (*PL* 23, 344).

A second passage that commands our interest is Jerome's interpretation of Jacob's vision at Bethel in which the angels ascend and descend the ladder. According to Jerome, we are to believe that all the angels on the ladder are saved, are among the "sheep," yet they are on higher and lower rungs. Only those angels who have descended completely off the ladder are among the "goats." Does Jovinian imagine that angels who have so descended will receive their inheritance?[361] Jerome's question to Jovinian is striking, because it concerns the exact problem Jerome will face in the Origenist controversy regarding the restoration or the nonrestoration of the devil. Jerome, against Jovinian, answers "no": the descended angels will *not* receive their inheritance. This is the same answer he will give eight or nine years later when defending himself against Rufinus's accusations of Origenism.

In whichever year between late 396 and 399 modern scholars place Jerome's treatise *Against John of Jerusalem*,[362] it nonetheless represents an earlier stage of Jerome's anti-Origenist attacks than the works composed in 401–402 and thereafter. Jerome's treatise against the bishop of Jerusalem was his reply to John's letter to Theophilus of Alexandria, in which John had attempted to clear himself of the charges of Origenist heresy that Epiphanius had levelled against him.[363] Writing (he says) three years after the clash between Epiphanius and John in Palestine,[364] Jerome chastizes John on a variety of issues: for the inappropriateness of his appeal to the bishop of Alexandria;[365] for his alleged prevarication about Epiphanius's friendly feelings toward him;[366] for raising the issue of Epiphanius's ordination of Jerome's brother Paulinianus outside the territory of his ecclesiastical jurisdiction as a "smokescreen";[367] for his attempt to clear himself of Origenist

---

[361] Jerome, *Adversus Jovinianum* II, 27 (*PL* 23, 338); see Genesis 28:12.

[362] A variety of opinions have been set forth: Grützmacher, *Hieronymus*, vol. 3: 18 (cf. vol. 1: 101) dates the *Contra Ioannem* to 398 or 399, but more recent commentators have pushed back the dating by a few years. See the discussion in Karl Holl, "Die Zeitfolge der ersten origenistischen Streits," 319 (Holl dates the *Contra Ioannem* to December 395 or January 396, shortly after Count Rufinus's death on November 27, 395, cf. *Contra Ioannem* 43. Cavallera, *Saint Jérôme*, vol. 1: 2, 34–35, favors fall or early winter of 396, and Kelly, *Jerome*, 207, opts for early 397. The earlier dating seems preferable (before Rufinus's departure from Palestine), although the reference in chapter 37 to Isidore's being under suspicion in Egypt again raises the possibility of a later dating (Theophilus only turned against Isidore after his

unsuccessful bid to seat Isidore on the episcopal chair of Constantinople in late 397). Perhaps Jerome refers to no "official" (i.e., Theophilan) condemnation of Isidore, but only to his *own* suspicions concerning Isidore's theology.

[363] For a summary of these confusing events, see Grützmacher, *Hieronymus*, vol. 3: chap. 10, #42; Cavallera, *Saint Jérôme*, vol. 1: 1, bk. 4; and Kelly, *Jerome*, chap. 18.

[364] So, Jerome debates the work: *Contra Ioannem* 1 (*PL* 23, 371).

[365] Jerome, *Contra Ioannem* 4; 5; 37 (*PL* 23, 374–375, 406–407).

[366] Jerome, *Contra Ioannem* 4; 14; 44 (*PL* 23, 374, 382–383, 412): Jerome lets his readers know that Epiphanius considered John a heretic.

[367] Jerome, *Contra Ioannem* 41 (*PL* 23, 410–411).

charges by piously condemning ancient heresies that were "corrected long ago";[368] and for his failure to address squarely the charges of Origenism that Epiphanius had made against him.[369] In the midst of this attack that so largely pertains to a precise historical moment, Jerome also notes the points of Origen's theology that he considers unorthodox.

Eight heretical points are listed by Jerome in section seven of his polemic against John. A close analysis of the charges reveals that the list is lifted directly from Epiphanius's accusatory letter to John (= Jerome, *Epistle* 51). The list is not, however, identical with that Epiphanius presents in *Panarion* 64: in Epiphanius's letter to John and in Jerome's *Against John of Jerusalem*, the charges include the restoration of the devil, not mentioned in *Panarion* 64. In addition, in both of the former works, the discussion of the loss of the "image of God" is placed at the end of the list, unlike *Panarion* 64.[370] Moreover, Jerome's list—like that in Epiphanius's letter to John—contains none of the confused argument on the resurrection body that Epiphanius had borrowed from Methodius and prominently inserted in *Panarion* 64.[371] The eight charges against Origen that appear in Jerome's *Against John of Jerusalem* are, in order:

1. The Son cannot see the Father nor the Holy Spirit the Son.

2. Souls had their origin as rational creatures that fell into bodies, construed as prisons; as in Epiphanius's letter to John, the Origenists are said on this point to appeal to Psalms 119:67, 116:7, and 142:7.[372]

3. The devil and demons will repent and come to reign with the saints.[373]

4. The "tunics of skins" of Genesis 3:21 are to be interpreted as bodies.

5. The resurrection of the flesh is denied in Origen's explication of Psalm 1.

6. Origen allegorized the geographical and physical reality of Paradise.

7. Origen allegorized the interpretation of the waters above the heavens and below the earth in his exegesis of Genesis.

8. Humans have lost "the image and likeness of God" through sin.[374]

Despite Jerome's heavy dependence on Epiphanius's list, he also demonstrates that he was a close reader of Origen. At some points, his own read-

---

[368] Jerome, *Contra Ioannem* 5; cf. 21 (*PL* 23, 375, 388). The accusation is of interest because Jerome himself used exactly the same technique a few years later: see above, p. 125 and below p. 150.

[369] Jerome, *Contra Ioannem* 5; 6; 8; 16; 21; 27–28; 41 (*PL* 23, 375–376, 377, 384–385, 388, 395–397, 410).

[370] See the discussion above, p. 92.

[371] See above, pp. 92–94.

[372] Epiphanius, *Ep. ad Ioannem Episcopum* (= Jerome, *Ep.* 51) 4 (*CSEL* 54, 402). *Pa-*

narion 64, 4, 5–8 (*GCS* 31², 412) lists the first two passages but lacks the third.

[373] In Epiphanius's *Letter to John of Jerusalem* (= Jerome, *Ep.* 51), the section on the restoration of the devil (5) occurs in the same position as in Jerome's rendition of the charge, between the fall of the rational creatures and the "coats of skins" (*CSEL* 54, 403).

[374] The list of charges runs from section 4 through section 6 of Epiphanius's letter (*CSEL* 54, 401–409).

ings of Origen provide him with a slightly more sympathetic approach to Origen than Epiphanius was willing to countenance. When, for example, Jerome takes up the debate over whether souls were created out of angels, he retorts that the question is not appropriately framed, since Origen never held this view. Rather, Jerome claims, for Origen, "angel" is the name of an office, not of a nature.[375] We know from *Panarion* 64,4 that Epiphanius, for his part, believed that Origen taught that pre-existent souls were "angels."[376] Moreover, although Jerome prefers to turn the issue of whether the Son "sees" the Father into an anti-Arian debate,[377] he at least—unlike Epiphanius—acknowledges Origen's rationale for the claim, that the Godhead is invisible and thus cannot be "seen".[378] Last although Jerome disagrees with Origen's teaching on the resurrection body, he has himself read Origen's *On the Resurrection, Exposition of Psalm 1,* and *Miscellanies*[379] in addition to *On First Principles,* and hence can make an independent judgment on the matter, unclouded by Methodius's confused description of Origen's teaching. This point is examined in more detail below.

Even though Jerome replicates Epiphanius's list of Origen's errors, he is obviously more interested in some charges than others. Although Jerome complains that John had responded to only three of the eight points Epiphanius had set forth against Origen's teaching,[380] Jerome himself concentrates heavily on just two: the debate over the soul's origin and that over the resurrection of the body. Surprisingly, he does not here seem particularly interested in the theme of the devil's restoration. Nor does he fault Origen's theology in detail for its implications concerning reproduction: Jerome merely raises the question in passing of what it could mean on Origenist grounds that Isaac, Samson, and John the Baptist are called children of promise, if it is an offense to be born with a human body. He cannot at the moment take the time to write against all of Origen's errors—but he piously adds that if Christ gives him a longer life, he will compose another book on the remaining issues.[381] Jerome's earlier discussions of marriage and childbearing would not, in any event, lead us to imagine that he would present himself as an ardent champion of reproduction.

Jerome devotes sections 16–22 of his treatise against John of Jerusalem to the question of the origin of the soul. He presses John to state plainly

[375] Jerome, *Contra Ioannem* 17 (PL 23, 385).
[376] Epiphanius, *Panarion* 64, 4 (GCS 31², 411).
[377] Jerome, *Contra Ioannem* 8 (PL 23, 377)—although in section 9, Jerome can mock John, "Nobody was accusing you of being an Arian" (PL 23, 378–379). This may not actually have been the case: see Yves-Marie Duval, "Sur les insinuations de Jérôme contre Jean de Jérusalem: De l'Arianisme á l'Origenisme," 353–374.
[378] Jerome, *Contra Ioannem* 9 (PL 23, 378).
[379] Jerome, *Contra Ioannem* 25 (PL 23, 392).
[380] Jerome, *Contra Ioannem* 6 (PL 23, 375–376).
[381] Jerome, *Contra Ioannem* 22 (PL 23, 389–390).

whether he accepts Origen's views that souls have a preexistent life as rational creatures before they acquire bodies, and that rational creatures (including the demons) will later be restored to their original condition so that God will be "all in all."[382] Faulting John for not knowing that Origen did *not* teach that souls were created from angels, Jerome nonetheless alleges that Origen's views were derived from pagan philosophy. With great assurance, he suggests that if John reads his *Commentaries on Ecclesiastes* and *on Ephesians*, written "about ten years ago," he like "thoughtful men" could note that Jerome's views were not those of Origen's.[383]

Jerome wants a plain answer from John: did the soul exist before the body? If so, how did it become attached to the body?[384] Or was it rather made at the same time as the body?[385] Or do humans receive their souls through propagation, bodies coming from bodies and souls from souls?[386] In this polemic against John, composed in about 397, Jerome is already completely confident of the correct position: that God *daily* creates souls, an activity consonant with his ongoing role as Creator. But if we receive a good soul from God directly, Jerome asks, how then did human degeneration occur? Even the good seed can degenerate into darnel and wild oats, he alleges, "because the cause of vices and virtues is not in the seed, but in the will of him who is born."[387] Jerome thus gives the precise answer that would be supplied by Pelagius and his followers a few years thereafter.[388] Although Jerome does not here register that he is dealing with one of the most perplexing and unresolved topics of late ancient philosophy and religion—a topic that would plague Augustine for years[389]—he would soon realize that the matter was far more complex (and dangerous) than he had assumed in 397. Soon he would learn to skirt the issue of the soul's origin so as to avoid falling into possible error.[390]

The second major defect of Origen's theology to which Jerome devotes detailed attention in his polemic *Against John of Jerusalem* concerns the resurrection state. The main thrust of Jerome's attack is that John had not affirmed the "resurrection of the flesh," only the "resurrection of the

---

[382] Jerome, *Contra Ioannem* 16, alluding to I Corinthians 15:28 (*PL* 23, 384). Jerome now recognizes this verse as a prime Origenist proof-text, rather than as supporting an anti-Arian polemic, as he had thought earlier: see above, pp. 126–127.

[383] Jerome, *Contra Ioannem* 17 (*PL* 23, 385–386); cf. 19 (*PL* 23, 387).

[384] Jerome, *Contra Ioannem* 20 (*PL* 23, 387).

[385] Jerome, *Contra Ioannem* 21 (*PL* 23, 388).

[386] Jerome, *Contra Ioannem* 22 (*PL* 23, 389).

[387] Jerome, *Contra Ioannem* 22 (*PL* 23, 389–390).

[388] See below, p. 219.

[389] For an exhaustive discussion of the topic see Robert J. O'Connell, *The Origin of the Soul in St. Augustine's Writings*.

[390] Jerome's correspondence with Augustine on this point perhaps alerted him to the possibilities of dangerous implications: see below, pp. 221–224. Note that in the *Apologia* II, 10 (*CCL* 79, 41–43), Jerome also impatiently implies that every right-thinking Christian knows that there is a correct answer to the question.

body,"[391] an omission that Jerome suspects cloaks an Origenist position.[392] For Jerome, Christians must affirm a fleshly resurrection that includes blood, veins, bones, sinews,[393] and all our organs, including the sexual ones that Origen denies we will have in the resurrection.[394] Jerome does not, however, misrepresent Origen's position. He reports that Origen believed that humans possessed a "seed" containing the "original principles" of the body's constitution that would ensure continuity of identity in the resurrection state,[395] despite the ultimate reversion of fleshly matter to the four elements from which it was created.[396] Even though he provides an informed rendition of Origen's view, Jerome finds Origen's witticisms about the absence of barbers and runny noses in the resurrection more shocking than humorous.[397] Although Jerome suspects that John will try to evade the charge of Origenism by claiming that he "thought that the body was the same as the flesh," this response will not exonerate him, since (Jerome claims) although all flesh is body, not all body is flesh.[398] According to Jerome, since Origen's arguments were designed to counter pagan mockery of Christians' belief in the resurrection body, it is not seemly for John or others to appropriate arguments that merely served as a sop to "heathens."[399] No longer, he implies, do we need to construct "apologies" for a pagan audience; the issue now centers on orthodoxy within or deviation from the Christian fold.

Despite Jerome's claim that he affirms a "same flesh" doctrine of the resurrection,[400] modern readers can note the ways in which he modifies the "physicality" of his stated position. Of course, he asserts, the flesh of the resurrection will be "glorious" and "immortal," unlike our present flesh.[401] Certainly we will not eat or drink in the afterlife,[402] nor use the sexual organs that Jerome nonetheless so adamantly asserts we will possess.[403] Moreover, he is aware that descriptions of Jesus' resurrection body in the

---

[391] Jerome, *Contra Ioannem* 25; 27 (*PL* 23, 392, 395–396). That Jerome's critique of John's views on the resurrection was indebted to Tertullian has been strongly argued by Yves-Marie Duval, "Tertullien contre Origène sur la résurrection de la chair dans le *Contra Iohannem Hierosolymitanum* 22–36 de saint Jérôme," 227–278.

[392] Jerome, *Contra Ioannem* 27 (*PL* 23, 396).

[393] Jerome, *Contra Ioannem* 27 (*PL* 23, 396).

[394] Jerome, *Contra Ioannem* 25 (*PL* 23, 392); see 31 for Jerome's repetition of "John will be John, and Mary, Mary" (*PL* 23, 390).

[395] Jerome, *Contra Ioannem* 26 (*PL* 23, 393–394).

[396] Jerome, *Contra Ioannem* 25 (*PL* 23, 392–393).

[397] Jerome, *Contra Ioannem* 26 (*PL* 23, 395).

[398] Jerome, *Contra Ioannem* 27 (*PL* 23, 395).

[399] Jerome, *Contra Ioannem* 32 (*PL* 23, 400).

[400] Jerome, *Contra Ioannem* 28 (*PL* 23, 397).

[401] Jerome, *Contra Ioannem* 29 (*PL* 23, 397–398).

[402] Jerome, *Contra Ioannem* 26; 34 (*PL* 23, 395, 404).

[403] Jerome, *Contra Ioannem* 31 (*PL* 23, 399–400); cf. to *Ep.* 108, 23 (*CSEL* 55, 340), in which an Origenist mocks Paula and other Christians who believe that we shall have (and thus presumably use) our restored sexual organs.

Gospels are ambiguous. Why, for example, did not Jesus' disciples recognize him on the road to Emmaus if he possessed the same fleshly body that he earlier had? Jerome improvises an answer: because Jesus "held their eyes" so that they would not recognize him.[404] As for the resurrected Jesus' passage through a closed door (John 20:26), Jerome suggests that by performing this act, Jesus displayed his spiritual state, just as he had manifested the materiality of his resurrection body by eating and drinking.[405] Jerome's advocacy of a "this flesh" resurrection body, like Epiphanius's,[406] is somewhat more qualified than his polemic at first sight suggests.[407]

The next few years show Jerome stepping up his anti-Origenist rhetoric. Although he still can praise Origen's *Contra Celsum* and *Miscellanies* for their adroitness in (respectively) countering pagan attacks and exploiting philosophy on behalf of the Christian faith,[408] Jerome continued to press the necessity of affirming the physicality of the resurrection body ("Paul will still be Paul, and Mary, Mary") against those heretics who take away Christians' certainty while holding out "vague promises."[409] Probably before the end of 399, Jerome wrote to Theophilus, stirring him to a more decisive stance against Origenists.[410] By 399, much had of course occurred within the Origenist debate: Rufinus had translated *On First Principles* into Latin and the translation had disturbed Jerome's Roman friends, prompting them to request from Jerome a more literal version of the work that would accurately reveal the errors of Origen.[411] The respective networks had been aroused to vigorous activity.

In his letter at the turn of the century responding to Pammachius's and Oceanus's request for a more literal translation of the *Peri Archōn*[412] (*Epistle* 84), Jerome at last registers a premonition of the danger to which he has exposed himself. In the preface to his translation of *On First Principles*, Rufinus had covered Jerome with praise for *his* translations of and commentaries upon Origen's work, thus surreptitiously suggesting that Jerome

---

[404] Jerome, *Contra Ioannem* 35 (*PL* 23, 405), alluding to the story in Luke 24:13–35.

[405] Jerome, *Contra Ioannem* 26 (*PL* 23, 395).

[406] See above, pp. 88, 94.

[407] As Yves-Marie Duval has noted, the resurrection of the flesh was not a topic disturbing Jerome's mind before 393: "Sur les insinuations," 360.

[408] Jerome, *Ep.* 70, 3–4 (*CSEL* 54, 703–706). This letter is dated by Cavallera to late 397 or early 398 (*Saint Jérôme*, vol. 1: 2, 46).

[409] Jerome, *Ep.* 75, 2 (*CSEL* 55, 31–32). This letter is dated by Cavallera to 399 (*Saint Jérôme*, vol. 1: 2, 46).

[410] Jerome, *Ep.* 63, 3 (*CSEL* 54, 586).

This letter is dated by Cavallera to the end of 399 (*Saint Jérôme*, vol. 1: 2, 39–40).

[411] For a summary of these events, see Grützmacher, *Hieronymus*, vol. 3: chap. 10, #46; Cavallera, *Saint Jérôme*, vol. 1: 1, bk. 4; Kelly, *Jerome*, chap. 20.

[412] Pammachius's and Oceanus's letter to Jerome is preserved as *Ep.* 83 of Jerome. Cavallera dates Jerome's response (= *Ep.* 84) to the winter of 398 or early 399 (*Saint Jérôme*, vol. 1: 2, 37–38), correcting Grützmacher's dating of 401 (*Hieronymus*, vol. 1: 100). In *Apologia* I, 24 (*CCL* 79, 24), Jerome claims that this letter was composed two years before the *Apology* he is presently writing.

stood in the Origenist camp.[413] Jerome is quick to distance himself from Rufinus's insinuation: his earlier praise of Origen and his translation of Origen's books had nothing to do with the issues of doctrine now under dispute; Jerome claims that he had always stuck to the "ethical issues" in Origen's teaching, leaving aside the speculative theories. Let the curious seek out his commentaries on Ecclesiastes and on Ephesians and they will see that he is no Origenist![414] Jerome asserts that as long as twenty years ago he had challenged Origen's interpretation of the seraphim of Isaiah 6:2 as the Son and the Holy Spirit, arguing instead that they symbolized the two Testaments.[415] Nor will he revert to the prevarications of Origenists who argue that since the Fathers at Nicaea never condemned Origen, neither should they.[416] Pointing out that the appeal to Nicaea is merely an evasion—but that nonetheless, Origen's theology is the root of Arius's subordinationism[417]—Jerome launches into a wholesale attack upon the erroneous views of Origen. Pride of place is given to the Origenists' advocacy of the "resurrection of the body" rather than the "resurrection of the flesh."[418] Moreover, Origen was also wrong in his teachings about the Son and the Holy Spirit, and about the fall of souls from heaven. As for the "restitution of all things" (Acts 3:21), the *apokatastasis*, its main difficulty according to Jerome is that it does not allow for a sufficient differentiation on the basis of moral behavior here and now. Rather, Gabriel and the devil, Paul and Caiaphas, virgins and prostitutes will all receive one and the same reward[419]—the exact argument that Jerome had forged in the controversy with Jovinian and that had become the linchpin of his anti-Origenist polemic.[420]

Interestingly, at this stage of the debate Jerome is willing to concede that in his youth he was overly enthusiastic for Origen. But bygones should be bygones. He writes that if his Origenist opponent who is addressed as a friend of his misguided youth—clearly Rufinus—is willing to return to the right path with Jerome in old age, Jerome will be all too happy to cease the debate.[421] Jerome claims that he would prefer to praise Origen even today, if others were not so avidly praising his errors.[422]

That Jerome could still appeal to Origen not just for his Scriptural learning and his knowledge of Hebrew, but for weightier—and even dangerous—points of theology, is further suggested by his response to Paulinus

---

[413] Jerome, *Ep.* 84, 1–2 (*CSEL* 55, 121–122).

[414] Jerome, *Ep.* 84, 2 (*CSEL* 55, 122).

[415] Jerome, *Ep.* 84, 3 (*CSEL* 55, 123–124); cf. *Ep.* 18A, 14 on the seraphim (*CSEL* 54, 91).

[416] Jerome, *Ep.* 84, 4 (*CSEL* 55, 125), with a probable veiled slap at either Rufinus or John of Jerusalem.

[417] Jerome, *Ep.* 84, 4 (*CSEL* 55, 125–126).

[418] Jerome, *Ep.* 84, 5 (*CSEL* 55, 126–127).

[419] Jerome, *Ep.* 84, 7 (*CSEL* 55, 129).

[420] See above, pp. 130–132.

[421] Jerome, *Ep.* 84, 6 (*CSEL* 55, 127–128); cf. *Apologia* III, 9 (*CCL* 79, 82).

[422] Jerome, *Ep.* 84, 7 (*CSEL* 55, 128).

of Nola in *Epistle* 85. When Paulinus inquired of Jerome how to reconcile passages such as Exodus 7:13 (the hardening of Pharoah's heart) and Paul's teaching in Romans 9 with the notion of free will, Jerome responded by suggesting that Paulinus read Origen's *On First Principles* (in Jerome's translation) as the best text addressing this thorny problem.[423] Although, Jerome says, some teachings of Origen are doubtless "objectionable," he tells Paulinus that he is not so boorish as to wish to condemn everything Origen wrote: surprising to the modern reader is Jerome's seeming lack of comprehension that Origen's proposed resolution to the thorny problems of theodicy were *exactly* the issues that might be considered highly "objectionable" by the turn to the fifth century. Jerome is especially eager to impress Paulinus with his consistent attitude toward Origen over time.[424] Yet at practically the same moment that he presses this judicious approach upon Paulinus—A.D. 400[425]—he is also congratulating Theophilus for his rout of the Egyptian Origenists[426] and reporting on his own anti-Origenist activities.[427]

If we accept Morin's dating of Jerome's *Fifty-Nine Homilies on the Psalms* to 401 or 402,[428] this work sheds further light on the state of Jerome's thinking about Origenism in these years. Far from his favorable treatment of Origen in the *Commentarioli on Psalms*, written about a decade earlier,[429] Jerome is now concerned to show his hand at anti-Origenist interpretation. The "mischief that returns upon the head" of the wicked (Psalm 7:16) is now taken as an injunction against the view that the devil will repent; Jerome tells his readers that the devil shall rather receive eternal punishment.[430] Commenting on Psalm 90:2 ("Before the mountains were brought forth . . ."), Jerome informs his audience that only heretics believe that souls existed "before mountains."[431] In a third passage, he attacks Origen by name: commenting on Psalm 79:11 ("Let the groans of the prisoners come in your face"), Jerome remarks that Origen referred this verse to the "groans" of angels imprisoned in bodies, fallen to earth from their heavenly home. To support such a view, Jerome adds, Origenists appeal to Romans 7:24, "Wretched man that I am, who shall deliver me from this body of death?' (a verse also cited as an Origenist proof-text in *Against*

---

[423] Jerome, *Ep.* 85, 2–3 (*CSEL* 55, 136–137).

[424] Jerome, *Ep.* 85, 4 (*CSEL* 55, 137).

[425] Cavallera dates *Epp.* 86 and 88 to 400, and *Ep.* 85 to "after 399" (*Saint Jérôme*, vol. 1: 2, 38; 89).

[426] Jerome, *Ep.* 86 (*CSEL* 55, 138–139).

[427] Jerome, *Ep.* 88 (*CSEL* 55, 141–142).

[428] See G. Morin, *Praefatio, CCL* 78, xi n.1. In the *Commentarioli*, Jerome remarks that twenty years earlier, the churches were in the hands of heretics (*CCL* 78, 285), i.e.,

Arians. The situation was corrected by Theodosius I's edict of 381 restoring basilicas to the Catholics. Questions regarding Jerome's authorship of the *Tractatus* are raised by Vittorio Peri, *Omelie origeniane sui Salmi: Contributo all' identificazione del testo latino.*

[429] See above, p. 125.

[430] Jerome, *Tractatus LVIIII in Librum Psalmorum* (*CCL* 78, 27).

[431] Jerome, *Tractatus LVIIII in Librum Psalmorum* (*CCL* 78, 119–120).

John of Jerusalem[432]) and Philippians 1:23, "I wish to be released and be with Christ." Jerome, by way of refutation, reminds his readers that the Greek original does not mean "be released" (*dissolvi*) but "return" (*reverti*)[433]—and "returning to Christ" from prison is better applied to Christian martyrs than to embodied angels.[434] Yet even from the vantage point of about 401, Jerome does not hesitate in the *Fifty-Nine Homilies on the Psalms* to repeat the Origenist interpretation of God's "footstool" (Psalm 99:5) as the human nature that Christ assumed from Mary.[435] Given Jerome's protest against the Origenist view of the resurrection body that was predicated on the notion of the constant change in human flesh,[436] also interesting is his comment on Psalm 144:4, "Man is like a breath, a passing shadow." We are always either growing or shrinking; our bodies change from moment to moment and are never the same.[437] Jerome does not seem aware that he may be undercutting his own ardently championed view of the identity of our flesh here and now with our flesh in the resurrection by advocating the notion of the body's constant flux.

Our knowledge of Jerome's charges against Origen is surprisingly little advanced by his *Apology against Rufinus*, dated either to 401–402[438] or to 402–403[439]—"surprisingly," because this treatise is by far the longest statement from Jerome pertaining to the Origenist controversy. The function of the work, however, is to remove from Jerome any taint of Origenism and to pin Origenist charges on Rufinus instead: the battle is now constructed as one directed more against the leader of the opposing network than against Origen. Jerome must distance himself from the interpretations of Origen he presented without criticism in the *Ephesians Commentary* (written "about eighteen years earlier," he reports),[440] and show that lurking beneath Rufinus's confession of faith to Anastasius of Rome lie Origenist views. Although Jerome had received only oral reports of Rufinus's attack upon him when he composed books I and II of his *Apology*,[441]

---

[432] Jerome, *Contra Ioannem* 17 (*PL* 23, 386).

[433] The Greek text reads that Paul has the desire "*eis to analusai kai sun Christo einai.*"

[434] Jerome, *Tractatus LVIIII in Librum Psalmorum* (*CCL* 78, 74–75, on Psalm 79:11). Jerome already conveniently seems to have forgotten that only a few years earlier, he had defended Origen against misrepresentation: Origen had *not* taught that angels become souls. See above, p. 134. On the theme of the body as a prison in Greek philosophy, Jerome, and Augustine, see Pierre Courcelle, "Tradition platonicienne et traditions chrétiennes du corps-prison (Phédon 62b; Cratyle 400c)," 406–443.

[435] Jerome, *Tractatus LVIIII in Librum Psalmorum* (*CCL* 78, 172, on Psalm 99:5);

cf. Origen, *In Isaiam*, Hom. 5, 1 (*PG* 13, 235).

[436] See above, p. 136.

[437] Jerome, *Tractatus LVIIII in Librum Psalmorum* (*CCL* 78, 315, on Psalm 144:4). There is also a second series of *Homilies on Psalms* ascribed to Jerome, but the dating of them is quite uncertain. Nonetheless, anti-Origenistic interpretation is given in comments on Psalms 16:7; 84:3; 84:7; 89:3; 89:6; 90:1; 94:2. The text of the second series is given in *CCL* 78, 355–446.

[438] Cavallera, *Saint Jérôme*, vol. 1: 2, 41.

[439] Grützmacher, *Hieronymus*, vol. 1: 101; Cavallera's date seems preferable.

[440] Jerome, *Apologia* I, 22 (*CCL* 79, 22).

[441] Jerome, *Apologia* I, 15; III, 1 (*CCL* 79, 14, 73).

his informants appear to have given him a very detailed account of Rufinus's accusations.

To distance himself from the Origenist views cited in the *Ephesians Commentary*, Jerome offers various disclaimers. First, he argues that it is the
correct style in commentary writing for the author to list several interpretations and let his readers choose the one they prefer.[442] Rufinus was mistaken in believing that each opinion Jerome cited was endorsed by him. In
fact, since he had already denied such views as that souls were made out of
angels, it would have been inconsistent for him to champion the same view
in other places.[443] Jerome also cites some passages in Ephesians on which,
he alleges, he expressed outright disagreement with Origen's interpretation. For example, commenting on Ephesians 1:4 ("He chose us before the
foundation of the world that we might be holy and unspotted before
him"), Jerome claims that he had discounted Origen's view that the verse
referred to the preexistent souls, although the words Jerome cites from the
Ephesians Commentary in his own defense do not address the question of
preexistence, but rather merely supply a moral rather than a cosmological
interpretation.[444] He asserts that his comments on Ephesians 1:20–21
plainly show his rejection of Origen's notion that heavenly powers are
changed into demons or humans; rather, he claims, he meant that angels
have different offices.[445] He was not wrong—and was not an Origenist—
when in the *Ephesians Commentary* he called the body the "chain" of the
soul,[446] for vice and disease are indeed "chains" in our present earthly
life.[447] Addressing Ephesians 4:16, Jerome states that although he had in
the *Commentary* mentioned Origen's view of the "restitution of all things,"
his emphasis was nonetheless to affirm that there will not be only rank in
the afterlife, but a variety of offices; otherwise, "the righteous and the sinners would be equal to each other." Jerome does not, however, now acknowledge that the very passage he cites from his *Ephesians Commentary*
claimed that humans would be restored to their paradisiacal condition and
that "the apostate angel shall begin to be that which he was by his creation"—the notion of the devil's restoration that Jerome now deems a heresy.[448] When he cited Origen's claim that in the afterlife, wives will be
turned into men and bodies into spirits so that there will be no differentiation of sex,[449] he meant only to teach that lust and sexual intercourse will
be absent from the afterlife, although sexual distinction will remain.[450]

---

[442] Jerome, *Apologia* I, 16; 22 (*CCL* 79, 14–15, 21).

[443] Jerome, *Apologia* I, 15 (*CCL* 79, 14). But see above, p. 134.

[444] Jerome, *Apologia* I, 22 (*CCL* 79, 21–22).

[445] Jerome, *Apologia* I, 23 (*CCL* 79, 23).

[446] Jerome's exegesis of Ephesians 3:1, in

his *Comm. ad Eph.* II (*PL* 26, 477).

[447] Jerome, *Apologia* I, 25 (*CCL* 79, 25).

[448] Jerome, *Apologia* I, 26–27 (*CCL* 79, 26–27).

[449] Cited in *Apologia* I, 28 (*CCL* 79, 27), commenting on Ephesians 5: 28–29.

[450] Jerome, *Apologia* I, 29 (*CCL* 79, 28–29).

With these explanations, Jerome thinks that he had successfully defended himself against any earlier association with the heretical opinions of Origen.

It is surprising to note that in levelling charges of Origenism against Rufinus, Jerome affords his readers a view of which opinions of Origen he deems particularly reprehensible. Several points in Rufinus's *Apology to Anastasius* seem highly suspicious to Jerome. First, he thinks that Rufinus must make clear his position on the origin of the soul—both the human soul in general, and the soul of Jesus in particular. Were souls formed earlier in heaven and sent down into bodies? Were souls generated by "traduction" along with bodies?[451] Or were souls sent into bodies after the latter were formed in the womb?[452] Rufinus's proclamation of ignorance on this matter[453] is, to Jerome, merely a cover for Origenist views. Jerome knows the answer to the question and boldly sets it forth: God forms souls every day and places them in the bodies who are born.[454] According to Jerome, Rufinus is neatly avoiding a condemnation of Origen's view that souls existed before bodies and were linked to them because of a sin committed in their prebodily state.[455]

A second point that Jerome finds suspicious in Rufinus's profession of faith concerns the resurrection state: Rufinus never confesses that it is "this very flesh" which will rise again in its bodily integrity. Does Rufinus believe that "Mary will still be Mary and John be John"? Or does he believe (with Origen) that the flesh will dissolve into nothing, reduced to the four elements from which it was made? Rufinus's claim that "no part of the body will be cut off" affords Jerome the opportunity to joke that Rufinus perhaps fears that we will rise without noses and ears (a jibe at the one-eared Ammonius?),[456] and that the new Jerusalem will be populated entirely with eunuchs.[457]

The third point in Rufinus's statement of faith questioned by Jerome concerns the salvation of the devil. Although Rufinus had written that the devil and his angels would inherit the "eternal fires," Jerome finds the statement unsatisfactory, since for Origen those "fires" were identified as the sinner's remorseful conscience. If Rufinus had truly rejected the notion of the devil's restoration, Jerome claims, he could have appealed to a number of Scriptural verses for assistance, including Ezekiel 28:19 ("You have come to a dreadful end, and shall be no more forever") and Job 41, on God's power over Leviathan.[458]

---

[451] Jerome, *Apologia* II, 4 (*CCL* 79, 36).

[452] Jerome, *Apologia* II, 10 (*CCL* 79, 42).

[453] Jerome, *Apologia* II, 8; 10 (*CCL* 79, 40, 41).

[454] Jerome, *Apologia* III, 28 (*CCL* 79, 100). See discussion above, pp. 134–135.

[455] Jerome, *Apologia* III, 30 (*CCL* 79, 102).

[456] See above, p. 46.

[457] Jerome, *Apologia* II, 5 (*CCL* 79, 37).

[458] Jerome, *Apologia* II, 7 (*CCL* 79, 38–39).

It is thus surprising to note that in only three passages of his entire *Apology* does Jerome actually identify for his readers the errors of Origen. The first such list, near the beginning of the Book I, includes an unspecified charge of Trinitarian error, to which is joined the fall of angels and of human souls, teachings about the resurrection and about the world ("or rather, about Epicurus's middle-spaces"), the restitution of all rational creatures to a state of equality, and "others much worse than these, which it would take too long to recite." All these errors Jerome has found in *On First Principles*.[459] In a second passage, Jerome reports that Origen was in error on the transmigration of souls, the infinite number of worlds, the assumption of various bodies by rational creatures, and the repeated suffering of Christ.[460]

The most detailed list of Origen's errors that Jerome recounts in his *Apology*, however, falls in Book II, 12. They are, in order: (1) that the Son is a creature and the Holy Spirit a servant; (2) that innumerable worlds will continue on into eternity; (3) that angels become human souls; (4) that Jesus' soul existed before his birth;[461] (5) that the resurrection body will not have the members that we now possess but will be "aerial," gradually dissolving into nothingness; (6) that there will be a restitution of all things, so that the devil, demons, and humans (whether they are Christians, Jews, or pagans) will be "of one condition and degree"; (7) that there will be a new world and different bodies for the souls that fall again after their restoration—so that men might be born as women and a virgin as a prostitute.[462]

Comparing this list to the one Jerome drew up about five years earlier in the *Against John of Jerusalem*, we note that not only is the order of charges different, but also several of the earlier charges have been dropped and new ones have been added. Some of the omissions are of interest. In 401–402, Jerome no longer wants to argue on the grounds that so plagued Epiphanius: the allegorizing of the geography of Eden and of the "tunics of skins."[463] Moreover, absent from his new list, and indeed, from his entire

[459] Jerome, *Apologia* I, 6 (CCL 79, 6): Jerome knows that Rufinus changed only the parts on the Trinity but did nothing to emend the other errors of Origen.

[460] Jerome, *Apologia* I, 20 (CCL 79, 19–20).

[461] The specific point about the soul of Jesus suggests that Apollinarianism was under discussion: was Jesus' soul truly human, or was it a "divine" soul? Theodore of Mopsuestia appears to misunderstand Apollinaris when he writes that Apollinaris taught that a divine element took the place of human feeling in Jesus (*Contra Apollinarium* [PG 66, 995]). Apollinaris does indeed deny a human *mind* to Jesus: see *Apodeixis*, frags. 76, 87, 97; *Ad Julianum*, frags. 150, 151; *Ad Diocaesareenses*, frag. 163, in *Apollinaris von Laodicea und seine Schule*, ed. Hans Lietzmann, 222, 226, 229, 247–248, 256. For discussions of Origen's teaching on Jesus' soul, see Rowan Williams, "Origen on the Soul of Jesus," 131–137; and Alain Le Boulluec, "Controverses au subjet de la doctrine d'Origène sur l'ame du Christ," 223–237.

[462] Jerome, *Apologia* II, 12 (CCL 79, 46–47).

[463] See above, p. 88.

three-volume *Apology*, is the charge that Origen taught that humans lost the "image of God": this allegation seems to have been far more important to the Egyptian and Greek-speaking participants in the debate than to Jerome.[464] The charge of subordinationism now emerges in refurbished form, no longer revolving around whether the Son "sees" the Father and the Holy Spirit, the Son.[465] Now, in 401–402, at the center of Jerome's charges are the origin of souls and their fall into bodies, the nature of the resurrection body, and the restoration of the devil, points also included in his list in *Against John of Jerusalem*.[466] New themes emerge as well: the innumerable worlds and the possibility of new "falls," with the consequent acquisition of different bodies. Moreover, Jerome shows himself responsive to the issues raised by Apollinarianism in his inclusion of the query about the origin of Jesus' soul and its attachment to his human body.[467]

Most striking of all, in this statement of charges, Jerome again declares his annoyance that in Origen's scheme, hierarchy will not be maintained into eternity: not only will the devil be placed in the same ranks as the cherubim and the seraphim, but it will not matter whether we were pagans or Jews rather than Christians. Moreover, Origen's notion that new falls may result in souls being clad with new bodies renders dubious the maintenance of proper ranking of men over women and virgins over prostitutes.[468] The issue of hierarchy, forged in the ascetic debates of the 380s and refined in his controversy with Jovinian, thus resonates throughout Jerome's anti-Origenist polemic.

In his letters from 402 on, Jerome manifests his newly heightened anti-Origenist stance. He now has more information about the Eastern branch of the controversy, no doubt derived from his translation of the letters of Theophilus. Thus when he sends Pammachius and Marcella his translation of Theophilus's festal letter of 402, he can in his cover letter refer to the exodus of the Tall Brothers from Egypt (his reference to "scars on our ears" may yet again call up the image of the earless Ammonius[469]). Jerome's cover letter indicates that he senses Theophilus's fading interest in attacking Origenists: he advises Pammachius and Marcella that if they find Theophilus's polemic against Origen in the enclosed festal letter wanting, they can refer back to Jerome's translation of the festal letter of 401, in which the charges against Origenism receive fuller treatment.[470]

In 404, while composing his memorial of Paula, Jerome details her refusal to be tricked by Origenist questions on God's justice or the resurrec-

---

[464] See above, pp. 51, 92.

[465] See above, p. 134.

[466] See above, p. 133, and *Contra Ioannem* 4; 5 (*CSEL* 54, 401–402, 403, 404).

[467] See n. 456 above.

[468] Jerome, *Apologia* II, 12 (*CCL* 79, 47).

[469] Jerome, *Ep.* 97, 2 (*CSEL* 55, 183); re-

call that Jerome had already translated Theophilus's Synodal Letter of 400 (= Jerome, *Ep.* 92, 1) with its reference to the Origenist who cut off his ear (*CSEL* 55, 148).

[470] Jerome, *Ep.* 97, 3 (*CSEL* 55, 184); the reference is to *Ep.* 96, the Festal Letter of Theophilus from 401.

tion body.[471] Given Jerome's opposition to Origen's teaching, it is interesting to note that he here accepts the view that the body is in constant flux—yet argues that these physical changes nonetheless do not render us different persons.[472]

In 406, writing to the monks Minervius and Alexander, Jerome is careful when citing Origen's *Commentary on I Thessalonians*, which contains an Origenist interpretation of resurrection,[473] to add that he does not always agree with the exegesis of the authors he cites. He adopts Paul's advice to "test everything and accept what is good" (I Thessalonians 5:21). Since Origen, despite his great learning, went astray on some points of doctrine, we should learn to mine the gold from the earth, but leave the rest behind.[474] In 407, writing to a Gallic woman named Hebydia, Jerome alleges that the notion of souls falling from heaven into bodies on the basis of diversity of merits acquired in a preexistent life is a "pagan" teaching derived from Pythagoras, Plato, and their disciples, some of whom try to introduce the view "under the pretext of Christianity."[475]

Only in 409–410, years after the height of the controversy, does Jerome for the first time make a systematic examination of Origen's *On First Principles* and list all its errors for his correspondent, Avitus. Beginning with Book I, he marches resolutely through the entire work. His letter to Avitus consists of nothing but citations from and paraphrases of Origen's book.[476] Although Jerome nowhere brings up the issue of allegorical interpretation of Genesis 1–3 or the theme of the human loss of God's image (issues he borrowed from Epiphanius when he composed his polemic *Against John of Jerusalem*),[477] all of the other points he had earlier attacked are here included. To these are added a few new items, such as that the sun, moon, and stars are alive;[478] that the "everlasting gospel" predicted in Revelation 14:6 will surpass our present Gospels as Christ's teaching surpasses that of the Old Testament;[479] and that all rational beings—angels, powers, virtues, and the "inner man"—are in some way of one essence with God.[480]

Having concluded his long and dispassionate survey of the errors in the

---

[471] Jerome, *Ep.* 108, 23 (*CSEL* 55, 339–340).

[472] Jerome, *Ep.* 108, 25 (*CSEL* 55, 343); see above, pp. 136–137.

[473] Jerome, *Ep.* 119, 9 (*CSEL* 55, 460–462). Also in 406, writing to Algasia, Jerome declares that if Origen had produced an exegesis of the parable of the dishonest steward (Luke 16:1–13), he would have referred to it; either the interpretation is lost, or Origen never wrote one (*Ep.* 121, 6 [*CSEL* 56, 26–27]).

[474] Jerome, *Ep.* 119, 11 (*CSEL* 55, 468).

[475] Jerome, *Ep.* 120, 10 (*CSEL* 56, 500).

[476] Jerome's list is useful in that it preserves Origen's wordings on the Father and the Son that Rufinus "doctored up." See Jerome, *Ep.* 124, 2 (*CSEL* 56, 97–98). For Jerome's citation of the *Peri Archōn* in this letter, and Koetschau's use of the citations in his edition of Origen's work, see Karl Müller, "Kritische Beiträge," 616–629.

[477] See above, p. 133.

[478] Jerome, *Ep.* 124, 4 (*CSEL* 56, 99).

[479] Jerome, *Ep.* 124, 12 (*CSEL* 56, 114).

[480] Jerome, *Ep.* 124, 14 (*CSEL* 56, 116–117).

Peri Archōn, Jerome adds but one point of his own interpretation: that it is "madness" to imagine (as Rufinus allegedly had) that by rendering more orthodox a few passages on the Son and the Holy Spirit, the entire impious work could be rescued.[481] Jerome warns Avitus to guard himself against the serpent and the scorpion if he reads Origen's book.[482] Since "scorpion" is one of Jerome's favorite code names for Rufinus,[483] there may here lie a hidden reference to the real target of Jerome's still-present wrath. Since Avitus had apparently asked Jerome to send a copy of his more accurate translation of Origen's *On First Principles* to supplant the pirated version he had seen, Jerome doubtless felt that he should protect his reputation as an anti-Origenist by appending to the translation a cover letter that detailed all the book's doctrinal errors. This time, there could be no mistaking *which* passages of Origen Jerome thought were blasphemous. He had doubtless been stung by Rufinus's earlier accusations regarding his *Ephesians Commentary.* Yet that Jerome was no longer in the midst of a heated controversy is suggested by his failure to discuss the various errors of Origen that he notes for Avitus: it is sufficient for Jerome's present purpose simply to make clear which opinions *are* erroneous.

Other letters from 409–410 onward devote less attention to the Origenist controversy, yet some references occur here and there. When correspondents ask him about the origin of the soul, Jerome refers them to his *Apology against Rufinus.*[484] Upon Marcella's death, he gives fulsome praise to her public attack upon Origenism in Rome.[485] He alludes to an unnamed heretic (probably Origen) who in his exegesis destroyed the historical reality of the land of Judea.[486] By 414, however, Jerome's references to Origenism in his letters have become the mere backdrop for his assault on a new heresy, Pelagianism. Thus in *Epistle* 130 to Demetrias and *Epistle* 133 to Ctesiphon, Jerome asserts that such issues in the Origenist controversy as the justice of God have led directly to the new heresy.[487] Of greatest interest for our understanding of the Origenist controversy, it is only now,

---

[481] Jerome, *Ep.* 124, 15 (*CSEL* 56, 117). For a discussion of the Trinitarian issue in the translation of *On First Principles*, see Basil Studer, "Zur Frage der dogmatischen Terminologie in der Lateinischen Übersetzung von Origenes' *De principiis,*" 403–414; and Gustave Bardy, *Recherches sur l'histoire du texte et des versions latines du De Principiis d'Origène,* esp. 134–137. Also see Heinrich Hoppe, "Rufin als Uebersetzer," 133–150; and M. Monica Wagner, *Rufinus, The Translator: A Study of His Theory and His Practice as Illustrated in His Version of the Apologetica of St. Gregory Nazianzen.*

[482] Jerome, *Ep.* 124, 15 (*CSEL* 56, 117).

[483] See, for example, *In Esaiam* X, *prologus*

(*CCL* 73, 396); *In Hiezechielem* I, *prologus* (*CCL* 75, 3).

[484] Jerome, *Ep.* 126, 1 (*CSEL* 56, 143); cf. *Apologia* II, 8–10; III, 30 (*CCL* 79, 40–43, 102).

[485] Jerome, *Ep.* 127, 9–10 (*CSEL* 56, 152–153). Marcella died after the sack of Rome in 410; Jerome's memorial of her comes from about two years later, probably 413 (Cavallera, *Saint Jérôme,* vol. 1: 2, 53).

[486] Jerome, *Ep.* 129, 6 (*CSEL* 56, 173). Cavallera (*Saint Jérôme,* vol. 1: 2, 54) dates the letter to 414.

[487] Jerome, *Epp.* 130, 16; 133, 3 (*CSEL* 56, 196–197, 244–247).

in the midst of the Pelagian controversy, that Jerome has any awareness of Evagrius Ponticus and his links to his now-dead enemies, Rufinus and Melania the Elder, and the close association of this group with the circle of Isidore and the Tall Brothers.[488] What Theophilus in all likelihood knew in 400[489] has only now, belatedly, crossed Jerome's consciousness.

It was not only in his letters from 402 on that Jerome attempts to distance himself from Origenist positions. After his skirmishes with Rufinus in the early years of the fifth century, Jerome returned to writing commentaries upon the Old Testament books. In these, we find him continuing to jab at Origenism and to suggest by his frequent attacks upon earlier heretics that he himself was entirely orthodox. Although he candidly admits that he had used Origen's commentaries on these same Biblical books in composing his own works,[490] he is now much more careful than before to distance himself from Origenism. In his *Commentary on Hosea*, completed in 406, Jerome faults Rufinus for making bad Latin from good Greek in his translation of *On First Principles*,[491] declares heretical the notion of the soul's fall from heaven,[492] and identifies as Origen's the idea of the fall of angels.[493] Writing on Daniel in 407, he acknowledges his debt to Origen at several points,[494] but criticizes Origen's teaching on the restoration of the devil, here identified with the king of Nineveh.[495] In the *Daniel Commentary*, Jerome's ardent desire to express degrees of hierarchy in the afterlife takes the form of an affirmation that in heaven "learned saints" will receive higher positions than "ordinary saints."[496]

In his *Commentary on Isaiah*, completed in 408–409,[497] Jerome again cites Origen's interpretations on a few issues,[498] yet carefully rules out the interpretation that the seraphim can be identified as the Son and the Holy Spirit[499] or that the devil will at the end repent.[500] In the *Ezekiel Commen-*

[488] Jerome, *Ep.* 133, 3 (CSEL 56, 246); cf. *Dialogus adversus Pelagianos, prologus* 1 (PL 23, 517–518).

[489] On Theophilus's possible knowledge of Evagrius, see above, pp. 107, 110–111, 114, 117.

[490] Jerome, *In Osee* I, *prologus* (CCL 76, 5); *In Zachariam* I, *prologus* (CCL 76A, 748); *In Malachiam, prologus* (CCL 76A, 902); *In Danielem, prologus* (CCL 75A, 774–775); *In Isaiam,* I, *prologus* (CCL 73, 4).

[491] Jerome, *In Osee* II (CCL 76, 55, citing Hosea 5:6–7). Jerome cites Terrence, *Eunuchus, prologus* 8: "de Graecis bona, Latina faciunt non bona."

[492] Jerome, *In Zachariam* I (CCL 76A, 763, citing Zechariah 2:1–2).

[493] Jerome, *In Malachiam, prologus* (CCL 76A, 902).

[494] Jerome, *In Danielem, prologus,* and comments on 4:8; 5:10; 9:24–27; 13:1–2 (CCL 75A, 774–775, 813, 824, 880, 945).

[495] Jerome, *In Danielem,* commenting on 3:29 and 4:36 (CCL 75A, 808–809, 818–819). See also above, p. 128, and Origen, *De principiis* I, 6, 2–3.

[496] Jerome, *In Danielem* IV (CCL 75A, 938, commenting on Daniel 12:3).

[497] See CCL 73, v; Cavallera, *Saint Jérôme,* vol. 1: 2, 52.

[498] Jerome, *In Isaiam* II; III (CCL 73, 40, 92, commenting on Isaiah 2:22 and 6:9–10).

[499] Jerome, *In Isaiam* III (CCL 73, 87, commenting on Isaiah 6:2–3).

[500] Jerome, *In Isaiam* VI; VII (CCL 73, 247, 273, commenting on Isaiah 14:20 and 17:12–14).

tary of 411–414,[501] the *Peri Archōn* is declared to be a "most impious book"[502] and the "heretical" notion of the body's dissolution is faulted.[503]

In his last Biblical commentary, the *Commentary on Jeremiah*, dated to the midst of the Pelagian controversy,[504] Jerome strikes frequently at Pelagius and his followers. Nonetheless, the theme of the book of Jeremiah—the capture of Jerusalem, the exile of the Jews in Babylon, and their return to their homeland—provides Jerome with inspiration to attack the Origenist theme of the fall and "exile" of souls from heaven and their eventual return to their original condition. Commenting on Jeremiah 1:4–5, Jerome discounts the (Origenist) exegesis that relates the verse to the preexistence of the soul.[505] The interpretation of Jerusalem, from whence the Jews were exiled, as "heaven" is deemed "foolish."[506] Such an interpretation "flees the truth of history" and dissolves the Jews' historical exile into mere allegory, the fall of the soul into the body.[507] Jerome knows that his opponents mock those who prefer historical exegesis and call them "clay-towners" (*pēlousiotas*)[508]—the nickname that in 398–399 Origenists had reportedly given to those, like Jerome, who affirmed a material resurrection body.[509] Moreover, any suggestion that humans eventually become demons is ruled out.[510] That Origen's views led straight to Pelagius's is the theme of Jerome's argument, to be detailed in another chapter.[511]

In addition to faulting Origenist positions in his later Biblical commentaries, Jerome also takes the opportunity they afford to criticize and mock Rufinus. In commentaries written while Rufinus was still alive, Jerome laughs at Rufinus's ineptness as a translator of *On First Principles*,[512] complains about the "scorpion" who rises up[513] ("the scorpion" has grumbled about his *Commentary on Daniel*),[514] and mocks the image of "Grunnius Corocotta Porcelli" teaching schoolboys.[515] Jerome's respect for his former friend did not increase after Rufinus's death, in 410 or 411:[516] in the prologue in his *Ezekiel Commentary*, he reports that the "scorpion" now lies

---

[501] See *CCL* 75, vii–viii; Cavallera, *Saint Jérôme*, vol. 1: 2, 52–53, 55).

[502] Jerome, *In Hiezechielem* VI (*CCL* 75, 236, commenting on Ezekiel 18:5–9).

[503] Jerome, *In Hiezechielem* XII (*CCL* 75, 587, commenting on Ezekiel 40:44–49).

[504] See *CCL* 74, vii; Cavallera, *Saint Jérôme*, vol. 1: 2, 55–56.

[505] Jerome, *In Hieremiam* I, 2 (*CCL* 74, 4, commenting on Jeremiah 1:4–5).

[506] Jerome, *In Hieremiam* IV, 12 (*CCL* 74, 183, commenting on Jeremiah 19:3b–5).

[507] Jerome comments on the following passages in Jeremiah: 13:18–19; 20:14–18; 24:1–10; 27:2–4; 27:9–11; 28:12b–14; 29:14–20 (*CCL* 74, 132, 194, 236, 262, 265, 273, 282–283).

[508] Jerome, *In Hieremiam* V, 66, 12 (*CCL*

74, 283, commenting on Jeremiah 29:9–11).

[509] Jerome, *Ep.* 84, 8 (*CSEL* 55, 131).

[510] Jerome, *In Hieremiam* V, 52, 2; 66, 10 (*CCL* 74, 265, 283, commenting on Jeremiah 27:9–11 and 29:14–20).

[511] See below, pp. 221–227.

[512] Jerome, *In Osee* II, *prologus* (*CCL* 76, 55).

[513] Jerome, *In Ioelem* I, *prologus* (*CCL* 76, 160).

[514] Jerome, *In Isaiam* X, *prologus* (*CCL* 73, 396).

[515] Jerome, *In Isaiam* XII, *prologus* (*CCL* 73A, 465).

[516] On 410 as the probable date of Rufinus's death, see Murphy, *Rufinus*, 212–213; C. P. Hammond, "The Last Ten Years of Ru-

buried in Sicily and can no longer "hiss" at him.[517] He jeers at Rufinus's naive belief that the *Sentences of Sextus* were written by the martyr Sextus and that the *Defense of Origen* was composed by the martyr Pamphilus rather than by Eusebius of Caesarea.[518] And he comments that the disciples of "Grunnius" continue to bark at him for his use of the Hebrew text of the Old Testament rather than the Greek translation.[519] In the *Jeremiah Commentary*, Jerome once more mocks "Grunnius's" belief that the martyred bishop of Rome, Sextus, had written the *Sentences* that bear his name.[520] And in this, his last commentary, Jerome frequently links Rufinus with Origen, Jovinian, and Pelagius.[521] Although Jerome was surely correct in linking Origen, Rufinus, and Pelagius in a network, he here fails to add that most important contemporary Origenist, Evagrius Ponticus.

Jerome's later Old Testament commentaries also suggest that he had been sensitized to the issue of anthropomorphic language in the Bible. Although he does not take the Origenist route of allegorizing all Scriptural language, he wants to distance himself from boorish interpretations of God's "members." Already by the opening years of the fifth century he knows that there is a party called "Anthropomorphites" whose views on the physical attributes of God must be combatted.[522] In his *Amos Commentary* of 406, Jerome names as "heretics" those who wish to depict God after a human likeness, supplying him with feet, eyes, ears, teeth, and other parts.[523] Since other heretics—perhaps Marcionites—have denounced the Old Testament because God there is said to possess such human characteristics as anger, Jerome is aware that "anthropopathic" language must be unpacked to convey a more spiritual sense.[524] So must such Biblical verses as Zechariah 14:4: God's "feet shall stand on the Mount of Olives."[525] When the prophet Isaiah represents God as declaring that his "soul hates" the new moons and feasts of the Israelites, we must decode this "anthropopathic" form of speech, since we know that God does not possess a soul.[526] And anyone who boasts that he "sees" God is plainly a heretic.[527] Thus Jerome, despite his occasional criticism of Origenist exegesis as

---

finus' Life and the Date of His Move South from Aquileia," 411.

[517] Jerome, *In Hiezechielem* I, *prologus* (CCL 75, 3).

[518] Jerome, *In Hiezechielem* VI (CCL 75, 236, commenting on Ezekiel 18:5–9). Rufinus is now deemed to be correct in the latter claim.

[519] Jerome, *In Hiezechielem* X (CCL 75, 475, commenting on Ezekiel 33:23–33).

[520] Jerome, *In Hieremiam* IV, 61, 4 (CCL 74, 210, commenting on Jeremiah 22:24–27).

[521] Jerome, *In Hieremiam* IV, 61, 6–7; IV, *praefatio*, 1; 4; V, 61, 6 (CCL 74, 211, 174,

175, 273, commenting on Jeremiah 22:24–27; 28:12b–14).

[522] Jerome, *Tractatus in Psalmos* (CCL 78, 145, commenting on Psalm 94:8–9).

[523] Jerome, *In Amos* I (CCL 76, 230, commenting on Amos 2:1–3).

[524] Jerome, *In Zachariam* I (CCL 76A, 758, commenting on Zechariah 1:14–16).

[525] Jerome, *In Zachariam* III (CCL 76A, 878, commenting on Zechariah 14:3–4).

[526] Jerome, *In Isaiam* I (CCL 73, 18, commenting on Isaiah 1:14).

[527] Jerome, *In Isaiam* IV (CCL 73, 130, commenting on Isaiah 9:8–13).

overspiritualized, sets himself apart from the Anthropomorphites of the Egyptian desert and elsewhere who had championed Scripture's language of physicality pertaining to God.[528]

A last way in which Jerome, after he was implicated for his use of Origen, proclaimed his own orthodoxy was by castigating earlier heretics for their views. Thus in the *Commentary on Matthew* of 398, he chastizes by name a dozen or more heretics ranging from the second-century Gnostics to Eunomius, with Mani and Marcion each receiving no less than six explicit references.[529] In his *Fifty-Nine Homilies on Psalms*, composed in the opening years of the fifth century, references to past heretics are also frequent, with Arians mentioned over a dozen times.[530] Likewise, Jerome's commentaries on the minor prophets, completed in 406, abound in notices of the earlier heretics. Of these, the *Amos Commentary* leads the list, naming heretics about fifteen times—including some mysterious *"Iberae ineptiae"* who appear to have dabbled with a form of Gnosticism.[531] Shortly after this time, however, the frequency of Jerome's attacks upon past heretics in his Biblical commentaries dwindles: his commentaries upon the much longer books of Isaiah (in about 408–409) and Ezekiel (411–414) contain fewer references to earlier heretics than do his much shorter commentaries on Amos and Hosea, composed in 406.[532] And by the time Jerome wrote his *Jeremiah Commentary* toward the end of his life, he had apparently abandoned all interest in *any* heresies except Origenism and Pelagianism, which he sees as deeply connected. Here, the one reference to former heretics (Arians) is made only to set up a mocking contrast between them and the Pelagians: whereas the impious Arians deny equality to the Son, Jerome's new opponents, the Pelagians, are so puffed up with pride that they fancy themselves like God.[533]

In sum, Jerome's assault on Origen was in several respects lukewarm, while his attack on his own present enemies was ferocious. He sought primarily to defend himself against charges of Origenism and to turn those charges against his foes. When we consider the theological issues, Jerome appears less cognizant of the Origenism flourishing in the Egyptian desert than Theophilus, and this despite his translation of several anti-Origenistic letters written by the Alexandrian archbishop. Jerome's focus is different: he was still fighting a Western controversy over asceticism and thus a major

---

[528] See above, Chap. 2.

[529] Jerome, *In Matheum* (*CCL* 77, 1, 11, 53, 57, 61, 86, 100, 102, 106, 113, 116, 122, 124, 126, 138, 197, 231, 276).

[530] Jerome, *Tractatus in Psalmos* (*CCL* 78, 16, 37, 86, 115, 149, 222, 224, 251, 285, 312, 337, 342, 345, 351).

[531] Jerome, *In Amos* (*CCL* 76, 220, 249, 250, 254, 258, 323): possibly Priscillianists?

[532] By my count, the *Commentary on Isaiah* mentions by name earlier heretics (aside from Origen) about thirteen times (*CCL* 73, 2, 6, 40, 99, 274, 357–358; *CCL* 73A, 506, 747, 759); and the *Commentary on Ezekiel*, about eight times (*CCL* 75, 101, 146, 164, 449).

[533] Jerome, *In Hieremiam* II, 1 (*CCL* 74, 59).

motif in his attack on Origenism lay in his insistence that moral hierarchy must be preserved and gradations of status in the afterlife upheld. Ascetic renunciation, not theological speculation, stands at the center of his religious concern.

SHENUTE'S VERSION OF ORIGENISM
AND HIS ANTI-ORIGENIST CHARGES

Whatever the progress of Christianization in Egypt during the fourth century, it was a progress nonetheless far from complete. The long life of Shenute, archimandrite of the White Monastery, which spanned the last half of the fourth century and the first half of the fifth,[534] abounds with interventions against a flourishing native paganism. His writings reveal that he and his supporters destroyed temples and idols at Atripe and Pneueit,[535] that he conducted services at which pagan temples were converted to Christian use,[536] and that he warred against the hieroglyphs in Egyptian shrines.[537] He boasts how he attacked the houses of pagan "idolators," slaughtered their animals, and repudiated their charges of "murder."[538] And like Theophilus before him, he claims in his sermons that the decisive sign of Christianity's triumph in Egypt lies in the dwindling of "idolatry."[539]

Thanks to Tito Orlandi's recent reconstruction of a Coptic treatise, *Against the Origenists*, and his convincing assignment of it to Shenute,[540] we now can affirm that Shenute had enemies other than pagans. That Origenism still constituted a problem for "orthodox" Christian leaders in the Thebaid in the mid-fifth century had earlier been suggested with the pub-

---

[534] On Shenute's life and activities, and teaching, see the classic study by Johannes Leipoldt, *Schenute von Atripe und die Entstehung des national ägyptischen Christentums*, and the more recent study by Janet Timbie, *Dualism and the Concept of Orthodoxy in the Thought of the Monks of Upper Egypt*, 1979.

[535] See Leipoldt, *Schenute*, 178–179; and of Shenute's own writings, "On the Idols of the Vicus Pneueit I" and "On the Wrongs of Shenute," in H. Weismann ed., tr., *Sinuthii Archimandritae, Vita et Opera Omnia*, Coptic, 84–85, 91; Latin, 47–48, 51–52.

[536] See Dwight W. Young, "Unpublished Shenoutiana in the University of Michigan Library," 26, for discussion of a sermon of Shenute that speaks of how "at the site of a shrine to an unclean spirit, there will henceforth be a shrine to the Holy Spriit"; see n. 537 for the text.

[537] See D. W. Young, "A Monastic Invec-

tive Against Egyptian Hieroglyphs," 348–360, esp. 353–354.

[538] Shenute, "Adversus Saturnum II," in *Vita et Opera Omnia*, Coptic, 81; Latin, 45. An English translation of this interesting scene is now provided by John Barns, "Shenute as a Historical Source," 156–159.

[539] Shenute, "Sermon on the Crucifixion," in H. Guérin ed., tr., "Sermons inédits de Senouti," 15–34: the Egyptians used to worship even bats, Shenute scoffs. For Theophilus's view, see p. 116 above, and *Epistula paschalis* (404) (= Jerome, *Ep.* 100) 11 (*CSEL* 55, 225).

[540] See Tito Orlandi, "A Catechesis Against Apocryphal Texts By Shenute and the Gnostic Texts of Nag Hammadi," 85–88; Shenute, *Contra Origenistas. Testo con introduzione e traduzione*, ed., tr. Tito Orlandi, 10–12.

lication of Dioscorus of Alexandria's letter to Shenute and his memorandum to Egyptian bishops in the area.[541] On first discovery and assessment of the Dioscoran evidence, however, the notion that Origenism had penetrated this far south was viewed with surprise: scholars expected to encounter Origenism at Alexandria and Nitria, but Dioscorus's correspondence proved that Origenism was deemed a danger throughout Upper Egypt as well, and at a later date than they had imagined likely.[542] Was the Origenism here noted perhaps merely an archaizing reference to the earlier controversy?

In his letter and memorandum, Dioscorus warns Shenute and the bishops against a priest named Elias, at large in Upper Egypt, who had been deposed for Origenism: although Elias had anathematized Origen and his doctrines, he later recanted. The bishop of Alexandria tells his correspondents that Elias should be driven from the Thebaid.[543] Moreover, Dioscorus is worried by the report that books and treatises of "the pest Origen and other heretics" are circulating in the Thebaid in the monastery of Parembole, at the former temple at Shmin (Panopolis), and elsewhere.[544] Although Herbert Thompson, commenting in 1922 on this correspondence, questioned whether Origenism still plagued Egypt at so late a date,[545] the reconstruction from fragments of the treatise *Against the Origenists* and the assignment of it to Shenute substantiate a revised interpretation: not only was Origenism still flourishing, it was Origenism of an Evagrian cast.[546]

In *Against the Origenists*, dated to about forty years after Evagrius's death,[547] we find a mix of Origenism and Gnosticizing motifs[548] that resurrects the question posed earlier by the association of the Nag Hammadi documents with Pachomian monasticism:[549] how close *was* the relationship between orthodox and heterodox forms of Christianity in the Egyptian desert during the fourth and fifth centuries? Leaving aside the issue of whether Evagrius himself was influenced by Gnosticism—a claim strenuously but not entirely successfully refuted by Gabriel Bunge[550]—we can

---

[541] See Herbert Thompson, "Dioscorus and Shenute," 367–376.

[542] Thompson, "Dioscorus," 369; Aloys Grillmeier, "La 'Peste d'Origène': Soucis du patriarche d'Alexandrie dus à l'apparition d'origénistes en Haute Egypte (444–451)," 236.

[543] Thompson ed., tr., "Dioscorus," Coptic, 370–373; English, 373–376; also now see Grillmeier, "La 'Peste.' "

[544] Thompson ed., tr., "Dioscorus," Coptic, 373; English, 376.

[545] Thompson, "Dioscorus," 369.

[546] Orlandi, "A Catechesis," 86, 89, 95; P. Du Bourguet, "Diatribe de Chenouté contre le démon," 21.

[547] Orlandi, *Shenute, Contra Origenistas*, 12.

[548] Orlandi, "A Catechesis," 85–86, 95.

[549] Orlandi, "A Catechesis," 95; cf. Grillmeier, "La 'Peste,' " 227–228. Two important articles that suggest some connections are John Barns, "Greek and Coptic Papyri from the Covers of the Nag Hammadi Codices," 7–18; and Frederik Wisse, "Gnosticism and Early Monasticism in Egypt," 431–440.

[550] Gabriel Bunge, "Origenismus-Gnostizismus: Zum geistesgeschichtlichen Standort des Evagrios Pontikos," esp. 28–35. The texts of Evagrius that Bunge uses to support his case (e.g., *Ad monachos* 43; 126;

nonetheless see that an Evagrian-type Origenism had meshed with a Gnosticizing cosmological speculation that Shenute claims was derived from "apocryphal books."[551] Recall that both the desert father Sopatros[552] and Theophilus of Alexandria[553] had earlier linked Origenist themes with "apocryphal books." In Shenute's treatise *Against the Origenists*, the cosmological speculation concerns the existence of a plurality of worlds,[554] and the celebration throughout these worlds (and even by God) of the Pasch.[555] Another claim, probably Gnostic in derivation, against which Shenute rails is that Mary did not really conceive Jesus,[556] and to this is linked the notion that Jesus should be considered an angel.[557] Although these four points do not appear together in any single Gnostic text of which I am aware, they nonetheless suggest an amalgamation of views that we know from a variety of Gnostic sources.[558]

The brunt of Shenute's attack, however, is against Origenist doctrine, not against Gnosticism *per se*. Many of the points he assails are ones found earlier in the anti-Origenist polemics of Epiphanius, Theophilus, and Jerome. Shenute thus faults the "allegorical" interpretation of Isaiah's sera-

---

127; *Antirrheticus* VIII, 56; *Gnosticus* 124) which warn against "false gnosis" and pit "true gnosis" over against it are highly unspecific as to what constitutes the "false gnosis." It is not evident to me that Evagrius is dealing with a genuine Gnostic opposition. Bunge argues that it is "false gnosis" *in Palestine* that is the center of Evagrius's concern (35–40).

[551] Shenute, *Contra Origenistas*, Orlandi ed., tr., Coptic, 14, 22; Italian, 15, 23; cf. Coptic, 36, 46; Italian, 37, 47. For a discussion of which apocryphal books we know circulated in Coptic, see Tito Orlandi, "Gli Apocrifi copti," 57–71.

[552] *Apophthegmata patrum* (Alphabetical), Sopatros (*PG* 65, 413); see above, p. 43.

[553] Theophilus, *Ep. paschalis* (401) (= Jerome, *Ep.* 96) 20 (*CSEL* 55, 180); see above, p. 114.

[554] Shenute, *Contra Origenistas*, Orlandi ed., tr., Coptic, 14, Italian, 15. Shenute rejects the notion of a plurality of worlds by an appeal to such Biblical verses as Genesis 1:1 and Jeremiah 31:35 (God created one sun and one moon), Orlandi ed., tr., Coptic, 14, 20; Italian, 15, 21.

[555] Shenute, *Contra Origenistas*, Orlandi ed., tr., Coptic, 22; Italian, 23. Shenute rejects the idea not only on the grounds that there is not a plurality of worlds, but also because the Pasch is a this-worldly institution: we should not involve the omnipotent God

in suffering and hunger.

[556] Shenute, *Contra Origenistas*, Orlandi ed., tr., Coptic, 28, 34; Italian, 29, 35. Over against this view, Shenute cites Isaiah 7:14, Matthew 1:18, and Luke 1:31 (Coptic, 30; Italian, 31). For Shenute, if Christ was not truly conceived, then he was not truly born; if he was not born, he was not a human, was not truly crucified, and the Christian faith is in vain. Conversely, in his *Christological Catechesis*, Shenute affirms the preexistence of Christ over against those who sceptically ask, "Then did he exist before being of the Holy Virgin?" Shenute calls such talk "Jewish." As the precise means by which Christ took flesh in the Virgin's womb, we should not inquire: we don't even know how human beings are born, let alone the Son of God. See L. Th. Lefort ed., tr., "Catéchèse Christologique de Chenouté," Coptic, 41–42; French, 43–44. Anti-Nestorian sentiments are expressed in Shenute, *Contra Origenistas*, Orlandi ed., tr., Coptic, 50, 52; Italian, 51, 53.

[557] Shenute, *Contra Origenistas*, Orlandi ed., tr., Coptic, 22; Italian, 23. Arian and Melitian views that subordinate the Logos are also attacked: Coptic, 24, 26; Italian, 25, 27. Shenute rails against those who oppose the use of the word "*homoousios*," Orlandi ed., tr., Coptic, 58; Italian, 59.

[558] Birger Pearson confirms the thesis that this grouping of themes seems novel for our known Gnostic texts.

phim as the Son and the Holy Spirit: the latter are of the very substance of the Godhead, not mere servants like the seraphim.[559] His point is the same one scored earlier by Jerome.[560]

A second charge familiar from Theophilus's critique[561] is that some Christians are refusing to pray to Jesus:[562] the fact that this charge appears in the writings of Theophilus and Shenute, but not in those of Epiphanius and Jerome, suggests that the issue was more pressing in Egypt than elsewhere. Who else than Christ, Shenute responds, could be our intercessor with God the Father?[563] Conversely, he calms the fears of those who worry that baptism in the name of Christ excludes the Godhead: when we name Jesus, he argues, we name the entire Trinity, Father, Son, and Holy Spirit.[564] That this discussion continued to disturb the Nitrian monasteries is undeniable from Guillaumont's discoveries at the Cells: in the material there uncovered, the devil was said to tempt monks to fear that if they prayed to Jesus alone, they had excluded the Father and the Holy Spirit.[565] To the contrary, Shenute argues, the name of Jesus should always be on our tongues. He provides his audience with a form of the "Jesus prayer":

> Seek for the fulfillment of these words and you will find them in your mouth
>   and in that of your children:
> When you celebrate a feast and rejoice: Jesus
> When you are anxious and grieving: Jesus
> Boys and girls repeat: Jesus
> He who draws water: Jesus
> He who flees before the barbarians: Jesus
> Those who see wild beasts or some frightening thing: Jesus
> Those who suffer pain or sickness: Jesus
> Those who are taken prisoner: Jesus
> Those who are the victims of corrupt judgments or who are unjustly treated:
>   Jesus
> It is enough for the name of Jesus to be on their lips and he is their salvation.
> He and his Father is their life.[566]

Other themes as well in Shenute's attack resonate with those of the earlier Origenist debates. One such topic to which Shenute devotes considerable attention is the theory of the preexistence and fall of souls, which he mocks: are we to believe that souls acquired bodies because they commit-

---

[559] Shenute, *Contra Origenistas*, Orlandi ed., tr., Coptic, 26; Italian, 27.

[560] See p. 127 above for references.

[561] See p. 108 above.

[562] Shenute, *Contra Origenistas*, Orlandi ed., tr., Coptic, 46, 58; Italian, 47, 59.

[563] Shenute, *Contra Origenistas*, Orlandi ed., tr., Coptic, 58; Italian, 59. I John 2:1

and Romans 8:34 are cited.

[564] Shenute, *Contra Origenistas*, Orlandi ed., tr., Coptic, 62; Italian, 63.

[565] See Antoine Guillaumont, "Une Inscription copte," 310, 325, and "The Jesus Prayer," 66–71, and above pp. 69–70.

[566] Shenute, *Contra Origenistas*, Orlandi ed., tr., Coptic, 62; Italian, 63.

ted adultery, engaged in calumny, or performed other "filthy acts" in the heavens? How could souls sin without being attached to bodies—or vice versa?[567] Instead, Shenute advocates a type of Creationist doctrine (souls as well as bodies are created "in the womb") and adduces Psalm 22:10 ("Upon thee was I cast from birth, and since my mother bore me thou hast been my God") and Luke 11:40 ("Did not he who made the outside make the inside also?") in support of his position. Moreover, if we believe—as Shenute appears to—that sinless men exist, how can we imagine that their souls sinned before they entered bodies? If souls sinned in heaven, how have they been able to become faithful in a world teeming with wickedness?[568] The Origenists apparently had used John the Baptist's demurrer that he was unworthy to loose Jesus' sandals (Mark 1:7) to argue that his soul had sinned before it entered his body. Shenute discounts this ingenious exegesis: John spoke out of humility and the fear of God; moreover, Jesus himself had testified that "no one greater" than John had been born of woman.[569] And in an argument reminiscent of the anti-Origenist polemics considered above,[570] Shenute adds that ordinary human generation is good and blessed by God: Genesis 1:22 and other verses so state. If the process by which souls and bodies are made and joined together is thus sanctified, Christians cannot affirm the Origenist view of the preexistence of the soul and its reception of a body as punishment.[571]

Another familiar point on which Shenute attacks the Origenists concerns the resurrection body. Some Origenists, Shenute reports, claim that the body is "of pigs" and *should* be cast off at the end. Shenute provides a moral argument to counter such a view: if the body is "pig-like," who made it that way? Was it not we ourselves, by our own deeds? That bodies are not in themselves evil is bolstered by the Biblical tale that the mere shadow of Peter's body was holy enough to cure many.[572] Moreover, some of those who denied the resurrection body were giving an allegorical interpretation to the story of the raising of Lazarus: according to them, Lazarus represents the *nous* and Mary and Martha are the "virtues" (*aretai*). Shenute responds: if Christ did not raise Lazarus and perform the other resurrections of which the Gospels speak, we call into question both Christ's own resurrection and all of his other miracles, thus destroying our hope for salvation.[573] Against those who hold the "pagan" (and Origenist) view that the body will dissolve into the four elements out of which it was composed (water, earth, air, and fire), Shenute argues that if God made man, a "liv-

---

[567] Shenute, *Contra Origenistas*, Orlandi ed., tr., Coptic, 26; Italian, 27.

[568] Shenute, *Contra Origenistas*, Orlandi ed., tr., Coptic, 28; Italian, 29.

[569] Shenute, *Contra Origenistas*, Orlandi ed., tr., Coptic, 46, 48; Italian, 47, 49.

[570] See Chap. 3 above for references.

[571] Shenute, *Contra Origenistas*, Orlandi ed., tr., Coptic, 48; Italian, 49.

[572] Shenute, *Contra Origenistas*, Orlandi ed., tr., Coptic, 32; Italian, 33, citing Acts 5:15.

[573] Shenute, *Contra Origenistas*, Orlandi ed., tr., Coptic, 44; Italian, 45.

ing" spirit (Genesis 2:7) from the earth and not from the other three elements, then God must have the power to resurrect our bodies from the earth at the end.[574]

A last point that disturbs Shenute is the Origenists' interpretation of the Lord's Supper as purely symbolic.[575] Not just pagans, but some of "ourselves" (i.e., Christians), he complains, hold that the bread and the wine are not really the body and blood of Christ, but only a *typos*. Shenute marshals Scriptural verses against this view (John 6:55 and Matthew 26:28) and faults the duplicity of clerics who pronounce the words over the elements, "This is my body given for you for the remission of sins," when they themselves do not believe that the bread and the wine bring eternal life. Such men should stop their mouths, for they in effect deny that God has the power to do anything he pleases,[576] in this case, to change the bread and the wine into the body and blood of Jesus.

We know from writings of Shenute other than *Against the Origenists* that he was troubled by those who questioned the reality of Jesus's body and blood in the Eucharist—and in some of them, the doubt is explicitly associated with Origenist views. For example, in what has been named the *Christological Catechesis*, Shenute warns against the teaching of Origen, which wounds hearts by raising the question, "How can the body and blood of Christ come from the bread and wine?" Shenute's retort is rhetorical: Is the one who made man from the earth incapable of making the bread and wine become Christ's body and blood?[577] The creation of man from the ground gives Shenute an analogy for the Eucharistic transforma-

---

[574] Shenute, *Contra Origenistas*, Orlandi ed., tr., Coptic, 40; Italian, 41.

[575] Apparently earlier, Shenute had encountered trouble with a different heretical interpretation of the Eucharist, which he associates with the Melitians. Shenute reports that they gorged themselves on bread and wine, deeming it mere physical food. Up to eighteen times a day they carried the Eucharistic bread to cemeteries and other places; they ate and drank so much that they not only became drunk, they also vomited. They defended their practice of "frequent communion," Shenute reports, by claiming that if a human sinned many times a day, he should take the Eucharistic bread often and his sins would be forgiven. See Shenute, "Two Instructions against the Heretics," in Guérin ed., tr., "Sermons inédits," Coptic, 106–108; French, 32–33.

A second kind of Eucharistic problem Shenute faced pertained to the country peasants, who having worked hard all day in the fields, ate a meal before they came to the Eu-

charist on Saturday evening. The count Chosroas, upon observing this custom, was shocked. Shenute provided him with a lenient explanation: the count is correct that it is not "fitting" to participate in the sacred mysteries "when the heart is full of bread and water"; nonetheless, we should recall that Jesus said that it was not what went into, but what came out of, a man's mouth that defiled him (cf. Matthew 15:17–20). How much worse it would be if the peasants were committing acts of fornication, violence, adultery, theft, and so forth. Shenute reminds the count rather pointedly of the injustices and greed displayed by magistrates. See Pierre Du Bourguet ed., tr., "Entretien de Chenouté sur les problèmes de discipline ecclésiastique et de cosmologie," Coptic, 111–112; French, 118–119.

[576] Shenute, *Contra Origenistas*, Orlandi ed., tr., Coptic, 30, 32; Italian, 31, 33.

[577] Note the same line of rhetorical argumentation in Epiphanius, *Ancoratus* 62 (*GCS* 25, 74–75), and n. 16 above.

tion: just as man did not move until God breathed on him and he became a living being (Genesis 2:7), so the bread and wine lie inert on the holy table, but become something more, the body and blood of the Lord, once the blessing has been pronounced and the Holy Spirit is sent down upon the elements. Just as bread and wine provide physical life for the human body, so the body and blood of the Lord provide spiritual life.[578]

Another teaching of Shenute on the Eucharist is preserved in a homily published by Amélineau early in this century. In it, Shenute rails against both those who give the Eucharist (i.e., priests) and those who receive it without believing that it is genuinely the body and blood of Christ. Those who deny this essential teaching have fallen prey to "false philosophy," have been led astray "by the wisdom of the psychic, demonic world." Such false Christians are "more wicked than those who do not know God." Shenute decries congregations who accept such impious views simply because they like their priests: for Shenute, such priests are "men of stone."[579]

That Shenute's treatise *Against the Origenists* reveals a type of Origenist theology associated especially with Evagrius seems clear. The subordination of Christ to the Godhead, the fear of praying to Jesus, the cosmological theory that rests on the soul's preexistence and fall, and the symbolic interpretation of both the resurrection body and of the Eucharist all point in the direction of an Evagrian piety, the details of which have been expounded in Chapter Two. Other scholars have noted specific points of Origenist teaching presented in the treatise, such as the indirect action of the devil on the tempted person's spirit, that suggest an Evagrian source.[580]

Although the four polemicists considered in this chapter attack many of the same points of Origenist theology and practice, each reveals his own religious concerns as well as the changing coloration of Origenism. Thus we have seen how Epiphanius's anti-Arian concern led him first to attack the "subordinationism" of Origen, but that soon he was more zealous to assail Origenist interpretations concerning the body. Although Theophilus's assault was ostensibly motivated more by his personal rancor against alleged Origenists than by a desire to uphold a narrowly defined "pure" doctrine, nonetheless he, too, charges Origenism with heterodox views on the body and reproduction. Jerome's approach was colored by his need to defend *himself* against charges of Origenism, but he also strongly pressed notions of moral hierarchy and of gradation of rank in the afterlife that he had developed in his ascetic debates some years earlier. And for Shenute,

---

[578] Shenute, "Catéchèse Christologique," Lefort ed., tr., Coptic, 93; French, 45.

[579] Shenute, "Homily 24," in E. Amélineau ed., tr., *Oeuvres de Schenoudi*, vol. II: 485–486.

[580] Du Bourguet, "Diatribe de Chenoute," 21.

the Gnosticizing variation of Origenism, that was an exotic development of Evagrian theology stands at the center of his polemic against those disturbing his monastic flock. Throughout the anti-Origenist writings of these four authors, concerns pertaining to Christian teachings regarding "the body" dominate. Neither "Origen" nor "Origenism" here provide stable targets for these anti-Origenist assaults.

Four polemicists, four Origenisms—but from Epiphanius, Theophilus, Jerome, and Shenute, we derive little sense of either Origenism's theological appeal or its coherence. It is to those accused of Origenist heresy and to their supporters that we must turn if we would fathom the attractiveness of these teachings to late fourth-century intellectuals. Rufinus will provide our case in point.

CHAPTER FOUR

Rufinus's Defense against
Charges of Origenism

R ufinus emerges on the scene of
ecclesiastical literature in the late 390s already pitched in the battle over
Origenism in Palestine, proffering an explanation that he no doubt hoped
would clear Origen's writings from the charge of heresy. Because he, unlike
Jerome, had no known career as a writer or translator of Origen's works
before his involvement in the Origenist controversy,[1] we have no earlier
material similar to that for Jerome by which we can test his Origenist sympathies in the 380s and early 390s. We can, however, safely posit that he
was early on well immersed in Origenist teaching: his reported eight years
of study with Didymus the Blind in the 370s provides one important clue;[2]
another is his association and correspondence with Evagrius Ponticus in
the 380s and 390s and his translation of a few of Evagrius's writings, to be
detailed below.[3]

The first datable extant literary works of Rufinus—his translation of
Pamphilus's *Apologia pro Origene* and his own addendum, *On the Adulteration of the Works of Origen*—reveal his already deep involvement in the
controversy: the preface to his translation of Pamphilus's *Apology* rebuts
Jerome's and Epiphanius's accusation that John of Jerusalem espoused Origenism. Pamphilus's *Apology* will provide Rufinus with some of the tools
for his later defense of Origen, which he will supplement with his own
theory of the "adulteration" of Origen's writings by heretics.

---

[1] Rufinus may have translated some works
by Evagrius Ponticus during this period, but
we cannot date these translations. Jerome delights to note that Rufinus made his debut as
an author only with his *Apology against Je-*

rome: see Jerome, *Apologia* I, 8 (CCL 79, 7).
[2] See Rufinus, *Apologia* II, 15 (CCL 20,
94).
[3] See below, p. 188.

A second translation project pertaining to Origen that Rufinus undertook before he turned his hand to Origen's *On First Principles* and to his *Apologies* of 400–401 was to render the anonymous *Dialogue with Adamantius* into Latin. (Rufinus either believed, or pretended to believe, that "Adamantius" was Origen himself, since the name was one that he and others used as an epithet for Origen.[4]) An investigation of Rufinus's writings from these first projects to his last and an exploration of his probable knowledge of Evagrian theology prompts the conclusion that Rufinus indeed supported at least a modified form of Origenism. Whether one then brands him a deceitful prevaricator, as did Jerome, or finds another explanation for his oft-repeated claims of his own orthodoxy, provides the problem for this chapter.

When the Roman nobleman Macarius in 398 requested Rufinus to translate Pamphilus's *Apologia pro Origene*, Rufinus obliged. Already in his preface to the translation, he stresses a point that will shortly assume centrality in his self-defense: that the pure faith passed down to us from Christian antiquity concerns only two essential items, the doctrines of the Trinity and of the Incarnation. Like our forefathers, we must affirm that the members of the Trinity are coeternal, of one nature, one power, and one substance. We must also hold that the Son of God was made man, suffered for our sins, and rose from the dead "in the very same flesh in which he suffered," from whence stems the hope of Christians.[5] Yet the nature of Christ's flesh leads Rufinus to focus immediately on the charge that Jerome had pressed against John of Jerusalem: that John had evaded an orthodox position on the resurrection by speaking only of a resurrection of the "body," not of the "flesh." According to Jerome, Christians must affirm the resurrection of the "flesh"—by which he meant skin, bones, blood, and genital organs.[6] Rufinus neatly attempts to collapse the distinction: "body" and "flesh" are merely two different ways of speaking of the same thing. Paul preferred the word "body"; the Creed uses the word "flesh." Vocabulary here makes no difference, Rufinus claims, as long as Christians confess that what rises is "whole and perfect," bearing the "same nature" we possess here and now—yet that what rises, "rises in power and glory," an "incorruptible and spiritual body," as Paul states in I Corinthians 15. This Scriptural position is taught in the church of Jerusalem by "the holy priest John," and it is Rufinus's own belief as well. To anyone who confesses otherwise, "anathema."[7] Thus in his opening gambit, Rufinus has tried to defuse the attack on Origenism's denial of a material resurrection body.

---

[4] See, for example, Rufinus's preface to his translation of Origen, *Hom. in Numeros* (*CCL* 20, 285); cf. Epiphanius, *Panarion* 64, 1.

[5] Rufinus, *praefatio*, Pamphilus, *Apologia*

pro Origene (*CCL* 20, 233–234).

[6] Jerome, *Contra Ioannem* 25–27 (*PL* 23, 392–396).

[7] Rufinus, *praefatio*, Pamphilus, *Apologia* (*CCL* 20, 234).

His translation of Pamphilus will provide him with further arguments useful in defending Origenist theology.

Pamphilus, writing to Christian confessors condemned to the mines of Palestine early in the fourth century, had composed his treatise to clear Origen from what he believed were unfair slanders of *On First Principles*.[8] Pamphilus begins by explaining Origen's rationale for writing the work and summarizing his theology in ways that suggests its orthodoxy. Next Pamphilus lists the specific objections made against points of Origen's teaching and attempts to show that they misrepresent his views by citing actual passages from his works. In the process, Pamphilus surveys a wide range of Origen's writings, not only *On First Principles* but also his many commentaries upon Biblical books (such as the *Commentary on Psalm 1*, known only through its citation by others[9]) and his now lost treatises such as the *De resurrectione*.[10]

Pamphilus begins his *Apology* with the justification that Origen himself had prefaced to the *On First Principles*: beyond the boundaries of what has been defined by the Church as handed down from the apostles and hence is set, there is room for questioning, for proposing different solutions to theological problems. No danger attends this process if the fixed teaching is given loyal adherence.[11] Thus Origen was, in Pamphilus's view, entirely free to discuss points that had not yet received firm definition. Moreover, Origen's speculations could even be deemed praiseworthy, for on many points he was countering the opinions of heretics.[12] *Which* heretics were conveniently identified by Origen himself in his *Commentary on Titus*, cited at length by Pamphilus: Marcionites, Basilidians, Tethianites (followers of Tatian? Sethianites?), Ebionites, Patripassians (Sabellians), and Cataphrygians (Montanists).[13] In addition to these designated heretical groups, there are others (probably Gnostics) whose positions are described but who are not named: those who say that souls are of diverse natures (these "speak iniquity of the Highest" [Psalm 73:8–9] and accuse God of injustice), and those who deny the power of free will to the soul.[14] Having allowed Origen to expound his own statement of purpose, Pamphilus catalogues numerous passages from Origen's writings that affirm such doctrines as the coeternity of the Son with the Father, the eternal generation of the Son,

---

[8] Pamphilus, *Apologia, praefatio* (PG 17, 541, 549).

[9] Origen's *Comm. in Genesim*, cited in Pamphilus, *Apologia* 3 (PG 17, 560–561).

[10] Origen's *De resurrectione* cited by Pamphilus, *Apologia* 6 (PG 17, 594–595); also Origen, *Comm. in Psalmos 1*, cited by Pamphilus, *Apologia* 6 (PG 17, 598).

[11] Pamphilus, *Apologia* 1 (PG 17, 549–

550), citing Origen, *De principiis, praefatio* 2–4.

[12] Pamphilus, *Apologia* 1 (PG 17, 552).

[13] Pamphilus, *Apologia* 1 (PG 17, 553–554), citing Origen, *Comm. in Titum*, at Titus 3:1–11 (on the heretics who will arise to corrupt apostolic tradition).

[14] Pamphilus, *Apologia* 1 (PG 17, 555), citing Origen, *Comm. in Titum*.

and exemption of the Holy Spirit from the status of "creaturehood."[15] Thus, Pamphilus concludes, Origen's teaching on the Trinity was "correct, orthodox, and catholic,"[16] despite wicked slanders directed against his views on the Son of God, allegorical exegesis, metempsychosis, and other points.[17] To the refutation of these slanders, Pamphilus devotes the rest of Book I of his treatise—and Book I alone is extant in Rufinus's translation.[18]

For our purposes, two items of Pamphilus's defense are conspicuous, for they become the subjects of heated debate in the Origenist controversy of the early fifth century. The first of these concerns the resurrection. Pamphilus attempts to exonerate Origen's teaching by citing a passage from *De resurrectione* in which Origen argues that it is not only the soul that is "crowned"; since the body as well underwent great labors, it too should receive a reward, or we would be accusing God of injustice.[19] Anti-Origenists such as Epiphanius later held that Origen denied this very point.[20] Most interesting, Pamphilus cites Origen's *Commentary on Psalm 1* (vs. 5), in which Origen claims that an *eidos* of body remains throughout life, despite the body's changes and flux, and that this *eidos* will be raised in glory.[21] This is the very passage on which Epiphanius will later focus to prove that Origen did *not* confess a true resurrection of the dead,[22] while for Pamphilus the passage proves that Origen *affirmed* a resurrection.[23] What "counts" as resurrection is the issue at stake. Their hermeneutical disagreement provides an instructive example of how the same passage in Origen's writings could be used by later commentators either to defend his orthodoxy or to charge his heterodoxy.

A second point of great dispute in the controversy of the fifth century concerned the origin and nature of the soul. Pamphilus declares that this is an issue that has not been given firm definition by the Church and thus by his and Origen's ground rules is open for discussion.[24] Diverse opinions have been proposed: for example, that souls come *ex traduce* with the body (probably incorrect, Pamphilus muses, since then the soul might be thought to die with the body), or that the soul is formed elsewhere and then "breathed" into the body. The position that the soul possesses the same substance as God should be ruled out, because God would then be

---

[15] E.g., Pamphilus, *Apologia* 3; 4 (*PG* 17, 559–560, 563, 564, 567).

[16] Pamphilus, *Apologia* 5 (*PG* 17, 577–578).

[17] Pamphilus, *Apologia* 5 (*PG* 17, 578–579).

[18] Originally there were six books to Pamphilus's *Apologia*: Jerome, *Apologia* I, 8 (*CCL* 79, 7).

[19] Pamphilus, *Apologia* 7 (*PG* 17, 594), citing Origen, *De resurrectione* 1.

[20] Epiphanius, *Panarion* 64, 72 (*GCS* 31², 523).

[21] Pamphilus, *Apologia* 7 (*PG* 17, 598–599), citing Origen, *Comm. in Psalmos 1*, on Psalm 1:5.

[22] Epiphanius, *Panarion* 64, 10–11 (*GCS* 31², 419–420).

[23] Pamphilus, *Apologia* 7 (*PG* 17, 600, 601).

[24] Pamphilus, *Apologia* 8 (*PG* 17, 603).

implicated in the soul's sin[25]: here Pamphilus perhaps aims at the Manichean solution to the problem, a solution that had not assumed this precise form in Origen's day. Since the Church has not pronounced on this matter, Pamphilus asserts, it is unreasonable to label someone who entertains a different opinion a heretic.[26] But, he continues, one essential criterion for a decision obtains: we must adopt a view that does not entail attributing injustice to the Creator, that does not blame God for the miseries of human life—for why some are born blind or with other disabilities, why some die young rather than old, why some reside in barbarian countries given over to impious superstition while others enjoy the civilities of life in the Roman Empire and the truth of the Christian confession. Any view of the soul's origin to which Christians ascribe must help them square the seeming injustices of life and varying human conditions with divine providence, with a confession that God is both good and just.[27] The range of options concerning the soul's origin, in other words, is deeply implicated in issues of theodicy. To be sure, Pamphilus has so stacked the argument that Origen's position on the original preexistent equality of souls emerges as the perfect solution to the dilemma. The concern here expressed by Pamphilus to preserve God's justice in the face of human and natural evil informed the Origenist position throughout the controversy and would inspire Pelagians a century later.

Having translated Pamphilus's *Apology*, Rufinus composed an addendum that addressed a perplexing question left unexplored by Pamphilus: Origen seemed to contradict himself in his own writings, at some points giving unorthodox interpretations that ran up against the more "correct" ones he posited elsewhere. This dilemma Rufinus proposed to solve for Macarius (and others) in his *On the Adulteration of the Works of Origen*, composed also in 397.[28] He sets the question: how could a man "so learned and wise" as Origen contradict himself—and not just over the long span of his literary career, but even from sentence to sentence? How could he say, for example, that nowhere in Scripture was the Holy Spirit called "created or made," yet go on to affirm that the Holy Spirit was made along with the other creatures? Having confessed that Father and Son were "of one substance," how could Origen write that the Son was created and of another substance? How could he speak of the resurrected Christ's flesh ascending to heaven and then deny that flesh is to be saved?[29] Rufinus

---

[25] Pamphilus, *Apologia* 9 (*PG* 17, 605–606).

[26] Pamphilus, *Apologia* 9 (*PG* 17, 606).

[27] Pamphilus, *Apologia* 9 (*PG* 17, 605).

[28] Murphy, *Rufinus*, 233.

[29] Rufinus, *De adulteratione* 1 (*CCL* 20, 7–8). Sulpicius Severus registers a similar query: how could Origen have differed so much from himself that in the "approved" sections of his work, "he has no equal since the age of the Apostles," while in the "condemned" sections, no one was more seriously in error (*Dialogus* I, 6)?

provides an ingenious answer: heretics interpolated Origen's works with their own wicked opinions. His thesis, he claims, is not novel. To prove his point, Rufinus lists several examples of interpolation in the writings of other Church Fathers: Eunomian arguments were interjected into (pseudo-) Clement's *Recognitions*,[30] subordinationist views into the writings of Clement of Alexandria,[31] Sabellian and Arian positions into those of Dionysius of Alexandria.[32] Indeed, Origen himself complained about the interpolation of his writings; as evidence, Rufinus cites at length from a letter of Origen expressing this complaint.[33] Latin writers, too, endured the treachery of interpolators: Hilary of Poitiers, Cyprian, and Jerome (not named, but clearly intended) were the victims.[34] Other calumniators of Origen disingenuously borrow his writings and then compose their *own* books out of them, one of whom even boasted that he had read six thousand of Origen's works[35]—a taunt obviously aimed at Epiphanius of Salamis.[36] Why should those who have devoted themselves less fully to Origen be branded with guilt, especially when they—like Rufinus himself—have kept their faith pure? Besides, Rufinus claims, even if he is not entirely correct about *which* passages were inserted into Origen's writing by heretics, "no danger" has resulted, thanks to God's benevolent assistance. He has been kept safe, more than can be said for the "evil speakers" who, he ominously concludes, will be shut out from the Kingdom of God.[37]

Thus, with these exercises behind him, when Rufinus received Macarius's further request to translate *On First Principles* in 398, he had his justification for doing so ready to hand. He informs Macarius that heretics and other "ill-disposed persons" have tampered with Origen's works so that he sometimes appears to contradict the orthodox opinions he had expounded elsewhere. Rufinus admits that he has omitted some passages in *On First Principles* at variance with these more orthodox statements elsewhere in Origen's writings. For some "misleading" points, he has substituted the more acceptable views found in other books of Origen.[38] He also repeats the position he had developed earlier, that even if he includes some of Origen's "novel opinions" on the rational creatures in his translations, these points do not touch the essence of the Christian faith and hence are harmless. Moreover, and importantly, he claims that perhaps "certain her-

---

[30] Rufinus, *De adulteratione* 3 (*CCL* 20, 9).

[31] Rufinus, *De adulteratione* 4 (*CCL* 20, 10).

[32] Rufinus, *De adulteratione* 5 (*CCL* 20, 10).

[33] Rufinus, *De adulteratione* 6–7 (*CCL* 20, 10–12). See also Henri Crouzel, "A Letter from Origen 'To Friends in Alexandria,' " 135–150. Parts of this letter are also cited by Jerome, *Apologia* II, 18 (*CCL* 79, 52–54).

[34] Rufinus, *De adulteratione* 10–13 (*CCL* 20, 14–16).

[35] Rufinus, *De adulteratione* 14–15 (*CCL* 20, 16–17).

[36] Jerome, *Apologia* II, 22; 13 (*CCL* 79, 58, 47); cf. *Ep.* 82, 7 (*CSEL* 55, 114).

[37] Rufinus, *De adulteratione* 14–16 (*CCL* 20, 16–17).

[38] Rufinus, *praefatio* 2, Origen, *De principiis* I (*CCL* 20, 245–246).

etics" have to be answered by these very teachings on the rational creatures[39]: although Rufinus does not here name Origen's conjectured opponents, they probably included Gnostics who posited an original diversity of natures that would account for the divergent present and future fates of individuals. For Rufinus, as for Origen, "determinism" in any form must be excluded from the Christian faith. It is indeed notable that Pamphilus and Rufinus are quick to situate the theological debates in which Origen himself was embroiled: thus they show themselves more sympathetic to a "historical" reading of Origen than do Epiphanius and Theophilus.

The point in Rufinus's preface that would most irritate Jerome, however, was his glowing tribute to Jerome's devoted and eloquent translations of Origen's writings. Although Rufinus does not dare to hope that his own modest efforts will resemble the beauty of Jerome's Latin rendering of Origen's *Homilies on the Song of Songs*, he nonetheless feels inspired by his predecessor[40]: Jerome has already translated "more than seventy" of Origen's homilies and some of his commentaries on the Pauline epistles.[41] That this public revelation of Jerome's exhaustive attention to Origen enraged Jerome—he was branded with guilt by association—is clear from his indignant responses in his letter to Pammachius and Oceanus[42] and in his own *Apology against Rufinus*.[43]

Other Greek texts that Rufinus translated between 398 and 400, when he wrote his *Apology* to Anastasius of Rome, would have further reinforced his claim that much in Origen's teachings was praiseworthy. Thus probably in 398,[44] he translated nine of Origen's *Homilies on Psalms 36–38* (37–39, in our numbering).[45] Although Rufinus states in his prologue to the dedicatee Apronianus, a relative of Melania the Elder,[46] that these homilies convey a simple, moral message understandable even by women (Apronianus's wife Avita appears to occupy his mind),[47] the points that Origen made in these homilies concern much more than elementary ethical injunctions: they relate to issues concerning the justice of God and providence. Several of Origen's themes are worthy of note.

Commenting on Psalm 36 (37), Origen had castigated those who complained that God's justice was not evident in the world. Why, they ask, does God permit impious men to achieve great success? It is a question, Origen notes, that heretics use to deny the goodness of the Creator God.[48]

[39] Rufinus, *praefatio*, Origen, *De principiis* III (*CCL* 20, 248).

[40] Rufinus, *praefatio* 1, Origen, *De principiis* I (*CCL* 20, 245).

[41] Rufinus, *praefatio* 2, Origen, *De principiis* I (*CCL* 20, 245).

[42] Jerome, *Ep.* 84 (*CSEL* 55, 121–134).

[43] Jerome, *Apologia* I, 1–3 (*CCL* 79, 1–4).

[44] *CCL* 20, x; Murphy, *Rufinus*, 234.

[45] Text in *PG* 12, 1319–1410.

[46] See *PLRE* I, 87.

[47] Rufinus, *prologus*, Origen, *In Psalmos 36–38* (*CCL* 20, 251).

[48] Origen, *Hom. in Psalmos 36 (37)* V. 5 commenting on Psalm 36(37):35–36 (*PG* 12, 1363–1364).

Why, the complainers ask, should we behave justly if we observe that the
righteous suffer while the unrighteous revel in happy prosperity? Origen
counsels his readers that our present life is like a passing shadow, that we
must await eternity for an equitable resolution to the dilemma:[49] eventually, neither the sinner nor the place of his sin shall exist any more.[50] In
these *Homilies on the Psalms*, Origen calls those who do not admit God's
providence "blasphemers,"[51] and even defines Christ himself as "justice."[52]
Origen here also teaches that God *always* stands ready to help and uphold
us, both before our "falls" and after them,[53] despite the fact that it is our
own negligence and sloth that prompted us to sin in the first place.[54] Like
a good father or tutor, God disciplines his children, but only to improve
and save them.[55] Issues of God's justice and providence, then, are deeply
embedded in these allegedly "simple" commentaries on the Psalms. Given
the subject matter, it is probably no accident that Origen here faults astrology for offering a wrong assessment of the workings of human life.[56] And
it is probably also no accident that the "heretics" Origen chastises in these
nine homilies on the Psalms are Gnostics (Valentinians, Marcionites, and
Basilidians),[57] who were believed to deny God's providential plan for the
universe.

Probably in the next year, 399,[58] Rufinus translated several sermons by
Basil of Caesarea and Gregory Nazianzen that doubtless reinforced his
claim that the very essence of true faith lay in correct Trinitarian doctrine,
especially in the refutation of Arianism's subordination of the Son.[59] In his
preface to Gregory's sermons, dedicated to Apronianus, Rufinus notes the
difficult period of Arian rule—Valens' reign—through which Gregory
(and he himself) had lived. Gregory's great triumph for orthodox Christianity, he informs Apronianus, was to win "multitudes" of Arian heretics
to the true faith.[60] Beyond the anti-Arian positions, Rufinus also found in
Gregory's sermons a critique of astrologers' attempts to fault the notion of

[49] Origen, *Hom. in Psalmos 35 (36)* II, 2
(*PG* 12, 1331).
[50] Origen, *Hom. in Psalmos 36(37)* II, 5
(*PG* 12, 1333–1334).
[51] Origen, *Hom. in Psalmos 38(39)* I, 5 (*PG*
12, 1394).
[52] Origen, *Hom. in Psalmos 36(37)* II, 1
(*PG* 12, 1329); *Hom. in Psalmos 38(39)* II, 1
(*PG* 12, 1402).
[53] Origen, *Hom. in Psalmos 36(37)* III, 8
(*PG* 12, 1343), commenting on Psalm
36(37):17; *Hom. in Psalmos 36(37)* IV, 2
(*PG* 12, 1354).
[54] Origen, *Hom. in Psalmos 37(38)* I, 1 (*PG*
12, 1370).
[55] Origen, *Hom. in Psalmos 37(38)* I, 1 (*PG*
12, 1370, 1372).

[56] Origen, *Hom. in Psalmos 36(37)* III, 6
(*PG* 12, 1341–1342).
[57] Origen, *Hom. in Psalmos 36(37)* II, 6
(*PG* 12, 1334); *Hom. in Psalmos 36(37)* III,
11 (*PG* 12, 1347); *Hom. in Psalmos 37(38)*
II, 8 (*PG* 12, 1378).
[58] Murphy, *Rufinus*, 234; *CCL* 20, x.
[59] See Rufinus's translation of Basil, *Hom.
VI* (*De fide*), 2 (*PG* 31, 1782–1784); his
translation of Gregory of Nazianzus, *Hom. I*
(*Apologeticus*), 36/37, 2; 38, 1; *Hom. III* (*De
luminibus*), 11, 4; 12, 1–5; *Hom. IV* (*De Pen-
tecoste*), 8, 5 (*CSEL* 46[1], 31–32, 121–123,
152).
[60] Rufinus, *praefatio*, Gregory of Nazianzus, *Orationes* (*CCL* 20, 255).

divine providence; according to Gregory, evil men blame fate or the stars for what actually is the result of their own negligence and idleness. The workings of God's benevolent providence they erroneously imagine to be only the "accidents of blind fortune."[61] That a manuscript of Rufinus's translations of Gregory Nazianzen came to be owned by either Melania the Elder or Melania the Younger[62] reinforces the notion that Rufinus belonged to a tight network of friends through which such literature circulated; if Melania's copy could be confirmed as the one read by Julian of Eclanum, further links in the network through which such literature passed might be established.[63]

Two other Greek texts that Rufinus translated in this period at first sight seem not to relate to the Origenist controversy, but some scholars have argued that they may nonetheless have possible associations with it. The first is Rufinus's translation of the (pseudonymous) letter of Clement of Rome to James of Jerusalem,[64] probably meant as a prologue to his translation of the Clementine *Homilies* that he undertook a few years later.[65] The content of the letter concerns Clement's support for the Petrine foundation of the Roman bishopric[66] and emphasizes the role of the Roman bishop in providing correct catechetical instruction for the "*animas rudes.*"[67] In itself, the letter appears to hold no meaning for the Origenist controversy, but it acquires a different and intriguing significance if we accept Eduard Schwartz's suggestion that Rufinus translated the letter for his protector, Siricius of Rome, who had refused to move against the Origenist sympathizers when called upon to do so.[68] If Schwartz's suggestion is correct—we have no proof for his position—there may be a hidden message in the letter's claim that the judgments of the Roman bishop should be heeded by all Christians, everywhere.[69]

A second text that Rufinus translated, probably in 399,[70] that contains no ostensible reference to the Origenist controversy is the *Sentences of Sex-*

---

[61] Gregory of Nazianzus, *Hom. IX (De Arianis)*, 10, 3 (*CSEL* 46¹, 276); cf. *Hom. III (De luminibus)*, 5, 2 (*CSEL* 46¹, 114), against astronomy and astrology.

[62] See Caroline Hammond Bammel, "Products of Fifth-Century Scriptoria Preserving Conventions Used by Rufinus of Aquileia: III, Nomina Sacra" (1979): 452, citing discussion in *CSEL* 46, xxx–xxxiii and *SC* 90, 178–179 n. 2.

[63] See Hammond Bammel, "Products," 374.

[64] Latin text in *GCS* 51, 375–387; Greek text in *GCS* 42, 1–22.

[65] In his epilogue to his translation of Origen's *Commentary on Romans* (*CCL* 20, 276–277), probably done after 405, Rufinus

reports that he translated the "letter of Clement" before he did his translation of the *Recognitions* (the latter, probably after 404): see Murphy, *Rufinus*, 113–114.

[66] *Ep. Clementis ad Iacobem* 1–2 (*GCS* 51, 375–376).

[67] *Ep. Clementis* 13, 1–3 (*GCS* 51, 382).

[68] Eduard Schwartz, "Unzeitgemässe Beobachtungen zu den Clementinen," 165; this early dating for the translation is disputed by Murphy, *Rufinus*, 115, on the grounds that Jerome and his circle don't know of it. Also see Jerome, *Ep.* 127, 9 (*CSEL* 56, 152).

[69] That James is the bishop of Jerusalem gives a nice connection to John of Jerusalem.

[70] Murphy, *Rufinus*, 234.

tus, the authorship of which became a subject of debate between Jerome and Rufinus.[71] For our present discussion, an important detail concerning Rufinus's handling of this collection is his announcement that he added maxims to those he found in the Greek original,[72] maxims that later dropped off in the process of the text's transmission. Otto Bardenhewer proposed that the extra "sentences" may well have been maxims of Evagrius Ponticus,[73] a view that Henry Chadwick also finds plausible.[74] In many ways, Chadwick writes, "Sextus is the direct precursor of Evagrius Ponticus, with whom indeed he is already conjoined both by Jerome and by the Armenian version of the sentences, though by the latter the connection is made from motives of sympathy and by the former from bitter hostility."[75] Thus even the seemingly "innocent" translations of Rufinus in the period from 398–400 may have been linked to Origenist interests and Origenist sympathizers.

A less "neutral" project undertaken by Rufinus in this period may be counted among the most important for his later defense of Origen: his translation of the so-called anonymous *Dialogue with Adamantius*, a work he brought forth as if it were a *Dialogue with Origen*. The view that Rufinus's translation was less than "innocent" has been posited by Vinzenz Buchheit, who argues that Rufinus must have known that the work was not by Origen—whose epithet "Adamantius" had led Christians to identify the central, orthodox participant in the *Dialogue* with Origen himself—but that he nonetheless feigned agreement with the identification in order to assist Origen's cause.[76] In fact, Rufinus explicitly identifies Adamantius with Origen in his Latin translation in a way that the Greek text does not.[77]

The character of Adamantius in the *Dialogue* is represented as debating heretics who are labelled Manicheans, Marcionites, Bardesanites, and Valentinians. Marcionite and Manichean views on the plurality of divine principles and on the nature of Scripture are roundly attacked, with Adamantius upholding the unity of the Old Testament and the New Testament

---

[71] Rufinus, *praefatio, Sexti Sententiae* (*CCL* 20, 259): Rufinus thought that the martyr bishop of Rome, Xystus, was the author. Jerome, who perhaps earlier imagined the author was a Christian (see his quotation in *Adversus Jovinianum* I, 49 [*PL* 23, 293]), came later to claim that the author was a Pythagorean philosopher: see Jerome, *Commentarius in Hiezechielem* VI (on Ezekiel 18:5–9) (*CCL* 75, 236); *Ep.* 133, 3 (*CSEL* 56, 246–247). Also see Henry Chadwick, *The Sentences of Sextus: A Contribution to the History of Early Christian Ethics*, 118–119.

[72] Rufinus, *praefatio, Sexti Sententiae* (*CCL* 20, 259).

[73] Otto Bardenhewer, *Geschichte der alt-*

kirchlichen Literatur, vol. III: 554.

[74] Chadwick, *Sentences*, 118.

[75] Chadwick, *Sentences*, 161–162.

[76] Vinzenz Buchheit ed., *Tyrannii Rufini Librorum Adamantii Origenis Adversus Haereticos Interpretatio*, xxxx, xxxxvii, xxxxviii; hereafter cited as *Dialogus*. See also Buchheit's earlier article, "Rufinus von Aquileja als Fälscher des Adamantiosdialogs," 314–328.

[77] In a speech by the interlocutor, Eutropius, in *Dialogus* V, 28, Rufinus adds to the Greek version's "Adamantius" the words, "Origenes, qui et Adamantius," thus making the identification complete for his Latin readers (Buchheit ed., 149–150).

deity.[78] The Law and the Gospel should not be separated, he claims, since both teach about justice *and* about mercy;[79] neither Jesus nor Paul dissolved the Law in the manner that Manicheans and Marcionites allege.[80] Moreover, Adamantius champions the power of human free will against various Gnostic positions:[81] our own negligence is the reason for sin, just as rust on a statue develops through later neglect and should not be attributed to the sculptor's ineptness.[82] Such views as these, in complete accord with Origen's, would occasion no surprise for readers who imagined that "Adamantius" really was Origen.

When they came to the debate on the resurrection, however, informed readers *should* have been surprised, since the position here expressed by Adamantius seems amazingly close to that of the anti-Origenist Methodius,[83] while the view ascribed to Adamantius's heretical opponent Marinus, a partisan of Bardesanes, replicates the opinion set forth by Origen in his *Commentary on Psalm 1*, verse 5. Adamantius begins the discussion by differentiating "flesh" from "body" in the afterlife. Although Christ had a heavenly body, we should not think that "flesh and blood and bones" have any place in heaven; for humans on earth, however, "flesh" and "body" mean the same thing.[84] It is immediately clear how useful this distinction will be for Rufinus's purposes: material substance is vanquished from the afterlife, but human speech is allowed a blurring of terms when it refers to our present existence.

As the allegedly heretical opponent, Marinus the Bardesanite, expounds his views, however, it becomes obvious that he has been assigned to "speak" the position of the historical Origen, although he draws more negative implications from them than Origen probably did. Since the substance of the body is always in a state of flux, Marinus inquires, at what age should we say that a human is resurrected? As a young boy, as a grown man, as an elder? Marinus highlights the fluidity of the body, which constantly changes its nature as old parts dissolve or are eliminated and as new parts develop through the nourishment we ingest.[85] Moreover, Marinus alleges, the human body is made from four elements—earth, water, air, and fire—and will resolve back into them upon death. How then could there be a resurrection when the parts have reverted to the elements out of which

---

[78] *Dialogus* I; II (Buchheit ed., 2–49).
[79] *Dialogus* I, 10–12 (Buchheit ed., 11–13); see Origen, *De principiis* II, 4–5.
[80] *Dialogus* II, 15 (Buchheit ed., 39).
[81] *Dialogus* III, 9; 10; IV, 9; 11 (Buchheit ed., 55, 56, 68, 70).
[82] *Dialogus* III, 13 (Buchheit ed., 58–59); cf. Pelagius, *Ep. ad Demetriadem* 8 (PL 30, 24), in which God is said to use the Law to file away the rust of ignorance and vice.

[83] Buchheit follows W. H. van de Sande Bakhuyzen (editor of the *GCS* edition of 1901), who shows that the author of the *Dialogue* is strongly indebted to Methodius: see Buchheit, 149.
[84] *Dialogus* V, 2 (Buchheit ed., 74–75). See Rufinus's use of this argument, p. 160 above.
[85] *Dialogus* V, 16 (Buchheit ed., 86–87).

they were created?[86] Thus Marinus denies that either the body or the flesh will be resurrected.[87] Did not Paul himself call the body a "chain" of the soul?[88] The evidence to which Marinus here appeals is similar to that in Origen's writings, although he does not affirm the continuation of the corporeal *eidos*, as Origen did. Marinus's opinions on the flux of the material body are the very ones often cited in horror by dismayed anti-Origenists to claim that Origen denied *any* notion of a resurrection.[89]

Adamantius ("Origen") for his part argues that our bodies remain basically the same throughout our lives: thus there is a unified "body" that can be raised.[90] His view is affirmed by the highly partisan interlocutor, Eutropius, who provides a biological corroboration: nourishment does not create a new bodily substance for us, but only preserves and restores that which we already have.[91] As for Marinus's claim that the body dissolves back into the four elements at death, Adamantius replies that God is at least as clever as human artisans, who can separate (for example) silver from air: cannot God, the creator of everything, separate out the parts of our bodies and reconstitute them? If he preserved whole the three boys in the fiery furnace and left Jonah alive for three days and nights in the depths of a whale, surely he can put back together the component parts of the body, even after it has returned to the earth.[92] Adamantius's argument here is derived from Methodius's anti-Origenist work *On the Resurrection*.[93] Adamantius further explains that when Paul in I Corinthians 15:50 wrote that no "flesh and blood" would inherit the Kingdom of God, he meant only that the shameful acts of humans given over to carnality would not be present in the Kingdom:[94] Adamantius implies that Paul affirmed a fleshly afterlife. By translating this anonymous *Dialogue*—now thought to have been composed around A.D. 330[95]—Rufinus gave publicity to a text supporting his claim that Origen was, as he asserts in his prologue, "catholic, ecclesiastical, and a *defensor* of dogma."[96] Whether or not Rufinus perpetuated a deliberate fraud, as Buchheit claims, is difficult to judge. Doubtless,

---

[86] *Dialogus* V, 18 (Buchheit ed., 88).

[87] *Dialogus* V, 20 (Buchheit ed., 90).

[88] *Dialogus* V, 21 (Buchheit ed., 90–91), citing Romans 7:24.

[89] Origen, *De principiis* II, 10, 3 (*GCS* 22, 175–176); *Contra Celsum* VII, 32 (*GCS* 20, 182–183); citations from (among other works) *Comm. in Psalmos 1* (on 1:5), in Epiphanius, *Panarion* 64, 12–16 (*GCS* 31[1], 421–429).

[90] *Dialogus* V, 16 (Buchheit ed., 87).

[91] *Dialogus* V, 17 (Buchheit ed., 88); cf. Methodius, *De resurrectione* I, 25, 4–5 (*GCS* 27, 251–252), also in Epiphanius, *Panarion* 64, 17, 6–10 (*GCS* 31[2], 428).

[92] *Dialogus* V, 18 (Buchheit ed., 89); cf. Methodius, *De resurrectione* I, 43, (*GCS* 27, 289–291).

[93] Fragments of the work in *GCS* 27.

[94] *Dialogus* V, 22 (Buchheit ed., 91–92); cf. Methodius, *De resurrectione* I, 52 (from Photius, *Bibliotheca* 234 [*PG* 103, 1125]: the "impassible body" does not mean that the members are changed, but that the body does not desire "carnal pleasures."

[95] Buchheit, *Tyrannii Rufini Librorum Admantii*, vii.

[96] Rufinus, *praefatio, Dialogus* (Buchheit ed., 1).

however, the entirely orthodox "Origen" presented in the *Dialogue* was useful for Rufinus's argument.

With the death of Siricius of Rome in November 399,[97] Rufinus found himself in a position less favorable than that which he had so far enjoyed since his return to the West. Whereas Siricius had refused to move against Origen's sympathizers and had even armed Rufinus with a document testifying that he had found Rufinus's views orthodox,[98] the new bishop of Rome, Anastasius, looked considerably less friendly. Indeed, after receiving in 400 Rufinus's statement of faith, the *Apologia ad Anastasium*,[99] Anastasius claimed in response that he didn't know who Origen was nor did he want to know—a startling testimony to the relative ignorance of Origen's theological works in the West. Anastasius nonetheless noted the effect that the translation of *On First Principles* had made on Roman Christians: he could not believe that Origen had even tried to maintain the orthodox faith. If the translator of the work (Rufinus) intended to make the book intelligible to Latin readers so that they might denounce it, fine— but was this the case?[100]

That this was *not* the reason Rufinus had translated *On First Principles* was made clear from the controversy that ensued. To be sure, Rufinus had undertaken the translation at Macarius's request, not on his own initiative, and he had done so in order to help Macarius answer the pressing arguments of the astral determinists, the *mathematici*[101]—reasons that might sound not merely plausible, but even laudable. Nonetheless, in his *Apologies* to Anastastius in 400 and to Jerome in 401, Rufinus was pressed to demonstrate his own theological correctness and to align Origen's teaching with Christian orthodoxy of his own day as much as possible.

By the time that Rufinus composed his *Apologia* for Anastasius, he had already left Rome. In this work, he urges Anastasius to use his confession of faith as a stick to drive off the "barking dogs" who attack him.[102] He reminds Anastasius that he had suffered for the orthodox faith at the hands of Arian heretics, a suffering that now prompts his defense of staunch orthodox teaching on the Trinity[103] and the Incarnation (including the resurrection of Jesus' "same flesh").[104] According to Rufinus, Jesus' fleshly resurrection gives Christians hope that they too will rise in the very flesh they now possess, without a single part cut off, but that their bodies will

---

[97] Murphy, *Rufinus*, 234.

[98] Jerome, *Apologia* III, 21; 24 (CCL 79, 92, 96).

[99] Text in CCL 20, 25–28. For a discussion of the argument that Rufinus borrowed heavily from Bachiarius's *De fide*, see Manlio Simonetti, "Note Rufiniane," esp. 140–152, questioning the ascription by J. Duhr, "Le 'De fide' de Bachiarius," 5–40, 301–331.

[100] Anastasius, *Ep.* 1 (*ad Ioannem Hierosolymitanem*), 3–4 (PL 20, 69–71).

[101] Rufinus, *Apologia* I, 11 (CCL 20, 44).

[102] Rufinus, *Apologia ad Anastasium* 1 (CCL 20, 25).

[103] Rufinus, *Apologia ad Anastasium* 2 (CCL 20, 25).

[104] Rufinus, *Apologia ad Anastasium* 3 (CCL 20, 26).

nonetheless be glorious and spiritual: this is the teaching of his home church, Aquileia, as well as that of Rome.[105] Rufinus willingly confesses that the devil merits eternal hellfire—but then, so do those who unjustly accuse their brothers.[106]

As for the origin of the soul, Rufinus refuses in the *Apologia ad Anastasium* to make a definite pronouncement. He reports to Anastasius that three views on the matter have been advanced: that the soul comes down with the body through human seed; that God continually makes new souls for the bodies being produced; and that God made souls long ago, now simply assigning one of them to a body as the occasion arises. The third view Rufinus identifies with Origen and "some others of the Greeks." Since the Church has not pronounced on these views, except to teach in a general way that God creates both souls and bodies, Rufinus sees no reason to decide which opinion is correct: he will leave the judgment on this question up to God.[107]

Rufinus also insists in the *Apologia ad Anastasium* that translators should not be held responsible for positions advanced by the authors of the works they translate. He explains for Anastasius his view concerning the interpolations in Origen's writings, and his substitution of "catholic" statements by Origen for more dubious ones. If Anastasius wants to ban for the future any further translation of Origen's books, that is his prerogative, but he does not have the power to undo the translations already completed:[108] a subtle reminder to Anastasius that Jerome *also* had translated Origen's works. He concludes with a rousing confession that he espouses the same faith as that held at Rome, Alexandria, Aquileia, and Jerusalem,[109] this last a rather impolitic addition, given that its bishop, John, was under suspicion of Origenist heresy. Jerome's assessment of the *Apologia ad Anastasium* was that Rufinus had protested overmuch about issues that were *not* matters of debate, such as the Trinity, but had failed to give straightforward responses on the disputed points in the present controversy over Or-

---

[105] Rufinus, *Apologia ad Anastasium* 4 (*CCL* 20, 26).

[106] Rufinus, *Apologia ad Anastasium* 5 (*CCL* 20, 26–27).

[107] Rufinus, *Apologia ad Anastasium* 6 (*CCL* 20, 27). Whether Rufinus tried to modify Origen's view in his translation of *On First Principles* is discussed by John Rist in "The Greek and Latin Texts of the Discussion of Free Will in *De Principiis*, Book III," 109–110. Commenting on Rufinus's translation of Origen's discussion of Jacob/Esau in Romans 9, Rist notes that Rufinus makes Origen's "preceding causes" that accounts for the relative honor and dishonor accorded the brothers apply to their life *in* the womb, not *before* it. Rist, however, thinks that Rufinus's modification relates to factors other than his "desire to conceal Origen's doctrinal unorthodoxy" (110). Rist does not note, however, that the origin of the soul was one of the most contested items of the Origenist controversy.

[108] Rufinus, *Apologia ad Anastasium* 7 (*CCL* 20, 27–28).

[109] Rufinus, *Apologia ad Anastasium* 8 (*CCL* 20, 28).

igen, such as the origin and fall of the soul, and the nature of the resurrection body.[110]

By 401, it appears that Rufinus had decided that the best defense was an offense: he would go on the attack himself. Jerome was his target. As I have detailed extensively elsewhere,[111] Rufinus's technique in the *Apologia contra Hieronymum* is to show that Jerome, in his earlier works, especially his *Commentary on Ephesians,* had cited Origen's opinions over and again— including ones now hotly disputed—without a suggestion that he disapproved of them. Since Jerome was keen to position himself against a variety of earlier heretics, why hadn't he included Origen among them if he now deems Origen's opinions so misguided?[112] Rufinus implies that Jerome was a fellow traveler in the Origenist camp long before he himself had written a word on the issue.

Moreover, in the *Apology against Jerome,* Rufinus strikes at his opponent in another way. Although Jerome now faults Rufinus for changing or omitting some words in his translation of *On First Principles,* the emendations that Rufinus made are nothing compared to the liberties that Jerome took in translating the Old Testament from Hebrew. Why was a new translation necessary? Had not the Septuagint been used without apostolic criticism from the earliest days of the Church?[113] Rufinus sneers at the "Jewish" tone of Jerome's translation, and mentions his hire of a Hebrew teacher whom Rufinus unflatteringly dubs "Barabbas."[114] The net result of Jerome's work on the Hebrew Old Testament, according to Rufinus, has been to remove from Scriptural status a book that provided an excellent lesson in chastity (*Susanna and the Elders*), to leave Christians open to Jewish mockery concerning such points as the species of plant Jonah sulked under at Nineveh, and to strengthen the unbelief of pagans, who now can see for themselves that Christians have no fixed truth to which they can turn.[115] Yet, his accuser notes, Jerome dares to protest about some minor omissions and emendations in Rufinus's translation of *On First Principles.*

In his *Apologia contra Hieronymum,* Rufinus once more explains the guidelines that he adopted in translating the *Peri Archōn.* Where Origen contradicted himself, Rufinus decided which view was genuinely Ori-

---

[110] Jerome, *Apologia* III, 4–8 (*CCL* 79, 36–40).

[111] Clark, "The Place of Jerome's Commentary on Ephesians," 141–171.

[112] Rufinus, *Apologia* I, 30 (*CCL* 20, 65).

[113] The argument pertaining to Jerome's translation from the Hebrew is found in Rufinus, *Apologia* II, 36–41 (*CCL* 20, 111–116). For a discussion of Jerome's Biblical translation, see C. H. Bammel, "Die Hexapla

des Origenes: Die *Hebraica Veritas* im Streit der Meinungen," 139–145.

[114] Cf. Rufinus, *Apologia* II, 36; 39; 41 (*CCL* 20, 111, 113–114, 115–116).

[115] Rufinus, *Apologia* II, 39 (*CCL* 20, 113–114): the reference is to Jerome's declaring *Susanna and the Elders* an apocryphal book; for the debate over Jonah's plant, see Augustine, *Ep.* 71 (= Jerome, *Ep.* 104, 5 [*CSEL* 55, 241]).

gen's.[116] Moreover, he claims that he carefully expounded his theory of interpolation of Origen's works by heretics.[117] He had not transmitted expressions that might "offend" Christians,[118] and he had passed over some few points that did not seem "edifying" to the faith.[119] He reasserts in this *Apology* that there is a difference between items of "belief" that Christians must espouse, such as in a Creator God, and those of "reasoning" about created entities, in which there is room for discussion and speculation.[120] Doctrines of the Church are one thing—and Rufinus staunchly upholds them—but some other points, he avers, have "nothing to do with faith in the deity."[121] That the devil might have a respite from punishment is one such view, billed by Rufinus as "mere opinion."[122] We may leave it to God to decide on the difficult points about which the Church, under divine guidance, had not declared.[123] For our part, we should behave like skillful masons, taking pieces of an old construction to build a new one. Thus Macarius could quite appropriately have used the "stones" of Origen's teachings to erect a new edifice suitable for the present; he would not have had to appropriate the whole Origenist "house".[124] Moreover, the function of the fortification that Macarius wished to build, Rufinus reminds Jerome, was to "repel a hostile attack":[125] Macarius's desire to have *On First Principles* in Latin translation had been motivated by entirely praiseworthy concerns. Here Rufinus again shows himself more willing than his opponents to give a historicized reading to Origen and Origenist theology. In addition, we are alerted to some theological issues underlying the dispute that had been obscured in the controversies over translation and Jerome's or Rufinus's "orthodoxy." Three points in particular emerge from a close reading of Rufinus's *Apology against Jerome*.

In Rufinus's judgment, the chief issue about which his "accusers from the East" (presumably Eusebius of Cremona)[126] raised the charge of heresy relates to questions in *On First Principles* I, 1: do the members of the Godhead "see" each other?[127] Rufinus's opponents allege that Origen on this point was heretical: to claim that the Son did not "see" the Father was taken by them as a sign of subordinationism, that is, Arianism. Rufinus responds that in this passage, Origen was not discussing differences among

---

[116] Rufinus, *Apologia* I, 14 (*CCL* 20, 47).

[117] Rufinus, *Apologia* I, 13; 15 (*CCL* 20, 46, 48).

[118] Rufinus, *Apologia* I, 20 (*CCL* 20, 54).

[119] Rufinus, *Apologia* II, 41 (*CCL* 20, 116).

[120] Rufinus, *Apologia* I, 15 (*CCL* 20, 48).

[121] Rufinus, *Apologia* II, 51 (*CCL* 20, 122).

[122] Rufinus, *Apologia* I, 35 (*CCL* 20, 70).

[123] Rufinus, *Apologia* I, 25 (*CCL* 20, 59).

[124] Rufinus, *Apologia* II, 44 (*CCL* 20, 117–118).

[125] Rufinus, *Apologia* II, 45 (*CCL* 20, 118).

[126] On Eusebius, see Rufinus, *Apologia* I, 19 (*CCL* 20, 53–54); Rufinus adds that it is acceptable to say "see" if we understand that we mean "as God sees," not as humans do.

[127] Origen, *De principiis* I, 1 (*GCS* 22, 16–27).

members of the Trinity[128] and thus his exposition should not be set in the context of the Arian–Nicene debate.[129] Rather, Origen here wished to express the notion that the Godhead is invisible, a characteristic that marks its essential difference from created things.[130] Once the locus of the debate is correctly positioned, Rufinus claims, readers can note against whom Origen *was* writing: Valentinus and the Anthropomorphites, who teach that God has a body. According to Rufinus, Origen believed that he could silence such heretics if he spoke of the members of the Godhead as "knowing" rather than "seeing" one another. Origen was attempting to teach these opponents that Father, Son, and Holy Spirit are equal in their invisibility—a perfectly correct expression of faith.[131] More to be feared than Origen's views are those of Rufinus's accusers, who have been overly hasty in "giving the hand" to persons espousing heretical opinions on the bodily nature of God.[132] Rufinus here attempts to tar members of Jerome's network with the brush of "Anthropomorphism."

Rufinus's discussion alerts us to contemporary resonances of the third-century debate he describes. Although it is highly improbable that Rufinus was worried about Valentinians in the opening years of the fifth century, the monasteries of the Egyptian desert had indeed been set astir by the Anthropomorphite debates of the late 390s that had issued in Theophilus of Alexandria's expulsion in A.D. 400 of the anti-Anthropomorphite monks, including the Tall Brothers and their Origenist supporters.[133] We know in fact that Rufinus a few years earlier had singled out one of his own present opponents as an Anthropomorphite: Epiphanius of Salamis, chief critic of Origen's alleged dissolution of material reality.[134] Rufinus claims, in contrast, that from his initial theological education, he had been correctly instructed by his teachers—presumably Chromatius of Aquileia and Didymus the Blind in person, and Gregory of Nazianzus through his writings—on the invisibility of the Trinity.[135] Rufinus thus underscores the usefulness of Origen's theology as polemic against both past and present theological deviance: what Origen had posited against various Gnostics could be appropriated for a critique of Anthropomorphism.

A second issue pertaining to bodiliness for which Rufinus attempts at least a modest defence of Origen's views concerns the resurrection. Rufinus admits that both Jesus and resurrected humans receive back "that very flesh" in which they died. But what does "that very flesh" mean? Rufinus claims that the "nature of the flesh" will remain; we will not be "mists and

[128] Rufinus, *Apologia* I, 18 (*CCL* 20, 51–52).

[129] See above, Chap. 3 on Epiphanius and Jerome.

[130] Rufinus, *Apologia* I, 18 (*CCL* 20, 52).

[131] Rufinus, *Apologia* I, 18 (*CCL* 20, 52).

[132] Rufinus, *Apologia* I, 17 (*CCL* 20, 50).

[133] See pp. 45–49 above.

[134] Jerome, *Apologia* II, 23 (*CCL* 79, 94).

[135] On Rufinus's knowledge of Gregory of Nazianzus and Didymus, see Murphy, *Rufinus*, esp. 44–47, 50, 115–118, and Rufinus, *Apologia* I, 45 (*CCL* 20, 81).

light vapors,"[136] nor will we receive someone else's members.[137] But it is not necessary, as Jerome insists, to name each and every bodily part that we will regain in the resurrection.[138] In fact, Jerome himself had wavered on the nature of the resurrection body, Rufinus reveals. Lately Jerome had mocked some women who were Origenist sympathizers when they tapped their breasts, bellies, and thighs, asking, "Is this poor, weak body to rise? If we are to be like the angels, we will have the nature of angels!"[139] How can Jerome face them honestly, Rufinus asks, when in his *Ephesians Commentary* he had affirmed the position that in the end, "women will become men"?[140] Is he now backtracking on his earlier view of the body's transformability?[141] Now, Jerome maintains that maleness and femaleness will persist in the future life, that our bodies will be equipped with genital organs (will we reproduce, Rufinus queries?), whereas in the *Ephesians Commentary*, he had affirmed neither the resurrection of the flesh nor that of the body.[142] Doesn't Jerome know Paul's teaching that the resurrection body will be spiritual and incorruptible?[143] The Church, Rufinus claims, has wisely taken a "middle path" between the theory of the body's total dissolution and that of its total transformation: the Origenist women, who tap their breasts and bellies, however, are *more* right than is Jerome.[144] Although Rufinus does not here adopt Origen's view wholesale, he is clearly willing to denounce Jerome's for its disturbing carnality.

Rufinus's attack now takes a nasty turn: did Jerome acquire such views on the preservation of bodily frailty in the resurrection from "his" Jews—that is, the ones from whom he learned Hebrew? Jews, Rufinus claims, have such a materialist view of the afterlife that they envision us enjoying carnal delights in the hereafter.[145] Did Jerome's teacher "Barabbas" inspire him "to hope for a resurrection not in power but in frailty, to make friends with the letter that kills rather than the spirit that gives life?"[146] It is Jerome, not Rufinus, who is in error with his talk about the weakness of the resurrection body,[147] talk derived from "Jewish" opinions.

To be sure, Rufinus does not here endorse Origen's notion of the resurrection body as a corporeal *eidos* that survives the physical body's dissolution. Nonetheless, compared with Jerome, he holds out for a more transformed (and more transformable), more spiritualized entity. As Peter Brown has expressed it, Jerome and the anti-Origenist party "did not wish their own bodies, and with their bodies, the landmarks of their own soci-

---

[136] Rufinus, *Apologia* I, 4 (*CCL* 20, 39).

[137] Rufinus, *Apologia* I, 6 (*CCL* 20, 41).

[138] Rufinus, *Apologia* I, 5 (*CCL* 20, 40).

[139] Jerome, *Ep.* 84, 6 (*CSEL* 55, 127), cited in Rufinus, *Apologia* I, 7 (*CCL* 20, 41).

[140] Jerome, *Comm. ad Eph.* III, on Ephesians 5:28 (*PL* 26, 533).

[141] Rufinus, *Apologia* I, 7 (*CCL* 20, 42).

[142] Rufinus, *Apologia* I, 24 (*CCL* 20, 58).

[143] Rufinus, *Apologia* I, 6 (*CCL* 20, 41).

[144] Rufinus, *Apologia* I, 7 (*CCL* 20, 42).

[145] Rufinus, *Apologia* I, 7 (*CCL* 20, 42).

[146] Rufinus, *Apologia* II, 15 (*CCL* 20, 95).

[147] Rufinus, *Apologia* II, 45 (*CCL* 20, 118).

ety, to be rendered evanescent by the vertiginous immensity implied in Origen's notion of the slow transformation of all created spirits."[148] For Jerome, the battle over the status of virginity had had its theological consequences: "Bodies defended with such care were not destined to melt away in some distant transformation. Far from being a superficial and transitory layer of the person, sexual differences, and the behavior appropriate to them, were validated for all eternity."[149] Once again, we note that the earlier debates over asceticism had implications for Jerome's stance during the Origenist controversy.

The third theological issue of the controversy returns us to Rufinus's stated motivation for the translation of *On First Principles*: he had not intended to incite a civil war, but to "repel a hostile attack,"[150] namely, from the *mathematici*, the astral determinists whose fatalism eviscerated the role of God's providential care for the universe. Recall that Macarius has been puzzled how best to respond to the astrologer's claims: thinking that Origen would provide him with the best answer, Rufinus had translated for him Pamphilus's *Apologia pro Origene*, but this work had only whetted Macarius's enthusiasm for the whole *Peri Archōn* being turned into Latin.[151]

The specific point at which Rufinus engages Jerome about the implication of Origen's teaching for God's direction and care for his creation is found in a criticism he makes of Jerome's *Commentary on Ephesians*. The verse in question is Ephesians 1:4, "God chose us before the foundation (*katabolēs*) of the world." One interpretation of the verse that Jerome had given pertained to God's foreknowledge and election of blessed individuals.[152] Jerome next referred to a second interpreter, "who tries to show that God is just," who holds that souls preexisted and received their place in the present world on the basis of their preexistent merits or demerits. The unnamed interpreter is plainly Origen.

Rufinus now, in his *Apology against Jerome*, proceeds to trap Jerome concerning Origen's rationale for adopting this specific cosmological theory, namely, his desire to show that God was just, that he had not arbitrarily fixed the fates of persons in this world. Origen's theory also had provided a solution for the suffering of seemingly righteous persons: perhaps some exemplary souls had not committed sins in their preexistent state, but nonetheless were "sent down to instruct and train sinful souls."[153] Why, if

---

[148] Peter Brown, *The Body and Society: Men, Women and Sexual Renunciation in Early Christianity*, 380.

[149] Brown, *The Body and Society*, 383.

[150] Rufinus, *Apologia* II, 45 (*CCL* 20, 118).

[151] Rufinus, *Apologia* I, 11 (*CCL* 20, 44–45).

[152] Rufinus, *Apologia* I, 26 (*CCL* 20, 60);

Jerome, *Comm. ad Eph.* I, on Eph. 1:4 (*PL* 26, 446–447).

[153] Rufinus, *Apologia* I, 27 (*CCL* 20, 61–62). The verse, "God is our refuge before the mountains were established" (Psalm 90:1–2), and references to the righteous who endured captivity in Babylon, are other examples used in Origenist exegesis.

Jerome accepted this position—Origen's—without comment earlier, does he now rush to condemn it? Rufinus puts the question sharply: does Jerome deny that God is just?[154] No one, he says, with the smallest shred of good sense would wish to do so.[155] Yet if Jerome agrees that God is just, does he not identify himself with the purpose of that older commentator, Origen, whose motivation for constructing his cosmological scheme was to uphold the justice of God by explaining present human fates on the basis of preexistent merits or demerits?[156]

In his *Ephesians Commentary*, Rufinus continues, Jerome had cited the views of an interpreter who held that the activities of preexistent souls explained why "some men are born poor and barbarian, in slavery and lacking power, while others are born wealthy Roman citizens, free and in robust health; why some are born in different countries, in different parts of the world." And, the unnamed interpreter had added, it is these antecedent causes that explain why God loved Jacob and hated Esau, why some became vessels of honor and others, vessels of dishonor.[157] If Jerome disagreed with this interpreter, he might have said so, just as he had expressed his displeasure at the opinions of Marcion, Valentinus and Arius.[158] We can see in retrospect that the answers of the unnamed interpreter (Origen) were designed to address in a different way the very questions that Macarius's opponents, the astral fatalists, had raised. For the latter, the configuration of the stars at an individual's birth held the key to his or her fate in life; no thought of God's justice or providence attended their schemes.

Although Jerome had labelled the Origenist answer "heathen," Rufinus advises him to rescind this rash judgment:

> Do not be so rash, my brother, as to condemn yourself unnecessarily. Neither you nor Origen are at once to be set down among the heathen if, as you have yourself said, you have written these things to vindicate the justice of God, and to make answer to those who say that everything is moved by chance or by fate: if, I say, it is from your wish to show that God's providence which governs all things is just that you have said the causes of inequality have been acquired by each soul through the passions and feelings of the former life which it had in heaven; or even if you said that it is in accordance with the character of the Trinity, which is good and simple and unchangeable that every creature should in the end of all things be restored to the state in which it was first created; and that this must be after long punishment equal to the length of all the ages, which God inflicts on each creature in the spirit not of one who is angry but of one who corrects, since he is not one who is extreme to mark

[154] Rufinus, *Apologia* I, 28 (CCL 20, 63).
[155] Rufinus, *Apologia* I, 27 (CCL 20, 61–62).
[156] Rufinus, *Apologia* I, 28 (CCL 20, 63).
[157] Rufinus, *Apologia* I, 29 (CCL 20, 64), citing Jerome's *Ephesians Commentary* I, on Ephesians 1:5–6 (*PL* 26, 449–450), commenting on Romans 9.
[158] Rufinus, *Apologia* I, 30 (CCL 20, 65).

iniquity; and that, his design like a physician being to heal men, he will place a term upon their punishment. Whether in this you spoke truly, let God judge; anyhow such views seem to me to contain little of impiety against God and nothing at all of heathenism, especially if they were put forward with the desire and intention of finding some means by which the justice of God might be vindicated.

I would not, therefore, have you distress yourself overmuch about these points, nor expose yourself needlessly either to penance or to condemnation.[159]

We can see from Jerome's response, the *Apology against Rufinus*, that it took him some time to comprehend the seriousness of Rufinus's point. In the first two books of the *Apology*, which he wrote before he actually had a copy of Rufinus's attack in hand,[160] he seems little concerned with the issues here explored. In Book I, he notes in one brief sentence that he had never claimed that the unnamed commentator he had cited in his *Ephesians Commentary* had successfully defended God's justice, only that he had *wished* to.[161] And in Book II, Jerome considers opinions about the soul's origin not in a context of discussion about God's justice and the diversity of human fates, but of Jesus' soul: if the soul that entered Jesus existed before his birth from Mary, it was not truly "his" soul.[162] One of Origenism's heresies, he claims, is to teach that the soul of Jesus existed before his birth from Mary:[163] Jerome here turns into a Christological issue what for Rufinus pertained to theodicy. That Jerome may have been prompted to do so after he had experienced a brush with Apollinarians, who had raised arguments about the soul of Jesus, is likely.[164]

Only in Book III of Jerome's *Apology*, after he had read for himself Rufinus's *Apologia contra Hieronymum* with its accompanying letter (now lost), from which Jerome quotes, did he comprehend that the issue of God's justice was not a minor one for his opponent. In the letter, Rufinus apparently had again confessed his ignorance on the question of the origin of souls. It is for him an unanswerable question, like asking, "What are the causes of the fountains and the wind? What makes the hail and the rain?" Jerome's reply mocks Rufinus: if one can't explain why a tiny ant is endowed with six feet when a huge elephant has only four, does that really mean that one can't know about the origin of souls? Jerome repeats the

---

[159] Rufinus, *Apologia* II, 12–13 (*CCL* 20, 92–93), translation cited from *NPNF*, 2nd series, vol. 3: 465.

[160] Jerome, *Apologia* I, 1; 3; 4; 21; III, 1 (*CCL* 79, 1, 3–4, 5, 20, 73).

[161] Jerome, *Apologia* I, 22 (*CCL* 79, 22).

[162] Jerome, *Apologia* II, 4 (*CCL* 79, 36): Jerome rules out the traducianist answer, for

then souls might perish with bodies; he favors the answer that God made the individual soul after the body was formed and then sent it into the body.

[163] Jerome, *Apologia* II, 12 (*CCL* 79, 46).

[164] Jerome, *Apologia* II, 20 (*CCL* 79, 56–57).

view that he knows is correct: God creates souls daily and sends them into bodies. But Rufinus, he suspects, will no doubt revert to the question of God's justice, whatever Jerome replies, complaining that Jerome's answer involves God in the sexual activities of adulterers and the incestuous, that is, the creators of the bodies. Rufinus will doubtless also want to know why it is that infants die young. The latter problem, Jerome remarks, was the subject of a treatise Didymus the Blind had composed for Rufinus, and adds that Didymus had also composed three books for himself on Hosea that addressed just such questions.[165] It is a great loss for scholarship on the Origenist controversy that none of Didymus's treatises on these subjects is extant.

Ridiculing his opponent, Jerome remarks that if Rufinus had not come West bearing the *Peri Archōn*, Macarius "would still be stuck among the *mathematici*, and all Christians would still be ignorant of what might be said against fatalism." Should Jerome pity himself because he lacks the great wealth of learning "about the cause of the sky and the stars" that Rufinus brought to Rome with him from his years of study in the East?[166] Jerome suggests that Rufinus secretly holds the Origenist position on the origin of souls, but won't admit it: he loves to avoid the burning questions everyone wants answered, but replies to ones that nobody asked.[167] To modern readers, however, it is evident that whatever wit Jerome here musters at Rufinus's expense, he has not addressed the problem of God's justice. All he concludes is that the ship in Macarius's dream that brought him treasures from the East, ostensibly come "to do away with the puzzle of the *mathematici*," had succeeded only "in loosing the faith of Christians."[168]

Although Jerome delighted to call Rufinus a "mole" and ridiculed the liveliness of his intellect,[169] the acuity of Rufinus's attack upon Jerome's *Ephesians Commentary*, as detailed in the previous chapter, and his clear focus on the pressing theological issues at stake in the controversy, suggest that a more favorable assessment of his capabilities is in order. F. X. Murphy, although sympathetic to Rufinus, writes of him in this way: "His critical faculties being a good deal less keen than those of Jerome, though, as events were to prove sharp enough when roused in self-defense, he adopted a more benevolent attitude toward Origen's mistakes."[170] Or, noting Rufinus's limitation of theological essentials to the doctrines of the Trinity and eternal salvation, Murphy adds:

[165] Jerome, *Apologia* III, 28 (*CCL* 79, 99–100). Didymus's treatise is not extant; for a fragment, see John of Damascus (*PG* 95, 1381 = PG 96, 520), noted in *CPG* II, 2564 (109).

[166] Jerome, *Apologia* III, 29 (*CCL* 79, 101).

[167] Jerome, *Apologia* III, 30 (*CCL* 79,

102).

[168] Jerome, *Apologia* III, 32 (*CCL* 79, 102).

[169] Rufinus, *Apologia* I, 1; 36 (*CCL* 20, 37, 70), cf. Jerome, *Apologia* I, 17 (*CCL* 79, 15–17).

[170] Murphy, *Rufinus*, 101.

In this matter, of course, it is his deficiency of doctrinal awareness that is at fault, not his good will or sincerity. He simply did not realize the dogmatic implications involved in the settlement of these questions. In these matters, his talents are considerably below the genius of Jerome.[171]

I would contest this assessment for two reasons: first, the same theological concerns that prompted Rufinus to look more favorably on Origen's views up to the year 401 are present in his writings from the last decade of his life, when ostensibly the part of the controversy that implicated him was largely over. These views, I submit, were not overturned by the anti-Origenist attack: they represent considered theological judgments on Rufinus's part.

Second, we must question whether Murphy's imputing theological ignorance to Rufinus is correct, given Rufinus's lengthy association with Evagrius Ponticus, his knowledge of some of Evagrius's writings, and his failure ever to criticize Evagrius's views. Rufinus's alleged "deficiency of doctrinal awareness" may be interpreted in quite a different way: that he was well aware of the Origenist positions espoused by his friends and looked for ways to mitigate the force of the attacks upon them and himself. To these points I now turn.

To the first issue: it seems clear that Rufinus's theological concerns remained constant even after the initial heat of the controversy had subsided; the views he defended in the heat of the controversy were not concocted in haste to "save" his orthodoxy. In 402 or 403, after his *Apology against Jerome*, Rufinus produced a work that bishop Chromatius of Aquileia had requested (with the stated purpose of taking the minds of his fellow countrymen off the Gothic invasion of Italy):[172] a translation into Latin of Eusebius of Caesarea's *Ecclesiastical History*, with the addition of two books by Rufinus that brought the history of the Church down to 395, the date of Theodosius I's death. The major theological events of the fourth century covered by Rufinus were the Arian controversy and the eventual triumph of Nicene Christianity. Yet to continue Eusebius's work with a strong endorsement of Nicene-Cappadocian theology was itself problematic, since Eusebius's own views had leaned toward Arianism and could not readily be claimed for what counted as "orthodoxy" in Rufinus's day. Through a series of omissions from and emendations of Eusebius's text, Rufinus managed to construct a more orthodox Eusebius. Thus, for example, the long panegyric Eusebius had delivered at Tyre, with its not entirely Nicene tone, is simply omitted by Rufinus on the grounds that "it didn't add any-

---

[171] Murphy, *Rufinus*, 102. Cf. Gustav Bardy's comments on Rufinus's "insignificant" role in the history of theology: *s.v.*, "Rufin," col. 159.

[172] Rufinus, *prologus*, Eusebius, *HE* (*GCS*

9[2], 951). For a discussion of earlier attempts to ascribe the two extra books to Gelasius, see P. Van den Ven, "Encore le Rufin Grec," 281–294, esp. 294.

thing to our knowledge of events."[173] He also changes some of Eusebius's expressions so that the coessentiality and coeternity of the son with the Father is better emphasized. For example, where Eusebius refers to the Son as "second after the Lord," Rufinus translates, "the Lord himself from the Lord."[174] Likewise, he omits Eusebius's reference to the Son's occupying the "second place in the Kingdom."[175] When Eusebius applies to Christ the words of Psalm 110:3 (in its Septuagint reading), "From the womb, before the daystar I begat thee," Rufinus adds a note not found in Eusebius that interprets the meaning of "begotten": not from a "foreign or external source," but from the very being of God the Father.[176]

In Rufinus's own version of fourth-century church history, large sections of his first book concern the struggles between the Arian and the Nicene parties; in his second book, he lauds the Cappadocian Fathers and rejoices at Arianism's diminished power.[177] For Rufinus, the notion that true faith consists in proper Trinitarian doctrine—and in not much else—is here confirmed.

Rufinus's theological sympathies emerge in various other ways in the *Ecclesiastical History* as well. To Eusebius's Book VI, dedicated largely to the life and work of Origen, Rufinus adds details based on his own independent knowledge. Oulton has catalogued eight passages[178] in which Rufinus adds information not found in Eusebius, for example, supplying details to the famous story of Origen's mother hiding his clothes so that her enthusiastic son could not join his father in martyrdom,[179] and to the account of Origen's assistance to the martyrs of Alexandria.[180]

Rufinus also takes the opportunity in his addition to the *Ecclesiastical History* to praise the activities of such Origenist-oriented desert fathers as the two Macarii, Isidore, and Pambo.[181] He proudly reports that he has met and conversed with them, and mentions the suffering they endured at the time of the Arian persecution of Catholic Christians in Egypt.[182] That devoted student to Origen, Didymus the Blind, also receives extravagant praise. Especially noted are Antony's words to Didymus—known also to Jerome[183]—that Didymus suffered no injury in being deprived of his

---

[173] Rufinus, *prologus*, Eusebius, *HE* (*GCS* 9², 952). See Eusebius's oration at Tyre, sections 10; 23; 25; 67; 68 (*HE* X, 4 [*GCS* 9², 865–866, 869–870, 881–882]). Also see J.E.L. Oulton, "Rufinus's Translation of the Church History of Eusebius," 156.

[174] Eusebius, *HE* I, 2, 9 (*GCS* 9¹, 14–15). This and the next examples are listed in Oulton, "Rufinus's Translation," 154–155.

[175] Eusebius, *HE* I, 2, 11 (*GCS* 9¹, 16–17).

[176] Eusebius, *HE* I, 3, 17–18 (*GCS* 9¹, 36–37).

[177] Rufinus, *HE* XI, 9; 15; 19 (*GCS* 9², 1014, 1017, 1020–1021, 1024).

[178] Oulton, "Rufinus's Translation," 160–164.

[179] His addition to Eusebius, *HE* VI, 2, 5 (*GCS* 9², 520–521).

[180] His addition to Eusebius, *HE* VI, 3, 4 (*GCS* 9², 524–525).

[181] Compare the list in Rufinus, *HE* XI, 8 (*GCS* 9², 1013–1014).

[182] Rufinus, *HE* XI, 4 (*GCS* 9², 1004–1005, 1007).

[183] Jerome, *Ep.* 68, 2 (*CSEL* 54, 677–

bodily eyes, for humans share these with mice, flies, and lizards; Didymus, rather, was blessed with heavenly eyes that "see" God's light.[184] Another pro-Origenist monk who is accorded special attention by Rufinus is John of Lycopolis, whose prophesies regarding political and military events were allegedly heeded by emperors.[185] Thus Rufinus in unobtrusive ways shows his admiration for Origen and for the Origenist monks of his own era.

In 403–404, Rufinus's translation of Origen's works proceeded apace: his Latin versions of the homilies on Joshua, Judges, Genesis, Exodus, and Leviticus all date from this period.[186] Especially in his commentaries on Joshua and Judges, Origen had countered the criticisms of Gnostics and Marcionites that these books revealed the bloody cruelty of the Old Testament God and his people: they claimed that God could not be the father of Jesus.[187] Such slanders of Scripture gave Origen cause to emphasize God's abundant mercy, to affirm that whatever punishments God metes out, he ultimately delivers each soul:[188] he abandons neither the circumcised nor the uncircumcised.[189] Especially in his *Homilies on Joshua*, Origen wished to rule out the notion that chance had governed Biblical events.[190] He also warns Christians of his own era against astrology; they mistakenly believe that through it they will discover "the secret of life and men's actions."[191] Rather, God's benevolent, providential care for the universe is shown in his assignment of "guardian angels" for humans and in his creation of the mysterious force that controls specific natural occurrences.[192] The "deceptions of the *mathematici*" cannot, Origen here avers, "separate us from the love of God that is in Christ Jesus" (Romans 8:39).[193] In his *Homilies on Genesis*, Origen again affirms that nothing in the universe happens apart from God's providence, although this claim does not mean that God wills each and every thing that occurs.[194] God's treatment of wicked people such as Pharaoh never means their "penal annihilation."[195] In trans-

---

678), written in 397; cf. *Ep.* 76 (*CSEL* 55, 35–36) written in 399.

[184] Rufinus, *HE* II, 7 (*GCS* 9², 1012–1013).

[185] Rufinus, *HE* II, 19; 32 (*GCS* 9², 1024, 1036), cf. the additions on John that Rufinus inserted into his Latin translation of the *Historia Monachorum* I, 1; 2 (*PL* 21, 391, 392).

[186] Murphy, *Rufinus*, 235.

[187] Annie Jaubert, "Introduction," *Origène, Homélies sur Josué. Texte latin, introduction, traduction et notes* (*SC* 71, 12–13); and see especially *Hom. in Jesu Nave* X, 2; XI, 6; XII, 3 (*SC* 71, 274, 291, 300).

[188] Origen, *Hom. in Jesu Nave* V, 5, on Joshua 8:28 (*SC* 71, 230).

[189] Origen, *Hom. in Jesu Nave* VI, 1 (*SC* 71, 178).

[190] Origen, *Hom. in Jesu Nave* XXIII, 4; XXV, 2 (*SC* 71, 464, 482).

[191] Origen, *Hom. in Jesu Nave* VII, 4 (*SC* 71, 204).

[192] Origen, *Hom. in Jesu Nave* XXIII, 3 (*SC* 71, 460, 462).

[193] Origen, *Hom. in Iudicum* II, 3 (*GCS* 30, 476–477).

[194] Origen, *Hom. in Genesim* III, 2 (*GCS* 29, 39–40).

[195] Origen, *Hom. in Exodum* III, 3 (*GCS* 29, 167)—although at the end of the passage, Origen says that Pharaoh was destroyed in the abyss.

lating these homilies of Origen on Old Testament books, Rufinus would have received powerful reminders of Origen's cosmological and theological scheme that was designed to uphold both the justice and the benevolence of God.

In probably 404, Rufinus translated an anonymously composed *Historia monachorum*, but added extra material to his Greek source that reveals his own fascination with the Egyptian monks.[196] Here, John of Lycopolis receives particular attention, about whom Rufinus can supply an eyewitness report.[197] He also adds to the Greek text a sermon John delivered against pride that stresses such points as the incorporeality and incomprehensibility of God.[198] Another hero about whom Rufinus has privileged information is one of the Tall Brothers, Ammonius, who with his Origenist supporters had recently been chased from the desert by Theophilus of Alexandria: of Ammonius, Rufinus writes that those who saw him testified "that nobody else of all the fathers had ever penetrated so deeply into the inner courts of complete wisdom."[199] Rufinus also furnishes more stories about the two Macarii.[200] Of greatest importance, he expands the material on Evagrius Ponticus, who is declared to be "most learned": it was thought, Rufinus reports, that "no other brother had ever achieved such knowledge of subtle and spiritual things."[201] Thus even the exercise of translating and supplementing the *Historia monachorum* gave Rufinus opportunity to praise the Origenist heroes of the Egyptian desert.

Perhaps also in 404, Rufinus composed his treatise *On the Apostles' Creed*.[202] Borrowing heavily from Cyril of Jerusalem's *Catechetical Orations* and other works,[203] Rufinus presents himself as an entirely orthodox churchman. Nonetheless, he stands fast by his earlier enunciated principle that there is a difference between what we as Christians must simply "believe" (i.e., that God is Father of the Son) and what is left open for discussion.[204] Although we say we "believe in" the Father, the Son, and the Holy Spirit, we don't say we "believe in" the Church or the resurrection of the flesh.[205]

In *On the Apostles' Creed*, more than elsewhere, Rufinus shows his concern for the critique of Christianity levelled by educated pagans, who had

---

[196] Greek text edited by André-Jean Festugière, *Historia monachorum in Aegypto. SH* 53 (1971); Latin translation, with Rufinus's additions, in *PL* 21.

[197] *Historia monachorum* 1 (*PL* 21, 391).

[198] *Historia monachorum* 1 (*PL* 21, 395–398).

[199] *Historia monachorum* 23 (*PL* 21, 445–446).

[200] *Historia monachorum* 28; 29 (*PL* 21, 449–455).

[201] *Historia monachorum* 27 (*PL* 21, 448–449).

[202] Murphy, *Rufinus*, 235; J.N.D. Kelly, *Rufinus, A Commentary on the Apostles Creed*, 9, suggests on the basis of Rufinus's discussion of the resurrection body in his two *Apologies* that the *Commentary* perhaps was written two or three years earlier.

[203] Kelly, *Rufinus*, 9–11.

[204] Rufinus, *Expositio symboli* 4 (*CCL* 20, 139).

[205] Rufinus, *Expositio symboli* 34 (*CCL* 20, 169–170).

attacked such notions as the virgin birth,[206] the "death of God" in Jesus,[207] the ease of forgiveness for horrendous sins,[208] and the resurrection of the flesh.[209] Against such pagan charges, Rufinus is eager to claim both that *all* men, whether Christian or not, act on the basis of "belief"[210] and that there is no opposition between Scriptural teaching and "natural reason."[211] The pagan objections, and Rufinus's answers, are reminiscent of the charges raised a few years later by Melania the Younger's still pagan uncle Volusianus, which Augustine attempted to answer in *Epistles* 135–138.[212]

As for his own adherence to correct doctrine, Rufinus is especially concerned to stress his Trinitarian orthodoxy, which the Creed recited at Aquileia had emphasized by adding to its confession of the Father that he was "*invisibilem et impassibilem*." This addition, Rufinus notes, was especially helpful in ruling out "heresy":[213] no doubt he has the Anthropomorphites in mind. Like Evagrius, he affirms that the unity of the Godhead is not numerical but absolute.[214] Like Origen, he likens the Son's generation to "brightness from light."[215] Perhaps also influenced by Origen is his point that the incorporeal substance of God cannot be introduced into bodies without a spiritual substance serving as a medium: the Son of God thus received a soul as the "medium" when he became human.[216] Another point ultimately deriving from Origen is that Christ's human flesh served as a "fishhook" to bait the devil.[217]

In *On the Apostles' Creed*, it is earlier heretics, not those of his own day, that Rufinus takes to task: Marcionites, Valentinians, Ebionites, Manicheans, Arians, Eunomians, Donatists, and Novatianists, as well as the followers of Paul of Samosata and of Photinus. None of these can claim to represent the "true church."[218] Having listed these heresies by name, Ru-

---

[206] Rufinus, *Expositio symboli* 9 (CCL 20, 146).

[207] Rufinus, *Expositio symboli* 17 (CCL 20, 153).

[208] Rufinus, *Expositio symboli* 38 (CCL 20, 174).

[209] Rufinus, *Expositio symboli* 39; 40 (CCL 20, 175–176).

[210] Rufinus, *Expositio symboli* 3 (CCL 20, 136–137).

[211] Rufinus, *Expositio symboli* 46 (CCL 20, 181–182).

[212] See Augustine, *Epp.* 135–138 (CSEL 44, 89–148).

[213] Rufinus, *Expositio symboli* 3 (CCL 20, 136). All possible allusions to the Origenist controversy are overlooked by Maurice Villain ("Rufin d'Aquilée, Commentateur du Symbole des Apotres," 129–156), who on this point mentions only the Patripassians (134). For a later criticism of these additions

by Maximus of Turin(?) in his *Explanatio Symboli*, see F. R. Montgomery Hitchcock, "The *Explanatio Symboli ad Initiandos* Compared with Rufinus and Maximus of Turin," 58–69, esp. 59–61.

[214] Rufinus, *Expositio symboli* 5 (CCL 20, 139); cf. Evagrius Ponticus ("Basil"), *Ep.* 8, 2 (PG 32, 248–249).

[215] Rufinus, *Expositio symboli* 7 (CCL 20, 142); cf. Origen, *De principiis* I, 2, 4 (GSC 22, 33).

[216] Rufinus, *Expositio symboli* 11 (CCL 20, 148); cf. Origen, *De principiis* II, 63; IV, 4, 4 (GCS 22, 142, 353): suggested by Kelly, "Introduction," *Rufinus*, 117–118 n. 76.

[217] Rufinus, *Expositio symboli* 14 (CCL 20, 151); see references in Kelly, "Introduction," *Rufinus*, 119–120n. 90 on Origen.

[218] Rufinus *Expositio symboli* 37 (CCL 20, 172–173): against those who say that the Holy Spirit is not of the same substance as

finus then describes a position against which he says that believers should "turn a deaf ear," but he does not name its adherents or designate them as "heretics." The position is plainly that of the Origenists:

> Keep clear also of those—if indeed such are to be found—who are alleged to say that the Son of God does not possess the same vision and knowledge of the Father as the Father does of Him, or that Christ's kingdom must have an end or that the resurrection of the flesh does not entail the complete restoration of its substance; and similarly, of those who deny the universality of God's righteous judgment, and who believe that the devil will be absolved from the damnation which is his desert. The ears of the faithful, I repeat, should be deaf to all such. Hold fast, on the other hand, to the holy church, which proclaims its faith in God the Father almighty, and His only Son Jesus Christ our Lord, and the Holy Spirit, as existing in one harmonious and indivisible substance, and believes that the Son of God was born from the Virgin, suffered for man's salvation, and rose again from the dead in the identical flesh with which He as born.[219]

Rufinus here obviously wants to dissociate himself from the most disputed points of Origenism, yet leaves some leeway of interpretation. First, he raises the suspicion that there may not even *be* any people who hold such ideas. Next, he blurs several points that were at the center of the dispute: even Origenists could say that the members of the Godhead "know" (but not "see") each other, and that the flesh is raised "in its substance," if "substance" is equated with corporeal *eidos*—although Rufinus adds a point not so compatible with Origenism, that Jesus was raised in the same flesh in which he was buried.

That the resurrection of the flesh was an issue calling for special attention is suggested by Rufinus's detailed treatment of the subject in chapters 39–45 of *On the Apostles' Creed*. Some of his arguments fit well with his Origenist interests, for example, that the resurrected state will be an "angelic" one,[220] and that "each individual flesh" has within it "an immortal principle" by means of which God will restore the bodily particles to a "proper form."[221] Although the "this flesh" affirmation of the Creed of Aquileia has a decidedly un-Origenist tone,[222] the notion of an "immortal principle" within the flesh that will survive is more in accord with Origen's position as expounded in his *Commentary on Psalm 1*.[223] Thus despite Rufinus's de-

---

the Father and the Son, Rufinus puns on Matthew 19:6: "man has put asunder what God has joined together."

[219] Rufinus, *Expositio symboli* 37 (*CCL* 20, 173–174); translation from Kelly, *Rufinus*, 76.

[220] Rufinus, *Expositio symboli* 39 (*CCL* 20, 175).

[221] Rufinus, *Expositio symboli* 41 (*CCL* 20, 177).

[222] Rufinus, *Expositio symboli* 41 (*CCL* 20, 177).

[223] Rufinus, *Expositio symboli* 41 (*CCL* 20, 176); cf. Origen, *Comm. in Psalmos 1* (1:5), in Epiphanius, *Panarion* 64, 12–16 *passim* (*GCS* 31², 421–429).

sire to present himself as unwaveringly orthodox, aspects of his confession still permit a modified Origenist interpretation.

In the years after his most intense debate with Jerome, Rufinus continued to translate Origen's writings. He reduced and rendered into Latin Origen's enormous *Commentary on Romans*,[224] a project that was to prove invaluable to Pelagius in the development of his theology. That Rufinus here sought to avoid further criticism for his attention to Origen is clear: he tells his audience in an epilogue that he has modified Origen's practice of raising thorny questions and then leaving them unsolved, for he knew that this lack of resolution irritated Latin readers.[225] He hopes that his translation will not again rouse "ill-disposed minds" to complain about his work and seek to "ruin" him. Men who have raised these objections simply "hate Origen."[226] We know that Rufinus's translations of Origen's writings occupied him to the end of his life: the last we hear him, he is in Sicily, a refugee from the Gothic invasion, translating Origen's *Homilies on Numbers* as a solace while he watches Rhegium burn.[227]

Two other late literary efforts by Rufinus were his rendering into Latin of the Pseudo-Clementine *Recognitions* and his composing, at Paulinus of Nola's request, a commentary on the *Benedictions of the Patriarchs*. The Pseudo-Clementine *Recognitions*, we may imagine, was not distasteful to his sympathies. In addition to recording a lively narrative, the work powerfully supports monotheism[228] and contains lengthy discussions of evil, free will, creation and providence.[229] Astrology is a topic receiving special attention.[230] Once more, Rufinus states in the preface to his translation that he hopes his efforts to bring this Greek "medicine" to the Latins will not be met with "evil eye and envious look."[231]

Although the *Benedictions of the Patriarchs*, written for Paulinus of Nola,[232] contains nothing explicit on the topics that fueled the Origenist controversy, as did the Clementine *Recognitions*, it is of interest to see Paulinus—who never was won for Jerome's camp—bonded with Rufinus in an affectionate correspondence at the end of Rufinus's life. We know that Melania the Younger and Pinianus, with whom Rufinus had been in Sicily

[224] Rufinus, *praefatio*, Origen, *Comm. in Romanos* (*CCL* 20, 275). See the detailed study of Caroline Hammond Bammel, *Der Römerbrieftext des Rufins und seine Origenes-Übersetzung*, esp. 43–104. She dates Rufinus's translation of Origen's *Romans Commentary* to 405/406 (45).

[225] Rufinus, *epilogus*, Origen, *Comm. in Romanos* (*CCL* 20, 276).

[226] Rufinus, *epilogus*, Origen, *Comm. in Romanos* (*CCL* 20, 276–277).

[227] Rufinus, *praefatio*, Origen, *Hom. in Numeros* (*CCL* 20, 285).

[228] Pseudo-Clement, *Recognitiones* II, 40–46 (*GCS* 51, 75–79). Rufinus says in his preface that he left out an "unclear discussion" on the unbegotten and begotten God (*GCS* 51, 4).

[229] Pseudo-Clement, *Recognitiones* IX, 4–32 (*GCS* 51, 259–319).

[230] Pseudo-Clement, *Recognitiones* IX, 16–29; X, 2–14 (*GCS* 51, 266–314, 324–335).

[231] Rufinus, *prologus*, Pseudo-Clement, *Recognitiones* (*GCS* 51, 4).

[232] Rufinus, *De benedictionibus patriarcharum* I (*CCL* 20, 189).

while he translated Origen's *Homilies on Numbers*, attempted to visit Paulinus at Nola on their exodus from Rome, but their ship was blown off
course and they never reached their destination.[233] Was Rufinus to have
accompanied them, to visit once more his old friend who had lavished such
praise on Melania the Elder and her circle?[234] Presumably so.

Thus we are led back to the question of Rufinus's network of Origenist
alliances before he returned West and translated the *Peri Archōn*. One sure
association is that with Evagrius Ponticus. It was to Rufinus and Melania
the Elder that Evagrius fled when he hastily exited Constantinople in
382;[235] it is Melania who is credited with curing him of his residual love-
sickness; and she and Rufinus are said to have started him on his monastic
career.[236] Now, thanks to Gabriel Bunge's research on the letters of Evagrius, we are in a better position to assess Evagrius's continued relationship
with Rufinus and Melania the Elder during the years he resided in the
Egyptian desert.[237] We know that letters went back and forth between
Evagrius in Egypt and Melania and Rufinus in Palestine,[238] although, unfortunately, all of Rufinus's correspondence has been lost. We also know
that Rufinus translated some works of Evagrius: definitely the *Sentences for
Monks and for Virgins*,[239] and possibly the *Chapters on Prayer*, of which he
was arguably the recipient.[240] Rufinus has also been posited as the translator of the *Practicus*, on the basis of evidence furnished by Gennadius.[241]

We can also posit that there were at least two "go-betweens" that connected Evagrius with the Mount of Olives community. The first is Palladius, who had lived in a monastery on the Mount of Olives for three years

[233] *Vita Melaniae Junioris* 19 (SC 90, 166, 168); cf. Rufinus, *praefatio*, Origen, *Hom. in Numeros* (CCL 20, 285).

[234] Paulinus of Nola, *Epp.* 29; 46; 47; *Carmen* 21.

[235] Palladius, *Historia Lausiaca* 38 (Butler ed., vol. 2: 118–119).

[236] Palladius, *Historia Lausiaca* 38 (Butler ed., vol. 2: 119–120).

[237] Bunge, *Evagrios Pontikos, Briefe*, 29.

[238] Bunge accepts as authentic *Epp.* 22, 32, and 36 to Rufinus; 31, 35, and 37 to Melania (*Briefe*, 184–187). The so-called "Epis-tle to Melania" he thinks was probably for Rufinus (199). In the Syriac manuscripts of the letters, *Epp.* 5, 7, 10, 19, 40, 44, and 49 also list Rufinus as the addressee, and *Epp.* 1 and 8 are addressed to Melania (Bunge, *Briefe*, 199, 30, 97n. 56, 331, 334, 336, 338, 344, 354, 355, 357, 358, 360, 364, 367, 391).

[239] Jerome, *Ep.* 133, 13 (CSEL 56, 246; Latin version of the *Sententiae ad fratres* and the *Sententiae ad virgines* are in PG 40,

1277–1286. On the *Sentences* to the women, see Wilmart, "Les Versions latines"; Elm "Evagrius Ponticus' *Sententiae ad Virginem*."

[240] John E. Bamberger, "Introduction," *Evagrius Ponticus, The Praktikos; Chapters on Prayer*, 51: the work is written for someone who had been a hermit in Egypt, who had had Macarius the Great as a teacher (as had Evagrius), who now lived a long way from Egypt, and who had requested before that the treatise be translated.

[241] So Johannes Quasten, *Patrology*, vol. 3: 172–173, citing material in Gennadius, *De viris inlustribus* 11; 17. Gennadius claims that he himself translated Evagrius's *Suggestions against the Eight Evil Thoughts* (presumably the *Antirrheticus*), the *Gnosticus*, and "a few collections of very obscure opinions" (*De viris inlustribus* 11). Gennadius's interest in Evagrius is especially significant, given the recent ascription by Yves-Marie Duval of a letter to Gennadius to Rufinus ("Le 'Liber Hieronymi,'" 182, 185).

during the 380s.[242] Palladius himself reports that he accompanied Melania the Elder and Silvia, sister of Count Rufinus, praetorian prefect of the East, on their trip from Jerusalem to Egypt.[243] In Egypt, he met Evagrius Ponticus, the Tall Brothers, and other Origenists;[244] he refers to Evagrius as his teacher.[245] That Palladius was back in Palestine at least briefly in 393 we know from a letter of Epiphanius, who warns against this sower of Origenist ideas now at work on Palestinian soil.[246] Bunge posits that Palladius was the person who carried the literary remains of Evagrius to Jerusalem after the monks were expelled from their desert retreat by Theophilus in the summer of 400; thus it may even have been in the monastery of Rufinus that some of Evagrius's writings were copied and preserved.[247] The importance of Rufinus and his circle in establishing and supporting monastic *scriptoria* for the copying of manuscripts has now been documented by Caroline Hammond Bammel in her extensive study of the early manuscript tradition surrounding Rufinus's translation of Origen's *Commentary on Romans*;[248] her investigations make plausible that Rufinus and his circle were also active in the translation and transmission of Evagrius's writings.

A second "go-between" has also been studied by Bunge. He posits that the Anatolius to whom Evagrius's trilogy of the *Practicus*, *Gnosticus*, and *Kephalaia gnostica* was sent, resided on the "holy mountain" in Jerusalem.[249] Anatolius surfaces in the Coptic (but not the Greek) version of Palladius's *Lausiac History* in the company of Melania the Elder in Egypt.[250] Like Melania, he was a Spaniard, and was earlier attached to the family of a Roman named Albinus,[251] who appears in the Greek version of the *Lausiac History* as an acquaintance of both Palladius and Evagrius Ponticus.[252] Anatolius, designated a *notarius* and an *archōn*,[253] presumably was a comfortably established official; he reportedly brought Pambo a present

---

[242] Palladius, *Historia Lausiaca* 44 (Butler ed., vol. 2: 131).

[243] Palladius, *Historia Lausiaca* 55 (Butler ed., vol. 2: 148).

[244] Palladius, *Historia Lausiaca* 11; 23; 35 (Butler ed., vol. 2: 34, 75, 101).

[245] Palladius, *Historia Lausiaca* 23 (Butler ed., vol. 2: 75).

[246] Epiphanius, *Ep. ad Iohannem Episcopum* (= Jerome, *Ep.* 51) 9 (*CSEL* 54, 412).

[247] Bunge, *Briefe*, 175–176, 52–53. Palladius speaks of "three books of Evagrius" (possibly three groups of books?) in the Coptic version of the *Lausiac History* (Amélineau ed., 114). Bunge suggests that perhaps we are seeing the start of a "corpus Evagrianum."

[248] See the three-part article by Hammond Bammel, "[Products] of a Fifth-Century Scriptorium Preserving Conventions Used by Rufinus of Aquileia" (1978): 366–391; 1979: 430–462; 1984: 347–393.

[249] See the dedication, and Bunge, *Briefe*, 34.

[250] Bunge, *Briefe*, 33; Palladius, *Historia Lausiaca* 2 (Coptic) (Amélineau ed., 99).

[251] Palladius, *Historia Lausiaca* 2 (Coptic) (Amélineau ed., 99, 100); Bunge, *Briefe*, 33.

[252] Palladius, *Historia Lausiaca* 26; 47 (Butler ed., vol. 2: 81, 137). Bunge also speculates that the name Albinus may indicate a member of Melania's family; her son married into the Caeionii, for whom Albinus was a common name (Bunge, *Briefe*, 98n. 76).

[253] Palladius, *Historia Lausiaca* 2 (Coptic) (Amélineau ed., 99–100, 101).

of 4,000 solidi.[254] Anatolius at some point apparently renounced public life for monastic contemplation. Bunge posits that the Anatolius known to Palladius is the same person who received the Evagrian trilogy while living in a monastery in Jerusalem—most likely, the monastery of Rufinus, which attracted a Latin population.[255] Bunge also posits that Evagrius may have met Anatolius during his stay at the Mount of Olives monastery in the early 380s.[256] If Bunge's reconstruction of Anatolius's association with Rufinus and Melania the Elder is correct—and indeed, his evidence carries conviction—a link between Evagrius and the Mount of Olives community is established that suggests that Evagrius's most important theoretical works were known there.

In the six letters of Evagrius that Bunge considers definitely addressed to Melania and Rufinus, we encounter nothing that suggests Origenist speculation: rather, the epistles express thanks to the monastic pair for their generous hospitality and spiritual support throughout the years.[257] In two cases, Evagrius refers to letters that he has received from them and to monastic visitors they sent from Jerusalem to visit him.[258] If, however, we add to this collection of six "definite" letters addressed to Rufinus and Melania the nine others that Bunge thinks can probably be assigned to them,[259] we encounter some noticeably Evagrian ideas. In these letters, we find references to *apatheia*,[260] to the theory of "pure prayer,"[261] to warnings against evil *logismoi*,[262] to complaints about the *eidōla* that disturb his mind.[263] Also in these epistles that possibly have Melania and Rufinus as their addressees, there are allusions to letters that Evagrius has received from them.[264]

Moreover, Evagrius probably corresponded with two other inhabitants of Jerusalem known to Rufinus and Melania: Anatolius and John of Jerusalem.[265] In a letter Bunge claims was addressed to Anatolius, Evagrius urges him to continue in the monastic rather than the public life.[266] Playfully elaborating on the names of cities and churches in Palestine, Evagrius urges Anatolius to pass from Bethlehem, symbolizing the practical life,[267] to the "resurrection," the "ascension," and—the very height of his jour-

[254] Palladius, *Historia Lausiaca* 2 (Coptic) (Amélineau, 100); cf. Socrates, *HE* IV, 23, on Pambo's refusing to count the gold he was given.

[255] Bunge, *Briefe*, 34.

[256] Bunge, *Briefe*, 35.

[257] Evagrius Ponticus, *Epp.* 22; 31; 32; 35; 36; 37.

[258] Evagrius Ponticus, *Epp.* 22, 1; 37, 1 (Frankenberg ed., 580–581, 590–591; Bunge tr., 234, 250).

[259] Evagrius Ponticus, *Epp.* 1; 5; 7; 8; 10; 19; 40; 44; 49.

[260] Evagrius Ponticus, *Epp.* 1, 2; 40, 3 (Frankenberg ed., 566–567; 592–593; Bunge tr., 211, 255).

[261] Evagrius Ponticus, *Ep* 1, 4 (Frankenberg ed., 566–567; Bunge tr., 212).

[262] Evagrius Ponticus, *Ep.* 7, 1 (Frankenberg ed., 570–571; Bunge tr., 220).

[263] Evagrius Ponticus, *Ep.* 7, 1 (Frankenberg ed., 570–573; Bunge tr., 220).

[264] Evagrius Ponticus, *Epp.* 5, 1; 44; 1 (Frankenberg ed., 568–569; 596–597; Bunge tr., 217, 259).

[265] Evagrius Ponticus, *Epp.* 2; 9; 24; 25; 50; 51.

[266] Evagrius Ponticus, *Ep.* 25, 1 (Frankenberg ed., 580–581; Bunge tr., 236).

[267] Bunge, *Briefe*, 349n. 21: Evagrius, *In Psalmos* 86, 5 (P5), identifies Bethlehem with the soul, the realm of *praktikos*.

ney—the "Mount of Olives."[268] It is of interest for understanding
Evagrius's evaluation of the Palestinian debates that Bethlehem is rated
lower than Jerusalem, and that the Mount of Olives represents the summit
of Anatolius's spiritual voyage. In this letter, Anatolius is also warned
against evil *logismoi*[269] and is urged to engage in self-examination at the
time of prayer to see if *apatheia* had been achieved.[270]

Of Evagrius's letters, Bunge thinks five were addressed to John of Jerusalem.[271] In them we find references that can reasonably be understood as
allusions to the dispute between John and Jerome's Bethelehem community. The recipient—presumably John—is said to fight against the "sticks,"
which Bunge interprets to mean John's excommunication of the monks in
Jerome's monastery.[272] Evagrius also informs his addressee that "eyewitnesses" have reported to him concerning John's gentle treatment of a stub-
born enemy: the "eyewitnesses," Bunge posits, may be Melania and Rufinus.[273] In one of the epistles, we learn that a previous letter had been
carried by "brother Palladius" from "your Holiness" (John) to Evagrius, a
letter that had apparently complained about the evils of the world that
clouded the priest's mind and heart.[274] If the letter carrier can be identified
with the Palladius of the Origenist controversy, the letter could have been
delivered to Evagrius upon Palladius's return from Palestine after his journey there in 393.[275]

None of the 21 Evagrian letters examined here, however, contains the
kind of cosmological speculation for which Jerome faulted Origenists. Yet
the central theological letter of Evagrius's epistolary corpus, customarily
known as the *Letter to Melania*,[276] contains just such speculation. That
Bunge thinks the letter was actually directed to Rufinus, not to Melania,
does not in any way damage, but rather strengthens, our argument regarding the Evagrian discussion known to Rufinus.[277] If the letter was indeed
received on the Mount of Olives by 397, we would have strong evidence

---

[268] Evagrius Ponticus, *Ep.* 25, 5 (Frankenberg ed., 582–583; Bunge tr., 237).

[269] Evagrius Ponticus, *Ep.* 25, 4 (Frankenberg ed., 582–583; Bunge tr., 237).

[270] Evagrius Ponticus, *Ep.* 25, 6 (Frankenberg ed., 582–583; Bunge tr., 237).

[271] Evagrius Ponticus, *Epp.* 2; 9; 24; 50;
51.

[272] Evagrius Ponticus, *Ep.* 24, 1–2 (Frankenberg ed., 580–581; Bunge tr., 235), and
Bunge's comment, *Briefe*, 347n. 4.

[273] Evagrius Ponticus, *Ep.* 24, 2 (Frankenberg ed., 580–581; Bunge tr., 235), and
Bunge's comment, *Briefe*, 347n. 4.

[274] Evagrius Ponticus, *Ep.* 51, 1 (Frankenberg ed., 598–599; Bunge tr., 263).

[275] See above, p. 96.

[276] Bunge rather consistently tries to rescue Evagrius for orthodoxy. Thus he refers
to the *Letter to Melania* as "a summa of his
[Evagrius's] mysticism," an attempt to deal
with "the one and the many" question
(*Briefe*, 140). Also see Bunge, "Origenismus–Gnostizismus," 24–54; and "Hénade
ou Monade? Au sujet de deux notions centrales de la terminologie évagrienne," 69–91.

[277] Bunge, *Briefe*, 199. His arguments: the
addressee is called "Lord"; nothing in the letter suggests that it was written to a woman;
the letter is unlike other letters of Evagrius
to Melania; other Syriac manuscripts do not
have the ascription to Melania (Bunge,
Briefe, 193–194; cf. Vitestam, "La Grande
Lettre," 4).

that Rufinus was fully aware of the speculation that Origen's teaching had promoted in the Egyptian desert by the late 390s. We would then be able to posit that Rufinus knew not only such practical treatises of Evagrius as the *Sentences for Monks, Sentences for Nuns,* and the *Chapters on Prayer,* but also the deeper, more "dangerous" ruminations of Evagrius that had contributed to the turmoil over Origenism in Egypt. And since Rufinus gives no notice that he disapproved of Evagrius's views, we might wonder if he did not deliberately mask the wilder manifestations of late fourth-century Origenism and instead align himself with a tamer variety of Origen's teaching.

In the *Letter to Melania* (possibly to be renamed the *Letter to Rufinus*) Evagrius posits that the created world is a revelation of the divine nature;[278] it is, in effect, the "letters" through which we learn "the intention, power, and wisdom" of the Creator.[279] The human mind is a "body" for the Son and the Holy Spirit, and can be assigned the same nature as the divine mind.[280] In the end, Evagrius claims, all plurality will be dissolved, the human body and soul will be raised to the level of mind, and "God will be all in all" (I Corinthians 15:28). Plurality and "names" came into existence as a result of the "movement," Evagrius's word for the preexistent fall of the minds.[281] The original minds, Evagrius continues, were "naked," but when they fell through their own free will, they descended to the level of soul, and from there they sank into bodies. Thus they lost the "image of God" and acquired the "image of the animals" (Romans 1:23), adopting an animal-like life, unable to raise the body because they themselves were corrupted.[282] In the end, however, after souls and bodies again become minds, all minds will flow back into God the Father like "torrents into the sea."[283] The nature of all rational beings is thus mingled with the nature of the Creator and becomes one with him in all respects for eternity.[284]

In this brief epitome of Evagrian theology, the alleged *Letter to Melania,* we find several of the very points that Jerome and other opponents of Origenism had decried: the preexistence of rational beings, the secondary status of the material creation, the "fall" from mind to soul to body, the ultimate transformation of the body so that there can be no "resurrection of the flesh," and the loss of the "image of God."[285] Even if Rufinus knew

---

[278] Evagrius Ponticus, *Ep. ad Melaniam* 2 (Frankenberg ed., 612–613; Parmentier tr., 9).

[279] Evagrius Ponticus, *Ep. ad Melaniam* 3 (Frankenberg ed., 614–615; Parmentier tr., 9).

[280] Evagrius Ponticus, *Ep. ad Melaniam* 4 (Frankenberg ed., 614–617; Parmentier tr., 10–11).

[281] Evagrius Ponticus, *Ep. ad Melaniam* 5 (Frankenberg ed., 616–617; Parmentier tr., 11–12).

[282] Evagrius Ponticus, *Ep. ad Melaniam* 9 Parmentier tr., 16–17).

[283] Evagrius Ponticus, *Ep. ad Melaniam* 6 (Frankenberg ed., 618–619; Parmentier tr., 12–13).

[284] Evagrius Ponticus, *Ep. ad Melaniam* 12 (Parmentier tr., 19–20).

[285] See Chap. 3.

only this one writing of Evagrius, he would have encountered a type of Origenism more developed than the views of Origen himself. His awareness that some forms of Origenism were considered "dangerous"—and that these suspicious views were held by deeply revered friends—may well have prompted him to affirm over and again that if a Christian held to an orthodox view of the Trinity and the Incarnation, speculative discussion about the created order was permissible, since it did not affect the "essence" of the faith. An investigation of Rufinus's network thus lends strong support to the hypothesis that he knew more of Evagrian theology than he was prepared to reveal to his opponents.

Far from being slow of mind, Rufinus appears to have possessed an astute theological sense of how far Origenist teaching could be pressed among Western Christians by the turn to the fifth century. In effect, he trimmed the essentials of the Christian faith to the theological agenda endorsed by the Cappadocian Fathers twenty years earlier, yet retained the driving concern of Origen's system, namely, to uphold God's love and justice simultaneously. Although Jerome and other opponents chose to gloss over this central affirmation, it was to enjoy a vigorous afterlife in the Pelagian controversy that followed.

From Origenism to Pelagianism

THE ISSUES

I doubt that at any time before or after the first three decades of the fifth century were a group of celibate men so concerned with babies. Whether they were discussing "babies-in-theory," or flesh-and-blood babies, is difficult to judge: the passion with which they detail the sufferings and death of infants[1] and their shrieks and wails upon receiving the baptismal waters,[2] might suggest the latter. How and why did babies capture the theological imagination of a generation? The answer, I think, lies in the fact that in this *topos* resided the point of greatest tension for those attempting at the same time to champion human freedom that allowed the assignment of praise and blame, to answer the thorny question of the soul's origin, and to uphold both the goodness and the power of God. The central importance of these issues finds its greatest urgency in the question of the suffering of children: theodicy here meets its hardest test.

The issue of God's justice, with its concomitant questions, had been left in abeyance with the condemnation of Origen's cosmic scheme that was the result of the Origenist controversy we have been exploring. Origen had provided a coherent framework in which questions of the origin of the soul, human free will, and God's justice and goodness could be discussed. Although the major participants of the Pelagian controversy, such as Au-

---

[1] Sources for the debate over the issues of babies between Augustine and Julian of Eclanum are found in *De nuptiis et concupiscentia* II, *Contra Julianum*, and *Opus imperfectum contra Julianum*.

[2] Augustine, *Contra Julianum* IV, 8, 42 (*PL* 44, 759); cf. *Sermo* 165, 6, 7 (*PL* 38, 906). For Augustine's early reflections on the bad behavior of babies, see *Confessiones* I, 7, 11 (*CCL* 27, 6).

gustine, had only partial knowledge of Origen's writings,[3] the larger issues that he had raised could not be avoided by later theologians even if they rejected his specific answers. The Pelagian controversy, I posit, provided an arena in which Origen's questions were answered in new and different ways.

We should recall once more the antideterminist context of Origen's theologizing. Over against various Gnostics and astral determinists, Origen pressed an interpretation of Scripture and a cosmic scheme that celebrated human freedom. From the preface to *On First Principles*, which claims that the Church holds as dogma that every rational creature has free will and is not subject to necessity (*contra* the astral determinists),[4] through his antiastrological polemic in his commentaries on the Old Testament,[5] to his long discussion of astrology preserved in *Philocalia* 23,[6] Origen stands firm against astral determinism. Likewise, he frequently criticized Gnostics (whether rightly or wrongly interpreted) for their implication that God is responsible for the world's injustice and cruelty.[7] To prove that "there is no unrighteousness with God" and that "God is no respecter of persons"[8]—later to be favorite Scriptural verses of the Pelagians—Origen explicates the "hard" Biblical passages in such a way that he excludes determinist explanations. Thus the divergent fates of Jacob and Esau relate to their merits in a previous existence;[9] "vessels of honor and dishonor" made *themselves* such either in a past or the present life;[10] and Pharaoh's "hardening" (*contra* the Gnostics) results from his own evil, not to his creation as a "lost nature."[11] Yet, Origen asserts, even in the midst of human stubbornness and error, God works to heal, to teach, to bring all back to their original blessed condition: although Pharaoh drowned, he was not de-

---

[3] O'Connell, *Origin*, 11, 102, 323–324; Pierre Courcelle, *Les Lettres greques en occident de Macrobe à Cassiodore*, 185–187. Berthold Altaner, "Augustinus und Origenes: Eine quellenkritische Untersuchung," 15–41, has a more generous estimate of Augustine's knowledge of Origen.

[4] Origen, *De principiis* I, *praefatio*, 5 (*GCS* 22, 12). It is of interest that this paragraph is followed immediately by a topic that Origen claims has *not* been so clearly defined: whether the soul is transmitted through human seed or had some different beginning; whether it was created or not; whether the soul is brought to the body from elsewhere (13).

[5] See, for example, Origen, *Hom. in Iudicum* II, 3 (*GCS* 30, 477); *Hom. in Jesu Nave* VII, 4 (*SC* 71, 4).

[6] Origen, *Philocalia* 23 (*SC* 226, 130–210), based largely on Origen's (now lost) *Commentary on Genesis*.

[7] E.g., Origen, *Hom. in Jesu Nave* X, 2; XII, 3 (*SC* 71, 274, 300); *De principiis* III, 1, (9) 8 (*GCS* 22, 208–209).

[8] Romans 9:14; 2:11, cited in Origen, *De principiis* I, 7, 4 (*GCS* 22, 90).

[9] Genesis 25:25–26; Malachi 1:2–3; Romans 9:10–13; and Origen, *De principiis* II, 9, 7; III, 1, 22 (20) (*GCS* 22, 170–171, 238–239); cf. II, 9, 5 (*GCS* 22, 168–169).

[10] Romans 9:18–21; see Origen, *De principiis* III, 1, 21 (20); II, 9, 8 (*GCS* 22, 235–238, 172).

[11] Exodus 7:3; Romans 9:17–18; Origen, *De principiis* III, 1, 7–10 (*GCS* 22, 204–211).

stroyed.[12] Since in no case can the sin of one person compel punishment for another, Exodus 20:5 (that "the sins of the parents are visited on their children to the third and fourth generations") cannot be taken literally.[13] The defects and sufferings that humans endure, such as congenital blindness, are to be explained either by one's demerits in a previous existence[14] or by the more beneficent theory that even some souls of high merit opt to suffer along with others in this life in order to assist the process of salvation.[15]

The "props" that undergirded Origen's argument of divine equity and human freedom were dismantled by the early fifth century. The notion that rational creatures had preexisted, then "fell" into bodies, and would after numerous ages and many "rises and falls" return to their original blessed unity was vigorously attacked by writers from Methodius to Jerome and Theophilus, as previous chapters detail. Augustine's response, although less personally vicious, was also resoundingly negative: chastising those who imagined that they might escape theological difficulties by positing that souls had a preexistence before they entered bodies, Augustine recoils from the theory of cyclic "rises and falls" that attends the scheme, for on it, the righteous man in Abraham's bosom could be cast down again into the flames. There would be no *security* against sinning once more. In contrast to Origen, Augustine believed that human history marches resolutely from its beginning in the Garden of Eden to its conclusion at the Last Judgment. Moreover, we must accept Scriptural teaching that we sinned "in Adam," not "outside of him,"[16] as Origen's theory of a precosmic fall might imply. Origen was a "most compassionate" thinker, Augustine concedes, but his views on these matters have been condemned by the Church and hence do not provide "correct" Christian answers to such admittedly difficult problems.[17]

Yet even if Origen's cosmic scheme would no longer be championed by the "orthodox," the pressure from determinists—which had stimulated Origen's views in the first place—had abated but little. Neither Manicheans nor *mathematici* had vanished by the later fourth century, and their explanations, revolving around lost and saved "natures," on the one hand, and

---

[12] Origen, *De principiis* III, 1, 14 (13) (*GCS* 22, 221); cf. *Philocalia* 27, 3–9 (*SC* 226, 278–300); cf. *Hom. in Exodum* III, 3 (*SC* 321, 104, 114): Pharaoh was scourged for his own good; but here, Origen has him "destroyed in the deep abyss."

[13] Origen, *De principiis* II, 5, 2 (*GCS* 22, 133–134).

[14] Origen, *De principiis* I, 8, 1 (*GCS* 22, 96–97).

[15] Origen, *De principiis* II, 9, 7 (*GCS* 22, 171).

[16] Augustine, *Ep.* 166, 9, 27 (*CSEL* 44, 582–584); cf. *De civitate Dei* XI, 23; XII, 14; 21; XXI, 17 (*CCL* 48, 341, 368–369, 377–379, 783); O'Connell, *Origin*, 291–293, 323–324.

[17] Augustine, *De civitate Dei* XXI, 17 (*CCL* 48, 783).

"fate," on the other, remained sufficiently compelling that all the theologians we consider here felt roused to assail one or both.

Although in his early years as a Christian convert Augustine had strongly attacked Manichean and astrological determinism, the attack on determinism became more problematic for him in his later years, when he hinged his theology to theories of original sin and predestination. Augustine's opponent, Julian of Eclanum, was quick to note that Mani's question, "If there is no natural sin, why baptize babies who clearly have done no wrong?"[18] found a resonance in Augustine's counterclaim to Julian that if one exempts infants who are subject to so many miseries from sin, one accuses God of injustice.[19] In order not to do so, Augustine came to insist, we must confess that original sin exists.[20] Augustine and Julian, we shall see, both attempted to answer the larger issues raised by the consideration of the wailing and expiring babies in order to address, in a new theological context, the issues of human freedom and God's justice. Their problems are those that were inevitably left over from the dissolution of the Origenist scheme.

Thus both sides in the Pelagian dispute affirmed human free will, although "free will" might receive a novel definition from Augustine in his claim that the will is indeed free—to choose wrong. Likewise, the origin of the soul had to be addressed. While the Pelagians and Jerome opted for a creationist solution, Augustine refused to declare himself publicly on this issue until the end of his life, backing off from the traducian view that would have been logical for him to adopt; rather, he "resolved" the issue through a theory of original sin that remained unconnected to any particular position on the soul's origin. God's goodness likewise received diverse explications. For Pelagius and his supporters, God's goodness was revealed in the traces he had left in human nature, and by his giving of the Law and of exemplary holy men, as well as Jesus, for our edification. For Augustine, God's goodness is signalled by his rescue of the elect from the "mass of perdition" in which all humans are doomed. To unpack these "Western" resolutions of the theological issues that Origen had so sharply posed for Christian theology is the aim of this chapter.[21]

---

[18] Julian of Eclanum, citing from Mani's *Letter to Patricius*, in Augustine, *Opus imperfectum contra Julianum* III, 187, 5 (*CSEL* 85¹, 487).

[19] Augustine, *Opus imperfectum* II, 236, 2; cf. I, 97 and II, 110 (*CSEL* 85¹, 349, 114, 242–243).

[20] Augustine, *Opus imperfectum* III, 2 (*CSEL* 85¹, 352); *Contra Julianum* III, 3, 8 (*PL* 44, 705–706).

[21] Peter Brown's assessment of the Pelagian controversy as a bridge between East and West is apt in this context: "Seen in terms of the previous opinions and allegiances of Roman aristocratic Christianity, Pelagianism appears, once again, as an incident in the relations between the Latin and Greek worlds" ("The Patrons of Pelagius," 72; *Religion and Society*, 226). For an important theological discussion of the links be-

"PRE-PELAGIAN" CONCERNS

The "Western" resolution of these theological issues did not, of course, emerge from a vacuum. Latin writers, as well as their Greek counterparts, had in the last decades of the fourth century and the opening years of the fifth wrestled with the questions of God's justice, the sin of Adam and Eve, and the origin of the soul (among other matters), but their discussions do not reveal a coherent solution to these problems; resolution would be left to their more theologically competent successors. Nonetheless, in the writings of theologians such as Ambrosiaster, Paulinus of Nola, and Rufinus the Syrian, we see issues coming to the fore that would dominate the controversy between Augustine and Pelagians. Before turning to the latter, I wish to indicate how some central problems of the Pelagian dispute emerge in the writings of these late fourth- and early fifth-century thinkers.

Let us begin with a consideration of Ambrosiaster, the name we give to the unknown author of a commentary on the Pauline epistles and of a work entitled *Questions on the Old Testament and the New Testament*,[22] written probably in the 370s or the early 380s.[23] The antideterminist cast of Ambrosiaster's thought is revealed in his response to two questions in particular, Question 115, "On Fate," and Question 127, "On the Sin of Adam and Eve." Nothing, Ambrosiaster asserts, is more contrary to Christian truth than the teachings of the *mathematici*. On their premises, the giving of the Law not only would have been in vain, but God as Lawgiver would be unjust and cruel to ordain commandments that ran contrary to the nature with which humans are born. How could a just God condemn a man for not doing what in fact it was impossible for him to do?[24] God's condemnation would be more than unjust; it would be criminal (*nefarius*).[25] The *vituperatio* would fall on the Creator, not on the creature,[26] for praise and blame can be assigned only to those who are capable of choosing.[27] After producing substantial evidence for the fragility of astrological explanation, Ambrosiaster concludes with the claim that supporters of the *ma-*

---

tween the controversies, see Hammond Bammel, "Adam in Origen," 62–93: "Augustine in attacking Pelagianism retained Origen's view of the human condition in this life as a fallen one but, because of his rejection of the theory of pre-existence, placed the whole burden of responsibility for his condition on Adam's sin and condemnation" (62).

[22] Critical edition of the remains of Ambrosiaster's *Commentary on the Pauline Epistles* in *CSEL* 81, 1–3; of his *Quaestiones Veteris et Novi Testamenti* in *CSEL* 50.

[23] Alexander Souter, *A Study of Ambrosiaster*, 166–174; Coelestinus Martini, *Ambrosiaster: De auctore, operibus, theologia*, 160.

[24] Ambrosiaster, *Quaestiones* 115, 1 (*CSEL* 50, 318).

[25] Ambrosiaster, *Quaestiones* 115, 2 (*CSEL* 50, 318).

[26] Ambrosiaster, *Quaestiones* 115, 7 (*CSEL* 50, 320).

[27] Ambrosiaster, *Quaestiones* 115, 5 (*CSEL* 50, 319–320).

thematici extirpate the root of faith that testifies to the *justitia* of the Creator.[28]

Against his determinist opponents, Ambrosiaster tackles some difficult questions posed by Scripture, through which he champions both God's justice and human freedom. He found—as did both Augustine and the Pelagians later—that this was an especially difficult problem when the suffering of children was at stake. Why, for example, were infants consumed in the fire of Sodom along with their parents (Genesis 19:25)? His answer seems theologically unsatisfactory: God wished to show just *how* dreadful the sin of the Sodomites had been by punishing the innocent children as well as the erring adults. Besides, Ambrosiaster assures his readers, God's action was in the children's best interests, for had they lived longer, they would have followed the example of their fathers. By suffering the fate they did here and now, they would be exempt from punishment in the future life.[29]

Children also emerge as the center of discussion in Question 14: how should we interpret Exodus 20:5, that the sins of the parents will be visited on the children to the third and fourth generation? How can such a claim be squared with the Scriptural affirmation that God is just? Anyone who implies that God is unjust is simply "demented." Ambrosiaster's solution is this: the children had continued in the wicked ways of their fathers, given over to the practice of idolatry. Thus they deserved their fate. The passage should rather remind us of God's *clementia*: he inflicted punishment *only* to the third and fourth generations, not to *millia millium*.[30]

How far we are from Augustinianism is revealed by Ambrosiaster's treatment of the question, "On the Sin of Adam and Eve." Nowhere does he deal with themes we might expect, such as the origin of the soul and the transmission (or nontransmission) of sin. Instead, Ambrosiaster's discussion is set squarely within the framework of the ascetic debate of the 380s and 390s: he uses the story of Adam and Eve to affirm both the goodness of marriage against its detractors (chiefly Marcionites and Manicheans[31]) and the appropriateness of clerical celibacy.[32]

Ambrosiaster's failure to address the questions of the soul and sin in his question on Adam and Eve does not mean that he neglected these issues entirely; he simply addressed them in other contexts. Elsewhere, he rejects

---

[28] Ambrosiaster, *Quaestiones* 115, 82 (*CSEL* 50, 349). For an excellent introduction to *Quaestio* 115, see David Hunter, "Ambrosiaster, Astral Fatalism and the Prehistory of the Pelagian Controversy." In his *Commentary on Romans* 8:7, Ambrosiaster adds the point that the study of astronomy leads humans to deny such basic Christian doctrines as the virgin birth and the resurrection of the body (*CSEL* 81¹, 260–263).

[29] Ambrosiaster, *Quaestiones* 13, 1–2 (*CSEL* 50, 37–39).

[30] Ambrosiaster, *Quaestiones* 14, 1–4 (*CSEL* 50, 39–41).

[31] Ambrosiaster, *Quaestiones* 127, 17–18 (*CSEL* 50, 406–407).

[32] Ambrosiaster, *Quaestiones* 127, 35–36 (*CSEL* 50, 415–416).

traducianism,[33] appealing to such Biblical evidence as that Eve is not said
to be taken from Adam "soul from soul" but "bone from bone," and Zechariah 12:1 and Isaiah 44:2.[34] He also, in another passage, claims that Adam
was subject to death because he disobeyed, but would have been given
immortality through the tree of life if he had not sinned.[35] In Question 19,
as well as in his *Commentary on Romans*, Ambrosiaster limits the effects of
Adam's sin to the death of the body.[36] There is no suggestion here of a
transmission of sin.

On the question of how to reconcile human free will with John 6:44
("no one comes to me if the Father does not draw him") and Romans
9:16–18,[37] Ambrosiaster argues that the "drawing" of the Father involves
no violence but rather should be interpreted as "attraction." Moreover,
Paul certainly does not attack free will in Romans 9: God knows on whom
to have mercy because he scrutinizes the person's inner disposition. Thus
the soul of a hypocrite can justly be hardened; it would, in any case, be
unjust for God to save someone who was not willing.[38] Ambrosiaster's
answer here is consonant with his discussion of Jacob and Esau in his *Romans Commentary*: God foreknew the future merits of the twins even before they were born, and thus he accepted one and rejected the other.[39]
That such themes suggest a certain "Pelagian" direction to Ambrosiaster's
thought has been noted by earlier commentators.[40] Nowhere, however,
does Ambrosiaster attempt to draw all these ideas together into a systematic and coherent presentation.

Nor does Paulinus of Nola succeed at this. Closely tied to the circle of
Rufinus and Melania the Elder, a correspondent of Jerome and Augustine,
and also knowledgeable about Pelagius, Paulinus must have been hard
pressed to keep his theological allegiances straight. A major motivating
force for Paulinus, as for Ambrosiaster, is the refutation of determinism.
Paulinus upholds God's providential care of the world over against the
insidious teachings of the astrologers and the partisans of fate who imagine
that "God takes holidays."[41] How can the stars be thought to control the

---

[33] Ambrosiaster, *Quaestiones* 23, 1 (*CSEL*
50, 49).

[34] Ambrosiaster, *Quaestiones* 23, 2 (*CSEL*
50, 49–50). Ambrosiaster adds that it would
be inappropriate for souls to come from
women, for "authority" is given only to men
(23, 3: 50–51).

[35] Ambrosiaster, *Quaestiones* 19 (*CSEL* 50,
45–46).

[36] Ambrosiaster, *Quaestiones* 19 (*CSEL* 50,
46); cf. *In Romanos* 7:22 (*CSEL* 81¹, 240).
For Ambrosiaster's position on Adam's sin,
see Julius Gross, *Entstehungsgeschichte des
Erbsünden Dogmas von der Bibel bis Augus-*
tinus, 230–237.

[37] Ambrosiaster, *Quaestiones* 75 (= 79), 1
(*CSEL* 50, 127–128).

[38] Ambrosiaster, *Quaestiones* 75 (= 79), 2
(*CSEL* 50, 128).

[39] Ambrosiaster, *In Romanos* 9:10–13
(*CSEL* 81¹, 310–317).

[40] Martini, *Ambrosiaster*, 109; Alfred J.
Smith, "The Latin Sources of the Commentary of Pelagius on the Epistle of St. Paul to
the Romans," 205.

[41] Paulinus of Nola, *Ep.* 16, 2 (*CSEL* 29,
115–116): probably a jab at Epicurean
teaching.

universe, he asks, when they are just "tiny fires"?[42] The Bible also teaches us that chance does not rule the seas: Moses controlled it with his rod,[43] and God's providence rescued Jonah from his watery distress.[44] Paulinus also received confirmation in his antideterminism from his study of Augustine's anti-Manichean writings:[45] they serve as his "Pentateuch" against the Manicheans, he tells Augustine.[46]

As for the sin of Adam, Paulinus's position lacks coherence. On the one hand, he affirms that Adam did not deserve to be completely excluded from Paradise since it was through another's craftiness that he had sinned; Adam deserved to be punished only for a time, not for eternity.[47] On the other hand, he writes that the "venom" of Adam infected the whole race, including himself, and claims, "In the state of natural goodness, I had my inner eyes open to innocence and closed to wickedness; but when I chose evil from that unfortunate food of the forbidden tree, I became blind, and, in addition, I learned unhappily about wickedness; I drank the knowledge of good and evil that brings death."[48] Whether Paulinus's opinions tend in a more "Pelagian" or "Augustinian" position on this point of Adam's sin would be hard to decide. And on the question of the origin of the soul, all we know is that Paulinus rejected the notion of transmigration,[49] as we might expect any Christian to do.

That Paulinus was interested in the problems that would fuel the Pelagian debate, however, is clear from the questions he addressed to his theologically minded correspondents. For example, at the outbreak of the Origenist controversy in Italy, Paulinus put to Jerome the question of how to explain "the hardening of Pharaoh's heart." He also asked Jerome how to interpret Romans 9:16 (that "it is not of him who wills or runs, but of God who shows mercy"). Don't such passages do away with free will?, he wonders. Moreover, does Jerome understand why Paul in I Corinthians 7:14 claims that children born of baptized parents are "holy," when without the gift of God's grace, received only later, they cannot be saved?[50] Astoundingly—given that he was upset by Rufinus's translation of *On First Principles* and by the development of Origenism—Jerome replies to Paulinus that these questions can best be answered by reading Origen's book in Jerome's own translation, not in Rufinus's.[51] The fact that the anonymous

[42] Paulinus of Nola, *Ep.* 16, 4 (*CSEL* 29, 117).

[43] Paulinus of Nola, *Carmina* 22, 98–104 (*CSEL* 30, 190–191).

[44] Paulinus of Nola, *Carmina* 22, 105–118 (*CSEL* 30, 191).

[45] Paulinus of Nola, *Epp.* 3, 2; 4, 1; 6, 2 (*CSEL* 29, 14, 19, 40).

[46] Paulinus of Nola, *Ep.* 4, 2 (*CSEL* 29, 20).

[47] Paulinus of Nola, *Ep.* 23, 44 (*CSEL* 29, 199).

[48] Paulinus of Nola, *Ep.* 30, 2 (*CSEL* 29, 263); cf. Augustine, *Ep.* 186, 12, 40–41 (*CSEL* 47, 78–80).

[49] Paulinus of Nola, *Ep.* 13, 25 (*CSEL* 29, 105).

[50] Jerome, *Ep.* 85, 2 (*CSEL* 55, 136). That Caelestius may also have written to Paulinus is suggested by Augustine, *De gratia Christi* I, 35, 38 (*CSEL* 42, 154).

[51] Jerome, *Ep.* 85, 3 (*CSEL* 55, 136–137).

Pelagian treatise, *On the Hardening of Pharaoh's Heart*, treats these very questions has prompted the hypothesis that the work might possibly have been written for Paulinus.[52] Clearly such questions fascinated Paulinus, but he had no developed theological scheme into which to integrate the disparate pieces.

A third writer, Rufinus the Syrian moves us closer to the circles in which the Pelagian controversy erupted—very close, if we believe Marius Mercator's report that it was Rufinus the Syrian who first brought to Rome from the East the notion that Adam and Eve were created mortal and injured only themselves, not their descendants, by their sin.[53] Marius Mercator's testimony gains support from Augustine's discussion of the Acts of the Council of Carthage in 411: when Caelestius was asked who in the Christian Church (besides himself) denied the notion of sin inherited from Adam, he replied that he had heard such a theory expressed by "the holy presbyter Rufinus" when he was staying with Pammachius in Rome.[54] Whether this Rufinus is the same Rufinus as Marius Mercator's, and whether he can be identified with Jerome's priestly friend who came from Bethlehem to Rome on a mission for Jerome, has been hotly debated.[55]

Likewise, the dating of Rufinus the Syrian's *Liber de fide* has been much discussed. If François Refoulé is correct (against Altaner) that the work predates Augustine's *De peccatorum meritis*,[56] and if we accept the traditional dating of *De peccatorum meritis* to 411–412,[57] we have in the *Liber*

Jerome shows no grasp of the import of Paulinus's second question, for he replies (5; 137–138) that Paulinus should read Tertullian's *On Monogamy*, in which he states that believers' children can be called "holy" because, as candidates for the faith, they have not fallen into idolatry. Jerome's memory failed him: Tertullian does not address this subject in *De monogamia*.

[52] De Plinval, *Essai*, 134; his proposal is rejected by Pierre Courcelle, "Paulin de Nole," 270–271.

[53] Marius Mercator, *Commonitorium, prologus* 3, 1 (*ACO* I, 5: 5). Marius Mercator's evidence regarding "Rufinus the Syrian" is being seriously challenged by Walter Dunphy; his argument will be published as "Marius Mercator on Rufinus the Syrian: Was Schwartz Mistaken?"

[54] Augustine, *De gratia Christi et de peccato originali* II, 3, 3 (*CSEL* 42, 168). On the role of Paulinus of Milan in bringing the accusation, see Angelo Paredi, "Paulinus of Milan," 209–210.

[55] Henri Marrou, "Les Attaches Orientales

du Pelagianisme," 463–465. Marrou's position is that Caelestius's Rufinus is not to be identified with Jerome's friend Rufinus—nor were either of them to be identified with Rufinus of Aquileia. Scholars who accept the identification of Caelestius's Rufinus with Jerome's Rufinus are Gerald Bonner, "Rufinus the Syrian and African Pelagianism," 35, 38; and Eugene TeSelle, "Rufinus the Syrian, Caelestius, Pelagius: Explorations in the Prehistory of the Pelagian Controversy," 61–65.

[56] François Refoulé, "Datation du premier concile de Carthage contre les Pélagiens et du *Libellus fidei* de Rufin," 47–49, argues against the view of Berthold Altaner that the *Liber de fide* was a response to Augustine's *De peccatorum meritis* and hence later; see Altaner, "De Liber de fide: Ein Werk des Pelagianers Rufinus des 'Syrers,' " 446–449. Altaner dates the work to between 413–428 on the grounds that the first time Augustine takes up the topic of the damnation of unbaptized infants is in *De peccatorum meritis*.

[57] O'Connell, *Origin*, 104, 113–114. In

de fide a work that makes an especially interesting transition from the Origenist to the Pelagian controversy. And if we further assume that the author was Jerome's emissary Rufinus and that he may have written the piece while he was on his Roman mission,[58] the *Liber de fide* would have been composed in the heyday of the Origenist controversy in Rome. Although the author does not rehearse the full catalogue of complaints against Origen that were current by the early fifth century, we suspect that he knew some of the ones he does recite from his contact with Jerome. Possibly he may also have read Epiphanius's attack upon Origen in the *Panarion*, although Rufinus's arguments do not cover all the points of Origen's theology—even some of the central ones—that Epiphanius found reprehensible. In any event, the *Liber de fide* provides an interesting "pre-Pelagian" stage of the discussion that aims to work a new theological resolution once Origen's scheme was rejected.

After covering the Trinitarian confession standard by his time, Rufinus the Syrian launches into an attack upon Origen's theology. To Rufinus's eyes, Origen denigrates the power and freedom of God by claiming that God could create only as much as he could control;[59] rather, God easily controlled the multitude of diverse beings that constituted the first creation.[60] The sun, moon, and stars were *not* among these, in Rufinus's view;[61] Origen was here guilty of the "Gentile error" of divination.[62] The first sin of the universe took place in Genesis 3, not in a precosmic state.[63] Punishments for both angelic and human beings will be everlasting, not temporary.[64] Especially reprehensible to Rufinus is Origen's view that souls were made before bodies—another illustration of "Gentile error." Moreover, Rufinus claims, Origen was inconsistent, at one time affirming that souls were created at the very beginning, and at another time, on the sixth day[65]—a point revealing that Rufinus did not comprehend well Origen's theory of the fall of minds to the status of souls. Last, Origen's allegorical interpretation led him away from an affirmation of bodies:[66] it wasn't *souls* who were called "male and female" and told to "Reproduce,

---

O'Connell's reconstruction, Book I of *De peccatorum meritis* as we now have it is an emended version that Augustine issued in its present form only in 417–418, when the Pelagian controversy was well developed.

[58] Implied in TeSelle, "Rufinus," 73; affirmed in Bonner, "Rufinus," 38, and in Mary William Miller, "Introduction," *Rufini Presbyteri Liber de Fide: A Critical Text with Introduction and Commentary*, 5–7, 10–11.

[59] Rufinus the Syrian, *Liber de fide* 17 (Miller ed., 72, 74).

[60] Rufinus the Syrian, *Liber de fide* 18

(Miller ed., 74, 76).

[61] Rufinus the Syrian, *Liber de fide* 21 (Miller ed., 80).

[62] Rufinus the Syrian, *Liber de fide* 22 (Miller ed., 82).

[63] Rufinus the Syrian, *Liber de fide* 20 (Miller ed., 78, 80).

[64] Rufinus the Syrian, *Liber de fide* 20; 25 (Miller ed., 78, 86).

[65] Rufinus the Syrian, *Liber de fide* 27 (Miller ed., 89).

[66] Rufinus the Syrian, *Liber de fide* 22 (Miller ed., 82).

multiply, and fill the earth." The material referent of these words proves that the first creatures were not living in the heavens.[67]

Having critiqued Origen's scheme Rufinus expounds views he considers more accurate. Almost all of his postulates represent what in retrospect we might call an early form of Pelagianism. Rejecting a traducian theory of the soul's origin,[68] Rufinus teaches that although the bodies of Adam and Eve were created capable of death, they would not have died if they had obeyed God; the tree of life would have conveyed immortality to them.[69] It is noteworthy that these views are strikingly like both Ambrosiaster's[70] and Theodore of Mopsuestia's, as reported by the editor of the Palatine Collection.[71] Adam and Eve's sin could not have been *so* horrendous, in any case, since by their own labors and afflictions they were saved from it, and Scripture never tells us that they sinned again.[72] Since Adam and Eve were saved, and since we learn that there were righteous people in the Scripture—Abel, Enoch, Elijah—only the "insane" would claim that wickedness passed through the whole human race because of the sin of one man; they imply either that God is unjust or that the devil is stronger than God.[73] Children could never be punished for their parent's sins.[74]

Questions of infant baptism bothered the author of *Liber de fide* as well. Since Rufinus rejected the view that infants die because of Adam's sin,[75] he also rejected the notion that unbaptized babies would suffer in hell.[76] On traducian theory, he notes, we might rather believe that the sanctity of their Christian parents passed to them.[77] Nonetheless, Rufinus advises infant baptism in order to give the children "spiritual birth," allow them to partake of the Kingdom of Heaven,[78] and regenerate them as coheirs of Christ.[79]

One striking feature of Rufinus the Syrian's anti-Origenist polemic is that it bypasses many of the central points deemed objectionable by Origen's fourth- and fifth-century critics. For example, although Rufinus the Syrian affirms the resurrection of the dead in the "same flesh" in which they

---

[67] Rufinus the Syrian, *Liber de fide* 27 (Miller ed., 88, 90). Cf. Epiphanius, *Panarion* 64, 65 (*GCS* 31², 506); see above, p. 91. There is, however, little else in Rufinus's exposition suggesting that he borrowed directly from Epiphanius's critique of Origen.

[68] Rufinus the Syrian, *Liber de fide* 28 (Miller ed., 90, 92).

[69] Rufinus the Syrian, *Liber de fide* 29 (Miller ed., 94).

[70] See above, p. 200 and below, p. 206.

[71] In *ACO* I, 5: 173–176.

[72] Rufinus the Syrian, *Liber de fide* 35; 36; 39 (Miller ed., 106, 108, 112).

[73] Rufinus the Syrian, *Liber de fide* 39 (Miller ed., 112).

[74] Rufinus the Syrian, *Liber de fide* 38 (Miller ed., 110).

[75] Rufinus the Syrian, *Liber de fide* 40 (Miller ed., 114).

[76] Rufinus the Syrian, *Liber de fide* 41 (Miller ed., 116, 118).

[77] Rufinus the Syrian, *Liber de fide* 40 (Miller ed., 114).

[78] Rufinus the Syrian, *Liber de fide* 40 (Miller ed., 114).

[79] Rufinus the Syrian, *Liber de fide* 48 (Miller ed., 126).

lived,[80] he nowhere faults Origen for espousing an inadequate theory of the resurrection, a notable omission in his anti-Origenist polemic. Despite his lengthy discussion of Trinitarian theology, Rufinus does not charge Origen with subordinationism, although he so chastises Arius and Eunomius.[81] The points on which Rufinus criticizes Origen's doctrine of God, in contrast, concern the supposed limitation of God's power and freedom.[82] Nor does Origen's theory of the *apokatastasis* especially bother Rufinus, except that he wishes to affirm a place of everlasting punishment.[83] The topic of Origen's theology around which Rufinus the Syrian frames his central objections concerns speculation on the precosmic state, the origin of souls, and their subsequent union with bodies. That from a critique of Origen's notion of souls, Rufinus moves to express his "Pelagian" notions indicates that he has selected for criticism the theories of Origen that will reinforce his own position on the original condition of human nature.

As we have earlier indicated, several of Rufinus the Syrian's views seem to resonate with Ambrosiaster's discussion on Adam and Eve's condition: he, like Ambrosiaster, denies the notion that Eve's soul was taken from Adam's ("bone from bone," not "soul from soul"). He quotes two of the same passages on God's creation of the human spirit as did Ambrosiaster: Zechariah 12:1 and Isaiah 44:2. Rufinus concludes that souls are crafted by God; they do not come *ex supposita materia*.[84]

A second resonance of Rufinus the Syrian's arguments on the soul and on Adam and Eve are with the teachings of Theodore of Mopsuestia derived from a work he wrote to attack Jerome's *Dialogue Against the Pelagians*. The authenticity of this piece, preserved in the *Palatine Collection*, has been hotly debated, Robert Devreesse rejecting the work as Theodore's,[85] Julius Gross defending its authenticity,[86] and Günter Koch offering a moderating position.[87] The views espoused in the treatises, in any case, are strikingly like those expressed by Rufinus the Syrian. Here it is helpful to recall Marius Mercator's claim that the origin of Pelagian teaching was with Theodore of Mopsuestia, and that it was Rufinus the Syrian who brought his views to Rome during the pontificate of Anastasius.[88]

---

[80] Rufinus the Syrian, *Liber de fide* 51 (Miller ed., 128).

[81] Rufinus the Syrian, *Liber de fide* 15; 52 (Miller ed., 70, 130).

[82] Rufinus the Syrian, *Liber de fide* 17; 18 (Miller ed., 72, 74, 76).

[83] Rufinus the Syrian, *Liber de fide* 20; 25 (Miller ed., 78, 86).

[84] Rufinus the Syrian, *Liber de fide* 28 (Miller ed., 90, 92).

[85] Robert Devreesse, *Essai sur Théodore de Mopsueste*, 102. Devreesse claims that the work is in any case directed against Augus-

tine (57).

[86] Julius Gross, "Theodor von Mopsuestia, ein Gegner der Erbsündenlehre," 1–15.

[87] Günter Koch, *Die Heilsverwirklichung bei Theodor von Mopsuestia*, 58–76.

[88] Marius Mercator, *Commonitorium*, prologus 3, 1 (*ACO* I, 5: 5). Here we must consider the possibility that if the author of the materials ascribed to Theodore in the *ACO* are *not* by him, someone else "made them up" to conform with the teachings of Rufinus the Syrian's *Liber de fide*. For a discussion of Pelagianism's Eastern connections, espe-

Theodore, like Rufinus, believes that Adam and Eve were created mortal in body and would have received immortality only later, had they remained obedient.[89] Both authors make light of the first sin: Theodore mocks those who imagine that God flew into a fury over this one offense and promulgated a universal sentence of sin and death because of it; God's wrath would then be *ultra modum iustitiae*.[90] Recall that Rufinus the Syrian claimed that the first couple made up for their one sin by their own efforts, and never sinned again.[91] Both reject the notion that children pay for their parents' sins, Ezekiel 18:1–4 being cited by each.[92] For both, the men deemed righteous in the Old Testament (reinforced by Hebrews 11) serve as proof that sin could not have been transmitted from Adam to his descendants. Theodore of Mopsuestia especially raises the case of Abel, "the first righteous man who lived and the first who died." If death were a penalty for sin (as his opponents, presumably Jerome, claim), how impious of God to allow Adam and Eve to go on living while Abel was killed! Enoch, who didn't die, provides another example to argue the nontransmission of sin.[93] Rufinus the Syrian uses the same examples: Abel was a "stranger to sins" and Enoch and Elijah were so pleasing to God that they did not see death. And what about Noah, whom God declared to be "just"?[94]

These parallel arguments lend weight to the view that what we label the "Augustinian" position on original sin was not well accepted either in the East or the West by the turn to the fifth century. Rufinus the Syrian, shadowy character that he is, may indeed have been of central importance for stimulating discussion of these issues in Latin circles. But neither he nor Paulinus nor Ambrosiaster provided a fully worked out scheme to advance them. Problems of God's justice in relation to human suffering, the origin

---

cially with Theodore, see Lionel Wickham, "Pelagianism in the East," esp. 205–208.

[89] Theodore of Mopsuestia, *Liber contra Hieronymum* 3; 5 (*ACO* I, 5: 174); cf. Theodore's commentary on Genesis 3:22, see R. M. Tonneau, ed., tr., "Théódore de Mopsueste, Interprétation (du Livre) de la Genèse (Vat. Syr. 120, ff. I–V)," 45–64; Syriac, 53–54; French, 61. As proof of the natural mortality of humans, Theodore adduces the fact that Jesus assumed a nature capable of death, even though he was exempt from sin (*Liber* 7, 176); if sin were part of our nature, Christ would have had to assume it. Compare the positions of Rufinus the Syrian, *Liber de fide* 29 (Miller ed., 94) and Ambrosiaster, *Quaestiones* 19 (*CSEL* 50, 45–46). For a helpful discussion of Theodore's views on Adam's sin and its consequences, see R. A. Norris, Jr., *Manhood and Christ: A*

Study in the Christology of Theodore of Mopsuestia, 178–188.

[90] Theodore of Mopsuestia, *Liber contra Hieronymum* 4; 5 (*ACO* I, 5: 174–175).

[91] Rufinus the Syrian, *Liber de fide* 35; 36 (Miller ed., 106–107). These views on the lightness of Adam and Eve's sin have resonance with Ambrosiaster's *Quaestio* 127: Adam and Eve are brought back to their original condition, but each with a *detrimentum*: for her, increased pains; for him, the sweat of work when the earth does not readily produce (*CSEL* 50, 412–413).

[92] Theodore of Mopsuestia, *Liber contra Hieronymum* 4 (*ACO* I, 5: 174); cf. Rufinus the Syrian, *Liber de fide* 38 (Miller ed., 110).

[93] Theodore of Mopsuestia, *Liber contra Hieronymum* 5 (*ACO* I, 5: 175).

[94] Rufinus the Syrian, *Liber de fide* 39 (Miller ed., 112).

of the soul, the sin of Adam and Eve, and related topics, all awaited fuller explication from the Pelagian camp, on the one side, and from Augustine, on the other.

THE PELAGIANS

The debate that erupted in the second and third decades of the fifth century between Pelagians and Augustinians centered both on interpretations of Scripture and on understandings of Church practices, for example, those associated with infant baptism. That neither Scriptural interpretation nor arguments about ecclesiastical praxis came from "neutral" observers is clear: as Theodore de Bruyn has noted in the case of Pelagius (and the observation could be extended to all the disputants), "exegetical decisions" are subordinated to "moral presuppositions."[95] Amid their varying interpretations, all participants in the controversy wished to square God's justice, power, and goodness with human freedom. By all the debaters, "Manichean" or "fatalist" explanations were ostensibly eschewed. In the section that follows, we turn first to the Pelagian response to these questions, questions once more raised for discussion with the rejection of Origen's answers.

The problem of which Pelagian treatises can be ascribed to Pelagius himself has raged since the late nineteenth century, exacerbated by the recovery of previously unidentified Pelagian works, or the reassignment of treatises previously known but ascribed to non-Pelagian authors. Thus Caspari located and edited six Pelagian documents,[96] Souter identified and edited Pelagius's *Commentary on the Pauline Letters*,[97] Plinval assertively claimed large bodies of the recovered Pelagian material for the heresiarch himself,[98] Morris reassigned most of Caspari's documents to "the Sicilian Briton"[99] (renamed "the Sicilian Anonymous" by Bonner),[100] and Evans argued that four of the Pelagian treatises whose author was unknown could be ascribed to Pelagius himself.[101] Although such debates leave nonspecialists confused regarding the validity of these claims, for our purposes it is fortunately not necessary to assign authorship for every treatise: the general structure of Pelagian argumentation will suffice.

Although Pelagius is sometimes declared to be more interested in "anthropology" than "theology," I think that theological concerns—the de-

---

[95] Theodore S. de Bruyn, "Pelagius's Interpretation of Rom. 5: 12–21: Exegesis Within the Limits of Polemic," 37–38.

[96] C. P. Caspari, *Briefe, Abhandlungen und Predigten aus den zwei letzten Jahrhunderten des kirchlichen Alterthums und dem Anfang des Mittelalters.*

[97] Alexander Souter, *Pelagius's Expositions*

of Thirteen Epistles of Saint Paul.

[98] Plinval, *Pélage*, esp. 44–45.

[99] John Morris, "Pelagian Literature," esp. 40.

[100] Gerald Bonner, *Augustine and Modern Research on Pelagianism*, 5–6.

[101] Robert F. Evans, *Four Letters of Pelagius*, esp. 31.

fense of God's holiness and justice—stand as the foundation of his views. A citation from his famous *Letter to Demetrias* suggests as much:

> Instead of thinking it a great privilege to be given commands by such an illustrious power . . . we talk back to God in a scornful and slothful way. We say, "This is too hard and difficult; we can't do it. We are only human, and we suffer from weakness of the flesh." Blind stupidity! Arrogant blasphemy! We ascribe to the Lord of knowledge the guilt of a twofold ignorance: that he is ignorant of what he created, and of what he commanded. We imply that God the Creator forgot human weakness and put upon us commands that a human cannot bear. In doing so, we ascribe injustice to the Just One and cruelty to the holy God, the first by complaining that God commands the impossible, and the second by assuming that God condemns us for what we cannot help. We think of God as seeking our condemnation rather than our salvation, which is sacrilegious even to imply. . . . No one knows the extent of our strength better than the one who gave it to us. . . . Because God is righteous, he does not command the impossible; because he is holy, he does not condemn us for what we could not avoid.[102]

Or, in the less well-known treatise, the *Expositio fidei catholicae*, the point is put more briefly: "If I say that I am not able (to avoid sin), I blaspheme God."[103] Far from being judged a cold-minded rationalist,[104] Pelagius is now seen as a thinker passionately concerned to construct a theology that avoided determinism—especially Manicheanism[105]—at all costs. God's absolute justice and nondetermination of human choice are points that ring loud in all Pelagian writings, whatever variations may be found on other issues. That these were the very issues that stirred Origen before him is probably not a coincidence, given the strong influence that "Greek" Christianity exercised on several of the Pelagian theologians.

Thus rejecting the Manichean solution,[106] yet also rejecting the Origen-

---

[102] Pelagius, *Ad Demetriadem* 16 (*PL* 30, 31–32).

[103] *Expositio fidei Catholicae* (*PLS* 1, 1685; cf. *De possibilitate non peccandi* 2, 2; 4, 2 (*PLS* 1, 1458–1459); *Ep.* "Humanae referunt," 2 (*PLS* 1, 1375–1376).

[104] The "rationalistic" side of Pelagius was stressed by Plinval, *Pélage*, 105; faulted by Torgny Bohlin, *Die Theologie des Pelagius und ihre Genesis*, 21.

[105] Commentators agreeing that the anti-Manichean stance of Pelagius's theology is of great importance are Bohlin, *Die Theologie*, 13ff., 41, 106; Robert F. Evans, *Pelagius: Inquiries and Reappraisals*, esp. 22; Wermelinger, *Rom und Pelagius*, 227; Theodore de Bruyn, *A Translation, With Introduction and*

Notes, of Pelagius's 'Commentary on Romans', 44, 61. Believing that the point has been overstressed is Georges de Plinval, "Points de vues récents sur la théologie de Pélage," 230.

[106] Anti-Manichean passages are found in such Pelagian primary sources as *De libero arbitrio* (*PLS* 1, 1540, 1543); *De vera circumcisione* 6; 7 (*PL* 30, 200, 201); *De castitate* 16 (*PLS* 1, 1499); *Ad Celantiam* 28 (*CSEL* 29, 456); Anianus, *praefatio*, John Chrysostom, *Hom. in Matthaeum* (*PL* 58, 625); *Libellus fidei* 10; 15 (*PL* 45, 1718). Anti-Manichean comments appear in thirteen passages in Pelagius's *Commentary on the Pauline Epistles* (my count): see his comments on Romans 1:2; 6:9; 7:7; 8:7; 9:5; I Corinthians 11:12;

ist answer that rested on souls having a heavenly preexistence before their bodily incorporation,[107] Pelagius consistently interprets the Pauline letters to exclude any hint of divine determinism. Thus, as is well known, Pelagius interprets passages that mention predestination to mean God's "fore-knowledge" of a person's future way of life,[108] an interpretation consonant with the person's "choosing to believe" and thus to acquire the power to become a son of God.[109] God, Pelagius claims, always calls those who are willing, not those who are unwilling.[110] God thus could foresee the future faith (or lack thereof) that Jacob and Esau would have.[111] That "God has mercy on whom he will" (Romans 9:15) means that God foreknows who will be *deserving* of his mercy.[112] Paul's words on Pharaoh in the same chapter of Romans mean to Pelagius that when Pharaoh exceeded the limit of wickedness by his sins, God punished him;[113] Pharaoh, in other words, had *already* made himself a "vessel of wrath."[114] In interpreting Romans 9, Pelagius thinks that Paul does not always speak in his own voice, but states objections that others might raise,[115] a device that conveniently rescues Paul from uttering verses repellent to Pelagian sympathies.

Pelagius's refusal to countenance any determination of human sinfulness from Adam is well illustrated by his treatment of Romans 5:12–15. That sin came into the world "through one man" is explained as meaning that Adam sinned and we followed him in sin.[116] As long as other humans sin, as Adam sinned, they too shall experience death.[117] In discussing these verses, Pelagius intriguingly refers to those "who oppose the transmission of sin," with whom he does not here clearly identify himself; it has been suggested that Pelagius may have had in mind the arguments of Rufinus the Syrian.[118] If, as has been posited, Pelagius's *Commentary on the Pauline*

15:45; II Corinthians 3:7; 13:1; Galatians 5:20; Colossians 1:16; Ephesians 2:20; I Timothy 6:4; 6:16.

[107] Pelagius, *In Ephesios* 1:4;1:10 (Souter ed., 345, 347); cf. both Pelagius's and Cae-lestius's *Libelli Fidei* (PL 48, 503–504).

[108] Pelagius, *In Romanos* 8:29 (Souter ed., 68–69); *In Ephesios* 1:11 (Souter ed., 347).

[109] Pelagius, *In Ephesios* 1:5 (Souter ed., 345–346).

[110] Pelagius, *In Romanos* 8:30 (Souter ed., 69).

[111] Pelagius, *In Romanos* 9:10 (Souter ed., 74).

[112] Pelagius, *In Romanos* 9:15 (Souter ed., 75).

[113] Pelagius, *In Romanos* 9:17 (Souter ed., 76). For an interpretation, see Faustus of Riez, *De gratia* II, 1 (CSEL 21, 58–60).

[114] Pelagius, *In Romanos* 9:22 (Souter ed.,

78).

[115] This interpretation is similar to that found in the Origen-Rufinus *Commentary on Romans*, in which the author also puts Ro-mans 9:14–19 in the mouth of an objector. See Alfred J. Smith, "The Commentary of Pelagius on Romans Compared with that of Origen-Rufinus, Part III," 163–164. Augus-tine criticized this exegetical technique: *De gestis Pelagii* 16, 39 (CSEL 42, 94–95).

[116] Pelagius, *In Romanos* 5:12 (Souter ed., 45); cf. Pelagius, *De natura*, cited in Augus-tine, *De natura et gratia* 9, 10 (CSEL 60, 238); and Julian of Eclanum, cited in Augus-tine, *Opus imperfectum* II, 56, 1; 61; 194 (CSEL 85¹, 203, 207–208, 309).

[117] Pelagius, *In Romanos* 5:12 (Souter ed., 45).

[118] DeBruyn, *A Translation*, 82, 126–127.

Epistles can be dated to 404–409,[119] we here see Pelagius grappling with arguments against the transmission of sin several years before he and his disciple Caelestius[120] confronted Augustine on this issue. The arguments that the opponents of sin's transmission raise, as reported by Pelagius in his *Commentary on Romans*, are that if Adam's sin injured everyone, even those who weren't sinners, then Christ's righteousness ought to save even nonbelievers; that baptized parents should not transmit the sin they have lost to their offspring; and that if only the flesh, not the soul, is passed from parents to children, then only the flesh, not the soul, should be punished. How unjust it would be for God to blame a person for "so ancient a sin," a sin that someone else committed, when Christianity teaches that God even forgives the sins that *we* commit.[121] How decisive these views, here presented by Pelagius without comment, would be for him and his followers is obvious.

The Pelagian claim that humans are able to fulfill God's commandments and to avoid sin rests not only on an understanding of God's justice and love, but also on a view of the strength of human nature and, as has recently been emphasized, on a powerful affirmation of baptism's power to create a completely new being.[122] As Pelagius details in many works, the goodness of human creation is revealed by the capacities given us by God,[123] which when strengthened by the provision of the Law, of exemplary holy men in the Bible, and of Christ,[124] suffice to enable us to will and to do the good. As Pelagius put it to Demetrias, "You confer your spiritual riches on yourself," a line that became somewhat of a *cause célèbre* in the controversy.[125]

Pelagius thus interprets Paul's view that we are not justified "by works of the Law" (Galatians 2:16) to mean "not by the Old Testament ceremo-

---

[119] Souter, *Pelagius's Expositions*, I, 189.

[120] Caelestius denied sin's transmission at the Council of Carthage (411); see Augustine, *De gratia Christi* II, 3, 3 (*CSEL* 42, 163); also see Souter, *Pelagius's Expositions*, I, 189. Augustine's views of which issues were still open for discussion differed considerably: *De gratia Christi* II, 23, 27 (*CSEL* 42, 185–186). A later Pelagian who composed the *Expositio interlinearis libri Job* interprets Job 1:20 ("naked came I into the world") as meaning "*nulla sorde peccati originalis aspersus*" (*PL* 23, 1477).

[121] Pelagius, *In Romanos* 5:15 (Souter ed., 46–47).

[122] A point especially emphasized by Bohlin, *Die Theologie*, 31–36.

[123] For example, in Pelagius's *De libero arbitrio*, fragments in Augustine, *De gratia Christi* I, 3, 4; 18, 19 (*CSEL* 42, 127, 140);

Ad Demetriadem 2–3 (*PL* 30, 17–19). Augustine argues that Pelagius stressed the goodness of creation at the expense of soteriology: *De natura et gratia* 34, 39 (*CSEL* 60, 261–262). For a detailed discussion of Pelagius's anthropology, based on his Pauline *Commentaries*, see Juan B. Valero, *Las Bases antropologicas de Pelagio en su tratado de las Expositiones*.

[124] Pelagius, *Ad Demetriadem* 4; 8 (*PL* 30, 20, 24–25); cf *In Colossenses* 1:10 (Souter ed., 452–453); *De libero arbitrio*, in Augustine, *De gratia Christi* I, 7, 8 (*CSEL* 42, 130–132). On these means of grace, see Gisbert Greshake, *Gnade als konkrete Freiheit: Eine Untersuchung zur Gnadenlehre Pelagius*, esp. 93–125.

[125] Pelagius, *Ad Demetriadem* 11 (*PL* 30, 28).

nial Law," although moral acts are *always* required for justification.[126] Although John writes that "if we say we have no sin, we deceive ourselves" (I John 1:8), we must always recall that if God *wants* us to be free from sin, we will be able to be so—and how impious it is to imagine that God does *not* want us to be free from sin! Never can we accuse "the just God" for our own wickedness.[127]

The Pelagian literature consistently repeats the point that *every* sin must be avoided,[128] that *all* of the commands must be kept.[129] One Pelagian author goes so far as to define a Christian as "a person who after baptism is free from sin,"[130] a view that he reinforces by insisting that the just God would not have given the commandments if he didn't expect us to keep free from sin by following them.[131] As Pelagius warns Demetrias, nothing, not even her vow of perpetual chastity, can make up for the failure to keep all the commandments.[132] The same advice he gives to a married woman, Celantia: no status in life is free from the requirement to keep God's commands.[133] Just one sin dishonors God.[134]

Baptism brings to perfection the gifts we have been given by creation and revelation. The washing away of "the old man" creates a new human being who is capable, with effort, to lead a life without sin.[135] Thus Paul can enjoin the Church to be "without spot or wrinkle" (Ephesians 5:27), for individual Christians who pass through the baptismal laver are just this.[136] Babies, too, although they are not born with sin, should be baptized into the Church's communion of the blessed.[137]

This high estimation of the baptized Christian's abilities led several Pelagian authors to adopt a view on the Last Judgment that was a precise opposite to the Origenist hope for the restoration of all things to their original goodness and unity. Pelagians derived from Matthew 25:31–46

---

[126] Pelagius, *In Galatas* 2: 16 (Souter ed., 315); cf. *De vita Christiana* 13 (*PL* 40, 1043). That true circumcision cannot be of the flesh is supported by an appeal to Job, a non-Israelite, in *De vera circumcisione* 11 (*PL* 30, 205–206).

[127] *Expositio fidei Catholicae* (*PLS* 1, 1685); cf. Pelagius's *Liber capitulorum*, cited by Augustine in *De gestis Pelagii* 30, 54 (*CSEL* 42, 107–108) and his *De natura*, cited in Augustine, *De natura et gratia* 43, 50 (*CSEL* 60, 270).

[128] For example, the *Fragmenta Pelagiana Vindobonensia* 6; 7 (*PLS* 1, 1564–1565).

[129] *Virginitatis laus* 3 (*PL* 30, 170); *De vita Christiana* 9 (*PL* 40, 1038).

[130] *Ep.* "Honorificentiae tuae," 1 (*PLS* 1, 1689).

[131] *Ep.* "Honorificentiae tuae," 1 (*PLS* 1, 1689).

[132] Pelagius, *Ad Demetriadem* 10 (*PL* 30, 26–27).

[133] *Ad Celantiam* 5; 22; 32 (*CSEL* 29, 440, 452, 459).

[134] *Ad Celantiam* 4 (*CSEL* 29, 438).

[135] Pelagius, *In Romanos* 9:1–2 (Souter ed., 72); *De libero arbitrio*, frag. 3 (*PLS* 1, 1543); *De poenitentia* 2 (*PL* 30, 250); *De divina lege* 2 (*PL* 30, 110). For the power of baptism to break evil custom in Pelagius's theology, see especially Bohlin, *Die Theologie*, 31–36.

[136] Augustine, *De gestis Pelagii* 12, 27–28 (*CSEL* 42, 80–82). Apparently Pelagius's reasoning convinced his Palestinian judges.

[137] Pelagius, *Libellus fidei* 17 (*PL* 48, 490); *Expositio fidei Catholicae* (*PLS* 1, 1684).

the message that there were only two places in the afterlife, one for the torment of sinners and the other for the blessed who had maintained righteousness.[138] Pelagius himself apparently accused Catholic Christians of "Origenism" on this very point. According to the record Augustine presents of the Synod of Diospolis that interrogated Pelagius, Pelagius was asked if he had written that on Judgment Day, sinners would receive no further forbearance, but would perish in the eternal fires. When the bishops present realized that Pelagius also included *Christian* sinners in this category, they registered alarm. Pelagius, however, stuck by his claim and cited Matthew 25:46 to them, adding that anyone who believed differently was an Origenist. The judges, who wished to disassociate themselves with Origenism, conceded Pelagius's point—much to Augustine's annoyance.[139] Pelagius's views on this matter are in accord with the rigorous understanding of the Last Judgment expressed elsewhere in Pelagian writings.[140]

These themes are nicely focused in the Pelagian treatise, composed about the turn to the fifth century,[141] on that most difficult of subjects, the hardening of Pharaoh's heart. The unknown author is concerned to refute uses of this passage that bolster "pagan fatalism"[142]—but he soon makes clear that his opponents are not genuine "pagans," but those who "try to introduce the teaching of fate under the color of grace,"[143] that is, Catholic Christians of a predestinarian stripe. After paying eloquent tribute to the role of both Mosaic and Christian Law in reshaping human nature to its original pristine condition,[144] the author announces his working herme-

---

[138] *De vita Christiana* 10 (*PL* 40, 1040); *De divina lege* 7 (*PL* 30, 116–117); *De malis doctoribus* 8, 2–3 (*PLS* 1, 1428–1429); *Virginitate laus* 6 (*PL* 30, 172); *De poenitentia* 6 (*PL* 30, 253).

[139] Augustine, *De gestis Pelagii* 3, 9; 10 (*CSEL* 42, 60–61). On Augustine's reading, some sinners will be *saved* by fire, not punished everlastingly by it. On Pelagius's use of the Matthew verses concerning the Last Judgment, see Evans, *Four Letters*, 97–98. That Augustine received his copy of the *Acts* of the Synod of Diospolis from Cyril of Alexandria is revealed in the newly published Epistle 4* of Augustine; see discussion in Wickham, "Pelagianism," 202.

[140] Especially in *De divina lege* 7 (*PL* 30, 117).

[141] The issue of the dating of the *De induratione* is complex. Germain Morin, the discoverer of the text, opted for the early fifth century: "Un Traité Pélagien inédit du commencement du cinquième siécle," 188. Plinval, who published the text, dates it to 397–

398 (*Essai*, 134); his view of an early dating is followed by Giovanni Martinetto, "Les Premières Réactions antiaugustiniennes de Pélage," 115–116, believing it a response to Augustine's *Ad Simplicianum*, and to Paulinus of Nola's questions to Pelagius and Jerome between 397–399; thus he argues that the Pelagian controversy starts in around 398 (115–116, 85). Those who think that the work should be dated several years later, since the author (perhaps) uses Rufinus's Latin translations of *On First Principles* and of Origen's *Commentary on Romans*, are TeSelle, "Rufinus the Syrian," 83–85, and Flavio G. Nuvolone-Nobile, "Problèmes d'une nouvelle édition du *De Induratione Cordis Pharaonis* attribué a Pélage," 115–116.

[142] *De induratione* 2 (Plinval ed., 139).

[143] *De induratione* 53; 2 (Plinval ed., 201, 139).

[144] *De induratione* 3–8 (Plinval ed., 138, 141, 143).

neutical principle: obscure and difficult texts (such as the one at hand) are to be interpreted through the "eyes" of lucid passages that require no complex interpretation, such as the Ten Commandments.[145] Those who do not appreciate the difference between these two types of texts might take Paul's words on Jacob and Esau, or the hardening of Pharaoh's heart, to mean that God was "an accepter of persons"[146]—a notion that was anathema to Pelagians.[147] The correct answer to the problem (since there is no *iniquitas* with God: Romans 9:14) is that God knew how people would turn out, who would love him and who would despise his ways, and dispensed his mercy on this basis.[148]

Using Pelagius's technique in his *Romans Commentary*, the author of *De induratione cordis Pharaonis* reminds his readers that Paul in Romans 9 is not always speaking in his own voice: sometimes he raises points made by objectors in order to answer them.[149] Since God "wants everyone to be saved" (I Timothy 2:4), we cannot interpret Romans 9 (as the heretics imply) to mean that God passes a sentence of condemnation on a man who performed well.[150] Since God wants everyone to be saved, we must believe that he addressed his commandments to everyone—even to Pharaoh.[151] The correct interpretation of the passage is that Pharaoh by his own deeds had reached such a state of cruelty that God was moved to deliver the suffering Israelites.[152] The verb tense gives us a clue: if God, rather than Pharaoh himself, were responsible for hardening Pharaoh's heart, he should have said, "I *have* hardened," not "I *will* harden." Although Pharaoh, in league with the devil, hardened his own heart,[153] yet even then the merciful God did not move to punish him until he was well advanced in wickedness.[154] In truth, the episode shows God's pity, for God did not wish Pharaoh to die;[155] he rather employed the physician's technique, threatening the sinner in the hope that he would retreat from his evil deeds.[156] What "hardening" ever occurs thus takes place by our own wills.[157] When Paul writes that "God has pity on whom he wishes and hardens whom he wishes" (Romans 9:15), he replies to the proud, to give them a lesson in humility.[158] Christian teaching insists that we have it in our power to

---

[145] *De induratione* 9; 10 (Plinval ed., 145, 147).

[146] *De induratione* 13 (Plinval ed., 151).

[147] See, e.g., *Ep.* "Honorificentiae tuae," 1 (*PLS* 1, 1689); Julian of Eclanum, *Libellus fidei* II, 3 (*PL* 48, 515).

[148] *De induratione* 13; 14 (Plinval ed., 151, 153).

[149] *De induratione* 18 (Plinval ed., 155, 157).

[150] *De induratione* 19 (Plinval ed., 157).

[151] *De induratione* 43 (Plinval ed., 189).

[152] *De induratione* 23 (Plinval ed., 161).

[153] *De induratione* 24 (Plinval ed., 163).

[154] *De induratione* 25 (Plinval ed., 163): when he was poised like a serpent to kill the Israelites (*De induratione* 27 [Plinval ed., 165, 167]).

[155] *De induratione* 26 (Plinval ed., 165).

[156] *De induratione* 32; 30 (Plinval ed., 171, 169).

[157] *De induratione* 35 (Plinval ed., 177).

[158] *De induratione* 38–39 (Plinval ed., 181, 183).

change ourselves from "vessels of dishonor" to "vessels of honor,"[159] and this by our own will.[160] Moreover, Pharaoh's fate had a salutary effect on the Israelites: not only did it give them physical freedom, it also stimulated them to righteous behavior.[161] In such ways as this were troubling Biblical passages rescued from the hands of "determinists" by Pelagian authors.

Commentators agree that the controversial issues of the Pelagian dispute sharpened with Caelestius. It was he, apparently, who raised the issue of the transmission of sin to the forefront of discussion, away from Pelagius's favorite topics of human nature and the freedom of the will.[162] At the Council of Carthage in 411, Caelestius testified that the question of whether or not sin is transmitted was "open" in the Church, and that some holy men, including Rufinus the Syrian, rejected the postulate.[163] Caelestius's condemnation by the Carthaginian Council did not impede his appeal to the bishop of Rome,[164] nor his later travels throughout the Mediterranean in search of support.[165] At the Synod of Diospolis in 415, the following points were alleged to summarize Caelestius's teaching:

> That Adam was created mortal and would have died whether he sinned or not;
> That Adam's sin injured only himself, not the human race;
> That the Law as well as the Gospel leads to the Kingdom;
> That there were men without sin before Christ's coming;
> That newborn babies are in same condition as Adam before the Fall;
> That it is not through Adam's Fall that the entire human race dies, nor through Christ's resurrection that it rises again.[166]

A second set of propositions ascribed to Caelestius also show the sharpened form in which he set the issues: that sin should not be defined as "what cannot be avoided," since it is based in the will; if persons "ought" to be without sin, then they are able to be so; it blasphemes God to say that he does not want us to be without sin; to hold that it is impossible to be without evil is a Marcionite and Manichean view; and that God would be unjust if he charged humans with sin for deeds that were impossible for them to avoid.[167]

[159] *De induratione* 40 (Plinval ed., 183).
[160] *De induratione* 54 (Plinval ed., 203).
[161] *De induratione* 45 (Plinval ed., 191, 193).
[162] Bonner, *Augustine*, 36; Pier Franco Beatrice, *Tradux peccati: alle fonti della dottrina agostiniana del peccato originale*, 54–55. For the central role of Caelestius in the determination of the North African debate, see Peter Brown, *Augustine of Hippo. A Biography*, 344–345.
[163] As reported in Augustine, *De gratia Christi* II, 3, 3 (*CSEL* 42, 168–169). For Caelestius's position, see Gross, *Entstehungs-geschichte*, 280–282.
[164] See Augustine, *Ep.* 157, 22 (*CSEL* 44, 471); Marius Mercator, *Commonitorium quod super nomine Caelestii* 36 (*ACO* I, 5: 66). For the history, see Wermelinger, *Rom und Pelagius*, 15–18, 141–146.
[165] Marius Mercator, *Commonitorium Caelestii* 35–36 (*ACO* I, 5: 65–66). For the history, see Plinval, *Pélage*, 259.
[166] Cited by Augustine in *De gestis Pelagii* 11, 23 (*CSEL* 42, 76). Also see Marius Mercator, *Commonitorium Caelestii* 36 (*ACO*, I, 5: 66).
[167] This list is a summary of the longer dis-

In the view of some scholars, Caelestius's position was close to that of Rufinus the Syrian's, although Caelestius's views appear more radical, for example, in his opinion that Adam would have died anyway, whether he sinned or not.[168] Gerald Bonner argues that since Caelestius stayed in North Africa longer than Pelagius, his form of Pelagian teaching may have interacted with the distinctively North African concerns of baptism and the purity of the Church, both topics that had been at the center of the Donatist controversy.[169] Although many details of Caelestius's career remain obscure,[170] two of his main theses were the denial that inherited sin was transmitted to infants, and yet the affirmation that they, like all Christians, should be baptized.[171]

In the affair of Caelestius, we receive a further glimpse of the likelihood that Augustine's views were not considered self-evidently correct everywhere in Latin Christendom: Pope Zosimus was willing to reconsider Caelestius's case in 417, after an African synod had condemned him[172] (the condemnation seems to have centered on his denial of original sin's transmission and on his views concerning infant baptism).[173] According to the record of Caelestius's *Libellus fidei* preserved in Augustine's *On the Grace of Christ and Original Sin*, Caelestius had taught that babies should be baptized to enable them to reach the Kingdom of Heaven.[174] When in 418 a Council of Carthage moved against those who refused to say that infant baptism was necessary *because* of the transmission of original sin, it seems that Caelestius's theology was their target.[175] Not the practice, but the stated *reason* for the practice, had become the standard for "orthodoxy."

---

cussion of Caelestius's propositions in Augustine, *De perfectione iustitiae hominis* 2, 1–7, 16 (*CSEL* 42, 4–14). For discussion, see Wermelinger, *Rom und Pelagius*, 31–34. The book from which these propositions were taken may be the same work of Caelestius which Jerome cites to Ctesiphon in *Ep.* 133, 5 (*CSEL* 56, 249).

[168] Bonner, *Augustine*, 28–29, 36.

[169] Bonner, *Augustine*, 36.

[170] Was Caelestius really a "disciple" of Pelagius? What was his relation to Julian of Eclanum? For these and other issues, see Wermelinger, *Rom und Pelagius*, 30n.153; 35ff.

[171] Caelestius's *Libellus fidei* is found in *PL* 48, 498–505. See discussion of his theology in Wermelinger, *Rom und Pelagius*, 45, 138; Beatrice, *Tradux peccati*, 44. For Caelestius's denial of original sin's transmission to infants, see the quotation in Augustine, *De gratia Christi* I, 33, 36; II, 6, 6 (*CSEL* 42, 153, 170).

[172] Zosimus, *Epp.* 2 and 3 (*PL* 20, 649–

661): the North Africans have been too hasty in dealing with the evidence and have allowed the testimony of unreliable witnesses to be admitted; see discussion in Wermelinger, *Rom und Pelagius*, 141–145.

[173] See Paulinus of Milan, *Libellus adversus Coelestium* 3 (*PL* 20, 713); discussed by Wermelinger, *Rom und Pelagius*, 155–156.

[174] Augustine, *De gratia Christi* II, 5, 5 (*CSEL* 42, 169–170) (cf. *PL* 48, 502–503); discussion in Wermelinger, *Rom und Pelagius*, 172–174.

[175] Wermelinger also argues that Zosimus's predecessor Innocent I probably did not accept the North Africans' belief that children must be baptized to be forgiven for original sin: see his explanation of Innocent, *Ep.* 181 in *Rom und Pelagius*, 124–130. Innocent was apparently not alarmed by Pelagius's *De natura* (Innocent, in Augustine, *Ep.* 183, 5 [*CSEL* 44, 729–730]). Zosimus, too, may never have agreed to the *tradux peccati* (Wermelinger, *Rom und Pelagius*, 215–216). Also see the fragment of Zosimus's

The broadening of the controversy to highlight the transmission of sin and its effect upon children provoked the debate that would provide Augustine with the sharpest opponent he had ever confronted: Julian of Eclanum. It was here that the Pelagian and the Augustinian positions became most clearly defined. The issue of how sin's transmission reflected on marriage and procreation now became central. After more than a decade of battle with this new opponent, Augustine was left in his final years, ironically, and somewhat pathetically, defending himself against Julian's charges of "Manichean fatalism"—the very notion that he had begun his career as a Catholic polemicist by combatting.

We know much less about Julian of Eclanum than we would like. Despite the extensive research and recovery of material at the turn of the century by Albert Bruckner,[176] our understanding of his theological position is less than complete—a situation not improved by the fact that his two major works of theology are preserved only as fragments by Augustine in his attempted refutation. We do know that after his failure to win papal approval for the Pelagian cause, he traveled East and spent time in the company of Theodore of Mopsuestia, whose *Commentary on Psalms* he translated.[177] The parallels between Julian's thought and that of Theodore, especially as contained in the materials preserved in the *Palatine Anthology*, are intriguing but remain largely unexplored. That Julian knew and used the *Commentary on Job* written by Theodore's brother, Polychronius of Apamea, in his composition of a commentary upon the same book,[178] is suggestive for other connections with Theodore and his circle.

On the Western front, Julian's connections are better known: the son of an Italian bishop, Memorius, he had married the daughter of Aemelius, bishop of Beneventum, who was one of the delegates sent from the West to Constantinople to support the cause of John Chrysostom.[179] The family was tightly linked to the circle of Paulinus of Nola, who wrote a poem for the occasion of Julian's wedding.[180] That this association would give him

---

Tractoria in Augustine, *Ep.* 190, 23 (*CSEL* 57, 159).

[176] Albert Bruckner, *Julian von Eclanum. Sein Leben und seine Lehre. Ein Beitrag zur Geschichte des Pelagianismus; Die vier Bücher Julians von Aeclanum an Turbantius. Ein Beitrag zur Charakteristik Julians und Augustins.* In addition to the fragments of Julian's writings preserved in Augustine and in Bede, we also have the notice preserved by Marius Mercator in his *Commonitorium* 3–4; 7 (*ACO* I, 5: 6–7, 9); see discussion in Serafino Prete, *Mario Mercatore. Polemista anitpelagiano*, 14–15, 36–37, 54.

[177] Bruckner, *Julian*, 46; Wermelinger, *Pe-*

lagius und Rom, 226–238; *CPG* II, 346 (3833). For Nestorius's complaints about Julian's pleas to the imperial court in Constantinople, see his *Epp.* 1, 1 and 2, 1 (to Pope Coelestine) (*PL* 48, 173–175, 178–179). For a brief summary of Julian's activities, see Aimé Solignac, "Pélage et Pélagianisme," *DS* 12, 2, cols. 2902–2908.

[178] See Adhemar d'Alès, "Julien d'Eclane, exégète," 322.

[179] Palladius, *Dialogus* 4 [15] (Coleman-Norton ed., 22).

[180] Paulinus of Nola, *Carmen* 25 (*CSEL* 30, 238–245).

an indirect tie to Melania the Elder and Rufinus in their final years seems likely. Such social connections suggest that we should expect to find Julian in a key position when the Origenist controversy shifted into the Pelagian debate, and he does not disappoint our expectation.

Julian's approach, like that of his Pelagian predecessors, was motivated by the desire to refute all varieties of fatalism. Writing to Rufus of Thessalonica after the appeal of the eighteen Italian bishops (spearheaded probably by Julian) had failed and Zosimus had approved an anti-Pelagian decree,[181] Julian complains that Catholics like Rufus and himself must stand against "Manichean profanity," namely, that of his Augustinian opponents who under the name of "grace" preach fatalism.[182] Their "Manichean" attitudes are manifested in a variety of ways. They curse the Old Law and deny that the blessed people of the Old Testament lived righteously.[183] Worse yet, the "new Manicheans" claim that the Old Testament Law was not given for the purpose of justifying the obedient, but rather to make the *causa peccati* more severe.[184] For Julian, such an argument implies blasphemy against God's providential care for the human race.

Another "Manichean" point against which Julian warred in his *Letter to Rufus* lay in the notion that "natural" evil (i.e., the belief that Adam's sin was transmitted) was the cause of sin.[185] Against this view, Julian argues that the transmission of sin could take place *only* on the hypothesis of traducianism, the view that the soul is begotten from soul as body from body—and this view, he claims, the Church curses. Adam passes no evil to others except death, which is not always so very evil, in any case.[186] Julian's allowance for the transmission of death, but not sin, from Adam links his position to that of Ambrosiaster, Theodore of Mopsuestia, and Rufinus the Syrian—suggesting that this theory was acceptable to several Christian thinkers of the period, although it was not the view held by his Pelagian colleague Caelestius.[187]

A line of anti-Manichean argumentation also emerges in the *Libellus fidei*. Here, Julian and his episcopal associates, in the course of condemning a list of heretics, arrive at the Manicheans. These are faulted for claiming that there are two supreme principles, of evil as well as of good, and the flesh is derived from the evil principle while the soul comes from the

---

[181] For the history, see Bruckner, *Julian*, 34–36; Wermelinger, *Rom und Pelagius*, 205–206, 235–238. Gisbert Bouwman notes that Garnier, who reconstructed the *Letter to Rufus* for the *PL*, arranged the fragments in a "very questionable" order (*Des Julian von Aeclanum Kommentar zu den Propheten Osee, Joel und Amos: Ein Beitrag zur Geschichte der Exegese*, 3).

[182] Julian, *Ad Rufum* (PL 48, 534).

[183] Julian, *Ad Rufum* (PL 48, 536). Julian objects to the Augustinian argument that the prophets and Apostles were not truly holy, just "less evil" than the rest of us (535). Cf. Julian, *Libellus fidei* III, 14 (PL 48, 521).

[184] Julian, *Ad Rufum* (PL 48, 534).

[185] Julian, *Ad Rufum* (PL 48, 535).

[186] Julian, *Ad Rufum* (PL 48, 535).

[187] See above, pp. 200, 204, 206.

good.[188] The bishops' point in ending their catalogue of heretics with the Manicheans becomes immediately obvious: it provides the springboard for an attack on "ones similar to this" (i.e., Augustinians), who, adhering to a view of "natural sin" say that marriage takes its rise from the devil.[189] Their view of the transmission of sin from Adam means that human sins result "from necessity."[190]

Even those works by Julian that are extant as only a few scattered fragments proclaim the anti-Manichean war. Thus in his *Exposition of the Song of Songs*, preserved by Bede, Julian announces that his aim in the work is to fight those who "under the name of Manicheans" dishonor the body, alleging that it is incapable of goodness and full of iniquity, from whence no righteousness can arise.[191] Likewise, in the few lines left of *De bono constantiae*, also preserved by Bede, Julian claims that he writes to defend the goodness of nature and the freedom of the will against "the perfidy of the Manicheans." His argument, it appears, praised the will's ability to lend "constancy" so that bodily members could be easily controlled.[192]

The most sustained criticism of Augustinian "fatalism"—the "new Manicheanism"—undoubtedly lay in Julian's *Ad Florum*, sizable portions of which are excerpted in Augustine's last mammoth writing, the *Opus imperfectum contra Julianum*. There the *tradux peccati* is dubbed "*Manichaeorum filia, vestra mater.*"[193] Julian begins by claiming that he had already written against "the supporters of Mani" in his *Ad Turbantium* (excerpted in Augustine's *Contra Julianum* and *De nuptiis* II), but that he will rehearse his argument again, since his earlier work does not seem to have accomplished its purpose.[194] Julian's strategic move in the *Ad Florum* is to claim that those who hold a doctrine of original sin are necessarily traducians:[195] in order to derive a transfer of sin from Adam to all humankind, they must link the soul to the seed.[196] But, Julian continues, anyone who thinks that souls are so transmitted is kin to Mani.[197] This identification of traducians and Manicheans is explicitly noted by Julian at least seven times in the *Ad Florum*.[198] And that Manichean fatalism is also linked to astrological fatal-

---

[188] Julian, *Libellus fidei*, III, 9 (*PL* 48, 520). Not all the opinions in the *Libellus fidei* are identical with what we know of Julian's ideas from other sources: see Wermelinger, *Rom und Pelagius*, 221.

[189] Julian, *Libellus fidei* III, 10; cf. III, 17 (*PL* 48, 520, 522).

[190] Julian, *Libellus fidei* III, 15 (*PL* 48, 521).

[191] Julian, *Expositio Cantici Canticorum*, in Bede, *In Cantica Canticorum* I (*PL* 91, 1069).

[192] Julian, *De bono constantiae*, in Bede, *In Cantica Canticorum* I (*PL* 91, 1072).

[193] Julian, *Ad Florum*, in Augustine, *Opus imperfectum* III, 29 CSEL 85¹, 367).

[194] Julian, *Ad Florum*, in Augustine, *Opus imperfectum* I, 1 (*CSEL* 85¹, 5).

[195] Julian, *Ad Florum*, in Augustine, *Opus imperfectum* I, 6 (*CSEL* 85¹, 9).

[196] Julian, *Ad Florum*, in Augustine, *Opus imperfectum* II, 178, 2 (*CSEL* 85¹, 298).

[197] Julian, *Ad Florum*, in Augustine, *Opus imperfectum* III, 173, (*CSEL* 85¹, 474).

[198] Julian, *Ad Florum*, in Augustine, *Opus imperfectum* I, 27; 66; 75, 1; II, 27, 2; 142; III, 10; 123 (*CSEL* 85¹, 23, 64, 90, 181, 265, 355, 440): my count.

ism is scored by Julian when he associates Augustine's teaching with "Chaldean and Manichean fantasies."[199]

Thus the question, Julian insists, rests on a disagreement about the soul's origin. Against opponents who must think that the soul comes "mixed with the seeds," Julian proclaims that the soul is created by God and then joined to the body; in other words, Julian is a creationist.[200] But Julian's point is not one that Augustine wants to address. As we shall see, Augustine consistently backs away from declaring himself on the origin of the soul:[201] he doesn't *know* how all humans can be said to be "in Adam,"[202] and he resents Julian's "taking refuge in a very obscure question about the soul."[203]

For Julian, "not compelling" and "not being compelled" are defining characteristics of God, manifest both in the Incarnation[204] and in God's more ordinary dealings with humans. The diverse destinies of humans are not decreed by God, who wishes all people to be saved (I Timothy 2:4). Since God is "no respecter of persons" (Romans 2:11), whether we are good or evil depends on our own wills,[205] and what is a matter of will is "not mixed with seeds."[206] Sins—human deeds—do not change human nature[207]; conversely, if sin were "inborn," it could not be effaced.[208]

This line of argumentation soon progressed to the issue of babies, where questions regarding God's justice received their sharpest form. How could a just God condemn an infant who had contracted sin not by its own volition but through its parents, Julian asks,[209] adding that it would be better not to believe in God at all than to believe that he exists but is unjust.[210] Since infants do not yet possess the power of volition, they cannot commit any offense.[211] On Augustine's theory of infant sinfulness, fetuses ought to have wills if they are to be accused of sin—but how can they have wills when they don't have souls and reason, both necessary for "the will" to

---

[199] Julian, *Ad Florum*, in Augustine, *Opus imperfectum* I, 82 (*CSEL* 85¹, 95).

[200] Julian, *Ad Florum*, in Augustine, *Opus imperfectum* II, 24, 1 (*CSEL* 85¹, 178); IV, 90 (*PL* 45, 1391).

[201] See, for example, Augustine, *Opus imperfectum* IV, 104 (*PL* 45, 1400); *Contra Julianum* V, 15, 53 (*PL* 44, 814).

[202] Augustine, *Opus imperfectum* II, 178, 2–3 (*CSEL* 85¹, 298–299).

[203] Augustine, *Contra Julianum* V, 4, 17 (*PL* 44, 794): Augustine affirms that even if he doesn't know which notion of the soul's origin is correct, "original sin is."

[204] Julian, *Libellus fidei* I, 5 (*PL* 48, 510).

[205] Julian, *Libellus fidei* II, 3 (*PL* 48, 515).

[206] Julian, *Ad Turbantium*, in Augustine, *Contra Julianum* VI, 9, 24 (*PL* 44, 837).

[207] Julian, *Ad Florum*, in Augustine, *Opus*

imperfectum I, 96 (*CSEL* 85¹, 111).

[208] Julian, *Ad Florum*, in Augustine, *Opus imperfectum* I, 61 (*CSEL* 85¹, 58).

[209] Julian, *Ad Turbantium*, in Augustine, *Contra Julianum* II, 1, 2 (*PL* 44, 673). For a discussion of the issue, see François Refoulé, "Misère des enfants et péché originel d'après saint Augustin," 341–362. Marius Mercator's response to Julian's view on the innocence of the newborn is to list 23 titles given to Jesus in the New Testament that show his redemptive mission (*Commonitorium* 14 [*ACO* I, 5: 15–19]); see discussion in Prete, *Mario Mercatore*, 55.

[210] Julian, *Ad Florum*, in Augustine, *Opus imperfectum* III, 9 (*CSEL* 85¹, 355).

[211] Julian, *Ad Turbantium*, in Augustine, *Contra Julianum* III, 5, 11 (*PL* 44, 707).

function?[212] Augustine, in effect, hands over the little ones to the devil.[213] Exhaling fumes more deadly than those of Lake Avernus, he delivers children to the flames before they are capable of choosing good or evil.[214] And all on account of someone's eating a piece of fruit, Julian scoffs.[215]

Such notions, Julian continues, must imply a certain understanding of baptism on Augustine's part. For if baptized parents still have original sin to pass on to their offspring, they must never have lost it.[216] Augustine must have a weak idea of baptism's efficacy, that it cleanses only "in part."[217] He must deny that we truly are made "new men" at baptism.[218]

And what is the function of infant baptism? For adults, Julian agrees, baptism is for forgiveness of sins and entry to the Kingdom of Heaven;[219] but what is the point of baptizing infants, who need no forgiveness of sins? Like several of his Pelagian colleagues, Julian affirmed the practice and declared that the same formula should be used for children as for adults.[220] In the *Libellus fidei*, he and his condemned episcopal colleagues appeal to the authority of John Chrysostom on this point, who wrote that although infants are not baptized because of defilement by sin, they should be baptized to increase their holiness and to bring them into the *fraternitas Christi*.[221] In the *Ad Florum*, Julian adds that baptism gives babies spiritual enlightenment, divine adoption, citizenship in the heavenly Jerusalem, sanctification, and possession of the Kingdom of Heaven.[222] To their natural birth are added gifts of grace that enhance their created goodness.[223] What they do *not* receive is forgiveness of a sin that they do not have.

Julian's most intriguing explanation of infant baptism comes in his *Letter to Rufus*. Baptism is necessary for persons of every age so that they may be adopted as children of God; they experience a regeneration, not an expiation. The analogy that Julian chooses to develop must have disturbed Augustine: just as Christ himself was "sprinkled" as a way of conforming him-

[212] Julian, *Ad Florum*, in Augustine, *Opus imperfectum* IV, 90 (*PL* 45, 1391).

[213] Julian, *Ad Florum*, in Augustine, *Opus imperfectum* I, 62 (*CSEL* 85¹, 58); VI, 23 (*PL* 45, 1555).

[214] Julian, *Ad Florum*, in Augustine, *Opus imperfectum* I, 48, 3 (*CSEL* 85¹, 37–38).

[215] Julian, *Ad Florum*, in Augustine, *Opus imperfectum* VI, 23 (*PL* 45, 1554–1555).

[216] Julian, *Ad Turbantium*, in Augustine, *Contra Julianum* VI, 7, 18 (*PL* 44, 833).

[217] Julian, *Ad Turbantium*, in Augustine, *Contra Julianum* VI, 13, 40 (*PL* 44, 843); cf. Julian, *Libellus fidei* III, 13 (*PL* 48, 521).

[218] Julian, *Ad Rufum* (*PL* 48, 534; cf. 536): Ephesians 5:27 teaches that we *do* become perfect in baptism.

[219] Julian, *Libellus fidei* I, 14 (*PL* 48, 513).

[220] Julian, *Libellus fidei* III, 19 (*PL* 48, 523).

[221] Julian, *Libellus fidei* IV, 10–11 (*PL* 48, 525–526), citing John Chrysostom, *Ad Neophytos*. See Sebastian Haidacher, "Eine unbeachtete Rede des hl. Chrysostomus an Neugetaufte," 168–193; and J.-P. Bouhot ed., "Version inédite du sermon 'Ad neophytos' de S. Jean Chrysostome, utilisés par S. Augustin," 27–41; the Latin text at 33–37; Greek fragments at 39–40.

[222] Julian, *Ad Florum*, in Augustine, *Opus imperfectum* I, 53, 3 (*CSEL* 85¹, 49).

[223] Julian, *Ad Florum*, in Augustine, *Opus imperfectum* V, 9 (*PL* 45, 1438); see discussion in François Refoulé, "Julien d'Eclane, théologien et philosophe," 49–51.

self to humanity rather than to remove the stain of any sin, of which his flesh was free, so likewise innocent infants, share a common human nature and thus should also receive baptism.[224] Although Augustine claims that Pelagians distinguished "eternal life" from "the Kingdom of Heaven" and allowed the former but not the latter to unbaptized infants,[225] this does not seem to have been a view pressed by Julian—nor for that matter, by Pelagius himself.[226]

Julian, we have seen, tried to move the argument regarding transmission of sin toward a discussion of the origin of the soul. This attempt, we shall see, was rejected by Augustine, who refused to pronounce himself on the matter, claiming that the theory of original sin did not require any particular view of the soul's origin for its support. His colleague and sometime sparring partner, Jerome, more readily accepted both a theory of original sin *and* a creationist position on the soul—but without a minute's worry on how these two might fit together. Thus we turn first to Jerome, before proceeding to Augustine's "solution."

JEROME

One of the great merits of Robert Evans' *Pelagius: Inquiries and Reappraisals* was that it brought Jerome to the forefront of the Pelagian controversy.[227] Although Augustine wrote against Pelagian teaching from 412 on,[228] he did not attack Pelagius by name until three years later.[229] Thus Jerome's anti-Pelagian notices from 414 on show that he predated Augustine as an explicit critic of Pelagius. What becomes clear from Jerome's discussion, however, is that he was fighting a somewhat different battle than was Augustine: for Jerome, the Pelagian debate was the continuation of both the ascetic and the Origenist controversies. And although Jerome, unlike Augustine, was an avowed creationist, he never worried about the details of how, on that supposition, original sin was transferred to the souls of infants. Here, as elsewhere, Jerome shows himself as less theologically probing than Augustine.

---

[224] Julian, *Ad Rufum* (PL 48, 535).

[225] Augustine, *Sermo* 294, 2–3 (PL 38, 1336–1339); *De peccatorum meritis* I, 20, 26 (CSEL 60, 25–26).

[226] See discussion of these points in François Refoulé, "La Distinction 'Royaume de Dieu-Vie Eternelle': est-elle Pélagienne?" 247–254.

[227] Evans, *Pelagius*, esp. 4.

[228] If we accept the traditional dating of the *De peccatorum meritis*, which is rejected by O'Connell; see above, n. 57.

[229] Brown explains this by the presence in Africa of highly placed protectors of Pelagius ("Patrons," *Religion and Society*, 218); Evans (*Pelagius*, 84–85, 89) notes that only in 415 did Augustine feel that his authority was being undermined, especially by Pelagius's use of his own earlier (anti-Manichean) writings that upheld free will (see *De natura et gratia*, a sustained attack upon Pelagius's *De natura*). In *De gestis Pelagii* 22, 46 (CSEL 42, 100–101), Augustine claims that he decided to refute the errors for what they were, rather than name individuals.

From early in his writing career—the *Commentary on Ecclesiastes*, dated to 388–389[230]—Jerome declares himself an opponent of traducianism. Commenting on Ecclesiastes 12:7 (that the flesh returns to the earth from which it was taken, and the spirit to God), Jerome pronounces "ridiculous" those who think that souls are produced along with bodies rather than being created directly by God. The author of Ecclesiastes rebukes such foolishness by claiming that the spirit returns to God, who is the author of souls.[231]

Decades later, in 412, Count Marcellinus and his wife Anapsychia wrote from North Africa to Jerome, requesting his opinion on the origin of the soul. In their letter (the contents of which we gather from Jerome's response), they had outlined various explanations: did the soul fall from heaven, as Pythagoras, the Platonists, and Origen believed? Is the soul part of God's essence, as the Stoics, Mani, and the Priscillianists claimed? Were souls created long ago and stored away? Or are they formed day by day; as John 5:17 ("My Father is working still . . .") might suggest? Or do souls come down by propagation, as Tertullian, Apollinaris, and "most Western writers" hold? Jerome's answer is casual: go look in my *Adversus Rufinum* for the answer. They can borrow a copy from Oceanus, or their bishop Augustine can give them oral instruction on "his opinion, or rather mine":[232] Jerome here incorrectly assumes that Augustine must be a declared creationist. In the *Adversus Rufinum*, Jerome had mocked his opponent for professing ignorance on the origin of the soul:[233] the correct answer, Jerome there claims, is to affirm that God creates souls daily and sends them into bodies.[234]

By 415, Jerome apparently had realized that the origin of the soul was a more pressing issue than he had assumed a few years earlier. In his *Epistle* 133, written shortly before his *Dialogue Against the Pelagians*,[235] Jerome responds to Ctesiphon's inquiries regarding Pelagius's teaching. Jerome frets that "many in the East" have been led astray by Pelagian teaching, which in his view revives the Pythagorean and Stoic teaching on *apatheia*.[236] Although the Pelagians claim that they hold out only for a *theoretical* possibility of human sinlessness—they do *not* claim that they or others have it[237]—Jerome is deeply suspicious of what he labels, in Greek, a doctrine of *anamartētos*. Others who held such a doctrine were Manichees—

[230] Dating in *CCL* 72, 248a.
[231] Jerome, *Comm. in Ecclesiasten* 12:7 (*CCL* 72, 357).
[232] Jerome, *Ep.* 126, 1; 3 (*CSEL* 56, 143, 145).
[233] Jerome, *Apologia* II, 8–10; III, 30 (*CCL* 79, 40–43, 101–102).
[234] Jerome, *Apologia* III, 28 (*CCL* 79, 100).

[235] Jerome, *Dialogus adversus Pelagianos*, *prologus* 1 (*PL* 23, 517); cf. Orosius, *Liber Apologeticus* 4, 6 (*CSEL* 5, 608).
[236] Jerome, *Ep.* 133, 1 (*CSEL* 56, 242).
[237] Jerome, *Ep.* 133, 2; cf. 11 (*CSEL* 56, 243–244, 257).

and Evagrius Ponticus.[238] This fascinating note shows that at long last, well after the fact of the Origenist controversy, Jerome has discovered Evagrius's teaching. He knows, for example, that Evagrius sent letters to virgins and monks, including to Melania the Elder, "whose name bears witness to the blackness of her wickedness"—perhaps referring to either the *Mirror for Nuns* or the famous Evagrian *Letter to Melania*. Evagrius also wrote a book of sayings on *apatheia* (the *Praktikos*?), to achieve which, Jerome sneers, one would have to be either a stone or God himself. Further, Jerome notes, Rufinus of Aquileia translated some of these Evagrian writings, so that they are now unfortunately accessible to Latin readers.[239]

Moreover, Jerome continues, the "new heretics" (i.e., the Pelagians) derive much of their teaching from Origen. In addition, they adopt Jovinian's postulate that baptized Christians cannot be tempted by the devil.[240] Jerome then unleashes his fury at women's role in the spread of heresy from the time of Simon Magus onward,[241] an attack that suggests that he believed that both Origenism and Pelagianism had found an especially enthusiastic reception among women.[242]

Other teachings of the Pelagians are also faulted in *Epistle* 133: by "grace," they merely mean God's commandments (thus doing away with the efficacy of prayer);[243] they transfer "sinlessness" from the divine to the human realm;[244] they claim that the heroes of the Bible were perfectly righteous.[245] Although they try to tar Jerome with the brush of "Manicheanism," it was not Jerome but God's apostle Paul who wrote the famous verses on human sinfulness in Romans 7, and who developed the metaphor of the potter and the clay in Romans 9, with corollary comments on vessels of honor and dishonor, and God's treatment of Jacob and Esau.[246] Jerome closes with a warning to Ctesiphon not to give Pelagius financial support: he would only assist in the spreading of heresy.[247]

Although in 415 Augustine had written Jerome a letter of inquiry about the origin of the soul,[248] Jerome did not address this issue either in his *Epistle to Ctesiphon* or in his *Dialogue with the Pelagians*—nor, as far as we know, did he ever respond to Augustine's request for information. This

---

[238] Jerome, *Ep.* 133, 3 (*CSEL* 56, 244–245).

[239] Jerome, *Ep.* 133, 3 (*CSEL* 56, 246). For the transfer of the Evagrian corpus to Palestine, see above, pp. 188–189.

[240] Jerome, *Ep.* 133, 3 (*CSEL* 56, 247); cf. *Adversus Jovinianum* II, 1 (*PL* 23, 295).

[241] Jerome, *Ep.* 133, 4 (*CSEL* 56, 248).

[242] See also Jerome, *Ep.* 133, 11 (*CSEL* 56, 258): the Pelagian heresy has won over many "who cleave to women and are assured that they cannot sin."

[243] Jerome, *Ep.* 133, 5 (*CSEL* 56, 248–249).

[244] Jerome, *Ep.* 133, 8 (*CSEL* 56, 252–253).

[245] Jerome, *Ep.* 133, 13 (*CSEL* 56, 259–260).

[246] Jerome, *Ep.* 133, 9 (*CSEL* 56, 254–255).

[247] Jerome, *Ep.* 133, 13 (*CSEL* 56, 260).

[248] Augustine, *Ep.* 166, to be considered below.

omission seems curious, given Jerome's declared position as a creationist. Somehow, he did not perceive that the origin of the soul was a key issue in the controversy he was waging with Pelagians. Instead, he strikes over and over at their alleged teaching on "sinlessness."

Jerome's fullest attack on Pelagian teaching comes in his *Dialogus adversus Pelagianos*, a work that reinforces the double thesis that Jerome saw the Pelagian dispute as a continuation of the Origenist controversy, and that his central concerns related to his views on ascetic striving. Just as the desert fathers had asked if *apatheia* were possible to achieve,[249] so Jerome considered the question in the context of Pelagian views regarding human agency and answered it with a resounding "no." Moreover, the *Dialogue* reflects Jerome's knowledge of the Palestinian councils that had approved Pelagius's teaching; the arguments and examples used by the Pelagian speaker in the *Dialogue*, Critobolus, parallel many of the points regarding the council discussions that are reported in *De gestis Pelagianorum* and by Orosius.[250]

In the *Dialogue*, Jerome repeatedly decries what he sees as the Origenist root of Pelagianism. Evagrius Ponticus is again faulted for imagining that perfectibility is possible, a view that makes him a bedfellow of Jovinian.[251] The Origenist heresy, Jerome claims, was spread further by Rufinus through his translation of *On First Principles*, and by Palladius[252]—an intriguing indication that Jerome had belatedly discovered Palladius's link to Evagrius, Rufinus, and Melania the Elder: his knowledge of Rufinus's network was apparently far from complete at the height of the Origenist debate.

The Origenist debate surfaces abruptly at several points in the text of the *Dialogue*. The spokesman for the "Catholic" position, Atticus, faults the Pelagian understanding of human perfectibility on the grounds that it takes away both the distinctions based on God's grace and those stemming from the variety of God's creation ("we might ask why we were made men and not angels"). He delivers a tirade against "your teacher, 'the Ancient' [*ho archaios*]"—that is, Origen[253]—who posited the equality of all rational beings at their creation and the diversity that resulted from their varying levels of descent. Embedded in Atticus's illustration is the very question

---

[249] See above, pp. 67–68, 83–84.

[250] The Catholic spokesman Atticus runs through a list of at least one hundred Pelagian propositions (see Jerome, *Dialogus* I, 32 [*PL* 23, 549]). Most points are standard Pelagian teaching, e.g., that the Kingdom of Heaven was proclaimed in the Old Testament (I, 31), that a man can be without sin and easily keep God's commands if he so chooses (I, 32), etc. Many of the points are

familiar from the charges against Pelagians raised in Carthage and at the Palestinian synods.

[251] Jerome, *Dialogus, prologus* 1 (*PL* 23, 518).

[252] Jerome, *Dialogus, prologus* 2 (*PL*, 519). Jerome also notes that Palladius aroused people against him for his (Vulgate) translation of Hebrew Scripture.

[253] Perhaps a pun on *Peri Archōn*?

that Rufinus had asked Jerome in a (now lost) letter that was answered in Jerome's *Apology against Rufinus*: why do huge elephants have only four feet when tiny fleas have six?[254] That is, how do we account for counter-intuitive diversity in the universe? Why does the created order frequently seem *not* to provide testimony for God's intelligent providence?

Moreover, Jerome in the *Dialogue* rules out Origen's teaching on the *apokatastasis*, including the restoration of the devil, as an appropriate Christian vision of the end time. But against the severity of Pelagian views on the Last Judgment, Catholics should hold that although the devil and impious heretics will be consigned to the eternal flames, Christians, even if sinful, will be saved after a period of chastisement.[255]

Last, Jerome concludes his *Dialogue* by again linking Origenism and Pelagianism: the Catholic spokesman, Atticus, exhorts his Pelagian interlocuter that if he believes that it is unjust to impute Adam's sin to others and that "those who could not sin"—that is, babies—have no need of remission, then he should "cross over to Origen," who thought that baptism was the "loosing of sins committed long ago in the heavens."[256] This is the closest that Jerome comes to affirming that a doctrine of original sin serves "structurally" to replace Origen's notion of the precosmic fall of the rational creatures: there must be *some* answer to explain human suffering and the Church's teaching of divine punishment that does not rest on the observed behavior of adult persons, yet makes them "accountable" for the penalties they endure.

Jerome also links the Origenist and Pelagian controversies to the earlier ascetic debate in the *Dialogue* through an appeal to Jovinian. The Pelagian who imagines that his "impassibility" allows him to mingle freely with women without the arousal of lust is called "Jovinian's heir"[257]—just as Evagrius, earlier in the *Dialogue*, had been linked with this teacher of perfectionism.[258] The arguments that Jerome had mounted over twenty years ago against Jovinian concerning degrees of human merit are here trotted out against Pelagian notions of perfectibility.[259] Jovinian's view that baptism renders Christians immune to temptation is seen by Jerome as reborn in Pelagian doctrine.[260] The Catholic spokesman, Atticus, advises a perusal of the *Adversus Jovinianum* to Pelagians, from which they would learn that

[254] Jerome, *Dialogus* I, 19 (*PL* 23, 536); cf. *Apologia* III, 28 (*CCL* 79, 100).

[255] Jerome, *Dialogus* I, 28 (*PL* 23, 544–546).

[256] Jerome, *Dialogus* III, 19 (*PL* 23, 618).

[257] Jerome, *Dialogus* II, 24 (*PL* 23, 588). It is interesting to see Jerome hurl an accusation at Pelagius that earlier had been directed at himself in Rome: see *Ep.* 45, 2–5 (*CSEL* 54, 324–327). Jerome seems especially piqued by Pelagius's success in attracting women to his cause: *Dialogus* III, 14; 16; I, 25 (*PL* 23, 611, 614, 542).

[258] Jerome, *Dialogus, prologus* 1 (*PL* 23, 518).

[259] Jerome, *Dialogus* I, 16 (*PL* 23, 532, 533); the same Biblical texts (John 14:2; I Cor. 15:41; Rom. 9:21) are used.

[260] Jerome, *Dialogus* III, 15; cf. III, 1 (*PL* 23, 613, 595).

although baptism gives remission for past sins, it provides no guarantees for the future: future righteousness requires much toil and effort, in addition to God's mercy.[261]

Such anti-Origenist and anti-Jovinianist arguments are folded into the anti-Pelagian arguments of the *Dialogue*. Although the treatise discusses at length issues of the will, grace, the goodness (or lack of thereof) in human nature,[262] the examples of allegedly righteous people named in Scripture, and other standard themes running throughout the debate, Jerome concentrates most strongly on the issues that Pelagius himself raised, not on those advanced by Caelestius and Julian. For example, there is almost no attention to the issue of the transmission of original sin and its implication for the justice of God. Only at the very end of the *Dialogue* does the Pelagian spokesman claim impatiently that he can no longer put off a burning question: what sin have little infants committed, infants who (in Jonah's words) "know not their right hand from their left"?[263] The Catholic respondent cites Paul in Romans 5, Cyprian's letter to Fidus on infant baptism, and several of Augustine's treatises;[264] but he has no arguments of his own to advance. Although the issue of God's justice had been raised in various ways throughout the *Dialogue*,[265] here, at the treatise's conclusion, the point that would dominate the discussion between Julian and Augustine is passed over with a final admonition that if Pelagians think that the doctrine of original sin is unjust, they had better go back to the Origenist solution.[266] It is here hard to judge whether Jerome is being uncustomarily perceptive or unusually dense.

In the same years in which Jerome was composing these anti-Pelagian treatises, he was also working on his *Commentary on Jeremiah*.[267] Here also, Jerome reveals that he considers the Pelagian controversy a continuation of the Origenist debate.[268] In the work's prologue, we learn that Pelagius had recently attacked Jerome's early *Commentary on Ephesians*, written in

---

[261] Jerome, *Dialogus* III, 1; cf. I, 22 (*PL* 23, 596, 539).

[262] Atticus, in pressing the theme of human sinfulness, uses a favorite Origenist text: Job 25:5 ("even the stars are unclean in God's sight") (*Dialogus* II, 24 [*PL* 23, 589]). For Origen, the text indicated that the astral bodies were rational creatures who "fell" (*De principiis* I, 7, 2 [*GCS* 22, 87]); for Atticus/Jerome, the text shows that humans must be *very* sinful if even the stars are unclean.

[263] Jerome, *Dialogus* III, 17 (*PL* 23, 614).

[264] Jerome, *Dialogus* III, 18–19 (*PL* 23, 615–617).

[265] Jerome, *Dialogus* I, 4; 6; 10; 23; II, 1; III, 5 (*PL* 23, 522, 523, 525, 540–541, 559,

601).

[266] Jerome, *Dialogus* III, 19 (*PL* 23, 618). It is interesting to note that Atticus thinks that Catholics are slandered as "Manicheans" because they favor the New Testament over the Old (*Dialogus* I, 31 [*PL* 23, 549]), not because of their denigration of the flesh and reproduction, the center of the accusation as directed at Augustine.

[267] The *Jeremiah Commentary* was begun about 414 and Jerome was still working on it in 416: see *CCL* 74, vii.

[268] Jerome, *In Hieremiam* IV, 41 (*CCL* 74, 210–211). Also see Claudio Moreschini, "Il contribuo di Gerolamo alla polemica antipelagiana," 61–71.

about 386; like Rufinus before him, his new attacker (an *"indoctus calumniator"*) does not know the rules of commentary writing—namely, that it is appropriate to list several interpretations and let the reader select the one he prefers.[269] By such a statement, Jerome means to let his readers know that not all the positions expressed in the *Commentary on Ephesians* were ones that he himself espoused.

Once again, it is the teaching on human perfection in both Origenism and Pelagianism that irritates Jerome: its partisans believe that the struggle is over.[270] They imagine that simply by following the Law, given as an *adiutorium*, they can live holy lives.[271] The Pelagian teaching on *apatheia* and *inpeccantia* is a dangerous carryover from the Origenists; the teaching originated with Pythagoras and Zeno, Jerome claims, but then infected the Christians through Origen, Rufinus, Evagrius Ponticus, and Jovinian.[272] Once again, we note the names of Evagrius and Jovinian linked for their alleged advocacy of perfectionism.

Thus Jerome fights the controversies of his past in his war against the Pelagians. Moreover, he fights the battle of the Pelagians' *own* past, that is, that of early Pelagianism: he seems not to sense the implications of the view of sin's transmission that were brought to the forefront by Caelestius and then Julian. Thus, although Jerome was an avowed creationist, he did not comprehend that he must bring his thesis on the soul's origin into conformity with his position on how original sin is transmitted. Whether "conformity" is *possible* on creationist grounds, Augustine was left to ponder. And that Augustine, the greatest thinker of the early Latin-speaking Church, could not resolve the question, leads one to reflect yet again whether Origenism did not, whatever its theological defects, at least provide a coherence that no other early Christian position—with the exception of Julian's version of Pelagianism—was able to match.

AUGUSTINE

Long before any Pelagians clouded his theological horizon, Augustine was interested in issues concerning determinism. As is well known and needs little further mention here, his campaign against Manicheanism marked his first polemical effort as a Christian convert. Less well explored is Augustine's interest in the questions—and the answers—posed by astral determinists. The question that especially caught Augustine's attention was the astrologers' claim that they could ex-

---

[269] Jerome, *In Hieremiam, prologus* 3 (CCL 74, 1).

[270] Jerome, *In Hieremiam* I, 17; VI, 6 (CCL 74, 15, 294).

[271] Jerome, *In Hieremiam* V, 5 (CCL 74, 238).

[272] Jerome, *In Hieremiam* IV, 1 (CCL 74, 174).

plain the diverse conditions of human life, a claim that Origen had set himself to refute in his attack on astral determinism in *On First Principles*.[273]

Augustine informs us in the *Confessions* that in his early life he was much intrigued by astrology.[274] He even hoped that the allegedly scientific approach adopted by astronomers and astrologers would help him to solve the questions concerning the sun, moon, and stars that had been wrongly answered by the Manicheans.[275] (To Augustine's great disillusionment, his would-be saviour, the Manichean Faustus, could not perform even the simple mathematical calculations necessary to deal with the astral bodies "scientifically.")[276] At long last, Augustine was "cured" of his penchant for astrology by the counsel of one wise friend[277] and by the discomforting results of "experiments" performed by another who showed that men born at exactly the same moment emerged with very different statuses in life. From these experiments, Augustine concluded that it must be pure luck if predictions based on the stars turned out to be true.[278]

A further disconfirmation of the truth of astrology was furnished by the young Augustine's reflection on the situation of twins: how can the discrepant destinies of Jacob and Esau be accounted for if astrological claims were true?[279] Since Jacob and Esau were conceived and born to the same parents at the same time, how, on the astrologer's premises, could their situations in life emerge so differently? Augustine will return to the example of Jacob and Esau in his exegesis of Romans 9 and in his debate with the Pelagians.

In the middle 390s, Augustine wrote his *Propositions on the Epistle to the Romans*, a piece directed against the Manichean interpretation of Paul.[280] Proposition 60 of the book concerns the fates of Jacob and Esau, as interpreted by Paul in Romans 9. Here, in an early attempt to address this vexed passage, Augustine claims that God chose Jacob and rejected Esau on the basis of his foreknowledge of Jacob's faith and Esau's unbelief.[281] God foreknew that Jacob would faithfully answer his call and merit the recep-

---

[273] Origen, *De principiis* I, *praefatio* 5 (*GCS* 22, 12–13). Later, Origen was accused of favoring astrology: Photius, *Bibliotheca* 117 (*PG* 103, 395); Theophilus of Alexandria, in Jerome, *Ep.* 92, 2 (*CSEL* 56, 150).

[274] Augustine, *Confessiones* IV, 3, 4; V, 3, 3; VII, 6, 8–10 (*CCL* 27, 41, 58, 97–99). Also see L. C. Ferrari, "Augustine and Astrology," 241–251; and E. Hendrikx, "Astrologie, Waarzeggerij en Parapsychologie bij Augustinus," 325–352.

[275] Augustine, *Confessiones* V, 3, 3; 5, 8; 7, 12 (*CCL* 27, 58, 60–61, 63).

[276] Augustine, *Confessiones* V, 7, 12 (*CCL* 27, 63).

[277] Augustine, *Confessiones* IV, 3, 5–6; VII, 6, 8 (*CCL* 27, 42–43, 97).

[278] Augustine, *Confessiones* VII, 6, 8 (*CCL* 27, 98).

[279] Augustine, *Confessiones* VII, 6, 10 (*CCL* 27, 99).

[280] Latin text and English translation in Paula Fredriksen Landes, *Augustine on Romans: Propositions from the Epistle to the Romans; Unfinished Commentary on the Epistle to the Romans*, ix.

[281] Augustine, *Prop.* 60, 9; 11 (Landes ed., 32).

tion of the Spirit, which in turn would enable him to perform good works. And Jacob would be accorded eternal life if by his free will he remained in the Spirit throughout his earthly days.[282] Thus according to Augustine's early interpretation of Romans, Paul does *not* abolish human free will in chapter 9.[283] As for the hardening of Pharaoh's heart, also mentioned in that chapter, we are to understand that God left Pharaoh to his own evil devices; God deserted him because of his impiety, and God's punishment of his unbelief was just.[284]

Augustine's early exegesis of Romans 9 is consistent with the position he had argued a few years before in *De libero arbitrio*,[285] although in the latter work he had argued philosophically, with little reference to Biblical texts. As stated in the first chapter of *On Free Will*, Augustine's central concern here is to show that God, who is both just and good, cannot be the author of evil.[286] Augustine thus rejects the views of those who hold that chance and accident rule rather than God's providence; by an appeal to the *patrocinium* of *fortuna*, they deny both God's judgment and human judgments.[287] Since Augustine confesses that God is both just and changeless, humans who suffer must be held to do so for sins they themselves have willed. In *On Free Will*, Augustine alludes to the difficulty of explaining the suffering and deaths of infants. He rejects the answer Origenists might pose (that the infants were paying for sins committed before they entered the human condition) and posits an alternative explanation, namely, that God is testing the adults who held their children dear.[288]

Such ideas concerning human freedom and God's justice posited by the young Augustine were similiar to those developed by Pelagius, not only because Pelagius had read Augustine's *De libero arbitrio*, but also because both theologies rest on an anti-Manichean (i.e., antideterminist), formulation of the problem.[289] Inevitably, questions of theodicy prompted Augustine in this work to consider theories of the soul's origin.[290] Yet later, in 412, when Count Marcellinus requested some explication of Augustine's position on the soul as he had expressed it in *De libero arbitrio* III,[291]

---

[282] Augustine, *Prop.* 60, 15 (Landes ed., 32).

[283] Augustine, *Prop.* 60, 2 (Landes ed., 30).

[284] Augustine, *Prop.* 62, 6–12; 16 (Landes ed., 34).

[285] *De libero arbitrio* was composed between 388 and 395: see chronological table B in Brown, *Augustine*, 74.

[286] Augustine, *De libero arbitrio* I, 1, 1–2 (*CCL* 29, 211).

[287] Augustine, *De libero arbitrio* III, 2, 5, 16 (*CCL* 29, 277).

[288] Augustine, *De libero arbitrio* III, 23, 66–88 (*CCL* 29, 314–315); Paula L. Fredriksen, *Augustine's Early Interpretation of Paul*, 180–190. It is of interest that Julius Firmicius Maternus (*Mathēseos* I, 7, 13 ff. and I, 8, 6) gives "fate" as the answer to the problems of the innocent sufferer and the deaths of newborns.

[289] Bohlin, *Die Theologie*, 50, 107.

[290] See Augustine, *De libero arbitrio* III, 11, 34, 118–119 (*CCL* 29, 295); see discussion in O'Connell, *Origin*, chap. 1.

[291] Augustine, *Ep.* 143, 5 (*CSEL* 44, 255);

Augustine proclaimed the matter "obscure":[292] probably he no longer wished to claim the views he had espoused two decades or more earlier.

From youth to old age, Augustine retained interest in the theories of the astrologers and took pains to refute them—and this despite his ever-growing propensity to predestinarian theory. Most interesting for our purposes, the question of Jacob and Esau still continues, in 397, to be posed by Augustine within the framework of *astrological* debate, perhaps because the antiastrological argument about the diverse fate of twins was easy to apply to the case of Jacob and Esau. According to Augustine in the *Ad Simplicianum*, the fact that Jacob and Esau were conceived by the same parents in the same moment leaves no room for the theories of the astrologers and the *genethliaci* (a type of astrologer who predicted an individual's life course on the basis of his moment of birth), for their fates were diverse: Jacob was loved by God and Esau hated. By the time Augustine wrote *Ad Simplicianum*, he had ruled out three views: that astral determinism provides an explanation for the diverse fates of Jacob and Esau;[293] that their fates were a result of God's foreknowledge of their respective deeds[294] (Pelagius's answer, although unbeknownst to Augustine in 397); and that their respective faith and unbelief made the difference in their situations, the solution Augustine had himself posited a few years before in his *Propositions on the Epistle to the Romans*, but now abandons on the basis of his new reading of Romans.[295] All now rests on God's decree alone. With this move in the *Ad Simplicianum*, William Babcock argues, "Augustine has, in effect, sacrificed both man's freedom and God's justice on the altar of the sheer gratuity of God's grace, unqualified by even a residual correlative with man's merit."[296] Augustine himself, of course, would rebut this assessment, but nonetheless struggled with the issue of human freedom and God's justice to the end of his days.

In pre-Pelagian works other than those cited above, Augustine vigorously rejects the validity of astrology and repudiates the moral consequences of its teaching. In *On Eighty-Three Diverse Questions*, for example,

---

see O'Connell, *Origin*, 118–129.

[292] Augustine, *Ep.* 143, 11 (*CSEL* 44, 261). Marcellinus then wrote to Jerome for assistance: see above, p. 222, and cf. Augustine, *Ep.* 190.

[293] Augustine, *Ad Simplicianum* I, 2, 3 (*CCL* 44, 25–27). On the interpretation of Romans 9 in this treatise, see Peter Gorday, *Principles of Patristic Exegesis: Romans 9–11 in Origen, John Chrysostom, and Augustine*, 168–169; and Fredriksen, *Augustine's Early Interpretation*, 196–208.

[294] Augustine, *Ad Simplicianum* I, 2, 11 (*CCL* 44, 36).

[295] Augustine, *Ad Simplicianum* I, 2, 5 (*CCL* 44, 29–30).

[296] William S. Babcock, "Augustine's Interpretation of Romans (A.D. 394–396)," 67. For an assessment more sympathetic to Augustine, see Alister E. McGrath, "Divine Justice and Divine Equity in the Controversy Between Augustine and Julian of Eclanum," 312–319. McGrath argues that Augustine's study of Romans in the mid-390s led him to abandon a Ciceronian view of justice (that each person is rendered what is due him), a view that Julian of Eclanum retained.

he employs the twins argument to combat the *mathematici*: whether one calculates by the moment of conception or by the moment of birth, astrology cannot account for the difference in the twins' fates. And in any case, astrological observation is not precise enough to calculate down to the very second.[297] A second example: in *On Christian Doctrine*, he mocks the man who, free when he consults the *mathematici* or the *genethliaci*, pays money to become a servant of Mars, Venus, and the stars.[298] Again in this treatise, he cites the case of twins who, although born under the same constellations, experience diverse fortunes.[299] And Augustine uses the same argument once more in the *De Genesi ad litteram*.[300] In this "literal" commentary on Genesis, Augustine also explains that when God refers to the astral bodies as "signs" in Genesis 1:14, he indicates that they should be used in navigation and for noting the change of the seasons,[301] not for being put to the evil uses of the astrologers. If we were to believe the astrologers, we would take away any reason for prayer, and would not be able to assign blame for evil actions.[302]

The case of twins, with Jacob and Esau as case-in-point, reappears in *Confessions*, Book VII, probably written in the last years of the fourth century: Augustine again argues that the very short interval between the births of twins cannot account for their diverse fates.[303] It is interesting that the presentation of the twins argument in *Confessions* VII, 6, is framed by a discussion about the origin of evil: where could evil have come from if God made all things good?[304] After considering astrology as a possible explanation for the diverse fates of humans and rejecting it, Augustine rounds out his discussion with an affirmation of the great justice by which God rules the universe, which we, mere mortals, cannot question.[305] The organization of this section of the *Confessions* shows how closely tied in Augustine's mind were the problems of astral determinism, human fate, and God's justice. Rejecting the astrologers' answer to these thorny questions, Augustine searched for more suitable theological resolutions.

From his first anti-Pelagian works onward, Augustine confronted the questions of human freedom and God's justice, as had Origen before him, but gave the questions a different solution, namely, the transmission of original sin from Adam to the entire human race. When his Pelagian

---

[297] Augustine, *De diversis quaestionibus LXXXIII* 45, 2 (*CCL* 44A, 68–69).

[298] Augustine, *De doctrina Christiana* II, 21, 32 (*CCL* 32, 55–56).

[299] Augustine, *De doctrina Christiana* II, 22, 33 (*CCL* 32, 56–57).

[300] Augustine, *De Genesi ad litteram* II, 17, 36 (*PL* 34, 278).

[301] Augustine, *De Genesi ad litteram* II, 14, 29 (*PL* 34, 275).

[302] Augustine, *De Genesi ad litteram* II, 17, 35 (*PL* 34, 278). The argument for prayer is also raised in *De civitate Dei* V, 1 (*CCL* 47, 128–129).

[303] Augustine, *Confessiones* VII, 6, 10 (*CCL* 27, 99).

[304] Augustine, *Confessiones* VII, 5, 7; 7, 11 (*CCL* 27, 96–97, 100).

[305] Augustine, *Confessiones* VII, 6, 10 (*CCL* 27, 99).

opponents declared that his theory was unfair to innocent sufferers such as babies and thus called into question God's justice, Augustine responded that original sin was the very doctrine *needed* to uphold God's justice, since without the premise of infants' sinfulness, we would have no way to account for their miseries—nor for what Augustine claimed was Church teaching, that the unbaptized ones who die will be cast into hell.[306]

In his first anti-Pelagian writing, *De peccatorum meritis*, conventionally dated to 411–412,[307] Augustine considers Paul's words on Jacob and Esau in Romans 9 and asks how the diverse fates of individuals can be accounted for. He rehearses the Origenist answer, without naming it as such, and rejects it: we did not sin earlier in the heavens and then pass down to the world in bodies that suited our degree of sinfulness. Although this myth *does* provide an explanation for the diversity of deserts, Augustine admits, the teaching is "an improbable fable," far removed from Christian teaching on God's grace.[308] Moreover, the Origenist solution is ruled out by Paul's words in Romans 9:11 (that Jacob and Esau were, respectively, elected and rejected, "although they were not yet born and had done nothing either good or bad").[309] The answer lies in the original sin we acquire by our natural births,[310] the "sinful flesh" of the parents acting as a conduit that allows the transfer of the "injury" to the child.[311] Yet Augustine here, as to the end of his anti-Pelagian writings, refuses to link his teaching with a particular theory on the origin of the soul. He asks whether the soul is propagated along with the body and replies that he does not know, since Scripture does not give "clear and certain proofs" on the point.[312] Augustine tries to ally Pelagius with him in his indecision, an attempt that seems dubious since Pelagians, when they declared themselves on the issue, were creationists.

Bypassing a theory of the soul's origin, Augustine instead substitutes a theory of original sin: "If the soul is *not* propagated," he asks, "where is the justice that infants, who have just been created and are free from the contagion of sin, should be compelled to suffer the passions and other fleshly

---

[306] On *Sermo* 294, see E. R. Fairweather, "Saint Augustine's Interpretation of Infant Baptism," II: 897–904.

[307] O'Connell opposes this dating, arguing that *De meritis* must have been emended after 415 because Augustine doesn't apprehend until that date that Romans 9:11 is the key verse to stand against the view of souls sinning in a heavenly preexistence (*Origin*, 13–14, 113–114, 104, 326). Refoulé, in contrast, accepts the traditional dating of *De meritis* and argues that the work is aimed at Rufinus the Syrian's *Libellus fide* ("Datation," esp. 47).

[308] Augustine, *De peccatorum meritis* I, 22, 31 (*CSEL* 60, 29–31).

[309] Augustine, *De peccatorum meritis* III, 9, 17 (*CSEL* 60, 143). On Augustine's qualification of Romans 9:11 to allow for a life before our "proper life," see O'Connell, *Origin*, 209–210, 243–244, 308–311.

[310] Augustine, *De peccatorum meritis* I, 9, 9 (*CSEL* 60, 10–11).

[311] Augustine, *De peccatorum meritis* III, 2, 2 (*CSEL* 60, 130).

[312] Augustine, *De peccatorum meritis* II, 36, 59 (*CSEL* 60, 127–128).

torments and even worse, the attacks of evil spirits?"[313] In other words, the trouble with the creationist option is that it allows no clear way to attribute sinfulness to babies—and if they are not sinful, how can we claim that they *deserved* the miseries they suffer? Augustine here sounds as if he might espouse the traducianist option, but doesn't. Probably the materialist notions of the soul that attached themselves to traducian theory were repellent to him.

Robert O'Connell, in *The Origin of the Soul in Augustine's Writings*, provides an exhaustive account of Augustine's struggle with the question of how we can be said to be "in Adam" when he sinned, so that *we* can be said to have sinned as well. O'Connell argues that Augustine gradually adopted the view that we had lives before our individual (*propria*) lives, a theory in accord with a notion of "the fall of the soul" that stems, O'Connell believes, from Plotinus's writings.[314] Thus Augustine will hold that we sinned, but before we were born into our "own, proper life."[315] O'Connell thinks that once Augustine developed this notion of the "proper life," he emended his already composed treatise *De peccatorum meritis* to claim that "even infants may be guilty with a guilt that is their own and yet a guilt contracted in a life that was not their 'proper' life."[316] This discovery gave Augustine a way to speak of prenatal sin, but one undergirded by a different theology than had supported Origen's scheme.[317] O'Connell argues that the new theory of the "life in Adam" as a precedent to one's "proper life" gave Augustine the tools to answer Pelagius's question of how infants without developed reason and wills could be said to sin: namely, that "we *were* Adam in his primal act of sinning."[318] Whether or not we deem this a sufficient "answer" to the Pelagian complaint against Augustine, O'Connell is surely on the right track in claiming that Augustine struggled to construct a view of the soul's origin and fall that would exempt him from the implications of Origenist cosmology, on the one hand, but answer the pressing problems of theodicy, on the other.

Augustine also tried to reason about original sin and its transmission to infants from the point of view of the Church's practice. Although his sermons are difficult to date, *Sermon* 294, "On the Baptism of Infants, Against the Pelagians," may stand relatively early in his anti-Pelagian period.[319] In this sermon, Augustine tried to reconcile the fate of infants who died without benefit of baptism—namely, eternal punishment—with the justice of God. Rejecting the view he reports some Pelagians held, that unbaptized

---

[313] Augustine, *De peccatorum meritis* III, 10, 18 (*CSEL* 60, 144).

[314] For the Neo-Platonic roots, see O'Connell, *Origin*, 38, 221, 337–350.

[315] O'Connell, *Origin*, esp. 196, 299–305, 308–310.

[316] O'Connell, *Origin*, 326.

[317] O'Connell, *Origin*, 15, 328.

[318] O'Connell, *Origin*, 335.

[319] Dating proposed in *Oeuvres complètes de Saint Augustin*, XVIII, 528n.1. See Fairweather, "Saint Augustine's Interpretation," 898–903.

babies are assured of eternal life because they have no sin, but cannot ascend to the Kingdom of Heaven without the sacrament,[320] Augustine replies that the parable of the Last Judgment in Matthew 25 affords us only two options: heaven or hell.[321] If unbaptized infants are excluded from the Kingdom of Heaven, there is no other place for them but the eternal flames,[322] and he adduces John 3:5 in support ("unless one is born of water and the Spirit, he cannot enter the Kingdom of God").[323] Interestingly, Augustine concedes that he hasn't yet found any really good reason for this position beyond Scripture, but he is sure that there must be one. In the meantime, we should not "condemn divine authority" because of our human weakness.[324]

In 414 and the years thereafter, Augustine appears to have gained further information on the Origenist position regarding the soul, and to have rejected it. Writing to Evodius in 414, he states that he "utterly rejects" (but gives no reason for doing so) the notion that the soul is cast into the body as into a prison, where it atones for "former actions of its own of which I know nothing."[325] In 415, probably prompted by Orosius's arrival from Spain and report to Augustine on Priscillianism and Origenism, Augustine has more to say about the soul. Orosius's informants have told him that although Origenists believe that the soul was created, they do not think that it came "from nothing." Orosius himself expresses doubt as to whether they have gotten Origen's position straight.[326] He goes on to list other errors of Origen: that all rational beings were derived from one principle and were assigned to their varying positions on the basis of merit; that the world was created to provide a place of purification for sinful souls; that the "eternal fires" are not really eternal; that the devil along with sinners will be restored in the end; that Christ will come to the various rational powers, assuming their own forms, as he assumed the "likeness of men."[327] But Orosius's report was not, we gather, of prime importance to Augustine for information on Origenist theories regarding the soul.[328] Au-

---

[320] See Refoulé, "La Distinction," 247–254 on this topic.

[321] Augustine, *Sermo* 294, 2–3 (*PL* 38, 1336–1337). Pelagius used this passage to condemn sinful adult Christians: see above, pp. 211–212.

[322] Augustine, *Sermo* 294, 4, 4 (*PL* 38, 1337–1338).

[323] Augustine, *Sermo* 294, 8, 9 (*PL* 38, 1340).

[324] Augustine, *Sermo* 294, 7, 7 (*PL* 38, 1339).

[325] Augustine, *Ep.* 164, 7, 20 (*CSEL* 44, 539); see O'Connell, *Origin*, 145–149.

[326] Orosius, *Commonitorium* 3 (*CCL* 49, 161). On Augustine's response to Orosius,

see J. A. Davids, *De Orosio et Sancto Augustino Priscillianistarum adversariis commentatio historica et philologica*, 247–254.

[327] Orosius, *Commonitorium* 3 (*CCL* 49, 161–162).

[328] In his *Liber apologeticus* 16, 3 (*CSEL* 5, 626), Orosius had faulted the doctrine of *anamartētos*; in his letter to Augustine that prefaces Augustine's *Ad Orosium*, he refers to Origen along with Priscillian (3 [*CCL* 49, 160–161]), but in neither passage does he convey any useful information on Origenism. For Orosius's failure to appreciate some of the nuances of Eastern and Pelagian theology, see A. Hamman, "Orosius de Braga et le pélagianisme," 346–355.

gustine responds that he understands why some have problems affirming that the soul came "from nothing" when it was created by the will of God; it is more proper to assert that it did not come "from matter."[329] Augustine next comments on various of the other points raised by Orosius,[330] but he does not center on the issue of creationism versus traducianism, as we might have expected.

Also in 415, Augustine seeks Jerome's views on the issue of the soul's origin in a letter that he sent (presumably) via Orosius.[331] On some points, Augustine reports, he feels certain, such as that the soul is not part of God, nor is it material.[332] But beyond this lie thorny questions of how the soul contracted the guilt that condemns infants who die unbaptized.[333] Years earlier, when he composed *On Free Will*, he had outlined four possible options concerning the soul's origin, and now Jerome, in his reply to Count Marcellinus, has added a fifth.[334] Since Augustine is sure that Jerome both believes in original sin[335] *and* holds a creationist position on the soul,[336] perhaps he can advise Augustine on how to harmonize the two affirmations. If souls are made daily, how do infants acquire sin? If they don't have sin at birth, it would not be compatible with God's justice to condemn them.[337] Augustine admits that his arguments in *On Free Will*, such as that by the suffering and death of children God reproves their parents, now seem unsatisfactory.[338] Origen's theory, resting on a notion of cycles, fails to provide any sense of final *security* for Christians or for their future happiness, and hence must be ruled out.[339] The problem becomes acute when we consider the issue of those who die unbaptized:[340] whatever opinion on the soul turns out to be "right" must be in accord with the Church's dogma that infants must be baptized to be saved from perdition.[341]

Jerome, as we have seen, chose not to respond to Augustine's inquiry on

---

[329] Augustine, *Ad Orosium* 2, 2 (*CCL* 49, 165–166).

[330] Augustine, *Ad Orosium* 5, 5–9, 12 (*CCL* 49, 168–175).

[331] Augustine, *Ep.* 166, 1, 2 (*CSEL* 44, 547); see discussion in O'Connell, *Origin*, 150–167.

[332] Augustine, *Ep.* 166, 2, 3–4 (*CSEL* 44, 548–553).

[333] Augustine, *Ep.* 166, 3, 6 (*CSEL* 44, 554–555).

[334] Augustine, *Ep.* 166, 3, 7 (*CSEL* 44, 555–557): that all souls are propagated from Adam's; that they are created singly for each person; that they were created earlier and are stored in heaven to the time that they are sent into (or alternatively, spontaneously join with) bodies. The fifth position raised in Jerome's letter (*Ep.* 126) is that the soul is an emanation of God's substance. See above, p. 222.

[335] Augustine, *Ep.* 166, 3, 6; 7, 21 (*CSEL* 44, 554, 577).

[336] Augustine, *Ep.* 166, 4, 8 (*CSEL* 44, 557).

[337] Augustine, *Ep.* 166, 4, 10; 6, 16 (*CSEL* 44, 560–561, 568–570).

[338] Augustine, *Ep.* 166, 7, 18–19 (*CSEL* 44, 571–574); cf. *De libero arbitrio* III, 23, 68, 229–230 (*CCL* 29, 315).

[339] Augustine, *Ep.* 166, 9, 27 (*CSEL* 44, 583).

[340] Augustine, *Ep.* 166, 7, 20 (*CSEL* 44, 574–575).

[341] Augustine, *Ep.* 166, 9, 28 (*CSEL* 44, 584–585).

the origin of the soul. I suspect that Jerome did not *know* the answer to Augustine's question; from his writings, we would not gather that he had even considered the issue problematic. It is highly significant that Augustine here presses Jerome hard on the notion of the soul's origin: Augustine has sensed that this question *must* be answered by anyone seeking to uphold creationism and original sin at the same time. Since Jerome did both, Augustine apparently—and incorrectly—assumed that he had considered the links between the two theories. Jerome, I think, had not. Augustine was thus thrown back onto his own resources: he turned to Oceanus to ask if *he* knew what Jerome's position was.[342]

In 417 (probably), we see Augustine making another attempt at addressing the problem in *Sermo* 165, an anti-Pelagian tract.[343] Without mentioning Origen by name, Augustine attacks the Origenist theory of souls: his hearers are enjoined to dismiss the "empty fables" of those who say that souls sinned first in heaven and receive bodies ("as if prisons") in accord with their sins. Paul's words in Romans 9:11 are again cited against the view.[344] Also to be corrected are those who imagine that each man dies only for his own sins, not for those of Adam: on this account, there would be no explanation for the deaths of babies, who do not yet have personal sin. Both Scripture (I Corinthians 15:22; Romans 5:12) and the experience of infants' deaths support the notion that original sin brings death. That babies have inherited sin from Adam is given support by a consideration of their vigorous resistance to baptism.[345]

By 418, a new dimension of the debate had made its appearance that would change its terms forever: the subject of marriage, sexual functioning, and reproduction had been raised in relation to the issue of original sin. In his treatises from this period, *De gratia Christi et de peccato originali*, *De civitate Dei* XIV, and *De nuptiis et concupiscentia* I[346]—that is, the works he wrote immediately before he learned of Julian's first onslaught against him—Augustine took on a new and difficult challenge, arguing that a theory of original sin's transmission does *not* harm "the good of marriage."[347]

Only between Book I and Book II of *De nuptiis et concupiscentia* did

---

[342] Augustine, *Ep.* 180 (*CSEL* 44, 697–700).

[343] The sermon is throughout an anti-Pelagian homily, centering on such topics as the necessity of grace, the insufficiency of the human will, and the death of infants because of the sin of Adam.

[344] Augustine, *Sermo* 165, 5, 6 (*PL* 38, 905).

[345] Augustine, *Sermo* 165, 6, 7 (*PL* 38, 906).

[346] For Augustine's discussion of the chronology of his and Julian's works, see his preface to the *Opus imperfectum* (*CSEL* 85¹, 3–4).

[347] See esp. *De gratia Christi* II, 33, 38–40, 46 (*CSEL* 42, 196–205); *De civitate Dei* XIV, 21–22 (*CCL* 48, 443–444); and *De nuptiis et concupiscentia* I, 4, 5–7, 8; 17, 19 (*CSEL* 42, 215–220, 231–232). In *De gratia Christi* II, 31, 36 (*CSEL* 42, 195), the view that infants are requited in this life for deeds they committed in another is attributed to "certain Platonists," and Romans 9:11 is adduced against them.

Augustine learn of Julian's polemic against him. Count Valerius, to whom Augustine had addressed Book I of the work, sent him "a few sentences" from Julian's *Ad Turbantium*,[348] to which Valerius requested Augustine's response. Whereas in Book I of *De nuptiis*, Augustine had largely reiterated points from his earlier writings on the "goods" of marriage and had affirmed the transmission of original sin to children even by regenerated parents, he now was forced to defend his views against Julian's complaint that they were "Manichean," a charge that Julian scored over and again in his "few sentences": the theory of original sin and its transmission degraded marriage and reproduction.[349] Julian repeatedly pressed Augustine to give a more precise account of "where the sin comes from." Does Augustine wish to fault gender differentiation, sexual intercourse, or fertility?[350] Does he imply that God made his image, man, for the devil?[351] Does Augustine imagine that infants have wills that they can be accused of sinning?[352] In several passages, Julian hints that the honor and justice of God are at stake. Was God so lacking in resources, he asks, that the only reward he could manage to bestow on holy men was to allow the devil to infuse them with "vitiation?"[353] Does Augustine, who *claims* that he believes in the goodness of reproduction, imagine that that God used the procreative act so that the devil could win dominion over human beings?[354] The implications of Julian's arguments are clear: and a God who would do such things is not worthy of the title.

With Book II of *De nuptiis*, Augustine begins the struggle that would occupy him throughout the rest of his life. His answer to Julian here, as elsewhere, is twofold: the Bible teaches a doctrine of original sin and Church practice confirms it. Romans 5 is the central court of appeal in the Bible.[355] For Church practice, Augustine points to the customs of the exorcism and exsufflation of infants before their baptisms. These practices show that infants are considered to be under "the power of darkness," from which they need release through baptism.[356] Cyprian is appealed to as a defender of infant baptism, and Augustine makes out that his martyred episcopal predecessor espoused the practice for the same reasons that he did, namely, for the erasure of original sin.[357]

[348] Augustine, *Opus imperfectum* I, *praefatio* 2 (*CSEL* 85¹, 3).

[349] Augustine, *De nuptiis* II, 3, 7; 19, 34; 23, 38; 29, 49; 29, 50 (*CSEL* 42, 258–259, 287–288, 291–293, 304–305, 305–307).

[350] Augustine, *De nuptiis* II, 4, 13 (*CSEL* 42, 264–265).

[351] Augustine, *De nuptiis* II, 16, 31 (*CSEL* 42, 284).

[352] Augustine, *De nuptiis* II, 27, 44 (*CSEL* 42, 297–298).

[353] Augustine, *De nuptiis* II, 13, 27 (*CSEL* 42, 280).

[354] Augustine, *De nuptiis* II, 27, 44 (*CSEL* 42, 298).

[355] Cited by Augustine in *De nuptiis* II, 5, 15; 8, 20; 27, 45; 27, 46; 27, 47; 29, 50 (*CSEL* 42, 266, 272, 298–299, 299–300, 302, 306).

[356] Augustine, *De nuptiis* II, 29, 50; 29, 51 (*CSEL* 42, 306, 307–308).

[357] Augustine, *De nuptiis* II, 29, 51 (*CSEL* 42, 307–308).

By the end of Book II of *De nuptiis*, the argument between Julian and Augustine has centered on babies. Augustine claims that it is on the "behalf of infants" that he labors in writing his treatise. He paints himself and his partisans as the merciful deliverers of babies over against Pelagians, whose position toward infants Augustine deems "cruel."[358] Augustine reasons that since Christ died for infants as well as for adults, they *must* be held guilty. To Julian's question, *"How* are they guilty?" Augustine can only respond, "How are they *not* guilty, since Christ died for them?"[359] "Jesus is Jesus even to infants," and to exempt them from salvation is a deadly trick of the Pelagians.[360] It is notable that in this treatise Augustine does not directly address the question of the origin of the soul, but this theme he will take up in treatises he wrote soon thereafter: *On the Soul and Its Origin* and *Against Two Letters of the Pelagians.*

In *De anima et ejus origine*, Augustine responds to a certain Vincentius Victor, who believed that the soul was material,[361] although he accepted a creationist position on the soul's origin.[362] Although he—unlike the Pelagians—thought that infants had original sin, Augustine reports, he excused them from it and granted them acceptance in Paradise.[363] It is no surprise to find Augustine upholding the incorporeality of the soul over against Vincentius Victor.[364] More surprising is that although Augustine claims that he does not know the origin of the soul and that we had best leave God's mysteries to God,[365] he unleashes an arsenal of criticisms against Vincentius Victor's attempt to prove that creationism is supported by Scripture. He takes the Biblical texts that his opponent had listed as "proof" and argues that a firm creationist line cannot be drawn from them[366]—and it is from Scripture alone, Augustine asserts, that we can draw our proofs for Christian doctrine.[367] Augustine is careful to state that he does not *object* to the creationist view; he just can't find any evidence in either reason or Scripture for its defense.[368]

Two points about the soul, Augustine thinks, *can* be strongly affirmed:

[358] Augustine, *De nuptiis* II, 35, 60 (*CSEL* 42, 318–319).

[359] Augustine, *De nuptiis* II, 33, 56 (*CSEL* 42, 313).

[360] Augustine, *De nuptiis* II, 35, 60 (*CSEL* 42, 319).

[361] Augustine, *De anima et ejus origine* I, 5, 5 (*CSEL* 60, 306).

[362] Augustine, *De anima* I, 14, 17 (*CSEL* 60, 317).

[363] Augustine, *De anima* I, 9, 11; II, 12, 17 (*CSEL* 60, 312, 351).

[364] Augustine, *De anima* I, 4, 4; 5, 5; IV, 12, 18–18, 28 (*CSEL* 60, 305–306, 306–307, 397–408).

[365] Augustine, *De anima* IV, 4, 5; 6, 8; 11, 16; 24, 38 (*CSEL* 60, 384, 388–389, 395, 418–419).

[366] Augustine, *De anima* I, 14, 17–17, 28 (*CSEL* 60, 317–329), discussing such verses as Isaiah 42:5; 57:16; John 20:22; Zechariah 12:1; II Maccabees 7:22–23; Acts 17:25, 28.

[367] Augustine, *De anima* III, 9, 12 (*CSEL* 60, 369–370). The story of Dinocrates from the *Passion of Perpetua and Felicitas* is counted as inadmissible evidence since it does not come from canonical Scripture.

[368] Augustine, *De anima* I, 19, 33 (*CSEL* 60, 333).

that souls were made by the Creator and that they are not of God's substance.[369] Beyond this, he desires a theory that will "vindicate God's righteous will."[370] How to construct such a theory here escapes him, except to deny the (Origenist) view that souls sinned in some state previous to this life and hence are condemned to a fleshly existence: Romans 9:11 stands against the theory.[371] Again he appeals to the necessity of baptism for entrance to the Kingdom of Heaven—and if all must be baptized to be saved, then all must be sinful.[372] Thus original sin emerges as the "answer" to the question about the soul,[373] even *without* any resolution of the problem of the soul's origin. For Augustine, our ignorance on this question furnishes one more example of how poorly we comprehend ourselves: we don't even recall if we once *did* know about the origin of the soul and "forgot," or whether we never knew. The mysteries of memory are beyond our grasp.[374] Nor is the soul's origin a point on which medical men can give us any assistance.[375]

Against Two Letters of the Pelagians was addressed to Boniface of Rome and attempted to refute the views of Julian and his Italian colleagues who had refused to sign Zosimus's *Tractoria*.[376] In these letters—examined above in the discussion of Julian[377]—the charge of "Manicheanism" had been levelled against Augustinian views,[378] the issue of the salvation of infants had been argued,[379] and the Church's baptismal practices examined.[380] In reply, Augustine once more rests his case with a refusal to pronounce on the origin of the soul, although he of course claims that infants contract original sin prior to birth.[381] Of interest for our argument, however, is the zeal with which Julian and his colleagues in their letters had pushed the charge of "fatalism," and the equal zeal with which Augustine defends himself against this allegation. Augustine tries rather to turn their accusation of fatalism back against *them*: if Pelagians do not accept the notion of preexistent merits or demerits, whether heavenly or earthly, as the explanation for why some babies die before they receive the good of

---

[369] Augustine, *De anima* IV, 24, 38 (*CSEL* 60, 418).

[370] Augustine, *De anima* IV, 11, 16 (*CSEL* 60, 395).

[371] Augustine, *De anima* I, 12, 15 (*CSEL* 60, 314).

[372] Augustine, *De anima* I, 11, 13; II, 12, 17 (*CSEL* 60, 313, 351–352).

[373] Augustine, *De anima* I, 13, 16; IV, 11, 16 (*CSEL* 60, 316–317, 395–396).

[374] Augustine, *De anima* IV, 6, 8–7, 10 (*CSEL* 60, 388–390). Augustine had been finishing *De Trinitate* and was much interested in memory; see O'Connell, *Origin*, 267–274. Note that in *De anima* IV, 6, 8 (*CSEL* 60, 388), Augustine still appears to

be contemplating a "fall of the soul."

[375] Augustine, *De anima* IV, 6, 7 (*CSEL* 60, 387–388).

[376] Augustine, *Contra duas epistolas Pelagianorum* I, 1, 3; II, 1, 1 (*CSEL* 60, 424, 460).

[377] See above, pp. 217–221.

[378] Augustine, *Contra duas epistolas* I, 2, 4; 5, 10; II, 1, 1 (*CSEL* 60, 425, 431, 460).

[379] Augustine, *Contra duas epistolas* I, 6, 11; IV, 4, 5; 5, 9 (*CSEL* 60, 431, 525, 529–530).

[380] Augustine, *Contra duas epistolas* II, 2, 3, (*CSEL* 60, 462–463).

[381] Augustine, *Contra duas epistolas* III, 10, 26 (*CSEL* 60, 518–519).

baptism, and if the Pelagians refuse to accept Augustine's solution (that it is only God's grace that permits some babies to live long enough to receive baptism before they expire), what other explanation is left to the Pelagians except that of "fate"?[382] But, claims Augustine, fate will not work as an explanation. He tries to prove his point by appealing to a hypothetical example: when twins were born to a harlot who left them to be exposed, one baby, but not the other, was rescued. Neither the infants nor the sinful parents had any merits of their own to account for why one of the babies was saved and baptized. But neither can astral determinism explain the diverse ends of the infants, since as twins, their constellations were exactly the same.[383] Their case can be compared to that of Jacob and Esau, Augustine notes. It is simply because God gives grace to Jacob that he is saved; and Esau, because he, like all of us, is taken from a sinful "mass," deserves God's rejection. This, says Augustine, is the correct interpretation of the story.[384]

We should pay close attention to Augustine's argument here: by a remarkably clever sleight-of-hand, Augustine has detached the twins example from the arsenal of the antideterminists (he himself earlier used the argument for this purpose) and has appropriated it to support his theory of predestination and the *massa peccati*. Despite his new predestinarian determinism, now bolstered by an antiastrological argument about the diverse fates of twins, Augustine remains convinced that the "vessels of wrath" that are rejected by God *deserve* their fate—for if they don't deserve it, God would be seen as unrighteous.[385] But *why* they "deserve" this treatment now hangs on the presumption of original sin, rather than on Origen's theory of precosmic or earthly sins, or on Pelagius's theory of God's foreknowledge of evil deeds and/or of actual evil deeds meriting punishment, or on Augustine's own early opinion regarding God's foreknowledge of a person's lack of faith.

Arguments about babies also occupy sections of Augustine's *Contra Julianum*. Church practice in exorcizing and exsufflating infants, Augustine argues, shows that Christian theology assumes that children are born in the grasp of "the power of darkness."[386] Their behavior at baptism—spitting and wailing—proves how much they resist God's saving grace.[387] Those who don't believe that babies are so delivered by God's grace (e.g.,

---

[382] Augustine, *Contra duas epistolas* II, 6, 11–12 (*CSEL* 60, 470–473). For Augustine and the Pelagians on infant baptism and the origin of the soul, see Fredriksen, *Augustine's Early Interpretation*, 238–250.

[383] Augustine, *Contra duas epistolas* II, 7, 14 (*CSEL* 60, 474–475).

[384] Augustine, *Contra duas epistolas* II, 7,

15; cf. II, 10, 22 (*CSEL* 60, 475–478, 483–484).

[385] Augustine, *Contra duas epistolas* IV, 6, 16 (*CSEL* 60, 538–540).

[386] Augustine, *Contra Julianum* VI, 5, 11 (*PL* 44, 829).

[387] Augustine, *Contra Julianum* IV, 8, 42 (*PL* 44, 759).

Julian) are enemies of children.[388] Yet Christ died for children, too,[389] as Julian's own father must have believed when he hastened with his infant son to the baptismal font, not knowing how ungrateful his son would later be.[390] Although Augustine refuses yet again to take a position on the soul's origin,[391] he insists that the doctrine of original sin must be upheld if for no other reason than to account for the sufferings of babies.[392]

And not only is it infants' early deaths that must be accounted for: birth defects also are cited as "proof" of the theory of original sin. If babies did not have evil from their origin, we cannot imagine them coming into the world with such deficiencies: "God forbid!" Augustine shudders.[393] Only justice and goodness can be ascribed to God,[394] so he is not to blame for the babies' plight. Since God in not unjust, he must be rendering to them what is due for sin.[395] Augustine once more offers a "logical" solution to such problems without adopting Origen's scheme.

Infants still occupy Augustine's mind in 428–429, when he wrote *On the Gift of Perseverance*. Here his predestinarian emphasis is at the fore. He admits that he made an error in *On Free Will* by claiming there that unbaptized infants would not be damned,[396] a view he has for years rejected.[397] But here, in *On the Gift of Perseverance*, Augustine wants to concentrate on the beneficent side of God's action. Since God is righteous in all he does, he assists even infants who "neither will nor run" (Romans 9:16), who in fact have no merits either of faith or of works. In contrast, there are some adults that God simply chooses not to help, even though he foresaw that if he worked miracles among them, they would have believed in him. We cannot "search out" God's judgments, but merely confess that "there is no unrighteousness with God" (Romans 9:14).[398] Such action of God *is* righteous, Augustine insists, since all of us deserve only punishment. Those who receive his help get something that they don't deserve; no one is wronged by his dispensation of a gracious gift to those whom he chooses.[399]

---

[388] Augustine, *Contra Julianum* III, 12, 25 (*PL* 44, 715).

[389] Augustine, *Contra Julianum* VI, 4, 8; 5, 13; 5, 14 (*PL* 44, 825, 829, 830–831).

[390] Augustine, *Contra Julianum* VI, 7, 17 (*PL* 44, 833).

[391] Augustine, *Contra Julianum* V, 4, 17; 15, 53 (*PL* 44, 794, 814).

[392] Augustine, *Contra Julianum* III, 3, 8–9 (*PL* 44, 705–706).

[393] Augustine, *Contra Julianum* III, 6, 13; cf. V, 15, 53 (*PL* 44, 709, 814).

[394] Augustine, *Contra Julianum* V, 10, 43 (*PL* 44, 809).

[395] Augustine, *Contra Julianum* II, 1, 3 (*PL* 44, 673).

[396] Augustine, *De dono perservantiae* 11, 27; 12, 30 (*PL* 45, 1009, 1010); cf. Augustine's retraction of some points in his earlier interpretation of Romans, in *De praedestinatione sanctorum* 3, 7; 4, 8 (*PL* 44, 964–965, 966).

[397] Augustine, *De dono perseverantiae* 9, 23 (*PL* 45, 1006).

[398] Augustine, *De dono perseverantiae* 11, 25 (*PL* 45, 1007).

[399] Augustine, *De dono perseverantiae* 12, 28; cf. 14, 35 (*PL* 45, 1009–1010, 1014): it is righteous of God to leave us in the "mass of ruin."

Most interesting, Augustine here centers on the issue of twins to make his point. Why is one twin child chosen and one rejected? The answer can be found in the parable of the laborers in the vineyard: the reward was simply from the graciousness of the master's will, and so it is with God and the twins.[400] It is not "fate" that decides the destiny of infants (as Pelagians like to call the gift of God's grace to some),[401] but God's providential direction of the universe.[402] Cleverly, Augustine argues that the fact that some children of believers die unbaptized (and hence are damned) shows that "God is no accepter of persons"; otherwise, he would assist the children of his devotees rather than those of unbelievers.[403] Augustine's Pelagian opponents probably did not relish his appropriation of their favorite Biblical verse.

In the *Ad Florum*, to which Augustine responded in his last book, the *Opus imperfectum contra Julianum*, Julian pushed his opponent one stage further: anyone who holds a theory of original sin's transmission, Julian claimed, *must* be a traducianist,[404] and to be a traducianist is equivalent to being a Manichean,[405] since both believe that evil natures are given to individuals at birth. Julian has no sympathy with Augustine's protest that he doesn't know the origin of souls[406] or how all humans are in one Adam.[407] In response, Augustine reverts to his earlier argument that it is Julian who is "cruel" to babies, for he doesn't allow them to be cured by the Savior's grace. Hasn't he read the angel's prediction to Joseph in Matthew 1:21, that Jesus would "save his people from their sins"?[408] To say, as Julian does, that babies suffer miseries when they have no sin is to say that God is unjust,[409] and thus inadvertently gives help to the Manicheans, who introduce an "evil nature" as an explanation.[410] And if we imply that infants' birth defects are attributed to an "evil and unjust artisan," we also aid the Manichean cause.[411] Without original sin, there would be no certainty that unbaptized infants who die are doomed as "vessels of dishonor."[412] From

[400] Augustine, *De dono perserverantiae* 8, 17 (*PL* 45, 1002–1003).

[401] Augustine, *De dono perserverantiae* 12, 29 (*PL* 45, 1010).

[402] Augustine, *De dono perserverantiae* 12, 31 (*PL* 45, 1011).

[403] Augustine, *De dono perserverantiae* 12, 31 (*PL* 45, 1012).

[404] Julian, *Ad Florum*, in Augustine, *Opus imperfectum* I, 6; 27; 66; 75, 1; II, 14; 142; 178, 1 (*CSEL* 85¹, 9, 23, 64, 91, 172, 297).

[405] Julian, *Ad Florum*, in Augustine, *Opus imperfectum* II, 27, 2; III, 10; 173 (*CSEL* 85¹, 181, 355, 474); IV, 5 (*PL* 45, 1342).

[406] Augustine, *Opus imperfectum* IV, 104

(*PL* 45, 1400).

[407] Augustine, *Opus imperfectum* II, 178, 3 (*CSEL* 85¹, 299).

[408] Augustine, *Opus imperfectum* I, 32; cf. I, 54; 117; II, 2; 236, 2–3 (*CSEL* 85¹, 24–25, 51, 134, 165, 349–350).

[409] Augustine, *Opus imperfectum* II, 236, 2 (*CSEL* 85¹, 349).

[410] Augustine, *Opus imperfectum* II, 110 (*CSEL* 85¹, 242–243).

[411] Augustine, *Opus imperfectum* III, 104 (*CSEL* 85¹, 424–425).

[412] Augustine, *Opus imperfectum* II, 117, 1–2 (*CSEL* 85¹, 249).

Augustine's standpoint, God's justice is under attack by anyone who thinks that human misery, from infancy on, is *not* the consequence of sin.[413] Original sin is therefore the necessary postulate for God's justice in Augustine's scheme, and the Church's baptismal practices serve as "proof" for the thesis.[414] It is remarkable that Augustine could argue the issue so meticulously and *still* avoid putting forth a theory of the soul's origin.

This outstanding "hole" in Augustine's theory—a hole that Origen had taken great care to plug in his own speculative scheme—is made embarrassingly manifest in a piece preserved as Pseudo-Jerome, *Epistle* 37.[415] Thought to have been composed within a decade or two after Augustine's death in 430, the treatise is constructed as a dialogue between Jerome and Augustine on the origin of the soul.[416] Although the author of the work,[417] perhaps constructing a school exercise in rhetoric,[418] calls both Jerome and Augustine "blessed,"[419] Jerome with his firmly argued creationist position appears to dominate the floundering Augustine—who, true to life, doesn't know what theory about the origin of the soul is correct. As we might suspect from this construction, the author of the work reveals himself as antitraducian in his introduction to the dialogue.[420] Rather than presenting Augustine as the superior theologian, the author casts him as pathetically begging his elder, Jerome, to instruct him on how the soul fell into sin,[421] on how the one soul of Adam came to be in his descendants.[422] Augustine is especially puzzled by how, on the creationist premise, sin could be ascribed to babies; "or, if they do not sin, where is the justice of God who makes them thus liable for the sin of another?"[423] How can infants be said to suffer justly the illnesses, hunger, thirst, demon possession, and other woes that they do, unless some evil lies behind the sufferings? Since the infants are not of an age to be held responsible for the performance of sinful deeds, some other solution needs to be posited,[424] for it is unimaginable that souls without guilt could be damned.[425] They must, therefore, be guilty.

---

[413] Augustine, *Opus imperfectum* I, 72, 3; 72, 6; II, 236, 2–3, (*CSEL* 85¹, 86, 87, 349).

[414] Augustine, *Opus imperfectum* III, 146, 1 (*CSEL* 85¹, 452–453); V, 9 (*PL* 45, 1439).

[415] See *Clavis Patrum Latinorum*, ed. E. Dekkers, 145 ("Pseudo-Hieronymus").

[416] Text in *PL* 30, 270–279.

[417] See Hans Von Schubert, *Der sogenannte Praedestinatus: Ein Beitrag zur Geschichte des Pelagianism*, 136–140.

[418] A suggestion made by Joseph Lien-hard.

[419] Pseudo-Jerome, *Ep.* 37, *praefatio* 7 (*PL* 30, 272).

[420] Pseudo-Jerome, *Ep.* 37, *praefatio* 3–5; 8–9 (*PL* 30, 270–271, 273).

[421] Pseudo-Jerome, *Ep.* 37 (*PL* 30, 274).

[422] Pseudo-Jerome, *Ep.* 37 (*PL* 30, 274).

[423] Pseudo-Jerome, *Ep.* 37 (*PL* 30, 275).

[424] Pseudo-Jerome, *Ep.* 37 (*PL* 30, 277; cf. 288).

[425] Pseudo-Jerome, *Ep.* 37 (*PL* 30, 278).

THEODICY

Pelagianism and Augustinianism have here been presented as two theological options, each driven by its own logic, to resolve the issue of how to reconcile God's justice with human freedom and suffering—especially the suffering of the innocent, of whom babies provide the exemplary case. The Pelagians, to whom the defense of God's justice was overridingly important, refused to entertain either the notion of demerits accrued in a former life (Origen's answer) or "original sin" (Augustine's answer). Although they apparently declined to give a *theological* explanation for the sufferings of the innocent,[426] this omission did not seem as significant to them as the "hole" that they found in Augustine's theory: that the transmission of original sin, which logically should have been linked to a traducianist position, was left by Augustine, at least in his published works, to float free of *any* view on the soul's origin. Rather, his postulate of original sin "stood in for" a theory of the soul's preexistence and fall into the body. It was Augustine's own, strikingly unique reconstruction of Origenist theodicy that was to influence all later Western theology.

---

[426] In this context, it is interesting to recall that the Pelagian Julian of Eclanum also refused to give a theological "explanation" for sexual desire, preferring to cite medical opinion on the "stirring up of the seed." See Julian in Augustine, *Contra Julianum* III, 13, 26 (*PL* 44, 715); and Elizabeth A. Clark, "Vitiated Seeds and Holy Vessels: Augustine's Manichean Past," in *Images of the Feminine in Gnosticism*, ed. Karen L. King, 367–401, esp. at 377; also printed in Clark's *Ascetic Piety and Woman's Faith: Essays on Late Ancient Christianity*, 291–349, esp. at 301; for Julian's anthropological arguments, 306–308. For an explication of Julian's views on "nature," see François Refoulé, "Julien d'Eclane," 66–72.

At the time when Origen composed his theological masterpiece, *On First Principles*, which was to become one focus of the later Origenist controversy, Christianity stood more open to varied expressions of the faith and required less in its affirmations of dogma than was the case one hundred and fifty years later. Considerable "tightening" of what constituted orthodoxy occurred in the intervening period, so that some questions debatable circa A.D. 230 were deemed dangerous by the turn to the fifth century. In the interim, "high" theology had centered on the doctrine of the Trinity: an exhausting sixty years and more of acerbic wrangling elapsed before an understanding of the *homoousia* permeated Christian theology at large. Thus when Rufinus of Aquileia insisted that he and other Christians were "orthodox" if they affirmed (only) the Incarnation of God in Jesus and the consubstantiality of members of the Godhead, he was pressing for a standard of orthodoxy that was itself in the process of being reconstructed.

Yet what had lapsed from consideration in the intervening years was just as important as what had been added: here as well, the teachings of Origen, as interpreted by later Origenists, often fell afoul of ecclesiastical scrutiny. By the first quarter of the fifth century, it struck many Christians as bizarre and unwelcome teaching for human intelligence to be thought akin to that of the sun, moon, and stars; for all rational beings including the devil to be deemed capable of sloughing off not just sin, but bodilessness itself, and of regaining their primordial contemplative ecstasy; for the justice of God to be confessed as the singular divine attribute that must be upheld at all costs. In the West particularly, the broad cosmic vision that had pervaded Origen's theology had shrunk: Christianity now clung more snugly to assertions of human sinfulness, ecclesiastical unity, and obedience to episcopal authority. This more rigid doctrinal dogmatism coupled with a retreat from issues of cosmology and theodicy created the religious grounding for the opposition to Origenism.

Yet another factor intervened between Origen's era and A.D. 400 that refocused the issues of the Origenist controversy: the development of an ascetic praxis and a theory to accompany it. In broad perspective, asceticism raised the question of the status of the body, of materiality itself. The question had, indeed, occupied the minds of second- and third-century Christian writers in their struggle with what they claimed was the Gnostic denigration of the created order, of reproduction, of the resurrection body. Ironically, although Origen's *own* project was cast in opposition to an alleged Gnostic "determinism" regarding "fixed natures,"[1] he was by the turn to the fifth century interpreted as a successor to the Gnostics in his denial that matter was part of the first creation or that it would be retained in the final spiritual unification of the universe, when God would be "all in all" (I Corinthians 15:28).

Origen's theology, in other words, became interwoven with the ascetic debate, centering especially on the writings of Jerome, that rumbled throughout the 380s and raged in the 390s. Thus the critiques of Origenism levelled by its opponents increasingly focused on issues pertaining to "the body," as I have shown especially in the cases of Epiphanius and Theophilus. The dispute surrounding the body also spilled over into the discussion of "the image of God": did humans retain it after the first sin, and did the phrase in any case imply that God was associated with corporeality? Did a teaching about "God's image" affect the way that Christians might understand the divine presence in the Eucharist and baptism? Did it influence issues of hermeneutics: was a "literal" or a "figurative" interpretation of Scripture to be preferred? Although the Trinitarian disputes of the fourth century doubtless left their mark on later discussions concerning language about God, the determining religious dispute with which the Origenist controversy of the late fourth and early fifth century intersected concerned asceticism. What to *our* contemporaries has sometimes appeared as a mere aberration of Christian praxis in late antiquity was, I posit, the core around which the ostensible controversy over Origen's writings wove and unwove itself.

Nor can the Origenist controversy be resolved into a dispute of "Easterners" versus "Westerners," "Greeks" versus "Latins." Although Origen's theology and speculative mysticism had a long career in the Greek-speaking world, "Westerners" such as Jerome, Rufinus, and Pelagius were all deeply engaged with Origen's spiritualizing exegesis and exploration of theological questions. Nonetheless, the person who came to epitomize

---

[1] See especially Peter J. Gorday, "*Paulus Origenianus*: The Economic Interpretation of Paul in Origen and Gregory of Nyssa," 145.

"Western" theology was Augustine, whose mind was barely touched by the Origenist dispute at the time it erupted. In his later theology, Augustine drew the line against Origenist speculation: the body belonged to the first creation (sexual intercourse would have been part of Paradise had sin not intervened) and would continue in some form in the afterlife; the affirmation of an *apokatastasis* was roundly denounced; and hierarchy of status was championed both here and in the hereafter. Banished was Origen's cosmic vision of the original and final unity of all rational creation. Through both his theological brilliance and his ecclesiastical politics, Augustine forged for the West a theology that, however broad its *social* and *historical* vision of the unity of humankind in sin, forfeited Origen's larger cosmological concerns. By refusing to answer the Origenist question of the soul's origin, Augustine in effect bypassed most of the Origenist (and anti-Origenist) discussion that occupied other Western theologians during his formative and mature years. What *might* have been the outcome had Augustine lived in Rome rather than Hippo Regius, or had read Greek texts with more ease, are unsettling—and unanswerable—questions.

Another aspect of my study has been to suggest how, given the admittedly fragmentary remains left to us, Origenist and anti-Origenist ideas threaded their way through social networks. Here, older scholarship on the relations between Jerome and Rufinus has more recently been supplemented by that of Antoine Guillaumont, Gabriel Bunge, and others. Bunge's work in particular has enabled me to proffer some hypotheses about the means by which Evagrius Ponticus, the central theoretician of latter-day Origenism, was connected to both Eastern and Western Origenist sympathizers. Attempting to take seriously my colleague Fredric Jameson's injunction that scholars should "always historicize," I have attempted to show how within these networks of hostility and friendship "theory traveled,"[2] to identify where possible the circuits through which the controversy developed, and to explore how previous relations of affection and enmity produced the material grounding by which Origenist ideas were disputed, disclaimed, and tempered to fit a new context of "orthodoxy." By stressing the social networks involved in the dispute, I have tried to suggest both how Origenist and anti-Origenist theories "traveled" to their new conceptual homes, and how persons whose names rarely appear in theology textbooks, such as Eusebius of Cremona, Melania the Elder, and Silvia, played strategic roles in these networks of transfer and patronage. Thus the wider aim of my study has been to probe the varying ways by which Origenist theory was grounded in the praxis of both asceticism and relationships.

[2] Edward Said's phrase: see his "Traveling Theory," in *The World, the Text and the Critic*, 226–247.

Peter Brown's assessment of the Pelagian controversy as an "incident in the relations between the Latin and Greek worlds"[1] also characterizes the Origenist debate: as we have seen, networks of friendship and enmity, support and rivalry, bound Palestine, Constantinople, Alexandria, and the Egyptian desert to Italy and North Africa. After the era detailed in this book, however, Eastern and Western Christianity increasingly went their own ways, paralleling the fate of the Roman Empire as a whole.

Origenism enjoyed a longer career in the East than in the West. After a relative lull of Origenist activity in the fifth century (recall, however, the Origenizing speculation of Shenute's monastic opponents)[2] the movement gained force in sixth-century Palestine, a development that is tempting to link with the preservation of Evagrius Ponticus's writings there.[3] The story of Origenism's revival among the monks of the New Laura, detailed in the *Life of St. Sabas*,[4] was explored for modern scholarship by Franz Diekamp in his monograph of 1899, *Die origenistischen Streitigkeiten im sechsten Jahrhundert und das fünfte allgemeine Concil*.[5]

Diekamp, writing before the recovery of much of Evagrius's literary cor-

---

[1] Peter Brown, "The Patrons of Pelagius," p. 72 (= *Religion and Society*, 226).

[2] See above, pp. 151–156; also see Guillaumont, *Les "Kephalaia Gnostica,"* 124n.1, for two further exceptions to the silence about Origenism in the fifth century.

[3] See above, p. 256 for discussion of Bunge's theory of the transfer of the Evagrian corpus to Palestine.

[4] Text published by Eduard Schwartz,

Kyrillos von Skythopolis, 85–200; English translation by R. M. Price, *Cyril of Scythopolis. The Monks of Palestine*.

[5] Münster: Verlag Aschendorff, 1899. A summary of events for English readers can be found in Derwas Chitty, *The Desert a City: An Introduction to the Study of Egyptian and Palestine Monasticism under the Christian Empire*, esp. chaps. 6–7.

pus, noted the difference between the 543 edict against Origenism and the anathemas pronounced by the Fifth Ecumenical Council in 553; the anathemas, he concluded, reflected a battle between "Isochrist" and "Protoctist" monks over Origenist and Christological issues.[6] Yet it was not until Antoine Guillaumont's discovery of the unexpurgated version of Evagrius's *Kephalaia gnostica* that the issues of this sixth-century conflict could be adequately explicated.[7] In Guillaumont's judgment, Evagrius's Christology was "absolutely identical" with that of the Isochrists (who believed that in the *apokatastasis* all believers would be one with Christ) and was the decisive aspect of Origenism singled out for condemnation in the anathemas of 553.[8] Moreover, Guillaumont was able to demonstrate that several of the anathemas cite or paraphrase sections of Evagrius's *Kephalaia gnostica*.[9] Thus it appears that a major flowering of Evagrian Origenism occurred in Palestine during the second quarter of the sixth century. In his monumental study Guillaumont describes how after the 553 condemnation of Origenism, Greek Christians continued to use Evagrius's ascetic works but abandoned his more speculative treatises.[10] In the Syriac church, on the other hand, where the Origenist controversy became deeply imbedded in disputes between and among Monophysites and Nestorians, Evagrius was "rescued" by severing his theology from that of Origen: while Origen's theology was pronounced heretical, Evagrius's was revered, albeit in sometimes expurgated form.[11]

In the Latin West, the influence of Origenist theology dwindled rapidly after the deaths of its major partisans shortly after the sack of Rome in 410. Evagrian Origenism lived on in the West (albeit in tamed and transmuted form) through the *Institutes* and *Conferences* of John Cassian, works in which he attempted to render palatable for fifth-century Gallic monasticism the teachings of the Egyptian desert. Surely a new study of Cassian is in order that takes into account recent scholarship on Origenism.[12] Ori-

---

[6] Diekamp, *Die origenistischen Streitkeiten,* 85–86.

[7] Guillaumont, *Les "Kephalaia Gnostica,"* pt. I, chap. 3, esp. 147–159.

[8] Guillaumont, *"Kephalaia Gnostica,"* esp. 156.

[9] Guillaumont, *"Kephalaia Gnostica,"* 156–159. Among the important consequences of Guillaumont's discovery is that the Koetschau text of Origen's *On First Principles* (which cites the 553 anathemas as if they contained Origen's own theology) should be redone (159n.118).

[10] Guillaumont, *"Kephalaia Gnostica,"* 166–167, 170. To a lesser extent, the same tendency is noticeable in the Latin church as well: Evagrius's more simple works, such as

the *Rule for Nuns,* were preserved and read throughout the Middle Ages. See D. A. Wilmart, "Les Versions latines," 143–153. Other treatises by Evagrius were preserved in Greek Christendom under the names of more "orthodox" writers, such as Nilus.

[11] Guillaumont, *"Kephalaia Gnostica,"* 166–170, and pt. II, chap. 1.

[12] Two studies of Cassian and Evagrius are worthy of note: Salvatore Marsili, *Giovanni Cassiano ed Evagrio Pontico* and Hans-Oskar Weber, *Die Stellung des Johannes Cassianus zur Ausserpachomianischen Mönchstradition.* The considerable recovery of Evagrian material (and scholarship on it) since 1961 suggests that new studies are in order. The exploration of the relationship between

gen's exegetical writings, however, either in Latin translation, or as incorporated into the treatises of such authors as Ambrose and Jerome, continued to influence the Western tradition of Biblical interpretation: here, Origen's works on the Song of Songs were notable.[13]

With the condemnation of both Origenism and Pelagianism, the last chances for a fruitful unification of Eastern and Western Christianity met with defeat. Their condemnation made effective in the West the flourishing of a Christian theology whose central concerns were human sinfulness, not human potentiality; divine determination, not human freedom and responsibility; God's mystery, not God's justice. Christendom was perhaps poorer for their suppression.

Cassian and Evagrius was no doubt hindered by the complete absence of Evagrius's name from Cassian's writings.

[13] See, for example, the study by E. Ann Matter, *The Voice of My Beloved: The Song of Songs in Western Medieval Christianity*.

BIBLIOGRAPHY

MAJOR PRIMARY SOURCES

English translations readily available in such series as *Ancient Christian Writers*, *Ante-Nicene Fathers*, *Fathers of the Church*, and *Nicene and Post-Nicene Fathers* are not cited in the bibliography.

Anonymous Pelagian literature:
   Ad adolescentem. PLS 1, 1375–1380.
   Admonitio Augiensis. PLS 1, 1699–1704.
   De castitate. PLS 1, 1464–1505.
   De divitiis. PLS 1, 1380–1418.
   De induratione cordis Pharaonis. (1) Ed., tr. Georges de Plinval (1947), *q.v.*; (2)
      PLS 1, 1506–1539.
   De malis doctoribus et operibus fidei et de iudicio futuro. PLS 1, 1418–1457.
   De poenitentia. PL 30, 249–253.
   De possibilitate non peccandi. PLS 1, 1457–1464.
   De vera circumcisione. PL 30, 194–217.
   Epistola honorificentiae tuae. PLS 1, 1687–1694.
   Epistola magnum cumulatur. PLS 1, 1694–1698.
   Expositio fidei catholicae. PLS 1, 1683–1685.
   Fragmenta Pelagiana Vindobonensia. PLS 1, 1561–1570.
   Virginitate laus. PL 30, 168–181.
   The Works of Fastidius. Ed., tr. R.S.T. Haslehurst. London: Society of SS. Peter
      and Paul Limited, 1927.
Agatonicus. "On Anthropomorphism." Tr. Tito Orlandi. "La cristologia nei testi
   catechetici copti." In *Cristologia e catechesi patristica*, ed. Sergio Felici, I, 217–
   219. Biblioteca di Scienze Religiose 31. Roma: Las, 1980.
Ambrosiaster. *Commentarius in Epistulas Paulinas.* Ed. H. J. Vogels. *CSEL* 81[1-3]
   (1966, 1968, 1969).
———. *Quaestiones Veteris et Novi Testamenti CXXVII.* Ed. A. Souter. *CSEL* 50
   (1908).

Ammon. *The Letter of Ammon*. In *The Letter of Ammon and Pachomian Monasticism*, ed., tr. James E. Goehring. Patristische Texte und Studien 27. Berlin/New York: Walter de Gruyter, 1986.

Anastasius I. *Epistolae*. *PL* 20, 68–76.

———. *Epistola ad Venerium*. In J. Van den Gheyn. "La Lettre du Pape Anastase Ier à S. Venerius, évêque de Milan, sur la condamnation d'Origène." *Revue d'Histoire et de Littérature Religieuses* 4 (1899): 1–12.

Apollinaris of Laodicea. *Opera, fragmenta*. In *Apollinaris von Laodicea und seine Schule*, ed. Hans Lietzmann (Tübingen: J.C.B. Mohr, 1904).

Apophthegmata Patrum. *PG* 65, 72–440; *PL* 73, 739–1062. French translations: (1) *Les sentences des Pères du désert. Les apophtegemes des Pères (Recension de Pélage et Jean)*. Tr. J. Dion and G. Oury. Solesmes: Abbaye Saint-Pierre de Solesmes, 1966. (2) *Les Sentences des Pères du desert. Collection alphabétique*. Tr. Lucien Regnault. Solesmes: Abbaye Saint-Pierre de Solesmes, 1981. (3) *Les Sentences des Pères du desert. Troisième recueil et tables*. Tr. Lucien Regnault. Solesmes: Abbaye Saint-Pierre de Solesmes, 1976. English translations: (1) (from the Syriac version) *The Wit and Wisdom of the Christian Fathers in Egypt*. Tr. E. A. Wallis Budge. Oxford: Oxford University Press, 1934. (2) *The Sayings of the Desert Fathers. The Alphabetical Collection*. Tr. Benedicta Ward. London: Mowbray, 1975.

Augustine. *Ad Orosium contra Priscillianistas et Origenistas*. Ed. K-D. Daur. *CCL* 49 (1985): 165–178.

———. *Ad Simplicianum (De diversis questionibus)*. Ed. A. Mutzenbecher. *CCL* 44 (1970).

———. *Confessiones*. Ed. L. Verheijen. *CCL* 27 (1971).

———. *Contra duas epistolas Pelagianorum*. Ed. C. Urba and J. Zycha. *CSEL* 60 (1913): 423–570.

———. *Contra Julianum*. *PL* 44: 641–874.

———. *De anima et ejus origine*. Ed. C. Urba and J. Zycha. *CSEL* 60 (1913): 303–419.

———. *De civitate Dei*. Ed. B. Dombart and A. Kalb. *CCL* 47; 48 (1955).

———. *De diversis quaestionibus LXXXIII*. Ed. A. Mutzenbecher. *CCL* 44A (1975): 11–249.

———. *De doctrina Christiana*. Ed. J. Martin. *CCL* 32 (1962): 1–167.

———. *De dono perseverantiae*. *PL* 45: 993–1034.

———. *De Genesi ad litteram*. *PL* 34: 245–466.

———. *De gestis Pelagii*. Ed. C. Urba and J. Zycha. *CSEL* 42 (1902): 51–122.

———. *De gratia Christi et de peccato originali*. Ed. C. Urba and J. Zycha. *CSEL* 42 (1902): 125–206.

———. *De libero arbitrio*. Ed. W. M. Green. *CCL* 29 (1970): 211–321.

———. *De natura et gratia*. Ed. C. Urba and J. Zycha. *CSEL* 60 (1913): 233–299.

———. *De nuptiis et concupiscentia*. Ed. C. Urba and J. Zycha. *CSEL* 42 (1902): 209–319.

———. *De peccatorum meritis*. Ed. C. Urba and J. Zycha. *CSEL* 60 (1913): 3–151.

———. *De perfectione iustitiae hominis*. Ed. C. Urba and J. Zycha. *CSEL* 42 (1902): 3–48.

———. *De praedestinatione sanctorum*. *PL* 44: 959–992.

————. *Epistulae*. Ed. A. Goldbacher. *CSEL* 34$^{1-2}$, 44, 57, 58 (1895, 1904, 1911, 1923).

————. *Epistolae ad Romanos inchoata expositio*. Ed. J. Divjak. *CSEL* 84 (1971): 145–181. English translation: *Augustine on Romans: Unfinished Commentary on the Epistle to the Romans*. Tr. Paula Fredriksen Landes. *SBL* Texts and Translations 23; Early Christian Literature Series 6. Chico, CA: Scholars Press, 1982.

————. *Oeuvres complètes de Saint Augustin évêque d'Hippone*. Tr. Péronne et al. 32 vols. Paris: Librarie de Louis Vivés, 1869–1873.

————. *Opus imperfectum contra Julianum*. Books I–III: Ed. M. Zelzer. *CSEL* 85^1 (1974). Books IV–VI. *PL* 45: 1337–1608.

————. *Sermones*. *PL* 38; 39.

Basil of Caesarea. *Epistulae*. Ed., tr. Marcella Forlin Patrucco. *Basilio di Cesarea, Le lettere I*. Torino: Società Editrice Internazionale, 1983.

Book of Paradise, Being the Histories and Sayings of the Monks and Ascetics of the Egyptian Desert by Palladius, Hieronymous and others. Ed., tr. E. A. Wallis Budge. 2 vols. London: Printed for Lady Meux, 1904.

Caelestius. *Libellus Fidei*. *PL* 48: 498–505.

Cassian, John. *Conlationes patrum XXIV*. Ed., tr. E. Pichery. *Conférences*. *SC* 42; 54; 64 (1955, 1958, 1959).

————. *Institutiones*. Ed., tr. J. C. Guy. *Institutions cénobitiques*. *SC* 109 (1965).

Codex Theodosianus. Ed. T. Mommsen. *Theodosiani libri xvi cum constitutionibus sirmondianis*. Berlin: Weidmann, 1905. English translation: *The Theodosian Code and Novels and the Sirmondian Constitutions*. Tr. C. Pharr. Reprint edition. New York: Greenwood Press, 1969.

Cyril of Alexandria. *Adversus Anthropomorphitas*. *PG* 76: 1065–1132.

Cyril of Scythopolis. *Vita Sabae*. Ed. Eduard Schwartz. *Kyrillos von Skythopolis*. *TU* 49, 2 (1939). English translation: *Cyril of Scythopolis. The Monks of Palestine*. Tr. R. M. Price. Kalamazoo: Cistercian Publications, 1991.

Didymus the Blind. *De Genesi*. Ed., tr. P. Nautin. *Didyme, Sur la Genèse: texte inédit d'après un papyrus de Toura*. 2 vols. *SC* 233; 244 (1976, 1978).

Epiphanius of Salamis. *Ancoratus*. *GCS* 25 (1915): 1–149.

————. *Epistula ad Iohannem Episcopum* (= Jerome, *Epistula* 51). *CSEL* 54 (1910): 395–412.

————. *Fragmenta* ("Against Images"), in Holl (1928), *q.v.*

————. *Panarion*. *GCS* 25; 31^2; 37^2 (1915, 1980, 1985).

Eusebius of Caesarea. *Historia ecclesiastica*. *GCS* 9$^{1-2}$ (1903, 1908).

Evagrius Ponticus. *Capita cognoscitiva* (*Skēmmata*), in Muyldermans (1931), *q.v.*

————. *Capita paraenetica*. *PG* 79: 1249–1252.

————. *Capitula XXXIII*. *PG* 47: 1264–1268.

————. *Commentarius in Ecclesiasten* (*fragmenta*), in Géhin (1979), *q.v.*

————. *De diversis malignis cogitationibus*. *PG* 79: 1200–1233.

————. *De octo vitiosis cogitationibus*. *PG* 40: 1272–1278. Tr. from Ethiopic: "Die Äthiopische Überlieferung des Abhandlung des Evagrius *Peri tōn oktō logismōn*." Tr. Otto Spies. *Oriens Christianus* 29 (1932): 203–228.

————. *De oratione*. *PG* 79: 1165–1200. English translation in *Praktikos* (Bamberger), *q.v.*

————. *De seraphim*; *De cherubim*, in Muyldermans (1946), *q.v.*

Evagrius Ponticus. *Epistula ad Melaniam*, in Parmentier (1985) and Vitestam (1964), *q.v.*

———. *Epistulae.* (1) Tr. Gabriel Bunge. *Evagrios Pontikos. Briefe aus der Wüste.* Sophia 24. Trier: Paulinus-Verlag, 1986. (2) in Van Lantschoot (1964), *q.v.*

———. *Epistula fidei* (= Basil, *Ep.* 8). *PG* 32:245–268.

———. *Fragmenta*, in Muyldermans (1931; 1934; 1938; 1952; 1963) and Hausherr (1939), *q.v.*

———. *Gnosticus.* Ed., tr. A. and C. Guillaumont. *Le Gnostique ou à celui qui est devenue digne de la science. SC* 356 (1989).

———. *Kephalaia gnostica.* Ed., tr. Antoine Guillaumont. *Les six centuries des "Kephalaia Gnostica" d'Evagre le Pontique. PO* 28, 1 (1958).

———. *Opera. Euagrius Ponticus.* Ed. W. Frankenberg. Abhandlungen der königlichen Gesellschaft der Wissenschaften zu Göttingen, philologisch-historische Klasse, n.f. 13, 2 (Berlin: Weidmann, 1912).

———. *Practicus.* Ed., tr. Antoine and Claire Guillaumont. *Traité Pratique ou le moine.* 2 vols. *SC* 170; 171 (1971). English translation: *Evagrius Ponticus. The Praktikos. Chapters on Prayer.* Tr. John E. Bamberger. Cistercian Studies Series 4. Spencer, MA: Cistercian Publications, 1970.

———. *Rerum monachalium rationes. PG* 47: 1252–1264.

———. *Skēmmata (Capita cognoscitiva)*, in Muyldermans (1931), *q.v.*

———. *Scholia in Proverbia.* Ed., tr. P. Géhin. *Scholiés aux Proverbes. SC* 340 (1987).

———. *Selections.* Tr. in E. Kadloubovsky and G.E.H. Palmer, eds. *Early Fathers from the Philokalia.* London/Boston: Faber and Faber, 1954.

———. *Sententiae.* (1) *PG* 40: 1277–1286. (2) *Sententiae ad monachos. Sententiae ad virginem.* Ed. Hugo Gressmann. "Nonnenspiegel und Mönchsspiegel des Euagrios Pontikos." *TU* 39, 4 (1913). (3) Latin versions: Wilmart (1911), *q.v.*

———. *Sermo sive dogmatica epistula de sanctissima trinitate* (pseudo-Basil, *Epistula* 8, *q.v.*)

Faustus of Riez. *De gratia.* Ed. A. Engelbrecht. *CSEL* 21 (1891): 3–96.

Gennadius. *De scriptoribus ecclesiasticis liber. PL* 58: 1059–1120.

———. *De viris inlustribus.* Ed. E. C. Richardson. *TU* 14, 1 (1896): 57–97.

Gerontius. *Vita Melaniae Junioris.* Greek text: Ed., tr. D. Gorce. *Vie de Sainte Mélanie. SC* 90 (1962). Latin text: Ed. Mariano del Tindaro Rampolla. *Santa Melania Giuniore, senatrice romana: documenti contemporei e note*: 3–40. Roma: Tipografia Vaticana, 1905. English translation of Greek text: Elizabeth A. Clark. *The Life of Melania the Younger, q.v.*, 25–82.

Gregory of Nazianzus. *Epistulae. PG* 37: 21–388; *PG* 46, 1101–1108.

———. *Orationum Gregorii Nazianzeni novem interpretatio.* Tr. Rufinus of Aquileia. Ed. A. Engelbrecht. *CSEL* 46¹ (1910).

Historia Monachorum in Aegypto. Ed. André-Jean Festugière. *SH* 53 (1971). Latin translation: Tr. Rufinus of Aquileia. *PL* 21: 387–462. English translation: *The Lives of the Desert Fathers: The Historia Monachorum in Aegypto.* Tr. Norman Russell. London: Mowbray; Kalamazoo: Cistercian Publications, 1981.

Jerome. *Adversus Helvidium (De perpetua virginitate B. Mariae). PL* 23: 193–216.

———. *Adversus Jovinianum. PL* 23: 221–352.

———. *Apologia contra Rufinum.* (1) Ed. P. Lardet. *CCL* 79 (1982). (2) Ed., tr. P. Lardet. *Saint Jérôme. Apologie contre Rufin. SC* 303 (1983).

———. *Chronicon*. Ed. R. Helm. *GCS* 24 (1913); 47² (1956).

———. *Commentarii in Prophetas Minores: Osee, Ioelem, Amos, Abdiam, Ionam, Michaeam*. Ed. M. Adriaen. *CCL* 76 (1969).

———. *Commentarii in Prophetas: Naum, Abacuc, Sophoniam, Aggaeum, Zachariam, Malachiam*. Ed. M. Adriaen. *CCL* 76A (1970).

———. *Commentarioli in Psalmos*. Ed. G. Morin. *CCL* 72 (1959): 177–245.

———. *Commentarius in Danielem*. Ed. F. Glorie. *CCL* 75A (1964).

———. *Commentarius in Ecclesiasten*. Ed. M. Adriaen. *CCL* 72 (1959): 249–361.

———. *Commentarius in Epistolam ad Ephesios*. *PL* 26: 467–590.

———. *Commentarius in Hiezechielem*. Ed. F. Glorie. *CCL* 75 (1964).

———. *Commentarius in Matheum*. Ed. D. Hurst and M. Adriaen. *CCL* 77 (1969).

———. *Contra Ioannem Hierosolymitanum*. *PL* 23: 371–412.

———. *Contra Vigilantium*. *PL* 23: 353–368.

———. *De viris inlustribus*. Ed. E. C. Richardson. *TU* 14, 1 (1896): 1–56.

———. *Dialogus contra Pelagianos*. *PL* 23: 517–618.

———. *Epistulae*. Ed. I. Hilberg. *CSEL* 54–56 (1910, 1912).

———. *Hebraicae quaestiones in Libro Geneseos*. Ed. P. de Lagard. *CCL* 72 (1959): 1–56.

———. *In Esaiam*. Ed. M. Adriaen. *CCL* 73; 73A (1963).

———. *In Hieremiam Prophetam*. Ed. S. Reiter. *CCL* 74 (1960).

———. *Tractatus in Psalmos*. Ed. G. Morin. *CCL* 78 (1958): 3–447.

John of Nikiu. *Chronicon*. Ed., tr. Hermann Zotenberg. *La Chronique de Jean, évêque de Nikiou. Texte éthiopien publié et traduit*. Paris: Imprimerie Nationale, 1883. English translation from the Ethiopic text: *The Chronicle of John, bishop of Nikiu*. Tr. R. H. Charles. London: Williams & Norgate, 1916.

Julian of Eclanum. *Ad Florum, fragmenta*. *Apud* Augustine, *Opus imperfectum contra Julianum, q.v.*

———. *Ad Turbantium, fragmenta*. (1) *Apud* Augustine, *Contra Julianum, q.v.* (2) Ed. Albert Bruckner, *Die vier Bücher Julianus von Aeclanum an Turbantius, q.v.*

———. *De bono constantiae, fragmenta*. *Apud* Bede, *In Cantica Canticorum*. *PL* 91: 1065–1077 *passim*.

———. *Epistula ad Rufum*. *PL* 48: 534–536.

———. *Expositio Cantici Canticorum, fragmenta*. *Apud* Bede, *In Cantica Canticorum*. *PL* 91: 1065–1077 *passim*.

———. *Expositio libri Iob. Tractatus Prophetarum Osee, Iohel et Amos. Opera de perditorum fragmenta*. Ed. L. De Coninck. *CCL* 88 (1977).

———. *Libellus fidei*. *PL* 48: 508–526.

Justinian. *Liber adversus Origenem*. *PG* 86, 1: 945–990.

Libanius. *Pro templis (Oratio XXX)*. In *Libanii Opera*. Ed. R. Foerster, III: 80–118. Leipzig: B. G. Teubner, 1906.

Macarius the Egyptian. *Homiliae PG* 34, 449–822. English translation: *Fifty Spiritual Homilies of St. Macarius the Egyptian*. Tr. A. J. Mason. Translations of Christian Literature: Series 1, Greek Texts. London: SPCK; New York: Macmillan, 1921.

Marius Mercator. *Commonitorium*. Ed. Eduard Schwartz. *ACO* I, 5: 5–23 (1924–1926).

Methodius. *De resurrectione.* Ed., tr. Nathanael Bonwetsch. *GCS* 27 (1917).

Moschus, John. *Pratum spirituale.* Ed., tr. M.-J. Rouët de Journel. *Le Pré spirituel.* *SC* 12 (1946).

Nestorius. *Epistulae. Apud* Marius Mercator. *PL* 48: 841–848.

Origen. *Commentarius in Epistolam ad Romanos.* (1) *PG* 14: 833–1292. (2) Ed. Caroline Hammond Bammel. *Der Römerbrief Kommentar des Origenes; kritische Ausgabe der Übersetzung Rufins, Buch 1–3.* Vetus Latina: Aus der Geschichte der Lateinischen Bibel 16. Freiburg im Breisgau: Verlag Herder, 1990.

———. *Contra Celsum.* Ed. P. Koetschau. *GCS, Origenes Werke 1–2* (1899). Tr. Henry Chadwick. Cambridge: Cambridge University Press, 1965.

———. *De principiis (Peri Archōn).* Ed. P. Koetschau. *GCS* 22 (1913). English translation: *Origen: On First Principles.* Tr. G. W. Butterworth. New York: Harper and Row, 1966.

———. *Epistula ad quosdam caros suos Alexandriam,* in Crouzel (1973), *q.v.*

———. *Homiliae in Exodum.* Ed., tr. M. Borret. *Homélies sur Exode. SC* 321 (1985).

———. *Homiliae in Ezechielem.* Ed., tr. M. Borret. *Homélies sur Ezechiel. SC* 352 (1989).

———. *Homiliae in Genesim.* Ed., tr. H. de Lubac and L. Doutreleau. *Homélies sur la Genèse. SC* 7bis (1976).

———. *Homiliae in Jesu Nave.* Ed., tr. A. Jaubert. *Homélies sur Josué. SC* 71 (1960).

———. *Homiliae in Leviticum.* Ed., tr. M. Borret. *Homélies sur le Lévitique.* 2 vols. *SC* 286; 287 (1981).

———. *Homiliae in Numeros.* Ed., tr. A. Méhat. *Homélies sur les Nombres. SC* 29 (1951).

———. *Homiliae in Psalmos* 35 (36)–38 (39). *PG* 12: 1319–1410.

———. *Opera.* Ed. P. Koetschau et al. *Origenes Werke.* 12 vols. *GCS* 2, 3, 6, 10, 22, 29, 30, 33, 35, 38, 40, 41 (1899–1955).

———. *Philocalia.* Ed., tr. E. Junod. *Philocalie 21–27. Sur le libre arbitre. SC* 226 (1976).

Orosius, Paulus. *Commonitorium.* Ed. K-D. Daur. *CCL* 49: 157–163 (1985).

———. *Liber apologeticum.* Ed. C. Zangemeister. *CSEL* 5 (1882): 601–664.

Pachomius. *Regula (fragmenta graeca).* Ed. A. Boon. *Pachomiana Latina.* Bibliothèque de la Revue d'Histoire Ecclésiastique 7. Louvain: Bureaux de la Revue, 1932: 169–182. Latin translation: In *Pachomiana Latina,* 13–74. Tr. Jerome. Ed. A. Boon. English translation: *Pachomian Koinonia: Pachomian Chronicles and Rules,* 141–167. Tr. Armand Veilleux. Cistercian Studies Series 46. Kalamazoo: Cistercian Publications, 1981.

Palladius. *Dialogus de vita S. Joannis Chrysostomi.* Ed. P. R. Coleman-Norton. Cambridge: Cambridge University Press, 1928.

———. *Historia Lausiaca.* Ed. Cuthbert Butler. *The Lausiac History of Palladius.* Texts and Studies VI, 1–2. 2 vols. Cambridge: Cambridge University Press, 1898, 1904. Coptic text: Ed. E. Amélineau. *De historia lausiaca.* Paris: Ernest Leroux, 1887. Syriac text: Ed. Réné Draguet. *Les Formes syriaques de la matière de Histoire Lausiaque.* 2 vols. *CSCO* 390, 398 = Scriptores Syri 170, 173 (1978).

Pamphilus. *Apologia pro Origene. PG* 17: 541–616.

Paulinus of Milan. *Libellus adversus Coelestium. PL* 20: 711–716.

Paulinus of Nola. *Carmina*. Ed. W. Hartel. *CSEL* 30 (1904).

———. *Epistolae*. Ed. W. Hartel. *CSEL* 29 (1894).

Pelagius. *Ad Celantiam*. Ed. W. Hartel. *CSEL* 29 (1894): 436–459.

———. *Ad Demetriadem*. *PL* 30: 15–45.

———. *De divina lege*. *PL* 30: 105–116.

———. *De libero arbitrio, fragmenta*. (1) *Apud* Augustine, *De gratia Christi, q.v.* (2) *PLS* 1: 1539–1543.

———. *De natura, fragmenta*. *Apud* Augustine, *De natura et gratia, q.v.*

———. *Expositiones XIII Epistularum Pauli*. Ed. Alexander Souter. (1) *Pelagius's Expositions of Thirteen Epistles of Saint Paul*. Texts and Studies IX. Cambridge: Cambridge University Press, 1926. (2) *PLS* 1: 1110–1374. English translation of *Commentarius in Romanos*: T. de Bruyn (1987), *q.v.*

———. *Libellus fidei*. *PL* 48: 488–491.

———. *Liber capitulorum, fragmenta*. *Apud* Augustine, *De gestis Pelagii, q.v.*

———. *De virginitate*. Ed. C. Halm. *CSEL* 1 (1866): 225–250.

———. *De vita Christiana*. *PL* 40: 1031–1046.

Photius. *Bibliotheca*. *PG* 103; 104: 10–356.

Pseudo-Clement. *Recognitiones*. Ed. B. Rehm. *Die Pseudoklementinen*. Vol. II: *Rekognitionen*. *GCS* 51 (1965).

Pseudo-Jerome. *Epistola* 37: *Dialogus sub nomine Hieronymi et Augustini*. *PL* 30: 270–280.

Rufinus of Aquileia. *De benedictionibus patriarcharum*. Ed., tr. Manlio Simonetti. *Les Bénédictions des patriarches*. *SC* 140 (1968).

———. *Historia ecclesiastica*. (1) Eusebius of Caesarea, *q.v.* (2) *PL* 27: 467–540.

———. *Opera*. Ed. M. Simonetti. *CCL* 20 (1961): *De adulteratione librorum Origenis*; *Apologia ad Anastasium*; *Apologia contra Hieronymum*; *Expositio symboli*; *De benedictionibus patriarcharum*; *Prologi et praefationes*.

Rufinus the Syrian. *Liber De Fide*. Ed., tr. Mary William Miller. Catholic University of America Patristic Studies 96. Washington, DC: The Catholic University of America Press, 1964.

Sancti Pachomii Vitae Graecae. Ed. F. Halkin. *SH* 19 (1932). French translation: *Les Pères du désert: textes choisis et presentes*: 87–126. Tr. Réné Draguet. Paris: Librairie Plon, 1949. English translation: *The Life of Pachomius: Vita Prima Graeca*. Tr. Apostolos N. Athanassakis. Early Christian Literature Series 2; *SBL* Texts and Translations 7. Missoula, MT: Scholars Press, 1975.

Shenute. *Christological Instruction*, in Lefort (1955), *q.v.*

———. *Contra Origenistas. Testo con introduzione e traduzione*. Ed., tr. Tito Orlandi. Roma: C.I.M., 1985.

———. *De certamine contra diabolum*, in Koschorke, et al. (1975), *q.v.*

———. *Diatriba contra diabolum*, in Du Bourguet (1961–1962), *q.v.*

———. *Discussions on Church Discipline and on Cosmology*, in Du Bourguet (1958), *q.v.*

———. *Discussion on the Duties of Judges*, in Du Bourguet (1956), *q.v.*

———. *Homilies of the Holy Week Lectionary*, in Burmester (1932), *q.v.*

———. *Opera*. Ed., tr. E. Amélineau. *Oeuvres de Shenoudi*. 2 vols. Paris: Ernest Leroux; 1907– .

Shenute. *Opera*. Ed. Johannes Leipoldt; tr. H. Weismann. *Sinuthii Archimandritas. Vita et Opera Omnia*. CSCO Scriptores Coptici, ser. 2, t. 4. Paris: E Typographeo Reipublicae, 1908.

———. *Sermones*, in Guérin (1904), *q.v.*

Socrates. *Historia ecclesiastica*. PG 67: 33–841.

Sozomen. *Historia ecclesiastica*. PG 67: 844–1629.

Sulpicius Severus. *Dialogus*. Ed. C. Halm. *CSEL* 1 (1866): 152–216.

Theodore of Mopsuestia. *Commentarius in Epistolas Pauli*. Ed. H. B. Swete. *Theodori Episcopi Mopsuesteni in Epistolas B. Pauli Commentarii: The Latin Version with the Greek Fragments*. 2 vols. Cambridge: Cambridge University Press, 1880, 1882.

———. *Homiliae catecheticae*. English translation: *A Commentary of Theodore of Mopsuestia on the Lord's Prayer and on the Sacraments of Baptism and the Eucharist*. Tr. A. Mingana. Woodbrooke Studies VI. Cambridge: W. Heffer and Sons, 1933.

———. *In Genesim, fragmenta*. Ed., tr. R. M. Tonneau. "Théodore de Mopsueste: Interprétation (du Livre) de la Genèse (Vat. Syr. 120, ff. I–V)." *Le Muséon* 66 (1953): 45–64.

———. *Liber contra Hieronymum*. Ed. E. Schwartz. *ACO* I, 5: 173–176.

Theodoret. *Historia ecclesiastica*. PG 82: 881–1280.

Theophilus of Alexandria. *Epistula ad Ammonem*. Ed. F. Halkin. *Sancti Pachomii Vitae Graecae*. SH 19 (1932): 121.

———. *Epistula ad ecclesiam Hierosolytanum*, in Nautin (1974), *q.v.*

———. *Epistula ad Epiphanium* (= Jerome, *Epistula* 90). *CSEL* 55 (1912): 143–145.

———. *Epistula ad Flavianum episc. Antiochenum*. In *The Sixth Book of the Select Letters of Severus, Patriarch of Antioch, in the Syriac version of Athanasius of Nisibus*, II: 303–308. Ed., tr. E. W. Brooks. London: Williams and Norgate, 1902–1904.

———. *Epistulae ad Hieronymum* (= Jerome, *Epistulae* 87; 89) *CSEL* 55 (1912): 140, 142–143.

———. *Epistula ad Horsiesium*. In *Papyruscodex*, ed. W. E. Crum (1905), *q.v.*, 12–17, 65–72. French translation: In *Les Vies coptes de Saint Pachôme et de ses premiers successeurs*, 389–390. Tr. L. Th. Lefort. Bibliothèque du *Muséon* 16. Louvain: Bureaux du *Muséon*, 1943.

———. *Epistula ad Theodosium Augustum*. In Bruno Krusch, *Studien* (1880) *q.v.*, 220–226.

———. *Epistulae festales*. (1) (= Jerome, *Epistulae* 96, 98, 100). *CSEL* 55 (1912): 159–181, 185–211, 213–232. (2) *Fragmenta*. PG 65: 48–60. (3) Armenian version: *apud* Timothy Aelurus. Ed. Karapet Ter-Mekerttschian and Erwand Ter-Mekerttschian. *Timotheus Älurus' des Patriarchen von Alexandrien Widerlegung der auf Synode zu Chalcedon festgesetzten Lehre*, 30, 105, 160, 161, 195. Leipzig: J. C. Hinrichs, 1908.

———. *Epistulae, fragmenta*. (1) PG 65: 61–64. (2) Ed. E. Schwartz. *ACO* I, 2: 41–42; I, 7: 91–92. (3) In F. Nau, "Une Lettre de Théophile, Patriarche d'Alexandrie, d'après la légende de Sérapion le Sindonite." *Revue de l'Orient Chretien* 9 (1914): 103–105.

———. *Fragmenta.* (1) In Declerck (1984), Ebied and Wickham (1970), and Richard (1938; 1975), *q.v.* (2) In *Doctrina Patrum de Incarnatione Verbi,* ed. Franz Diekamp, *q.v.,* 180–183. (3) In Severus of Antioch. *Liber contra impium grammaticum.* Ed. Joseph Lebon. *CSCO* 101 (= Scriptores Syri 50): 317–318; *CSCO* 102 (= Scriptores Syri 51): 234 (1952). (4) In *Codex Vaticanus gr. 1431: eine antichalkedonische Sammlung aus der Zeit Kaiser Zenos*: 36, 38. Ed. Eduard Schwartz. Abhandlungen der Bayerischen Akademie der Wissenschaften, philosophisch-philologische and historische Klasse 32, 6. München: Bayerischen Akademie der Wissenschaften, 1927. (5) In Zacharias Rhetor. *Historia ecclesiastica.* German translation: *Die Sogenannte Kirchengeschichte des Zacharias Rhetor,* 48–49. Tr. K. Ahrens and G. Krüger. Scriptores Sacri et Profani 3. Leipzig: B. G. Teubner, 1899.

———. *Homilia.* Ed., tr. Maurice Brière. "Une Homélie inédite de Théophile d'Alexandrie." *Revue de l'Orient Chretien* 18 (1913): 79–83.

———. *Homilia de crucifixione et in bonum latronem.* Tr. F. Rossi. *Memorie della Reale Accademia delle scienze di Torino,* ser. 2, t. 35: 244–250. Torino: Ermano Loescher, 1884.

———. *Homilia de paenitentia et abstinentia.* Ed., tr. E. A. Wallis Budge. "The Discourse of Archbishop Theophilus, Which He Pronounced on Repentance and Continence, and Also How a Man Must Not Neglect to Repent Before the Last Times Come Upon Him." In *Coptic Homilies in the Dialectic of Upper Egypt, ed. from the Papyrus Codex Oriental 5001 in the British Museum,* E. A. Wallis Budge ed., 65–79, 212–225. London: Trustees of the British Museum, 1910.

———(?). *Homilia de resurrectione Lazari et de apertione gehennae.* Tr. Sirarpie Der Nersessian. "A Homily on the Raising of Lazarus and the Harrowing of Hell." In *Biblical and Patristic Studies in Memory of Robert Pierce Casey,* ed. J. Neville Birdsall and Robert W. Thomson, 219–234. Freiburg: Herder, 1963.

———(?). *Homilia in Petrum et Paulum.* Tr. H. Fleisch. "Une Homélie de Théophile d'Alexandrie sur l'honneur de St. Pierre et de St. Paul." *Revue de l'Orient Chretien* 10 (1936): 371–419.

———. *Homilia X, In mysticam coenam. PG* 77: 1016–1029. French translation: in Richard (1937), *q.v.*

———(?). *In Esaiam VI, 1–7.* Ed. G. Morin. *Anecdota Maredsolana* 3, 3 (1903): 103–122.

———. *Responsio ad synodo Constantinopoli. Apud* Pelagius the Deacon. *In defensione trium capitulorum*: 9–10, 70–71. Ed. R. Devreesse. Studi e Testi 57. Città del Vaticano: Biblioteca Apostolica Vaticana, 1932.

———(?). *Sermo de ecclesia s. familiae in monte Qusquam.* Ed., tr. A. Mingana. "The Vision of Theophilus." In *Woodbrooke Studies: The Christian Documents in Syriac, Arabic, and Garshuni,* III: 8–92. Cambridge: W. Heffer and Sons, 1931.

———. *Synodica epistula ad Palaestinos et ad Cyprios episcopos* (= Jerome, *Epistula* 92). *CSEL* 55 (1912): 147–155.

Tyrannii Rufini librorum Adamantii Origenis, adversus haereticos interpretatio. Studia et Testimonia Antiqua I. Ed. Vinzenz Buchheit. München: Wilhelm Fink, 1966.

Vita Olympiadis. Ed. A.-M. Malingrey. *Jean Chrysostome, Lettres à Olympias. Vie Anonyme d'Olympias. SC* 13bis (1968): 406–448.

Zacharias Rhetor. *Historia ecclesiastica.* Ed., tr. E. W. Brooks. *CSCO* 83; 84; 87; 88 (= *Scriptores Syri* 38; 39; 41; 42) (1953).

Zosimus. *Historia nova.* Ed. L. Mendelssohn. Leipzig, 1887; reprint, Hildesheim: Georg Olms Verlag, 1963. English translation: *New History.* Tr. Ronald T. Ridley. Byzantina Australiensia 2. Sydney: Australian Association for Byzantine Studies, 1982.

Zosimus (pope). *Epistolae. PL* 20: 640–686.

SECONDARY SOURCES

Alexander, Paul G. "An Ascetic Sect of Iconoclasts in Seventh Century Armenia." In *Late Classical and Medieval Studies in Honor of Albert M. Friend, Jr.,* ed. Kurt Weitzmann, 151–160. Princeton: Princeton University Press, 1955.

Alexandrina. Hellénisme, judaïsme et christianisme à Alexandrie. Mélanges offerts au P. Claude Mondésert. Paris: Les Editions du Cerf, 1987.

Altaner, Berthold. "Augustinus und Origenes: Eine quellenkritische Untersuchung." *Historisches Jahrbuch* 70 (1951): 15–41.

———. "De Liber de fide: Ein Werk des Pelagianers Rufinus des 'Syrers.' " *Theologische Quartalschrift* 130 (1950): 432–449.

———. "Wer ist der Verfasser des Tractatus in Isaiam VI, 1–7?" *Theologische Revue* 42 (1943): 147–151.

Amand, David. *Fatalisme et liberté dans l'antiquité grecque.* Université de Louvain, Recueil de travaux d'histoire et philologie, 3rd ser., no. 19. Louvain: Bibliothèque de l'Université, 1945.

Antin, Paul. "Rufin et Pélage dans Jérôme, Prologue 1 *In Hieremiam.*" *Latomus* 22 (1965): 792–794.

Arbesmann, Rudolph. "The 'Daemonium Meridianum' and Greek and Latin Patristic Exegesis." *Traditio* 14 (1958): 17–31.

Armantage, James Walter. *Will the Body Be Raised? Origen and the Origenist Controversies.* Ph.D. dissertation, Yale University, 1970.

Armstrong, A. H. "Some Comments on the Development of the Theology of Images." *Studia Patristica IX* (= *TU* 94), 3, ed. F. L. Cross (1966): 117–126.

Augustinus Magister. Congrès International Augustinien. Paris, 21–24 Septembre 1954. 3 vols. Paris: Etudes Augustiniennes, n.d.

Babcock, William S. "Augustine's Interpretation of Romans (A.D. 394–396)." *Augustinian Studies* 10 (1979): 55–74.

———, ed. *Paul and the Legacies of Paul.* Dallas: Southern Methodist University Press, 1990.

Baldini, Antonio. "Problemi della tradizione sulla 'distruzione' del Serapeo di Alessandria." *Rivista storica dell' Antichità* 15 (1985): 97–152.

Balthasar, Hans Urs von. "Metaphysik und Mystik des Evagrius Ponticus." *Zeitschrift für Aszese und Mystik* 14 (1939): 31–47.

———. "Die Hiera des Evagrius." *Zeitschrift für Katholische Theologie* 62 (1939): 86–106, 181–206.

Bammel, Caroline Hammond. See also Hammond, C. "Adam in Origen." In *The Making of Orthodoxy,* ed. R. Williams, *q.v.,* 62–93.

————. "Die Hexapla des Origenes: Die *Hebraica Veritas* im Streit der Meinungen." *Augustinianum* 28 (1988): 124–149.

————. "Products of Fifth-Century Scriptoria Preserving Conventions Used by Rufinus of Aquileia: III." *Journal of Theological Studies* n.s. 30 (1979): 430–462.

————. "Products of Fifth-Century Scriptoria Preserving Conventions Used by Rufinus of Aquileia: Script." *Journal of Theological Studies* n.s. 35 (1984): 347–393.

————. *Der Römerbrieftext des Rufins und seine Origenes-Übersetzung.* Vetus Latina: Aus der Geschichte der Lateinischen Bibel 10. Freiburg: Verlag Herder, 1985.

Banton, Michael P. *The Social Anthropology of Complex Societies.* New York: Frederick A. Praeger, 1966.

Bardenhewer, Otto. *Geschichte der altkirchlichen Literatur.* Freiburg in Breisgau: Verlag Herder, 1912.

Bardy, Gustave. *Didyme l'Aveugle.* Etudes de Théologie historique 1. Paris: Gabriel Beauchesne, 1910.

————. "Faux et fraudes littéraires dans l'antiquité chrétienne." *Revue d'Histoire Ecclésiastique* 32 (1936): 5–23, 275–302.

————. *Recherches sur l'histoire du texte et des versions latines du 'De Principiis' d'Origène.* Mémoires et travaux des Facultés Catholiques de Lille 25. Paris: Edouard Champion, 1923.

————. "Rufin d'Aquilée." *Dictionnaire de Théologie Catholique* 14, 1 (1939): 153–160.

Barnes, J. A. *Social Networks.* Addison-Wesley Module in Anthropology 26. Reading, MA: Addison-Wesley Publishing Co., 1972.

Barns, John. "Greek and Coptic Papyri from the Covers of the Nag Hammadi Codices." In *Essays on the Nag Hammadi Texts in Honour of Pahor Labib*, ed. M. Krause, 7–18. Nag Hammadi Studies 6. Leiden: E. J. Brill, 1975.

————. "Shenute as a Historical Source." In *Actes du Xe Congrès International de Papyrologues. Varsovie-Cracovie, 3–9 Septembre 1961*, ed. Józef Wolski, 151–159. Wroclaw: Polish National Academy of Sciences, 1964.

Baur, Chrysostome. "S. Jérôme et S. Chrysostome." *Revue Bénédictine* 23 (1906): 430–436.

Baynes, Norman H. "Idolatry and the Early Church." In Baynes, *Byzantine Studies and Other Essays*, 116–143. London: Athlone Press, 1955.

Beatrice, Pier Franco. *Tradux peccati: alle fonti della dottrina agostiniana del peccato originale.* Studia Patristica Mediolanensia 8. Milano: Vita e Pensiero/Università Cattolica del Sacro Cuore, 1978.

Beyer, Hans-Veit. "Die Lichtlehre der Mönche des vierzehnten und des vierten Jahrhunderts, erörtert am Beispiel des Gregorios Sinaïtes, des Evagrios Pontikos und des Ps.-Makarios/Symeon." *Jahrbuch der Österreichischen Byzantinistik* 31 (1981): 473–512.

Block, Ned, ed. *Imagery.* Cambridge, MA: MIT Press, 1981.

Bohlin, Torgny. *Die Theologie des Pelagius und ihre Genesis.* Uppsala Universitets Årsskrift 1957: 9. Uppsala: A.-B. Lundequistska Bokhandeln; Wiesbaden: Otto Harrasowitz, 1957.

Boissevain, Jeremy. *Friends of Friends. Networks, Manipulators and Coalitions.* New York: St. Martin's Press; London: Macmillan, Ltd., 1974.

Boissevain, Jeremy. "When the Saints Go Marching Out: Reflections on the Decline of Patronage in Malta." In *Patrons and Clients*, ed. E. Gellner and J. Waterbury, *q.v.*, 81–96.

———, and J. Clyde Mitchell, eds. *Network Analysis: Studies in Human Interaction*. The Hague: Mouton & Co., 1973.

Bonner, Gerald. *Augustine and Modern Research on Pelagianism*. Saint Augustine Lecture, 1970, Villanova University. Villanova, PA: Villanova University Press, 1972.

———. "How Pelagian Was Pelagius?" In *Studia Patristica IX* (= *TU* 94), ed. F. L. Cross, 350–358. (1966).

———. "Rufinus the Syrian and African Pelagianism." *Augustinian Studies* 1 (1970): 30–47.

Bouché-Leclercq, Auguste. *L'Astrologie grecque*. Paris: Ernest Leroux, 1899.

Bouhot, J.-P. "Version inédite du sermon 'Ad neophytos' de S. Jean Chrysostome, utilisée par S. Augustine." *Revue des Etudes Augustiniennes* 17 (1971): 27–41.

Bousset, Wilhelm. *Apophthegmata: Text Überlieferung und Charakter der Apophthegmata Patrum. Zur Überlieferung der Vita Pachomii. Euagrios-Studien*. Tübingen: J.C.B. Mohr [Paul Siebeck] Verlag, 1923.

Bouwman, Gisbert. *Des Julian von Aeclanum Kommentar zu den Propheten Osee, Joel und Amos: Ein Beitrag zur Geschichte der Exegese*. Analecta Biblica 9. Roma: Pontifico Instituto Biblico, 1958.

Brochet, J. *Saint Jérôme et ses ennemis*. Paris: Albert Fontemoing, 1905.

Brown, Peter. "Aspects of the Christianization of the Roman Aristocracy." *Journal of Roman Studies* 51 (1961): 1–11. Reprinted in Brown, *Religion and Society, q.v.*, 161–182.

———. *Augustine of Hippo. A Biography*. Berkeley: University of California Press, 1969.

———. *The Body and Society: Men, Women and Sexual Renunciation in Early Christianity*. New York: Columbia University Press, 1988.

———. "The Patrons of Pelagius: The Roman Aristocracy Between East and West." *Journal of Theological Studies* n.s. 21 (1970): 56–72. Reprinted in Brown, *Religion and Society, q.v.*, 208–226.

———. "Pelagius and His Supporters: Aims and Environment." *Journal of Theological Studies* n.s. 19 (1968): 93–114. Reprinted in Brown, *Religion and Society, q.v.*, 183–207.

———. *Religion and Society in the Age of St. Augustine*. New York: Harper & Row, 1972.

Bruckner, Albert. *Julian von Eclanum. Sein Leben und seine Lehre. Ein Beitrag zur Geschichte des Pelagianismus*. TU 15, 3 (1897).

———. *Die Vier Bücher Julians von Aeclanum an Turbantius. Ein Beitrag zur Charakteristik Julians und Augustins*. Neue Studien zur Geschichte der Theologie und der Kirche 8. Berlin, 1910; reprint, Aalen: Scientia Verlag, 1973.

Bruyn, Theodore S. de. "Pelagius's Interpretation of Rom. 5: 12–21: Exegesis Within the Limits of Polemic." *Toronto Journal of Theology* 4 (1988): 30–43.

———. *A Translation, With Introduction and Notes, of Pelagius's "Commentary on Romans."* Ph.D. dissertation, Toronto School of Theology, 1987.

Buchheit, Vinzenz. "Rufinus von Aquileja als Fälscher des Adamantiosdialogs." *Byzantinische Zeitschrift* 51 (1958): 314–328.

Bunge, J. G. (Gabriel). *Akēdia: Die geistliche Lehre des Evagrios Pontikos von Überdruss.* Koinonia IX. Köln: Luthe-Verlag, 1983.

———. "Evagre le Pontique et les deux Macaire." *Irēnikon* 56 (1983): 215–227, 323–360.

———. *Das Geistgebet. Studien zum Traktat "De Oratione" des Evagrios Pontikos.* Koinonia XXV. Köln: Luthe-Verlag, 1987.

———. "Hénade ou Monade? Au Subjet de deux notions centrales de la terminologie evagrienne." *Le Muséon* 102 (1989): 69–91.

———. "Origenismus—Gnostizismus: Zum geistesgeschichtlichen Standort des Evagrios Pontikos." *Vigiliae Christianae* 40 (1986): 24–54.

———. "Palladiana I: Introduction aux fragments coptes de l'Histoire Lausiac." *Studia Monastica* 32 (1990): 79–129.

Burmester, O.H.E. "The Homilies or Exhortations of the Holy Week Lectionary." *Le Muséon* 45 (1932): 21–70.

Caspari, C. P. *Briefe, Abhandlungen und Predigten aus den zwei letzten Jahrhunderten des Kirchlichen Alterthums und dem Anfang des Mittelalters.* Christiana, 1890; reprint, Bruxelles: Culture et Civilization, 1964.

Cavallera, F. *Saint Jérôme. Sa vie et son oeuvre.* 2 vols. Etudes et documents 2. Louvain: Spicilegium Sacrum Lovaniense Bureaux; Paris: H.and E. Champion, 1922.

Chadwick, Henry. "Origen, Celsus, and the Resurrection of the Body." *Harvard Theological Review* 41 (1948): 83–102.

———. "Rufinus and the Tura Papyrus of Origen's Commentary on Romans." *Journal of Theological Studies* n.s. 10 (1959): 10–42.

———. *The Sentences of Sextus: A Contribution to the History of Early Christian Ethics.* Cambridge: Cambridge University Press, 1959.

Chadwick, Owen. *John Cassian.* 2nd ed. Cambridge: Cambridge University Press, 1968.

Chaîne, M. "La Double Recension de l'Histoire Lausiaque dans la version copte." *Revue de l'Orient Chrétien* 25 (1925): 232–275.

Chavoutier, Lucien. "Querelle Origéniste et controverses trinitaires à propos du Tractatus Contra Origenem de Visione Isaiae." *Vigiliae Christianae* 14 (1960): 9–14.

Chesnut, Glenn F. *The First Church Histories. Eusebius, Socrates, Sozomen, Theodoret and Evagrius.* Théologie historique 46. Paris: Editions Beauchesne, 1977.

Chitty, Derwas J. *The Desert a City. An Introduction to the Study of Egyptian and Palestinian Monasticism under the Christian Empire.* Crestwood, NY: St. Vladimir's Seminary Press, 1966.

Clark, Elizabeth A. "Elite Networks and Heresy Accusations: Towards a Social Description of the Origenist Controversy." *Semeia* 56 (1991): 81–107.

———. *The Life of Melania the Younger: Introduction, Translation, Commentary.* Studies in Women and Religion 14. Toronto: Edwin Mellen Press, 1985.

———. "The Place of Jerome's Commentary on Ephesians in the Origenist Controversy: The Apokatastasis and Ascetic Ideals." *Vigiliae Christianae* 41 (1987): 154–171.

Clark, Elizabeth A. "Theory and Practice in Late Ancient Asceticism: Jerome, Chrysostom, and Augustine," *Journal of Feminist Studies in Religion* 5 (1989): 25–46.

———. "Vitiated Seed and Holy Vessels: Augustine's Manichean Past." In *Images of the Feminine in Gnosticism*, ed. Karen L. King, 367–401. Philadelphia: Fortress Press, 1988. Also in Clark, *Ascetic Piety and Woman's Faith: Essays on Late Ancient Christianity*, 291–349. Studies in Women and Religion 20. Lewiston: Edwin Mellen Press, 1986.

Collins, Randall, ed. *Sociological Theory 1983*. San Francisco: Jossey-Bass Publishers, 1983.

Cornélis, H. "Les Fondements cosmologiques de l'eschatologie d'Origène." *Revue des Sciences Philosophiques et Théologiques* 43 (1959): 32–80, 201–247.

Courcelle, Pierre. *Les Lettres grecques en occident de Macrobe à Cassiodore.* Bibliothèque des Ecoles Françaises d'Athènes et de Rome 159. Paris: E. de Boccard, 1948.

———. "Paulin de Nole et Saint Jérôme." *Revue des Etudes Latines* 25 (1947): 250–280.

———. "Tradition platonicienne et traditions chrétiennes du corps-prison (Phédon 62b; Cratyle 400c)." *Revue des Etudes Latines* 43 (1965): 406–443.

Crouzel, Henri. "Les Critiques adressées par Méthode et ses contemporains à la doctrine origénienne du corps ressuscité." *Gregorianum* 53 (1972): 679–716.

———. "La Doctrine origénienne du corps ressucité." *Bulletin de Littérature Ecclésiastique* 81 (1980): 175–200, 241–266.

———. *Les Fins dernières selon Origène.* Hampshire: Variorum, 1990.

———. "L'Hadès et la Géhenne selon Origène." *Gregorianum* 59 (1978): 291–329.

———. "A Letter from Origen 'To Friends in Alexandria.'" Tr. J. D. Gauthier. In *The Heritage of the Early Church: Essays in Honor of the Very Reverend Georges Vasilievich Florovsky*, ed. David Neiman and Margaret Schatkin, 135–150. Orientalia Christiana Analecta 195. Roma: Pont. Institutum Studiorum Orientalium, 1973.

———. *Origen: The Life and Thought of the First Great Theologian.* Tr. A. S. Worrall. San Francisco: Harper and Row, 1989.

———. "Origène a-t-il tenu que la regne du Christ prendrait fin?" *Augustinianum* 26 (1986): 51–61.

———. *Théologie de l'image de Dieu chez Origène.* Théologie 34. Aubier: Editions Montaigne, 1956.

Crum, W. E. *Catalogue of the Coptic Manuscripts in the British Museum.* London: British Museum, 1905.

———. *Coptic Ostraca from the Collections of the Egypt Exploration Fund, the Cairo Museum and Others.* London: Egypt Exploration Fund, 1902.

———. *Der Papyruscodex saec. VI–VII der Phillippsbibliothek in Cheltenham: Koptische Theologische Schriften.* Strassburg: Karl J. Trübner, 1915.

Daitz, E. "The Picture Theory of Meaning." In *Essays in Conceptual Analysis*, ed. Antony Flew, 53–74. London: Macmillan; New York: St. Martin's Press, 1966.

D'Alès, Adhemar. "Julien d'Eclane, exégète." *Recherches de Science Religieuse* 6 (1916): 311–324.

Davids, J. A. *De Orosio et Sancto Augustino Priscillianistarum adversariis commentatio historica et philologica.* The Hague: A. N. Govers N. V., n.d.

Dechow, Jon F. *Dogma and Mysticism in Early Christianity: Epiphanius of Cyprus and the Legacy of Origen.* North American Patristic Society Monograph Series 13. Macon, GA: Mercer University Press, 1988.

———. "The Heresy Charges Against Origen." In *Origeniana Quarta*, ed. L. Lies, *q.v.*, 112–122.

———. "Origen and Early Christian Pluralism: The Context of His Eschatology." In *Origen of Alexandria*, ed. C. Kannengiesser and W. L. Petersen, *q.v.*, 337–356.

———. "Third-Century Resurrection Controversy: Methodius, on the Resurrection." Paper presented at the North American Patristics Society, 27 May 1988.

Declerck, José. "Thèophile d'Alexandrie contre Origéne: Nouveaux fragments de l'*Epistula Synodalis Prima* (CPG 2595)." *Byzantion* 54 (1984): 495–507.

Dekkers, E., ed. *Clavis Patrum Latinorum.* 2nd edition. *Sacris Eruditi* 3 (1961).

Delobel, R., and M. Richard. "Théophile d'Alexandrie." *Dictionnaire de Théologie Catholique* 15, 1: 523–530 (1946).

Der Nersessian, S. "Une Apologie des images du septième siécle." *Byzantion* 17 (1944–1945): 58–87.

———. "Image Worship in Armenia and Its Opponents." *Armenian Quarterly* 1 (1946): 67–81.

Devreesse, Robert. *Essai sur Théodore de Mopsueste.* Studi e Testi 141. Città del Vaticano: Biblioteca Apostolica Vaticana, 1948.

Diekamp, Franz. *Doctrina Patrum De Incarnatione Verbi: Ein griechisches Florilegium aus der Wende des siebenten und achten Jahrhunderts.* Münster in Westf.: Verlag Aschendorff, 1907.

———. *Die origenistischen Streitigkeiten im sechsten Jahrhundert und das fünfte allgemeine Concil.* Münster: Verlag Aschendorff, 1899.

Dihle, Albrecht. "Philosophische Lehren von Schicksal und Freiheit in der frühchristlichen Theologie." *Jahrbuch für Antike und Christentum* 30 (1987): 14–28.

Dölger, Franz Joseph. "Drei Theta als Schatzsicherung u. ihre Deutung durch den Bischof Theophil von Alexandrien." *Antike und Christentum* III (1932): 189–191.

Draguet, Réné. "L'Histoire Lausaique: Une oeuvre écrite dans l'esprit d'Evagre." *Revue d'Histoire Ecclésiastique* 41 (1946): 321–364; 42 (1947): 5–49.

———. "Un Morceau grec inédit des vies de Pachôme apparié à un texte d'Evagre en partie inconnu." *Le Muséon* 70 (1957): 267–306.

Drioton, Etienne. "La Discussion d'un moine anthropomorphite Audien avec le patriarche Théophile d'Alexandrie en l'année 399." *Revue de l'Orient Chrétien*, 2ᵉ ser., 10 (= 20) (1915–1917): 92–100, 113–128.

Driscoll, Jeremy. "Gentleness in the *Ad Monachos* of Evagrius Ponticus." *Studia Monastica* 32 (1990): 295–321.

Du Bourguet, Pierre. "Diatribe de Chenouté contre le Démon. *Bulletin de la Société d'Archéologie Copte* 16 (1961–1962): 17–72.

———. "Entretien de Chenouté sur le devoirs des Juges." *Bulletin de l'Institut Français d'Archéologie Orientale* 55 (1956): 85–109.

Du Bourguet, Pierre. "Entretien de Chenouté sur les problèmes de discipline ecclésiastique et de cosmologie." *Bulletin de l'Institut Français d'Archéologie Orientale*
57 (1958): 99–142.

Duhr, J. "Le 'De Fide' de Bachiarius." *Revue d'Histoire Ecclésiastique* 24 (1928): 5–
40, 301–331.

Durand, Matthieu-Georges de. "Evagre le Pontique et le 'Dialogue sur la vie de
saint Jean Chrysostome.'" *Bulletin de Littérature Ecclésiastique* 3 (1976): 191–
206.

Duthoy, Robert. *The Taurobolium. Its Evolution and Terminology.* Leiden: E. J.
Brill, 1969.

Duval, Yves-Marie. "Julien d'Eclane et Rufin d'Aquilée: du Concile de Rimini à la
répression pélagienne. L'intervention impériale en matière religieuse." *Revue des
Etudes Augustiniennes* 24 (1978): 243–271.

———. "Le 'Liber Hieronymi ad Gaudentium': Rufin d'Aquilée, Gaudence de
Brescia et Eusèbe de Crémone." *Revue Bénédictine* 97 (1987): 163–186.

———. *Le Livre de Jonas dans la littérature chrétienne grecque et latine: Sources et
influence du commentaire sur Jonas de Jérome.* Paris: Etudes Augustiniennes, 1973.

———. "Pélage est-il le censeur inconnu de l'Adversus Iovinianum à Rome en 393?
ou: du 'Portrait-Robot' de l'hérétique chez S. Jérôme." *Revue d'Histoire Ecclésiastique* 75 (1980): 525–557.

———. "Saint Cyprien et le roi de Ninive dans l'*In Jonam* de Jérome: La conversion des lettrés à la fin du IVe siècle." In *Epektasis,* ed. J. Fontaine and C. Kannengiesser, *q.v.,* 551–570.

———. "Sur les Insinuations de Jérome contre Jean de Jérusalem: de l'Arianisme à
l'Origénisme." *Revue d'Histoire Ecclésiastique* 65 (1970): 353–374.

———. "Tertullian contre Origène sur la résurrection de la chair dans le *Contra
Iohannem Hierosolymitanum,* 23–36 de saint Jérôme." *Revue des Etudes Augustiniennes* 17 (1971): 227–278.

Ebied, R. Y., and L. R. Wickham, "A Collection of Unpublished Syriac Letters of
Timothy Aelurus." *Journal of Theological Studies* 21 (1970): 321–369.

Eisenstadt, S. N., and Louis Roniger. "Patron–Client Relations as a Model of
Structuring Social Exchange." *Comparative Studies in Society and History* 22
(1980): 42–77.

Elm, Susanna. "Evagrius Ponticus' *Sententiae ad Virginem.*" *Dumbarton Oaks Paper*
45 (1991): 265–295.

Evans, Robert F. *Four Letters of Pelagius.* New York: Seabury Press, 1968.

———. "Pelagius, Fastidius, and the Pseudo-Augustinian *De Vita Christiana.*"
Journal of Theological Studies n.s. 13 (1962): 72–98.

———. *Pelagius: Inquiries and Reappraisals.* New York: Seabury Press, 1957.

Evelyn-White, Hugh G. *The Monasteries of the Wâdi 'N Natrûn. Part II: The History
of the Monasteries of Nitria and of Scetis,* ed. Walter Hauser. New York: Metropol-
itan Museum of Art, 1932.

Fabre, Pierre. *Essai sur la chronologie de l'oeuvre de Saint Paulin de Nole.* Publications
de la faculté des lettres de l'Université de Strasbourg, fasc. 109. Paris: Société
d'Edition "Les Belles Lettres," 1948.

———. *Saint Paulin de Nole et l'amitié chrétienne.* Bibliothèque des Ecoles Françaises d'Athènes et de Rome 167. Paris: de Boccard, 1949.

Fairweather, E. R. "Saint Augustine's Interpretation of Infant Baptism." In *Augustinus Magister, q.v*, II: 897–904.

Favale, Agostino. *Teofilo d'Alessandria (345c.–412): Scritti, vita e dottrina.* Biblioteca del "Salesianum" 41. Torino: Società Editrice Internazionale, 1958.

Ferguson, John. *Pelagius.* Cambridge: W. Heffer and Sons, 1956.

Ferrari, L. C. "Augustine and Astrology." *Laval Théologique et Philosophique* 33 (1977): 241–251.

Floëri, Fernand. "Le Pape Zosimus et la doctrine augustinienne du péché originel." In *Augustinus Magister, q.v.*, II: 755–761.

Florovsky, George. "The Anthropomorphites in the Egyptian Desert." In *Akten des XI. Internationalen Byzantinistenkongresses, München 1958*, ed. F. Dölger and H.-G. Beck, 154–159. München: C. H. Beck, 1960.

———. "Origen, Eusebius, and the Iconoclastic Controversy." *Church History* 19 (1950): 77–96.

Fontaine, Jacques, and Charles Kannengiesser, eds. *Epektasis: Mélanges patristiques offerts au Cardinal Jean Daniélou.* Paris: Beauchesne, 1972.

Fowden, Garth. "Bishops and Temples in the Eastern Roman Empire A.D. 320–435." *Journal of Theological Studies* 29 (1978): 53–78.

Frank, Karl Suso. *Grundzüge der Geschichte des Christlichen Mönchtums.* Darmstadt: Wissenschaftliche Buchgesellschaft, 1975.

Frede, Hermann Josef. *Ein Neuer Paulustext und Kommentar.* Band I: *Untersuchungen.* Vetus Latina: Aus der Geschichte der Lateinischen Bibel 7. Freiburg: Herder, 1973.

Fredriksen, Paula L. *Augustine's Early Interpretation of Paul.* Ph.D. dissertation, Princeton University, 1979.

Geerard, Mauritius, ed. *Clavis Patrum Graecorum.* Volumen II: *Ab Athanasio ad Chrysostomum.* Turnhout: Brepols, 1974.

———, ed. *Clavis Patrum Graecorum.* Volumen III: *A Cyrillo Alexandrino ad Iohannem Damascenum.* Turnhout: Brepols, 1979.

Geffcken, Johannes. *The Last Days of Greco-Roman Paganism.* Tr. Sabine MacCormack. Europe in the Middle Ages: Selected Studies, 8. Amsterdam: North Holland Publishing Company, 1978.

Géhin, Paul. "Un nouvel inédit d'Evagre le Pontique: son Commentaire de l'Ecclésiaste." *Byzantion* 49 (1979): 188–198.

Gellner, Ernest, and John Waterbury, eds. *Patrons and Clients in Mediterranean Societies.* London: Duckworth, 1977.

Gendle, Nicholas. "Cappadocian Elements in the Mystical Theology of Evagrius Ponticus." In *Studia Patristica* XVI (= *TU* 129), ed. Elizabeth A. Livingstone, II (1985): 373–384 .

Gianotto, Claudio. "Melchisedek e lo Spirito santo: Alcuni aspetti della pneumatologia eterodossa tra il III e il IV secolo." *Augustinianum* 20 (1980): 587–593.

Goldschmidt, R. C. *Paulinus' Churches at Nola. Texts, Translations and Commentary.* Amsterdam: N. V. Noord-Hollandsche Uitgevers Maatschappij, 1940.

Gorday, Peter. "*Paulus Origenianus*: The Economic Interpretation of Paul in Origen and Gregory of Nyssa." In *Paul and the Legacies of Paul*, ed. William S. Babcock, *q.v.*, 141–163.

———. *Principles of Patristic Exegesis: Romans 9–11 in Origen, John Chrysostom, and*

Augustine. Studies in the Bible and Early Christianity 4. New York: Edwin Mellen Press, 1983.

Gordini, Gian Domenico. "Il monachesimo romano in Palestina nel IV secolo." In *Saint Martin et son temps: Mémorial du XVIᵉ centenaire des débuts du monachisme en Gaule, 361–1961*, 85–107. Studia Anselmiana 46. Roma: Herder, 1961.

———. "Origine e sviluppo del monachesimo a Roma." *Gregorianum* 37 (1956): 220–260.

Gould, Graham. "The Desert Fathers, the Laity, and the Church." Paper given at the Eleventh International Conference on Patristic Studies, Oxford, 20 August 1991.

———. "Doctrines of the Image: Origenism and the Monks." Paper given at the *Colloquium Origenianum Quintum*, Boston College, 18 August 1989.

Granfield, Patrick, and Josef A. Jungmann, eds. *Kyriakon: Festschrift Johannes Quasten*. 2 vols. Münster Westf.: Verlag Aschendorff, 1970.

Granovetter, Mark S. "The Strength of Weak Ties." *American Journal of Sociology* 78 (1973): 1360–1380.

———. "The Strength of Weak Ties: A Network Theory Revisited." In *Sociological Theory 1983*, ed. R. Collins, q.v., 201–233.

Greshake, Gisbert. *Gnade als konkrete Freiheit: Eine Untersuchung zur Gnadenlehre Pelagius*. Mainz: Matthias Grünewald Verlag, 1972.

Gribomont, Jean. "Marc l'Ermite et la christologie évagrienne." *Cristianesimo nella Storia* 3 (1982): 73–81.

Grillmeier, Aloys. "Das 'Gebet zu Jesu' und das 'Jesus-Gebet': Eine neue Quelle zum 'Jesus-Gebet' aus dem Weissen Kloster." In *After Chalcedon: Studies in Theology and Church History*, ed. C. Laga, J. A. Munitz, and L. Van Rompay, 187–202. Orientalia Lovaniensia Analecta 18. Leuven: Departement Oriëntalistiek/Peeters, 1985.

———. "Markos Eremites und der Origenismus: Versuch einer Neudentung von Op. XI." In *Überlieferungsgeschichtliche Untersuchungen*, ed. Franz Paschke. *TU* 125 (1981): 253–283.

———. "La 'Peste d'Origéne': Soucis du patriarche d'Alexandrie dus à l'apparition d'origénistes en Haute Egypte (444–451)." In *Alexandrina*, q.v., 221–237.

Gross, Julius. *Entstehungsgeschichte des Erbsünden Dogmas von der Bibel bis Augustinus*. München: Ernst Reinhardt Verlag, 1960.

———. "Theodor von Mopsuestia, ein Gegner der Erbsündenlehre." *Zeitschrift für Kirchengeschichte* 65 (1953/1954): 1–15.

Grützmacher, Georg. *Hieronymus: Eine biographische Studie zur alten Kirchengeschichte*. 3 vols. Studien zur Geschichte der Theologie und der Kirche X, 2. Berlin, 1906; reprint, Aalen: Scientia Verlag, 1969.

Guérin, H. "Sermons inédits de Senouti (Introduction, texte, traduction)." *Revue Egyptologique* 11 (1904): 15–34.

Guillaumont, Antoine. "Evagre et les anathématismes anti-origénistes de 553." In *Studia Patristica* 3, 1 (*TU* 78), ed. F. L. Cross (1961): 219–226.

———. "Le Gnostique chez Clément d'Alexandrie et chez Evagre le Pontique." In *Alexandrina*, q.v., 195–201.

———. "Histoire des moines aux Kellia." *Orientalia Lovaniensia Periodica* 8 (1977): 187–203.

————. "Une Inscription copte sur la 'Prière de Jesus.' " *Orientalia Christiana Periodica* 34 (1968): 310–325.

————. "The Jesus Prayer among the Monks of Egypt." *Eastern Churches Review* 6 (1974): 66–71.

————. *Les "Kephalaia Gnostica" d'Evagre le Pontique et l'histoire de l'Origénisme chez les Grecs et chez les Syriens.* Patristica Sorbonensia 5. Paris: Editions du Seuil, 1962.

————. "Un philosophe du désert: Evagre le Pontique." *Revue de l'Histoire des Religions* 181 (1972): 29–56.

————. "Le Rôle des versions orientales dans la récuperation de l'oeuvre d'Evagre le Pontique." *Académie des Inscriptions and Belles-Lettres, Comptes Rendus* 1985: 64–74.

————, and Claire Guillaumont. "Contemplation." *DS* 2: 1775–1785.

————. "Demon: Evagre le Pontique." *DS* 3: 196–205.

————. "Evagre le Pontique." *DS* 4, 2: 1731–1744.

————. "Le Texte véritable des 'Gnostica' d'Evagre le Pontique." *Revue de l'Histoire des Religions* 142 (1952): 156–205.

Gundel, Wilhelm, and Hans Georg Gundel. *Astrologumena: Die astrologische Litteratur in der Antike und ihre Geschichte.* Sudhoffs Archiv Beihefte 6. Wiesbaden: Franz Steiner Verlag, 1966.

Guy, Jean-Claude. *Jean Cassien. Vie et doctrine spirituelle.* Collection Théologie, Pastorale et Spiritualité, Recherches et Synthèses IX. Paris: P. Lethielleux, 1961.

Haidacher, Sebastian. "Eine unbeachtete Rede des Hl. Chrysostomus an Neugetaufte." *Zeitschrift für katholische Theologie* 28 (1904): 168–193.

Haller, Wilhelm. *Iovinianus. Die Fragmente seiner Schriften, die Quellen zu seiner Geschichte, sein Leben und seine Lehre. TU* 17, 2 (1897).

Hamman, A. "Orosius de Braga et le Pélagianisme." *Bracara Augusta* 21 (1968): 346–355.

Hammond, Caroline P. *See also* Bammel, C. Hammond. "The Last Ten Years of Rufinus' Life and the Date of his Move South from Aquileia." *Journal of Theological Studies* n.s. 28 (1977): 372–427.

————. "A Product of a Fifth-Century Scriptorium Preserving Conventions Used by Rufinus of Aquileia: I and II." *Journal of Theological Studies* n.s. 29 (1978): 366–391.

Hanson, Richard, and Henri Crouzel, eds. *Origeniana Tertia. The Third International Colloquium for Origen Studies.* (University of Manchester 7–11 September 1981). Roma: Edizioni dell' Ateneo, 1985.

Harl, Marguerite. "La Préexistence des âmes dans l'oeuvre d'Origène." In *Origeniana Quarta*, ed. L. Lies, *q.v.*, 238–258.

Hausherr, Irénée. "Appendice au fasc. 69: Les versions syriaque et arménienne d'Evagre le Pontique." *Orientalia Christiana* 24 (1931): 38–40.

————. "Eulogios-Loukios." *Orientalia Christiana Periodica* 6 (1940): 216–220.

————. *Noms du Christ et voies d'oraison. Orientalia Christiana Analecta* 157. Roma: Pont. Institutum Orientalium Studiorum, 1960.

————. "Nouveaux fragments grecs d'Evagre le Pontique." *Orientalia Christiana Periodica* 5 (1939): 229–233.

Hausherr, Irénée. "L'Origine de la théorie orientale des huit péchés capitaux." *Orientalia Christiana* 30 (1933): 164–175.

———. "Le Traité de l'oraison d'Evagre le Pontique (Pseudo-Nil)." *Revue d'Ascétique et de Mystique* 15 (1934): 34–93, 113–170.

Hendrikx, O. "Astrologie, Waarzeggerij en Parapsychologie bij Augustinus." *Augustiniana* 4 (1954): 325–352.

Hengstenberg, Wilhelm. "Pachomiana mit einem Anhang über die Liturgie von Alexandrien." In *Beiträge zur Geschichte des christlichen Altertums und der byzantinischen Literature: Festgabe Albert Ehrhard*, ed. A. M. Koeniger, 228–252. Bonn: Kurt Schroeder Verlag, 1922.

Hickey, Anne Ewing. *Women of the Roman Aristocracy as Christian Monastics.* Studies in Religion 1. Ann Arbor: UMI Research Press, 1987.

Hitchcock, F. R. Montgomery. "The *Explanatio Symboli ad Initiandos* Compared with Rufinus and Maximus of Turin." *Journal of Theological Studies* 47 (1946): 58–69.

Holl, Karl. *Gesammelte Aufsätze zur Kirchengeschichte. II: Der Osten.* Tübingen: J.C.B. Mohr [Paul Siebeck], 1928.

———. "Die Schriften des Epiphanius gegen die Bilderverehung" (1916). Reprinted in Holl, *Gesammelte Aufsätze, q.v.*, 351–387.

———. "Die Zeitfolge der ersten origenistischen Streits." (1916). Reprinted in *Gesammelte Aufsätze, q.v.*, 310–350.

Hoppe, Heinrich. "Griechisches bei Rufin." *Glotta* 26 (1937): 132–144.

———. "Rufin als Uebersetzer." In *Studi dedicati alla memoria di Paolo Ubaldi*, 133–150. Pubblicazioni della Università Cattolica del Sacro Cuore, ser. 5, 16. Milano: Società Editrice "Vita e Pensiero," 1937.

Hunt, E. D. "Palladius of Helenopolis: A Party and Its Supporters in the Church of the Late Fourth Century." *Journal of Theological Studies* n.s. 24 (1973): 456–480.

———. "St. Silvia of Aquitaine: The Role of a Theodosian Pilgrim in the Society of East and West." *Journal of Theological Studies* n.s. 23 (1972): 351–373.

Hunter, David. "Ambrosiaster, Astral Fatalism and the Prehistory of the Pelagian Controversy." Paper given at the North American Patristic Society, Loyola University of Chicago, 24 May 1990.

Isetta, Sandra. "Lo spirito della tristezza e dell'accidia in Giovanni Cassiano: una sintesi filosofica, teologica e scientifica." *Civiltà Classica e Cristiana* 6 (1985): 331–347.

Jones, A.H.M., J. R. Martindale, and J. Morris, eds. *The Prosopography of the Later Roman Empire.* Vol. I: *A.D. 260–395.* Cambridge: Cambridge University Press, 1971.

Junod, Eric. "L'*Apologie pour Origène* par Pamphile: état de la question et perspectives nouvelles." Paper delivered at *Colloquium Origenianum Quintum*, Boston College, 14–18 August 1989.

Kannengiesser, Charles. *Athanase d'Alexandrie, évêque et écrivain: Une lecture des traité contre les ariens.* Théologie historique 70. Paris: Beauchesne, 1983.

———, and W. L. Petersen, eds. *Origen of Alexandria: His World and His Legacy.* Notre Dame: University of Notre Dame Press, 1988.

Kelly, J.N.D. *Early Christian Doctrine.* 2nd ed. New York: Harper and Row, 1960.

———. *Jerome: His Life, Writings, and Controversies.* New York: Harper and Row, 1975.

Kitzinger, Ernst. "The Cult of Images in the Age Before Iconoclasm." *Dumbarton Oaks Papers* 8 (1954): 83–150.

Klostermann, E. "Die Schriften des Origenes in Hieronymus' Brief an Paula." *Sitzungsberichte der königliche preussischen Akademie der Wissenschaften zu Berlin* 1897, 2: 855–870.

Kock, Günter. *Die Heilsverwirklichung bei Theodor von Mopsuestia.* Münchener Theologische Studien II, 31. München: Max Hueber Verlag, 1965.

Koopmans, G. H. "Augustine's First Contact with Pelagius and the Dating of the Condemnation of Caelestius at Carthage." *Vigiliae Christianae* 8 (1954): 149–153.

Koschorke, Klaus, Stefan Timm, and Frederik Wisse. "Shenute: De Certamine contra Diabolum." *Oriens Christianus* n.s. 59 (1975): 60–77.

Krusch, Bruno. *Studien zur Christlich-Mittelalterlichen Chronologie: Der 84Jährige Ostercyclus und seine Quellen.* Leipzig: Verlag Von Veit, 1880.

Labate, Antonio. "L'Esegesi di Evagrio al libro dell' Ecclesiaste." In *Studi in onore di Anthos Ardizzoni*, 485–490. Roma: Edizioni dell' Ateneo & Bizzarri, 1978.

Lackner, Wolfgang. "Zum Zusatz zu Epiphanios' von Salamis Panarion, Kap. 64." *Vigiliae Christianae* 27 (1973): 56–58.

———. "Zur profanen Bild des Evagrios Pontikos." In *Hans Gerstinger Festgabe zum 80. Geburtstag*, 17–29. Graz: Akademische Druck, 1966.

Ladner, Gerhart B. "The Concept of the Image in the Greek Fathers and the Byzantine Iconoclastic Controversy." *Dumbarton Oaks Papers* 7 (1953): 1–34.

Lanne, Emmanuel. "La 'Prière de Jésus' dans la tradition égyptienne: témoignage des psalies et des inscriptions." *Irēnikon* 50 (1977): 163–203.

Lataix, Jean. "Le Commentaire de Saint Jérome sur Daniel." *Revue d'Histoire et de Littérature Religieuses* 11 (1897): 164–173.

Lazzati, Giuseppe. *Teofilo d'Alessandria.* Pubblicazioni della Università Cattolica del Sacro Cuore (Milan), s. 4, 19. Milano: Società Editrice 'Vita e Pensiero,' 1935.

Lebon, Joseph. "Sur quelques fragments de lettres attribuées à Saint Epiphane de Salamine." In *Miscellanea Giovanni Mercati* I, 145–174. Studi e Testi 121. Città del Vaticano: Biblioteca Apostolica Vaticano, 1946.

LeBoulluec, Alain. "Controverses au subjet de la doctrine d'Origéne sur l'ame du Christ." *Origeniana Quarta*, ed. L. Lies, *q.v.*, 223–237.

———. "De la croissance selon les Stoïciens à la résurrection selon Origène." *Revue des Etudes Grecques* 88 (1975): 143–155.

Leclercq, Jean. "L'Ancienne Version latine des Sentences d'Evagre pour les moines." *Scriptorium* 5 (1951): 195–213.

Lefort, L. Theodore. "Catéchèse Christologique de Chenoute." *Zeitschrift für ägyptische Sprache* 80 (1955): 40–55.

———. "A propos d'un aphorisme d'Evagrius Ponticus." *Bulletin de la Classe des Lettres et des Sciences Morales et Politiques, Académie Royale de Belgique.* 5 ser., 36 (1950): 70–79.

———, tr. *Les Vies coptes de Saint Pachôme et de ses premiers successeurs.* Bibliothèque du Muséon 16. Louvain: Bureaux du Muséon, 1943.

Leipoldt, Johannes. *Schenute von Atripe und die Entstehung des national ägyptischen Christentums*. Leipzig: J. C. Hinrichs, 1903.

Leroux, Jean-Marie. "Jean Chrysostom et la querelle origéniste." In *Epektasis*, ed. J. Fontaine and C. Kannengiesser, *q.v.*, 335–341.

Leroy, Julien. "Le Cénobitisme chez Cassien." *Revue d'Ascétique et de Mystique* 43 (1967): 121–158.

Liebeschuetz, J.H.W.G. *Barbarians and Bishops: Army, Church, and State in the Age of Arcadius and Chrysostom*. Oxford: Clarendon Press, 1990.

————. "Friends and Enemies of John Chrysostom." In *Maistor: Classical, Byzantine and Renaissance Studies for Robert Browning*, ed. Ann Moffatt, 85–111. Byzantina Australiensia 5. Canberra: Australian Association for Byzantine Studies, 1984.

Lies, Lothar, ed. *Origeniana Quarta. Die Referate des 4. Internationalen Origeneskongresses*. Innsbrucker Theologische Studien 19. Innsbruck/Wien: Tyrolia Verlag, 1987.

Lorenz, Rudolf. "Die Anfänge des abendländischen Mönchtums im 4. Jahrhundert." *Zeitschrift für Kirchengeschichte* 77 (1966): 1–61.

Maas, Paul. "Die Ikonoklastische Episode in dem Brief des Epiphanios an Johannes." *Byzantinische Zeitschrift* 30 (1929–1930): 279–286.

Markus, R. A. "Pelagianism: Britain and the Continent." *Journal of Ecclesiastical History* 37 (1986): 191–204.

Marrou, Henri. "Les Attaches Orientales du Pelagianisme." *Académie des Inscriptions et Belles-lettres, Comptes Rendus*, 1968: 459–472.

Marsili, D. Salvatore. *Giovanni Cassiano ed Evagrio Pontico. Dottrina sulla carità e contemplazione*. Studia Anselmiana Philosophica Theologica V. Roma: Herder, 1936.

Martindale, J. R., ed. *The Prosopography of the Later Roman Empire*. Vol. II: *A.D. 395-527*. Cambridge: Cambridge University Press, 1980.

Martinetto, Giovanni. "Les Premières Réactions antiaugustiniennes de Pélage." *Revue des Etudes Augustiniennes* 17 (1971): 83–117.

Martini, Coelestinus. *Ambrosiaster: De auctore, operibus, theologia*. Spicilegium Pontificii Athenaei Antoniani 4. Roma: Pontificum Athenaeum Antonianum, 1944.

Matter, E. Ann. *The Voice of My Beloved. The Song of Songs in Western Medieval Christianity*. Philadelphia: University of Pennsylvania Press, 1990.

Matthews, John. *Western Aristocracies and Imperial Court, A.D. 364-425*. Oxford: Clarendon Press, 1975.

Mayer, Adrian C. "The Significance of Quasi-Groups in the Study of Complex Societies." In *Social Anthropology*, ed. M. Banton, *q.v.*, 97–122.

McGrath, Alister E. "Divine Justice and Divine Equity in the Controversy Between Augustine and Julian of Eclanum." *Downside Review* 101 (1983): 312–319.

McNabb, Vincent. "Was the Rule of St. Augustine Written for St. Melania the Younger?" *Journal of Theological Studies* 20 (1919): 242–249.

Melcher, Robert. *Der 8. Brief des hl. Basilius, ein Werk des Evagrius Pontikus*. Münsterische Beiträge zur Theologie 1. Münster i. W.: Verlag Aschendorff, 1923.

Meyvaert, Paul. "Excerpts from an Unknown Treatise of Jerome to Gaudentius of Brescia." *Revue Bénédictine* 96 (1986): 203–218.

Mitchell, J. Clyde. "The Concept and Use of Social Networks." In *Social Networks in Urban Situations: Analyses of Personal Relationships in Central African Towns*, ed. J. Clyde Mitchell, 1–46. Manchester: Manchester University Press, 1969.

————. "Networks, Norms and Institutions." In *Network Analysis*, ed. J. Boissevain and J. C. Mitchell, *q.v.*, 15–35.

————. "Social Networks." *American Review of Anthropology* 3 (1974): 279–299.

Mitchell, W.J.T. *Iconology: Image, Text, Ideology*. Chicago/London: University of Chicago Press, 1986.

————. "Spatial Form in Literature: Toward a General Theory." In *The Language of Images*, ed. W.J.T. Mitchell, 271–299. Chicago: University of Chicago Press, 1980.

Moine, Nicole. "Melaniana." *Recherches Augustiniennes* 15 (1980): 3–79.

Montcheuil, Yves de. "La Polémique de Saint Augustin contre Julien d'Eclane d'après l'*Opus Imperfectum*." *Recherches de Science Religieuse* 44 (1956): 193–218.

Moreschini, Claudio. "Il contribuo di Gerolamo alla polemica antipelagiana." *Cristianesimo nella Storia* 3 (1982): 61–71.

Moretus, Henri. "Les Bénédictions des Patriarches dans la littérature du IVᵉ au VIIIᵉ siècle." *Bulletin de littérature Ecclésiastique* 11 (1909): 398–411.

Morin. Germain. "La Lettre de l'Evêque Maxime à Théophile d'Alexandrie." *Revue Bénédictine* 11 (1894): 274–278.

————. "Les Monuments de la prédication de Saint Jérôme." *Revue d'Histoire et de Littérature Religieuses* 1 (1896): 393–434.

————. "Un Traité pélagien inédit du commencement du cinquième siècle." *Revue Bénédictine* 26 (1909): 163–188.

————, ed. *Anecdota Maredsolana* 3, 3 (1903).

Morris, John. "Pelagian Literature." *Journal of Theological Studies* n.s. 16 (1965): 26–60.

Müller, Karl. "Kritische Beiträge." *Sitzungsberichte der preussischen Akademie der Wissenschaften* (1919: 1): 616–629.

Murphy, Francis X. "Melania the Elder: A Biographical Note." *Traditio* 5 (1947): 59–77.

————. *Rufinus of Aquileia (345–411). His Life and Works*. Studies in Medieval History, n.s. 6. Washington, D.C.: Catholic University of America Press, 1945.

————. "Rufinus of Aquileia and Paulinus of Nola." *Revue des Etudes Augustiniennes* 2 (1956): 79–91.

Muyldermans, J. "Evagre le Pontique: *Capita Cognoscitiva* dans les versions syriaque et arménienne." *Le Muséon* 47 (1934): 73–106.

————. "Evagriana Coptica." *Le Muséon* 76 (1963): 271–276.

————. "Evagriana"; "Evagriana: Note Additionelle A." *Le Muséon* 44 (1931): 37–68, 369–383.

————. "Evagriana: Le Vatic. Barb. Graecus 515." *Le Muséon* 51 (1938): 191–226.

————. "Une Nouvelle Recension du *De octo spiritibus malitiae* de S. Nil." *Le Muséon* 52 (1939): 235–274.

————. "*Sur les séraphins et sur les chérubins* d'Evagre le Pontique dans les versions syriaque et arménienne." *Le Muséon* 59 (1946): 367–379.

————. "Le Teneur du *Practicus* d'Evagre le Pontique." *Le Muséon* 42 (1929): 74–89.

Muyldermans, J. *A travers la tradition manuscrite d'Evagre le Pontique. Essai sur les manuscrits grecs conservés à la Bibliothèque Nationale de Paris*. Bibliothèque du *Muséon* 3. Louvain: Bureaux du *Muséon*, 1932.

————, ed., tr. *Evagriana Syriaca. Textes inédits du British Museum et de la Vaticane.* Bibliothèque du *Muséon* 31. Louvain: Publications Universitaires/Institut Orientaliste, 1952.

Nagel, Peter. *Die Motivierung der Askese in des alten Kirche und der Ursprung des Mönchtums. TU* 95 (1966).

Nau, F. "La Version syriaque de la vision de Théophile sur le séjour de la Vierge en Egypte." *Revue de l'Orient Chrétien* 15 (1910): 125–132.

Nautin, Pierre. "Etudes de chronologie hiéronymienne (393–397)." *Revue des Etudes Augustiniennes* 18 (1972): 209–218; 19 (1973): 69–86; 213–239; 20 (1974): 251–284.

————. "La Lettre de Théophile d'Alexandrie à l'église de Jérusalem et la réponse de Jean de Jérusalem (juin–juillet 396)." *Revue d'Histoire Ecclésiastique* 69 (1974): 365–394.

————. *Origène: sa vie et son oeuvre*. Christianisme Antique 1. Paris: Beauchesne, 1977.

Niemeijer, Rudo. "Some Applications of the Notion of Density to Network Analysis." In *Network Analysis*, ed. J. Boissevain and J. C. Mitchell, *q.v.*, 45–64.

Noble, Mary. "Social Network: Its Use as a Conceptual Framework in Family Analysis." In *Network Analysis*, ed. J. Boissevain and J. C. Mitchell, *q.v.*, 3–14.

Nolan, John Gavin. *Jerome and Jovinian*. The Catholic University of America Studies in Sacred Theology, 2nd ser., 97. Washington, D.C.: Catholic University of America Press, 1956.

Norris, R. A., Jr. *Manhood and Christ: A Study in the Christology of Theodore of Mopsuestia*. Oxford: Clarendon Press, 1963.

Nuvolone-Nobile, Flavio G. "Problèmes d'une nouvelle édition du *De Induratione Cordis Pharaonis* attribué a Pélage." *Revue des Etudes Augustiniennes* 26 (1980): 105–117.

O'Connell, Robert J. *The Origin of the Soul in St. Augustine's Writings*. New York: Fordham University Press, 1987.

O'Laughlin, Michael. "The Anthropology of Evagrius Ponticus and Its Sources." In *Origen of Alexandria*, ed. C. Kannengiesser and W. Petersen, *q.v.*, 357–373.

————. *Origenism in the Desert: Anthropology and Integration in Evagrius Ponticus*. Th.D. dissertation, Harvard University, 1987.

Opelt, Ilona. *Hieronymus' Streitschriften*. Heidelberg: Carl Winter-Universitätsverlag, 1973.

Opitz, H.-G. "Theophilos von Alexandrien." In *RE* 5A, 2 (1934): 2149–2165.

Orlandi, Tito. "A Catechesis Against Apocryphal Texts by Shenute and the Gnostic Texts of Nag Hammadi." *Harvard Theological Review* 75 (1982): 85–95.

————. "La cristologia nei testi catechetici copti." In *Cristologia e catechesi Patristica*, ed. Sergio Felici, I, 213–229. Roma: Las, 1980.

————. "Un frammento copto Teofilo di Alessandria." *Rivista degli Studi Orientali* 44 (1969): 23–26.

————. "Gli Apocrifi copti." *Augustinianum* 23 (1983): 51–71.

————. "Uno scritto di Teofilo di Alessandria sulla distruzione del Serapeum?" *La Parola del Passato* 121 (1968): 295–304.

————. "Theophilus of Alexandria in Coptic Literature." In *Studia Patristica* XVI (= *TU* 129), ed. Elizabeth A. Livingstone, II (1985): 100–104.

Ostrogorsky, Georg. *Studien zur Geschichte des byzantinischen Bilderstreites.* Historische Untersuchungen 5. 1929; reprint, Amsterdam: Verlag Adolf M. Hakkert, 1964.

Oulton, J.E.L. "Rufinus's Translation of the Church History of Eusebius." *Journal of Theological Studies* 30 (1929): 150–174.

Paredi, Angelo. "Paulinus of Milan." *Sacris Erudiri* 14 (1963): 206–230.

Pargoire, Jules. "Rufinianes." *Byzantinische Zeitschrift* 8 (1899): 429–477.

Parmentier, Martin. "Evagrius of Pontus' 'Letter to Melania.' " *Bijdragen, tijdschrift voor filosofie en theologie* 46 (1985): 2–38.

Patterson, L. G. "*De libero arbitrio* and Methodius' Attack on Origen." In *Studia Patristica* XIV (= *TU* 117), ed. Elizabeth A. Livingstone (1976): 160–166.

————. "Notes on *De Cibis* and Methodius' View of Origen." In *Origeniana Tertia*, ed. R. Hanson and H. Crouzel, *q.v.*, 233–243.

————. "Who Are the Opponents in Methodius' *De Resurrectione*?" In *Studia Patristica* XIX, ed. Elizabeth A. Livingstone, 221–229. Leuven: Peeters, 1989.

Pelikan, Jaroslav. *The Christian Tradition: A History of the Development of Doctrine.* Vol. 2: *The Spirit of Eastern Christendom (600–1700).* Chicago: University of Chicago Press, 1974.

Peri, Vittorio. *Omelie origeniane sui Salmi: Contributo all'identificazione del testo latino.* Studi e Testi 289. Città del Vaticano: Biblioteca Apostolica Vaticana, 1980.

Petersen, Joan M. "Pammachius and his Houses." In *Studia Patristica* XII (= *TU* 115), ed. Elizabeth A. Livingstone, I (1975): 443–448.

Pietri, Charles. "Esquisse de conclusion: Augustine d'Hippone." In *Jean Chrysostome et Augustin. Actes du Colloque de Chantilly, 22–24 septembre 1974*, ed. C. Kannengiesser, 283–305. Théologie historique 35. Paris: Editions Beauchesne, 1975.

Plinval, Georges de. *Essai sur le style et la langue de Pélage.* Collectanae Friburgensia, n.s. 31. Fribourg en Suisse: Librarie de l'Université, 1947.

————. *Pélage: Ses ecrits, sa vie et sa reforme.* Lausanne: Libraire Payot, 1943.

————. "Points de vues récents sur la théologie de Pélage." *Recherches de science religieuse* 46 (1958): 227–236.

Prete, Serafino. *Mario Mercatore. Polemista antipelagiano.* Scrinium Theologicum XI. Torino: Marietti, 1958.

Preuschen, Erwin. *Palladius und Rufinus. Ein Beitrag zur Quellenkunde des ältesten Mönchtums.* Giessen: J. Ricker, 1897.

Refoulé, François. "La Christologie d'Evagre et l'origénisme." *Orientalia Christiana Periodica* 27 (1961): 221–266.

————. "Datation du premier concile de Carthage contre les Pélagiens et du *Libellus fidei* de Rufin." *Revue des Etudes Augustiniennes* 9 (1963): 41–49.

————. "La Distinction 'Royaume de Dieu-Vie Eternelle': est-elle Pélagienne?" *Recherches de Science Religieuse* 51 (1963): 247–254.

————. "Evagre fut-il origéniste?" *Revue des Sciences Philosophiques et Théologiques* 47 (1963): 398–402.

Refoulé, François. "Immortalité de l'âme et résurrection de la chair." *Revue de l'Histoire des Religions* 163 (1963): 11–52.

———. "Julien d'Eclane, théologien et philosophe." *Recherches de Science Religieuse* 52 (1964): 42–84, 233–247.

———. "Misère des enfants et péché originel d'après saint Augustin." *Revue Thomiste* 63 (1963): 341–362.

———. "Rêves et vie spiritualle d'après Evagre le Pontique." *La Vie spirituelle* 14 (1961): 470–516.

Regnault, Lucien. "La Prière continuelle 'monologistos' dans la littérature apophtegmatique." *Irēnikon* 47 (1974): 467–493.

Reitzenstein, Richard. *Historia monachorum und Historia Lausiaca. Eine Studie zur Geschichte des Mönchtums und der frühchristlichen Begriffe Gnostiker und Pneumatiker*. Göttingen: Vandenhoeck & Ruprecht, 1916.

Richard, Marcel. "Les Ecrits de Théophile d'Alexandrie." *Le Muséon* 52 (1939): 33–50.

———. "Les Fragments exégétiques de Théophile d'Alexandrie et de Théophile d'Antioche." *Revue Biblique* 47 (1938): 387–397.

———. "Une Homélie de Théophile d'Alexandrie sur l'institution de l'Eucharistie." *Revue d'Histoire Ecclésiastique* 33 (1937): 46–54.

———. "Nouveaux Fragments de Théophile d'Alexandrie." *Nachrichten der Akademie der Wissenschaften in Göttingen* 1975, 2: 57–65.

Riedinger, Utto. *Die Heilige Schrift im Kampf der griechischen Kirche gegen die Astrologie*. Innsbruck: Universitätsverlag Wagner, 1956.

Riggi, Calogero. "Catechesi escatologica dell' 'Ancoratus' di Epifanio." *Augustinianum* 18 (1978): 163–171.

———. "La forma del corpo risorto secondo Metodio in Epifanio (Haer. 64)." In *Morte e immortalità nella catechesi dei Padri del III–IV secolo*, ed. Sergio Felici, 75–92. Biblioteca di Scienze Religiose 66. Roma: Libreria Ateneo Salesiano, 1985.

———. "Origene e Origenisti secondo Epifanio (Haer. 64)." *Augustinianum* 26 (1986): 115–142.

Rist, John. "The Greek and Latin Texts of the Discussion of Free Will in *De Principiis*, Book III." In *Origeniana: Premier colloque international des études origéniennes*, ed. Henri Crouzel, Gennaro Lomiento, and Josep Rius-Camps, 97–111. Quaderni di Vetera Christianorum 12. Bari: Instituto di Letteratura Cristiana Antica, Università di Bari, 1975.

Romaniuk, Kasimierz. "Une Controverse entre saint Jérôme et Rufin d'Aquilée à propos de l'épître de saint Paul aux Ephésiens." *Aegyptus* 43 (1963): 84–106.

Rondeau, Marie-Josèphe. "Le Commentaire sur les Psaumes d'Evagre le Pontique." *Orientalia Christiana Periodica* 26 (1960): 307–348.

———. *Les Commentaires patristiques du Psautier. Vol. I: Les Travaux des pères grecs et latins sur le Psautier. Recherches et bilan*. Orientalia Christiana Analecta 219. Roma: Pont. Institutum Studiorum Orientalium, 1982.

Rousseau, Philip. *Ascetics, Authority, and the Church in the Age of Jerome and Cassian*. Oxford: Oxford University Press, 1978.

———. "Cassian, Contemplation and the Cenobitic Life." *Journal of Ecclesiastical History* 26 (1975): 113–126.

Rousselle, Aline. *Porneia: On Desire and the Body in Antiquity*. Tr. Felicia Pheasant. Oxford: Basil Blackwell, 1988.

Sage, Athanase. "Le Péché originel dans la pensée de saint Augustin, de 412 à 430." *Revue des Etudes Augustiniennes* 15 (1969): 75–112.

Said, Edward. *The World, the Text and the Critic.* Cambridge, MA: Harvard University Press, 1984.

Saller, Richard P. *Personal Patronage under the Early Empire.* Cambridge: Cambridge University Press, 1982.

Salzman, Michele. "Aristocratic Women: Conductors of Christianity in the Fourth Century." *Helios* 16 (1989): 207–220.

Schenke, Hans-Martin. "Ein koptischer Evagrius." In *Graeco-Coptica: Griechen und Kopten im byzantinischen Ägypten,* ed. Peter Nagel, 219–230. Halle-Wittenberg: Martin-Luther-Universität, 1984.

Schubert, Hans von. *Der Sogenannte Praedestinatus: Ein Beitrag zur Geschichte des Pelagianism. TU* 24, 2 (1903).

Schwartz, Eduard. "Palladiana." *Zeitschrift für die Neutestamentliche Wissenschaft* 36 (1937): 161–204.

———. "Unzeitgemässe Beobachtungen zu den Clementinen." *Zeitschrift für die Neutestamentliche Wissenschaft* 31 (1932): 151–199.

Schwartz, Jacques. "La Fin du Serapeum d'Alexandrie." In *Essays in Honor of C. Bradford Welles,* 97–111. American Studies in Papyrology 1. New Haven: American Society of Papyrologists, 1966.

Scott, Alan. *Origen and the Life of the Stars: A History of an Idea.* Oxford Early Christian Studies. Oxford: Clarendon Press, 1991.

Seeck, Otto. *Geschichte des Untergangs der antiken Welt.* 6 vols. Berlin: Siemenroth & Troschel, 1897–1920.

Shisha-Halévy, Ariel. "Commentary on Unpublished Shenoutiana in the British Library." *Enchoria* 6 (1976): 29–61.

———. "Unpublished Shenoutiana in the British Library." *Enchoria* 5 (1975): 53–108.

Simonetti, Manlio. "Note Rufiniane." *Rivista di Cultura Classica et Medioevale* 2 (1960): 140–172.

Smith, Alfred J. "The Commentary of Pelagius on Romans Compared with that of Origen-Rufinus, Part III." *Journal of Theological Studies* 20 (1919): 127–177.

———. "The Latin Sources of the Commentary of Pelagius on the Epistle of St. Paul to the Romans." *Journal of Theological Studies* 19 (1918): 162–230; 20 (1919): 55–177.

Solignac, Aimé. "Pélage et Pélagianisme." *DS* 12, 2: 2889–2942 (1986).

Souter, Alexander. *A Study of Ambrosiaster.* Texts and Studies VII, 5. Cambridge: Cambridge University Press, 1905.

Stancliffe, Claire. *Saint Martin and his Hagiographer: History and Miracle in Sulpicius Severus.* Oxford: Clarendon Press, 1983.

Stark, Rodney, and William Sims Bainbridge. "Networks of Faith: Interpersonal Bonds and Recruitment to Cults and Sects." *American Journal of Sociology* 85 (1980): 1376–1395.

Studer, Basil. "Zur Frage der dogmatischen Terminologie in der Lateinischen Übersetzung von Origenes' *De principiis.*" In *Epektasis,* ed. J. Fontaine and C. Kannengiesser, *q.v.,* 403–414.

———. "Zur Frage des westlichen Origenismus." In *Studia Patristica IX* (= *TU* 94) ed. Elizabeth A. Livingstone, II (1966): 270–287.

TeSelle, Eugene. "Rufinus the Syrian, Caelestius, Pelagius: Explorations in the Pre-history of the Pelagian Controversy." *Augustinian Studies* 3 (1972): 61–95.

Thelamon, Françoise. "Modèles de monachisme oriental selon Rufin d'Aquilée." In *Aquileia e l'oriente mediterraneo*, I: 323–352. Udine: Arti Grafiche Friulane, 1977.

———. *Païens et Chrétiens au IVe siècle: L'apport de l' 'Histoire ecclésiastique' de Rufin d'Aquilée*. Paris: Etudes Augustiniennes, 1981.

Thoden van Velzen, H.U.E. "Coalition and Network Analysis." In *Network Analysis*, ed. J. Boissevain and J. C. Mitchell, *q.v.*, 219–250.

Thompson, Herbert. "Dioscorus and Shenoute." *Bibliothèque de l'Ecole des Hautes Etudes: Recueil d'Etudes Egyptologiques* 233 (1922): 367–376.

Thümmel, Hans Georg. "Die bilderfeindlichen Schriften des Epiphanios von Salamis." *Byzantinoslavica* 47 (1986): 169–188.

Tibiletti, Carlo. "Giovanni Cassiano. Formazione e dottrina." *Augustinianum* 17 (1977): 355–380.

Timbie, Janet. *Dualism and the Concept of Orthodoxy in the Thought of the Monks of Upper Egypt*. Ph.D. dissertation, University of Pennsylvania, 1979.

Tonneau, R. M. "Théodore de Mopsueste, Interpretation (du Livre) de la Genèse (Vat. Syr. 120, ff. I–V)." *Le Muséon* 66 (1953): 45–64.

Trigg, Joseph Wilson. *Origen: The Bible and Philosophy in the Third-Century Church*. Atlanta: John Knox Press, 1983.

Valero, Juan B. *Las Bases antropologicas de Pelagio en su tratado de las Expositiones*. Pubblicaciones de la Universidad Pontificia Comillas Madrid, ser. 1, 18; I, 11. Madrid: UPCM, 1980.

Van Andel, G. K. "Sulpicius Severus and Origenism." *Vigiliae Christianae* 34 (1980): 278–287.

Van den Ven, P. "Encore le Rufin Grec." *Le Muséon* 59 (1946): 281–294.

Van Lantschoot, Arnold. "Un Opuscule inédit de Fr. C. Conybeare." *Le Muséon* 77 (1964): 121–135.

Van Loy, René. "Le 'Pro Templis' de Libanius." *Byzantion* 9 (1933): 7–39, 388–404.

Van Ommeslaeghe, Florent. "Jean Chrysostome et le peuple de Constantinople." *Analecta Bollandiana* 99 (1981): 329–349.

Veilleux, Armand. "Chénouté ou les écueils du monachisme." *Collectanea Cisterciensia* 45 (1983): 124–131.

Villain, Maurice. "Rufin d'Aquilée, commentateur du Symbole des Apotres." *Recherches de Science Religieuse* 31 (1944): 129–156.

———. "Rufin d'Aquilée, l'étudiant et le moine." *Nouvelle Revue Théologique* 64 (1937): 1–33, 139–161.

———. "Rufin d'Aquilée—La Querelle autour d'Origène." *Recherches de Science Religieuse* 27 (1937): 5–37, 165–195.

———. "Rufin d'Aquilée et l'Histoire Ecclésiastique." *Recherches de Science Religieuse* 33 (1946): 164–210.

Villecourt, Louis. "La Date et l'origine des 'Homélies Spirituelles' attribuées à Macaire." *Comptes Rendus des Seances de l'Academie des Inscriptions et Belles-Lettres* (1920): 250–258.

———. "La Grande Lettre grecque de Macaire: Ses formes textuelles et son milieu littéraire." *Revue de l'Orient Chrétien*, ser. 3, 2 (= 22) (1920–1921): 29–56.

Viller, Marcel. "Aux sources de la spiritualité de S. Maxime: Les oeuvres d'Evagre le Pontique." *Revue d'Ascetique et de Mystique* 11 (1930): 156–184, 239–268.

Vitestam, Gösta. "Second Partie de traité, qui passe sous le nom de 'le Grand Lettre d'Evagre le Pontique a Mélanie l'Ancienne.' " *Scripta Minora 1963-1964*: 3–29. Lund: C.W.K. Gleerup, 1964.

Voguë, Adalbert, de. "Les Fragments coptes de l'Histoire Lausiaque: L'édition d'Amélineau et le manuscrit." *Orientalia* 58 (1989): 326–332.

———. "Un Morceau célèbre de Cassien parmi des extraits d'Evagre." *Studia Monastica* 27 (1985): 7–12.

———. "Palladiana II: La version copte de l'Histoire Lausiaque." *Studia Monastica* 32 (1990): 323–339.

———. "Les Sources des quatre premiers livres des *Institutions* de Jean Cassien. Introduction aux recherches sur les anciennes règles monastiques latines." *Studia Monastica* 27 (1985): 241–311.

Wagner, M. Monica. *Rufinus, the Translator: A Study of His Theory and His Practice as Illustrated in His Version of the Apologetica of St. Gregory Nazianzen.* Catholic University of America Patristic Studies 73. Washington, D.C.: Catholic University of America Press, 1945.

Walsh, P. G. "Paulinus of Nola and the Conflict of Ideologies in the Fourth Century." In *Kyriakon*, ed. P. Granfield and J. Jungmann, *q.v.*, II: 565–571.

Watt, J. W. "Philoxenus and the Old Syriac Version of Evagrius' *Centuries*." *Oriens Christianus* 64 (1980): 65–81.

Weber, Hans-Oskar. *Die Stellung des Johannes Cassianus zur Ausserpachomianischen Mönchstradition.* Beiträge zur Geschichte des alten Mönchtums und des Benedictinerordens 24. Münster Westfalen: Verlag Aschendorff, 1961.

Weingood, Alex. "Patronage and Power." In *Patrons and Clients*, ed. E. Gellner and J. Waterbury, *q.v.*, 41–51.

Weiss, Hans-Friedrich. "Zur Christologie des Shenute von Atripe." *Bulletin de la Société d'Archéologie Copte* 20 (1969–1970): 177–209.

Wellman, Barry. "Network Analysis: Some Basic Principles." In *Sociological Theory 1983*, ed. R. Collins, *q.v.*, 155–200.

Wenzel, Siegfried. "*Akēdia*. Additions to Lampe's Patristic Greek Lexicon." *Vigiliae Christianae* 17 (1963): 173–176.

Wermelinger, Otto. *Rom and Pelagius. Die theologische Position der Römischen Bishöfe im Pelagianischen Streit in den Jahren 411-432.* Päpste und Papstum 7. Stuttgart: Anton Hiersemann, 1975.

Wickham, Lionel. "Pelagianism in the East." In *The Making of Orthodoxy*, ed. R. Williams, *q.v.*, 200–213.

Wiesen, David. *St. Jerome as a Satirist.* Ithaca: Cornell University Press, 1964.

Wilken, Robert S. "Free Choice and Divine Will in Greek Christian Commentaries on Paul." In *Paul and the Legacies of Paul*, ed. William S. Babcock, *q.v.*, 123–140.

Williams, Rowan. "Origen on the Soul of Jesus." In *Origeniana Tertia*, ed. R. Hanson and H. Crouzel, *q.v.*, 131–137.

———, ed. *The Making of Orthodoxy: Essays in Honour of Henry Chadwick.* Cambridge: Cambridge University Press, 1989.

Wilmart, André. "La Lettre spirituelle de l'Abbé Macarius." *Revue d'Ascétique et de Mystique* 1 (1920): 58–83.

Wilmart, André. "Les Versions latines des Sentences d'Evagre pour les vierges." *Revue Bénédictine* 28 (1911): 143–153.

Winkelmann, Friedhelm. "Einige Bemerkungen zu den Aussagen des Rufinus von Aquileia und des Hieronymus über ihre Übersetzungstheorie und -Methode." In *Kyriakon*, ed. P. Granfield and J. Jungmann, *q.v.*, II: 432–547.

Wisse, Frederik. "Gnosticism and Early Monasticism in Egypt." In *Gnosis. Festschrift für Hans Jonas*, ed. B. Aland, 431–440. Göttingen: Vandenhoeck & Ruprecht, 1978.

Wolf, Eric R. "Kinship, Friendship, and Patron-Client Relations in Complex Societies." In *The Social Anthropology of Complex Societies*, ed. Michael Banton, *q.v.*, 1–22.

Young, Dwight W. "A Monastic Invective Against Egyptian Hieroglyphs." In *Studies Presented to Hans Jakob Polotsky*, ed. D. W. Young, 348–360. East Gloucester, MA: Pirtle and Polson, 1981.

———. "Unpublished Shenoutiana in the University of Michigan Library." In *Scripta Hierosolymitana* 28: *Egyptological Studies*, ed. Sarah Israelit-Groll, 251–267. Jerusalem: Magnes Press of Hebrew University, 1982.

Zöckler, Otto. *Evagrius Pontikus. Seine Stellung in der altchristlichen Literatur- und Dogmengeschichte*. Biblische und Kirchenhistorische Studien 4. München: C. H. Beck, 1893.

I N D E X